The power of the past

_____

The power of the past

Essays for
Eric Hobsbawm

Edited by
PAT THANE,
GEOFFREY CROSSICK
and
RODERICK FLOUD

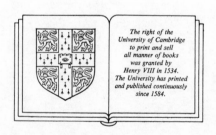

The right of the
University of Cambridge
to print and sell
all manner of books
was granted by
Henry VIII in 1534.
The University has printed
and published continuously
since 1584.

CAMBRIDGE UNIVERSITY PRESS

Cambridge
London   New York   New Rochelle   Melbourne   Sydney

EDITIONS DE LA MAISON DES SCIENCES DE
L'HOMME
Paris

Published by the Press Syndicate of the University of Cambridge
The Pitt Building, Trumpington Street, Cambridge CB2 1RP
32 East 57th Street, New York, NY 10022, USA
296 Beaconsfield Parade, Middle Park, Melbourne 3206, Australia
and
Editions de la Maison des Sciences de l'Homme
54 boulevard Raspail, 75270 Paris Cedex 06

First published 1984

Printed in Great Britain at the University Press, Cambridge

Library of Congress catalogue card number: 83-25235

British Library Cataloguing in Publication Data

The power of the past.
1. Hobsbawm, E.J.   2. Europe – Economic
conditions – 19th century – Addresses, essays,
lectures
I. Thane, Pat   II. Crossick, Geoffrey
III. Floud, Roderick   IV. Hobsbawm, E.J.
330.94'02'8   HC240

ISBN 0–521–25525–2
ISBN 2–7351–0084–4   (France only)

TM

Contents

List of Contributors   *Page*   vii

Introduction. Capitalism and its pre-capitalist heritage   1
   PAT THANE and GEOFFREY CROSSICK

1 The politics of class struggle in the history of society: an appraisal of
   the work of Eric Hobsbawm   13
   EUGENE D. GENOVESE

2 Working class and sociability in France before 1848   37
   MAURICE AGULHON

3 Men and women in the Parisian garment trades: discussions of family
   and work in the 1830s and 1840s   67
   JOAN WALLACH SCOTT

4 Craft traditions and the labour movement in nineteenth-century
   Germany   95
   JÜRGEN KOCKA

5 Structures of subordination in nineteenth-century British industry 119
   RICHARD PRICE

6 The First of May 1890 in France: the birth of a working-class ritual 143
   MICHELLE PERROT

7 Civic rituals and patterns of resistance in Barcelona, 1890–1930   173
   TEMMA KAPLAN

8 English landed society in the nineteenth-century   195
   F.M.L. THOMPSON

9   British and European bankers 1880–1914: an 'aristocratic bourgeoisie'?   215
JOSÉ HARRIS and PAT THANE

10   Problems of Jewish assimilation in Austria–Hungary in the nineteenth and twentieth centuries   235
PETER HANAK

11   Alternatives to class revolution: Central and Eastern Europe after the First World War   251
IVÁN T. BEREND

12   Vicissitudes of feudalism in modern Poland   283
ANTONI MACZAK

Index   299

Contributors

Maurice Agulhon, *Université de Paris I*
Iván T. Berend, *Karl Marx University, Budapest*
Geoffrey Crossick, *University of Essex*
Eugene D. Genovese, *University of Rochester*
Peter Hanak, *Institute of History, Hungarian Academy of Sciences*
José Harris, *St Catherine's College, Oxford*
Temma Kaplan, *University of California, Los Angeles*
Jürgen Kocka, *University of Bielefeld*
Antoni Maczak, *University of Warsaw*
Michelle Perrot, *Université de Paris VII*
Richard Price, *University of Maryland*
Joan Wallach Scott, *Brown University*
Pat Thane, *Goldsmiths' College, London*
F.M.L. Thompson, *Institute of Historical Research, University of London*

Introduction. Capitalism and its pre-capitalist heritage

PAT THANE and GEOFFREY CROSSICK

These essays have been gathered together as a tribute to Eric Hobsbawm on his retirement from his chair at Birkbeck College. The problems involved in compiling a collection that was necessarily limited in size yet also thematically coherent will be obvious to anyone familiar with the diversity of his work and influence, and they are indeed further testimony to both. His work has ranged widely in time, though lying mainly in the period from the late eighteenth to the early twentieth centuries; in subject matter, from jazz to the Fabians;[1] and in geographical scope. Those who have been influenced, inspired, or personally and generously helped by him are similarly various in intellectual, geographical and age range. The choice of contributors and of topics was therefore unusually difficult, though much assisted by the simultaneous plans for a complementary volume edited by Raphael Samuel and Gareth Stedman Jones, which enabled more people to express their appreciation of Eric Hobsbawm and his work than would otherwise have been possible.

In selecting a theme we chose what appears to us to be the central theme of much of his work. This was the dialectical relationship between capitalism and its pre-capitalist heritage; what is revolutionized or what is adapted or rejected from the older societies in the process of transition to full industrial capitalism; the process by which, within certain limits, the pre-capitalist heritage shapes and informs economic, social, political and cultural change among all social groups, and within the society as a whole. All of the essays in this collection bear upon this theme, with the exception of Eugene Genovese's introductory assessment of Eric Hobsbawm's work. Most of them were discussed at a conference held at King's College, Cambridge in July 1982.

It is not our concern, nor that of our contributors, to draw up a balance sheet of what does and what does not change over time. Still less are we pursuing the now fashionable, but in our view questionable, strategy in historical writing of emphasizing the continuities in historical experience, playing down the significance and the effect of change and discontinuities in the past. To do so would

1

provide a strange tribute indeed to a historian whose most widely read book is *The Age of Revolution*. Our concern is rather to explore the intensely complex nature of the process of change during the growth of industrial capitalism; in particular the ways in which older social, economic, political and cultural forms – whether they be structures, institutions, movements, ideologies, rituals, vocabulary – help to shape the new, and in that process find themselves reshaped. A new type of society did not spring up fully formed in the nineteenth century, relatively untouched by the past; nor was what remained of the old society mere vestigial survivals, but active agents, and not necessarily agents of progress. As several of these essays stress – particularly those by Kocka, Price, and Harris and Thane – historians have often worked with models of change inherited from Marx, the classical economists and classic social theorists, which all assumed a greater rapidity and totality of change than appears to have occurred. One consequence has been an excessive stress on the role of new groups – the factory proletariat and the industrial bourgeoisie in particular – in creating the new society, with a resulting neglect of such supposedly declining groups as the landed aristocracy and craft workers who loom so large in this book.

A fuller and more accurate assessment of the process of change requires that we free ourselves from rigid presuppositions, categories and concepts, from narrow conceptions of the nature and purpose of history, and from romantic interpretations of it. As Genovese points out, freedom from these constraints has characterized Eric Hobsbawm's own work and has been perhaps his greatest influence. For Hobsbawm, the historian's role is to contribute to the writing of that 'history of society' which is no compartmentalized 'social history' abstracted from the history of power, politics or economics, but quite the reverse. The 'history of society' must attempt to integrate historical inquiry, to seek out the complex relations among these separate but associated processes, in pursuit of the central issue of how power, in all its dimensions, is constructed, maintained and exercised in any given society, or in any set of international relationships.

The essays in this volume reveal such concerns and approaches. They all contribute to the organizing theme, but they do so across a range of different issues now regarded as important by historians. One of Eric Hobsbawm's great achievements lies in his contribution to that broadening of the concerns of historians and, more significantly, to the elaboration of the way these concerns fit together in a more integrated and more creative historical analysis. Some central interests of recent historical writing flow from this, and they are important elements within this book. There is, at the outset, the recognition that change since the late eighteenth century has been complex and by no means unilinear, and that groups once thought simply to have 'declined', notably artisans and landed aristocrats, have played formative roles within it. The precise nature of these roles is now being explored: that of artisans in shaping the culture, ideology and organizations of the developing working class; whether aristocracies have indeed, as has been recently argued, maintained hegemony over European bourgeoisies and hence, presumably, over everyone else. This implies close attention to the subtle forces shaping classes; to their composition; their experiences and the ideas, vocabulary and ritual through which they sought to make sense of them; and the meaning and explanation of those ideologies, including many once dismissed as 'utopian' (such as co-operativism) or underestimated (such as nationalism); and to those forces which may fragment them internally, perhaps with disabling results.

Maurice Agulhon opens by analysing the process whereby working-class identity and solidarity were created out of the great variety of material and cultural experiences of the working population in different trades, whether in the home, workshop, fields or factory. He shows how the leading role in the formation of a distinctive ideology and forms of organization in France in the decades before 1848 was taken not by classic factory proletarians, but by craft workers in old-established but changing trades. Work and sociability intertwine as he reconstructs the process whereby material circumstances and custom brought them together in the workshop, the lodging house, the café, in associations devoted to leisure or to mutual support. Political ideas and action grew out of institutions initially and perhaps primarily devised for sociability; institutions that grew fast during the July Monarchy, in part as the people emulated the bourgeois associational model; and it was the discussions and conversations built around the sociability of daily life that sharpened the discovery of shared needs and grievances. Consciousness and organization thus grew not only from economic and political experiences but through the development of patterns of social behaviour which helped to shape the content, the language and the form of political and economic aspirations and action. Chief among these aspirations was that for a democratic republic of mutually supportive co-operative workshops. Agulhon helps us to comprehend the passionate defence of the democratic and social republic.

Agulhon raises a theme explored more fully by Joan Scott: the fact that for Parisian tailors of the 1830s and 1840s proletarianization meant not the move to the factory, but being forced from the relative independence of the workshop to the sweated labour of the whole family in the home. Indeed, she adds to the increasing realization that the family work unit cannot be seen simplistically as something displaced by industrialization. Amongst Parisian tailors it was no inheritance from the past, destined for destruction, but in many small-scale trades the creation of nineteenth-century industrialization. Family production was an area into which many retreated as they struggled to cope with the economic difficulties created by the capitalist transformation of small-scale production. Scott's discussion of an experience which stretched through much of Europe in these decades enables her to draw together two themes so often separated, those of labour history and of gender and work. She demonstrates how the experiences of the family in relation to work shaped workers' economic and social ideals in a manner which did not consign work, family, leisure, politics and culture to separate and unrelated spheres of existence. This conception of life, both real and ideal, as an indivisible and non-alienated totality was – as Kocka, Price, Perrot and Kaplan all in different ways suggest – central to the worldview, the 'moral economy' of artisans and other labouring people in Western Europe in early industrialization. Artisanal ideals and culture developed in part as a reaction to proletarianization, but they were more precisely about the way that process of subordination to the forces of capital was experienced as a challenge and an affront to expectations and cultures of daily life that found their roots in older ideals of independence, morality and community. That is why so many of the workers' movements and activities discussed in the early essays here were essentially popular, drawing on a wider world of the ordinary people that would include many not strictly wage earners, those producers and traders who complete the social world of the European urban working class for a good part of the nineteenth century. The transition from communal to class solidarities was no sudden one. The ambiguities remain as late as the periods examined by Perrot and Kaplan.

Scott also demonstrates how the reform strategies of male and female workers – tailors and seamstresses – differed as a result not only of their different work experiences but of long-established gender distinctions, in their beliefs about the relationship between work, home and family. In spite of such differences, however, they united on a common conception of a co-operativist form of social, political and economic organization which incorporated a conception of family roles quite distinct from prevalent bourgeois conceptions of the family (above all in the belief that mothers had a right to as well as a need for paid employment, but in non-exploitative conditions which made adequate provision for child care), which were appropriate for their needs, as bourgeois family ideals were not, and which were, in principle, capable of realization. They did not represent a mere nostalgic clinging to the past but were proposals for a different and better future, developed out of the way present experience was interpreted and understood through long-held notions and ideals.

In the later nineteenth century, as Scott points out, both male and female French workers did seek to consign mothers to a separate social sphere, free from paid work. This process must be related, in as yet insufficiently explored ways, to a wider splintering of the artisan economy (with its assumptions of morality and regulation) with the advance of industrial capitalism, a theme also referred to in different contexts by Kocka and Price. The importance of the artisan experience in the formation of the working class and its ideology is well established in the historiography of France, where large-scale industry developed late and slowly, and where the egalitarian rhetoric of a victorious revolution offered a vocabulary to artisan protest, while the structures and assumptions of a corporatist past gave it a moral and associationist critique of the present.

Jürgen Kocka points out that the similar role of journeymen and other handworkers in the cultural and political organizations of the German working class in the 1830s and 1840s and in the trade unions and socialist organizations of the 1860s and 1870s has been overlooked. He argues that, as in France and Britain, their role must not be seen as a simple matter of the protests of a declining economic group against the engulfing tide of industrialization, protests rooted in long-established craft guilds. In fact, in Germany as elsewhere, the numbers of workshop-based independent craftsmen expanded alongside and in close association with the growth of factories, though not without themselves changing. Their movements were not primarily defensive, but constituted a highly developed if ultimately unsuccessful offensive against the ideology and institutions of industrial capitalism. This alternative artisan moral economy was, as in France, essentially co-operativist and as critical of narrowly defensive and divisive artisan traditions and strategies as of capitalist social, political and economic relations. German journeymen in particular had little reason for enthusiasm for the survivals of the old guild structure which functioned to conserve the authority and privileges of masters against themselves. Kocka sums up his interpretation, in asserting that 'it was not only, perhaps not even primarily, the conflict between capital and labour ... which produced those challenges, frictions, frustrations and propensity to protest out of which the early working-class movement grew, but also, more importantly, the conflict between the traditional culture and capitalist modernization'. Although they might not all agree with the firmness of Kocka's order of priority there, the theme and the reinterpretation connect with those of Agulhon, Scott and Price here, as well as those of others outside this volume. Early labour protest was fuelled by fury against the offence to family life, to patterns of leisure as well as of work organization, but above all to the artisan's sense of independence, the desire to control his or her own life, which capitalism meant to working people; offences the more resented because they could envisage an alternative way forward which could conserve all that they valued whilst extending it and benefiting from new forces of production, but whose realization was endlessly frustrated. This alternative has been dismissed as 'utopian' or 'immature' because its origins and meaning have been misunderstood, but it served, for a while at least, to unite workers across boundaries of gender, trade and region, a unity which underpinned later, different movements. Not, of course, all or even most workers; Kocka points out that some trades were changed too little, others too much (to the point of destruction) to play a significant part in the process. For those which did, artisan traditions facilitated common action even where formalized institutions did not exist. Journeymen of the same trade often maintained contact with one another beyond local boundaries, facilitated by their tradition of mobility, their shared trade-specific symbols and rites, qualifications and work experiences, benefit societies, shared language and loyalties.

If in this sense and by all these means the working class was 'made' in Western Europe in the first half of the nineteenth century, it was, as Kocka, Scott and also Price suggest, united by a moral economy which could not retain its coherence against an assault determined to splinter the social, economic and political spheres. However, the sense of artisan independence long continued to shape the actions of labouring people. This is the theme of Richard Price's discussion of the English working class, in which he explores more fully than other contributors the dynamics of the contest for cultural and economic control between 'master' and 'servant', as they were designated by English labour law until the 1870s, at which point they became, significantly, 'employer' and 'workman'.

Price stresses the key role in British industrial production of craftsmen working in small units. They too experienced industrial capitalism as not just an assault upon their working lives but upon their entire culture, as employers recognized as clearly as they that work did not occupy a distinct social space and that habits of work were indissolubly linked with those of home and leisure; hence to establish work and time discipline they had also to control non-work time and its uses, establish a hegemony beyond the workplace, discipline workers to value higher incomes above longer leisure (whether drinking, family time or whatever), to abandon the old culture for a new. In Britain, Price argues, this was a longer and slower struggle than elsewhere, and fluctuating and uneven in its outcome. However, its very length in association with the slow development of British capitalism enabled British craft workers to establish a degree of autonomy in the workplace, which they were able to transpose to new structures of work as they developed, and which shaped and limited the techniques of control available to employers. It was and remained a struggle over independence, which Price describes as 'the key concept of a heightened and more unitary working-class consciousness'. An early outcome in England, as elsewhere (not explored by Price), was co-operativism, but again one of the victories of capitalism was to force the division of economic, political and cultural struggles so that in Britain by the 1870s 'industrial conflicts began to be conceptualized as economic struggles for rewards', which may have divided craft from craft more in Britain than in Germany. Kocka points out the greater craft exclusiveness of British unions compared with those of Germany in the later nineteenth century, as Price in his turn emphasizes the greater strength of craft autonomy in Britain, which has survived profoundly to influence the later history of British industrial relations and the British labour movement.

Both these essays uncover the importance of the craft tradition – whether embodied in corporate structures or more informal traditions of 'the trade' – in shaping the developing working-class movements of nineteenth-century Europe. German master artisans reaffirmed the authority and the corporate controls of the craft guilds in 1848, while their British counterparts had for twenty years or more been detaching themselves from workplace culture and artisanal traditions and expectations, thus seeking long before their journeymen to escape the influence and restrictions of the past. Here are the origins of Price's industrial conflicts over customary rights, as an expression of a fundamental rejection of processes under way in early nineteenth-century Britain. Here perhaps is one of the sources of the continuing craft traditions within British labour history.

Yet, and perhaps especially in those countries in which industrial capitalism developed more slowly, the older moral economy long retained a hold, as Michelle Perrot suggests in her study of the first May Day in France. The unifying desire of the active supporters of May Day was the 'three eights', the right to eight hours each of work, leisure and sleep, a totality each of whose elements had equal importance. She shows the remarkable extent to which this call appealed to great numbers of labouring people despite differences of region, gender, occupation and ideology, and the way their responses differed, shaped as they were by their cultural and immediate material experiences. It was not a movement based primarily on the workplace nor was it directed chiefly against employers, but was an appeal to the *state* for redress, suggestive both of the specific development of French industrial capitalism by 1890 and of the more assertive role ascribed to the French state compared with that of Britain. Is this a positive role for the state, rooted in republican memory and its symbols? The appeal was unsuccessful and Perrot's account suggests as much about the weakness and divisions among French workers as about their unity and strength.

So too does Temma Kaplan's account of the recurrent and often moving demonstrations of the working people of Barcelona against ultimately unassailable state authority. Again, the forms and language of working-class protest were, as in the first French May Day, profoundly shaped by custom – demonstrations took the paths of religious processions, workers asserted their rights through the symbolic occupation of public space, spurred by offences against popular morality as well as by claims against repression and for improved conditions. She shows how the popular cultures of urban life, and also the more community-based and even elite-based rituals, became a complicated means of popular resistance to oppression and repression. Shared traditions were a force for unity amongst otherwise disparate groups; the meaning of ritual could change in response to new experiences and thus new needs, but through its familiar form people could comprehend the meaning of action without the need to make it explicit. Kaplan stresses that that was all the more important when overt opposition was impossible.

This issue of the force of culture and custom is a central theme of the book. In part it demonstrates the use of older rituals and forms for new struggles, and the way the use of the old form gives shape to the meaning of the new struggle. Culture is not just a medium. Can customary expression act in essentially conservative ways, holding people in older frameworks of social analysis and understanding? Many of the essays in this book show the ambiguities of the relationship. Indeed, since Joan Scott can show how the response of French working women when faced with economic pressures was more creative about social relationships than was the response of men, could part of the explanation not lie in the absence of the older craft corporatist assumptions that shaped so much of French (male) artisans' responses? Perrot tells us most here about the power of ritual and custom. She shows how nineteenth-century socialists were anxious to create a new ritual, but did so by drawing on an older, a much older, vocabulary of visual and verbal symbols, and added to it the idea of the great day of manifestations, whose roots in the *journées* of the Revolutions gave added force to ruling-class fears. Fêtes and festivals thus were a powerful language, given meaning by the symbols that were used. May Day was to supplant the 14th of July, the workers' republic was to be asserted, and as she shows, at Doyet-Les-Mines the interweaving of working-class consciousness and republican faith showed how impossible are such absolute transformations of symbol and expression.

The mobilization of working people in nineteenth- and early twentieth-century Europe to maintain or achieve some independence within states, economic systems, and indeed cultures that were dominated by others is impressive, and its dynamics important, but by whom they were dominated and by what means is more often assumed than analysed. If artisans and their experiences played a more central role in shaping the modern working class than was long thought, 'pre-industrial' landed aristocracies showed no greater enthusiasm for the grave to which Marx and many classical economists too enthusiastically assigned them. A central theme in the history of industrial capitalism is what Peter Hanak describes as 'the adaptability of ruling elites'. As F.M.L. Thompson shows, great landowners played an essential role in its economic development, and there is a revived fashion for asserting their continued pre-eminence in the political, administrative and cultural life of industrial Britain, to a point at which they are claimed to have maintained hegemony over the bourgeoisie and thus over society as a whole. Of course, their immense wealth and power at the outset of industrialization gave them enormous opportunities which were exploited to the full by many, but they were themselves changed by the experience. It is quite wrong to think in terms of an 'aristocratic tradition', pickled and preserved through the upheavals of the nineteenth century. Certain rituals and poses were retained – robes, titles, an appearance of 'amateurism', an overt disdain for 'trade', and of course landownership itself – but these were now kept not as empty traditions but because they served new functions in maintaining the landowners' changed role in changed societies.

As Harris and Thane argue, although the aristocracy and their descendants retained much power they not only shaped but were changed by their relations with other classes and by their involvement in new forms of activity, so that by 1914 a great hereditary landowner in Britain or elsewhere had more in common with a banker or a steelmaster than with his *ancien régime* ancestor. He was not entirely transformed, and he was still well aware of the ways in which he differed from such wealthy bourgeois, but this is not the central issue. That is the matter of whether landowners as a group wielded power commensurate with that of their ancestors, politically, economically or socially. They plainly did not, though they retained more in some countries than in others. Similarly in relation to the European bankers with whom Harris and Thane maintain a running comparison with aristocrats: if they had ever been the dependent servants of courts and nobles in early modern Europe (and that is doubtful), they changed their economic and political character in the course of industrialization as emphatically as did the aristocrats with whom they so frequently mixed. This chapter reminds us of the distorting effects of that revisionism in historical writing which sees the only alternative to transformation as the continuity of old patterns. The precise relationships between and within landowning and bourgeois groups and of both to states – which Genovese rightly describes as 'not a mere reflex of class interest . . . a political centre with considerable autonomy and yet ultimately compelled to act in the interests of the propertied class' – remain even less understood than the relationships and the divisions within the populace and the working class.

One source of division at all levels of society was religion and ethnicity, which Peter Hanak introduces in his study of the Jews of Austria-Hungary. Here the universal European experience of an interpenetration of old landowning and new business and professional elites – a process fraught with tension – was fundamentally influenced by the fact that the latter were overwhelmingly Jews of recent migration. Comparisons between the experiences of Western and East-Central Europe in the nineteenth and twentieth centuries have to be treated with care, in view of the profound differences between the societies in which capitalism expanded fastest and which were mostly independent liberal democracies, and that combination of failing imperial power, dependent status and weak peripheral economies described by Berend, which characterized Central and Eastern Europe. Yet Hanak's description of the processes whereby the Jews' own culture (whose homogeneity he rightly questions) gave shape to their behaviour and environment, and was in turn changed by it, as they to varying degrees assimilated to those sectors of the host societies which were, however ambiguously, most prepared to receive them and whose values were closest to their own, is a study of the complex interplay of tradition and change whose

10   Pat Thane and Geoffrey Crossick

significance goes beyond his immediate subject. Indeed, the study of cultural and ethnic assimilation is almost a perfect case of the analytical theme of this collection, for it involves the dialectical relationship between historical forces (economic life, culture, social and demographic structures, religion) each of which are changed, and continue to be changed, by the very process of interaction that the historian is exploring and calls assimilation. Hanak's argument is of further interest, for his description of the 'assimilation to the nobility in public and preservation of the bourgeois in business and Jewish culture in private life' of successful Central European Jews is a further thrust against those who would simplify aristocratic-bourgeois relations in recent history.

Another and far more tragic one is the all too evident fact that the Jews of East and Central Europe never assimilated so successfully as to be simply accepted, nor did the old elites maintain sufficiently confident authority to accept them. Amid the upheavals and misery of Central and Eastern Europe during and after World War I, as Iván Berend describes, the old elites could hold on strongly enough to defeat the forces of revolution from below, but not to subdue them entirely or to retain power on the old basis in a radically changed political world and a deteriorating economic situation. This could only be done by a new kind of movement which drew upon both the old and the new, which could feed off widely held grievances and ideals – against the excesses of failed capitalism, yet also against the destructive forces of class conflict, above all for a unifying and restoring nationalism. Fascism proved itself as capable as any movement of mobilizing and transforming long-held sentiment, symbol and ritual in the forging of a spirit of unity.

Berend's comments upon the drive in the countries of East and Central Europe in the 1920s and 1930s to throw off their peripheral political and economic status, and the national movements that resulted have a certain contemporary relevance, as obviously does Maczak's concluding piece. His description of how certain economic structures and cultural responses may have survived through six hundred years of change in Polish history, though with profoundly altered meaning and content for rulers and ruled, both bears upon the central theme of the volume and is a suitable note on which to conclude a tribute to a historian whose history and politics have never been dissociated.

NOTE

1 See Keith McClelland, 'Bibliography of the writings of Eric Hobsbawm', in Raphael Samuel and Gareth Stedman Jones (eds.), *Culture, Ideology and Politics. Essays for Eric Hobsbawm* (London 1982), pp. 332–63.

ACKNOWLEDGMENTS

The editors are grateful to the Maison des Sciences de l'Homme, the Nuffield Foundation, King's College, Cambridge and the British Academy for their financial support for the conference in Eric Hobsbawm's honour at which earlier versions of most of the essays in this volume were first discussed; to Birkbeck College for the provision of secretarial facilities; and to Antony Polonsky for his assistance with the final preparation of chapter 12. The following people, through their participation in the conference, helped in the final shaping of the papers: Robert Browning, David Blackbourn, Logie Barrow, Virginia Berridge, Gill Burke, David Goodway, Istvan Hondt, Patrick Joyce, Victor Kiernan, Heinz Lubasz, Wolfgang Mommsen, Alastair Reid, Raphael Samuel, John Saville, Deborah Valenze, Bernd Weisbrod and Jonathan Zeitlin.

1

The politics of class struggle in the history of society: an appraisal of the work of Eric Hobsbawm

EUGENE D. GENOVESE

At first and deceptive glance Eric Hobsbawm has influenced Marxist historiography much less than some of his contemporaries, although few if any serious historians, Marxist or no, have remained without a large debt to his work. No 'Hobsbawm School' has arisen, nor should we expect one to arise. Hobsbawm, in concentrating on the development of the 'school' associated with the political movement to which he has dedicated his life, has advanced a Marxism at once living, coherent, undogmatic, and with hegemonic prospects. His specific achievements on a breathtaking array of subjects, the product of his exceptional talent, have added up to a demonstration of the superiority of historical materialism as method and worldview. For his students – for all who endeavour to write Marxist history today – to be 'Hobsbawmian' means to be Marxist, neither more nor less, although it does not mean that we must accept all his views, judgments, and interpretations, any more than he himself accepts all of Marx's.

Hobsbawm has generally eschewed direct participation in the ideological struggles that have rent Marxist historiography and have pitted Marxists against radicals who, when they do not repudiate theory altogether, assert one or another variant of 'humanist' idealism. Yet his work has constituted a powerful defence of historical materialism, most notably by its consistent demonstration that it can take full account of art, science, religion, ideology, and even social psychology without surrendering to the disguised subjectivism of 'critical theory', the romance of lower-class 'culture', or assorted other fads. From his earliest work he has subscribed to the essential materialist viewpoint expressed in his Preface to *The History of Marxism*: 'Both the thought and practice of Marx and of subsequent Marxists are the product of their times, whatever their permanent intellectual validity or practical achievement.'[1] Thus he has vigorously defended the theoretical outline of historical development that Marx provided in his famous Preface to the *Introduction to the Critique of Political Economy* – 'marvellous', 'neglected', 'superb'[2] – without ever allowing himself to become imprisoned in its categories.

13

Hobsbawm rejects unilinear readings of historical materialism and of the historical record, although some ambiguity arises from one of his rare ritualistic bows to received doctrine. I cannot imagine what he means by writing: 'Certainly no Marxist would deny that the forces which made for economic development in Europe operate everywhere, though not necessarily with the same results in different social and historical circumstances.'[3] Despite this puzzling concession to the unilinearists, who normally prefer to assimilate pre-capitalist economic formations to 'feudalism', he turns the tables on them. In yielding, in general formulation, to this tendency toward assimilation, Hobsbawm immediately returns the discussion to a consideration of the possibility that some forms of 'feudalism', perhaps most, showed no signs of evolving toward capitalism: 'It is very doubtful whether we can speak of a *universal* tendency of feudalism to develop into capitalism.'[4]

Constant attention to material conditions and the forces of production puts a healthy distance between Hobsbawm and such dogmatisms as unilinearism and leftwing subjectivism. In general, and especially in his crowning work on society since the French and Industrial Revolutions, he balances the objective and subjective elements in historical process. He does not confuse class with class consciousness or reduce the one to the other – a sleight of hand that renders Marxism useless for the interpretation of pre-industrial societies. As Hobsbawm observes, class consciousness appeared rarely before the advent of industrial capitalism. He might well add that if Marxism, with its projected centrality of class struggle, only becomes useful when historians reach the eighteenth century, then it has little to offer beyond a set of insights into a brief period and a special set of problems.

The reduction of class to class consciousness obscures everything of importance. The elaboration and defence of historical materialism require a discrete consideration of categories and a constant effort to identify and, as it were, measure the conscious aspects of class and class struggle. If class and class struggles as such have not shaped historical process through their objective development, then our theory is wrong.

Hobsbawm's clearest discussion of these problems appears in an essay on class consciousness in history, the principal theses of which receive substantial support in his histories.[5] He begins by noting that Marx used 'class' in two senses: (1) according to the objective criterion of human relation to the means of production, especially as exploiters and exploited; and (2) according to the subjective criterion of class consciousness. Marx and Engels used class in the first sense to open the *Communist Manifesto* and in 'what we might call Marx's macro-theory'. He adds, 'Class in the full sense only comes into existence at the historical moment when classes being [*sic*: begin] to acquire consciousness of themselves as such' – that is, largely with the appearance of industrial capitalism.[6]

Hobsbawm's discussion displays the tendency that plagues all who focus primarily on the history of capitalism – the tendency to feel uncomfortable with the objective meaning of class and to hurry to a consideration of modern conditions. Thus he comes close to denying his own careful distinction: 'For the purpose of the historian, the student of micro-history, or of "history as it happened" (and of the present "as it happens") as distinct from the general and rather abstract models of the historical transformation of societies, class and the problem of class consciousness are inseparable'.[7] Now, since he accepts Marx's view that classes have existed since the breakup of communal society, whereas class consciousness 'is a phenomenon of the modern industrial era',[8] he comes close to denying the centrality of class struggles to pre-industrial history. For if historians must focus on what actually happened, if classes are inseparable from the problem of class consciousness, if self-conscious classes only arose with the industrial era – then we remain with a pre-industrial world in which objectively defined classes lack class consciousness, are therefore hardly classes at all, and cannot readily be taxed with much of a historical role.

Hobsbawm's own writing on pre-capitalist societies and his other statements in the essay 'Class Consciousness in History' suggest that he intends no such meaning.[9] 'The absence of class consciousness in the modern sense,' he writes, 'does not imply the absence of classes and class conflict. But it is evident that in the modern economy this changes quite fundamentally.'[10] He resolves the apparent contradiction by advancing a hypothesis that deserves the fullest exploration by Marxist historians: throughout history classes have responded to objective pressures by actions that, at their height, have included at least a rudimentary sense of themselves as classes. Despite occasional lapses from his customary clarity of formulation, Hobsbawm's struggle with the vexing problem of the subjective aspect of class remains powerful, even if its full development must necessarily be the collective result of much specialized, individual work. But another, almost submerged side to that contribution helps explain his apparent hesitations while it promises to enrich both Marxist theory and Marxist politics.

In elaborating his ideas on proletarian class consciousness, Hobsbawm, echoing Lenin, insists that its flowering requires formal organization as the carrier of class ideology. 'Bourgeois or middle-class movements,' he observes, 'can operate as "stage armies of the good", proletarian ones can only operate as *real* armies with *real* generals and staffs.'[11] But he does not leave the matter where Lenin had left it. First, he argues, without formal organization for action the proletariat must 'remain as subaltern as the common people of the pre-industrial past'.[12] This judgment implicitly criticizes attempts to read popular culture as inherently political in a positive sense or, worse, as a substitute for politics. Second, he says flatly that Marxists must rethink the idea that the proletariat has been cast by history as the grave-digger of capitalism. In exploring the political ramifications of this viewpoint, he notes:

> The crucial problem for socialists is that revolutionary socialist regimes, unlike bourgeois ones, arise not out of a class, but out of a characteristic combination of class and organization. It is not the working class itself which takes power and exercises hegemony, but the working class *movement* or party, and (short of taking an anarchist view) it is difficult to see how it could be otherwise. In this respect the historical development of the USSR has been quite logical, though not necessarily inevitable.[13]

Hobsbawm thus lays the groundwork for insisting that, more often than not, the bourgeoisie has not so much made the bourgeois revolutions as it has been made by them. And further back of the bourgeois epoch, questions arise about the role of force, including revolutionary force, in historical change. For it is one thing to cite the class struggles in, for example, ancient slave society, and another to assert that slaves, coloni, peasants, and urban proletarians and lumpenproletarians proved the revolutionary carriers of the feudalism that replaced slave society. Hobsbawm demonstrates throughout his histories that such formulas will not serve. And it remains inescapable that the socialist revolutions of our century have, with the partial exception of the Russian, been won by movements with a proletarian ideology but other than a proletarian social base.

Hobsbawm's view must be understood in the context of his positive reading of Marx's Preface to the *Introduction to the Critique of Political Economy*:

> Marx sought to establish the general mechanism of *all* social change: the formation of social relations of production which correspond to a definite stage of development of the material forces of production; the periodic development of conflicts between the forces and relations of production; the 'epochs of social revolution' in which the relations once again adjust themselves to the level of the forces.[14]

Hobsbawm observes that the Preface does not contain the word 'class': 'For classes are merely special cases of social relations of production at particular – though admittedly very long – periods of history.'[15] This insight, perhaps more his own than Marx's, despite its origins in Marx's thought, calls for a radical rethinking of the thesis of history as the story of struggles for control of the social surplus and the emphasis on classes in those struggles. It invites attention to the importance of social differentiation in pre-class societies as well as in socialist societies and to struggles for the social surplus between whole communities and peoples.

In pursuing these theoretical questions, Hobsbawm has called for a 'history of society' and has been practising what he has been preaching.[16] I refer here not to his impressive integration of art, science, religion, technology, and so much else, especially in his great work on the nineteenth century, for that integration constitutes more a tribute to his encylopaedic range and intellectual depth than to his method.[17] What historian would not like to do as much? And if few can even make the attempt without embarrassing themselves, the failure of the many ordinarily says much more about the limits of talent than about the seriousness of intentions. Nor does his work stand as an attempt, even if more successful than most, to write 'global history', in the manner of those *annalistes* who offer lush trees that do not add up to a forest or, worse, add up to an ideologically constructed and imaginary forest.

Hobsbawm understands society as pre-eminently political, and he brings to centre stage that particular, historically essential politics which permits us to extract the dynamics of process from a frustrating maze of endless information. Perhaps in no other way has he so firmly established himself as an 'orthodox' Marxist while never hesitating to discard what has proven inadequate, dated, or wrong in Marxist thought. He has, for example, focused on the problem of the relation of the bourgeois-democratic to the proletarian revolution and has accepted the challenge from which Marxist historians normally shrink: the failure of an international proletarian revolution. His many-sided contribution to an anatomy of that failure has flowed from his mastery of the history of society as a whole. Those who, in contrast, try to write the history of the working class with scant attention to the national bourgeoisies and residual aristocracies and to the hegemony of ruling-class culture have invariably ended by obscuring the outcome. For the working class, whatever its cultural achievements, did not storm the Winter Palaces of Western Europe. It rarely even tried.

In unravelling this story, Hobsbawm has demonstrated the value of an intellectually disciplined political commitment that constructively dictates the questions without prejudging the answers. He has demonstrated thereby that the vantage point of historical materialism has no worthy rival for those who would both see the nineteenth century whole and understand the roots of the protracted crises of socialism as well as capitalism in the twentieth century.

Hobsbawm's work on the nineteenth century, the centrepiece of his life's work, contains a hard critique of the 'labouring poor' and the emerging industrial proletariat. His communist politics prove decisive here. Never does he succumb to a gnashing of teeth, to retrospective rebukes, to condemnation of the dead for having disappointed the expectations of their heirs. His balanced critique of strengths and weaknesses proceeds on the assumption that only an accurate and unsentimental history – a history that, while politically engaged, resists ideological impositions – can serve the ends of a socialist movement that expects to win.

His harsh critique of the revolutions of 1848 faces a reality unpalatable to many Marxists and others on the Left. That he demolishes so many of Marxism's most cherished myths quietly and without ruffling too many sensibilities testifies to his self-control and aversion for partisan polemics. It may also explain the apparent failure of many of his leftwing readers to notice or at least appreciate fully the range and depth of his implicit attack on reigning pieties. Hobsbawm does not mince words about the much heralded, eagerly awaited great revolution of 1848:

> It failed, universally, rapidly and – though this was not realized for several years by the political refugees – definitively. Henceforth there was to be no general social revolution of the kind envisaged before 1848 in the 'advanced' countries of the world. The centre of gravity of such social revolutionary movements, and therefore of twentieth-century socialist and communist regimes, was to be in the marginal and backward regions. . . .. The sudden, vast and apparently boundless expansion of the world capitalist economy provided political alternatives in the 'advanced' countries.[18]

Hobsbawm notes that the 'labouring poor' drove the revolutions of 1848 well beyond the political demands of even the radical bourgoisie, only to suffer a crushing defeat once the issue had been joined as one of Order versus Social Revolution. He provides a devastating reply to the celebrants of the culture of the labouring classes: 'The labouring poor . . . lacked the organization, the maturity, the leadership, perhaps most of all the historical conjuncture, to provide a political alternative.'[19] The defeats of 1848 and after emerge from his account as the result both of the strength of the bourgeoisie – its economic performance, however flawed, and above all its ability to master popular politics – and the weakness of the labouring poor and the working class, whose celebrated autonomous culture could not save them from the increasing lure of bourgeois nationalism and their own inability, despite heroic efforts, to forge the class unity requisite for a struggle for power.

Hobsbawm, developing this theme throughout his work, illuminates both the historical record and current struggles. In 'Methodism and the Threat of Revolution in Britain', for example, he writes: 'As Lenin argued – a specialist on the subject – a deterioration of the conditions of life for the masses, and an increase in their political activity, is not enough to bring about a revolution. There must also be a crisis in the affairs of the ruling order, and a body of revolutionaries capable of directing and leading the movement.'[20] Accordingly, 1830, not 1848, emerges as the great turning point after the French Revolution. For although the revolutions of 1848 unleashed 'the communist spectre that was haunting Europe', their defeat exorcized it. Their defeat destroyed the possibilities for an international social revolution and confirmed politically the economic power of the solid bourgeoisie. After Hobsbawm's delineation of the political contours of the period, working-class history cannot plausibly be written without full and careful attention to the bourgeoisie.

Hobsbawm betrays no astonishment at the evidence that workers frequent taverns in which their conversation over drinks departs from bourgeois standards and rejects some bourgeois values. Probably, no historian of labour overmatches his respect and sympathy for workers, his vast knowledge of their living and working conditions, and his disdain, itself born of respect for the people he is writing about, for all attempts to romanticize their dissent or to pretend that it may be substituted for engaged politics.

He often does write of the culture of workers, peasants, village artisans and labourers, and others. Some of his finest, and certainly his angriest, writing concerns their oppression, the indignities to which they have been subjected, and the courage and resourcefulness with which they have fought back. Nowhere does he come so close to losing his temper as in his outburst against those historians who slight 'what industrial capitalism actually did to people's feelings as well as to their bodies'.[21] Throughout such books as *Primitive Rebels, Bandits, Labouring Men, Revolutionaries*, not to mention *The Jazz Scene*, he combines respect for the efforts of labouring people to fashion their own lives with a refusal to minimize the terrible extent to which they have been victims and have, in consequence, developed some unattractive, self-destructive, and socially dangerous tendencies. Hobsbawm does some blunt speaking in his appreciative analysis of the Captain Swing rising: 'The condition of the southern labourer was such that he required only some special stimulus – admittedly it would have to be exceptionally powerful to overcome his demoralized passivity – to produce a very widespread movement.'[22]

Hobsbawm's judicious treatment of the strength and weakness of the people with whose struggles for justice he passionately identifies appears in especially moving form in his studies of social bandits. That treatment, which eschews judgments from on high about how people ought to have lived, fought, and died, constitutes a necessary political evaluation for anyone who takes his or her political commitments seriously. *Primitive Rebels* and *Bandits* explore the limits of popular resistance under given historical conditions and are unsparing about the negative and even ghastly features of banditry. While delineating the circumstances in which various kinds of rebels can become revolutionary and the circumstances in which they deserve the respect of revolutionaries, he prettifies neither men nor movements. His portrait of Salvatore Giuliano gives that attractive thug all the respect and sympathy he had any reason to expect – actually, too much for my taste – but it leaves no doubt about the character of the man and the social effects of his activity. Or more generally: 'To be terrifying and pitiless is a more important attribute of this bandit than to be a friend of the poor.'[23]

Hobsbawm's treatment of these questions prepares us for a paradox in his big books on industrial capitalist society. For there is much less in them than some might demand about working-class culture and related matters. Yet *The Age of Revolution, The Age of Capital*, and *Industry and Empire*, taken together and especially if supplemented by the essays in *Labouring Men* and *Revolutionaries*, come as close to providing that 'history of society' as anything available.

Hobsbawm does not slight the cultural achievements of the working class. He notes that a labour movement began to emerge as a way of life during the first half of the nineteenth century, and that by 1848 the risings of the labouring poor were making the revolutionary demand for a new kind of society. Instead of rejecting the 'old' labour history's emphasis on working-class organization and direct political intervention, he enriches it through attention to the cultural dimension. At his hands culture illuminates problems of class struggle; it does not substitute for them. Thus he contributes significantly to an explanation of the failure of the working class during the nineteenth century without denigrating its struggles and everyday efforts. As part of that project he provides a skilful dissection of the forces for disunity in the working class – another subject of capital importance that requires much more attention than it has been getting from labour historians.[24]

In a peerless exploration entitled 'Society Since 1914', which implicitly challenges the uncritical celebration of working-class culture as an end in itself, Hobsbawm demonstrates that the British workers have indeed won impressive battles on the cultural front, only to find themselves unable to win the political war.[25] The twentieth century has brought a substantial net improvement in the standard of living and a noteworthy if inadequate deterioration in the bases of inequality, but the white-collar workers, who generally have earned no more than the best paid industrial workers, have found their status, relative to that of the mass of industrial workers, gravely compromised. Those white-collar workers and the less affluent among the middle classes saw their most revered status symbols crumble after World War II. The servants went first, and then, to make matters intolerable, clothing became standardized and no longer marked status. The political and ideological malaise of the working class, which long predated the current economic slump, has not arisen from economic hardship, for the working class has provided the very centre of the new mass-consumer economy. Hobsbawm effectively argues that the working class, especially the young workers, have increasingly set the pace for popular culture and that strong elements of social dissent have gone into the making. But he insists that it has accompanied political malaise rather than a heightened revolt against capitalism – that it is one thing to grasp the cultural dimension of politics and another to pretend that culture can substitute for politics.

In 'Karl Marx and the British Labour Movement' he makes short work of those who would dismiss the working-class experience of Marx's day and ours as a matter of *embourgeoisement*. Marx and Engels knew that workers were not turning into modest copies of the middle class; that was not, and is not now, the point.[26] Rather, 'The peculiarity of Britain is that it was the oldest, for a long time the most successful and dominant, and almost certainly the stablest capitalist society, and that its bourgeoisie had to come to terms with a proletarian majority of the population long before any other.'[27] From this perspective, he can provide a sound historical analysis of the political and cultural advance of the British working class, shed light on its divisions, and explain much of its current dilemma without imposing his own political preferences and thereby slipping into wishful thinking.

These studies of industrial societies and peoples, buttressed by the studies of pre-industrial, yield important theoretical insights into the nature and inter-relations of social classes:

> Class is not merely a relationship between groups, it is also their coexistence within a social, cultural, institutional framework set by those above. The world of the poor, however elaborate, self-contained, and separate, is a subaltern and therefore in some sense incomplete world, for it normally takes for granted the existence of the general framework of those who have hegemony, or at any rate its inability for most of the time to do much about it. It accepts their hegemony, even when it challenges some of its implications because largely it has to. Ideas, models, and situations in which action becomes possible tend to reach it from the outside, if only because the initiative that changes conditions on a national scale comes from above or because the mechanisms for diffusing ideas are generally outside.[28]

He disposes of the confused objection that deference to elites should not be assumed, and demonstrates that such deference, presumed or actual, is not the issue. 'The popular classes,' he writes, 'fall under the influence of the hegemonic culture because it is in a sense the only culture that operates as such through literacy – the very construction of a standard national language belongs to the literate elite. The very process of reading and schooling diffuses it, even unintentionally.'[29] As he so often does, he adds secondary theses to guide theoretical and empirical work on a variety of subjects. He rejects the mechanistic notion that high culture can be understood simply as propaganda. 'Rather, popular ideas cannot be understood without recalling the hegemony of high culture' – a generalization he defends in part by a sensitive reading of Ernesto Ragionieri's work on Tuscany, in which high culture emerges as a primary medium for a popular revolt against stultifying tradition.

And he adds two arresting suggestions: that nineteenth-century bourgeois culture, with its theoretical invitation to mass participation, did indeed appeal, if in different ways, to different classes; and that the traditional peasants spurned it not so much because it was anti-traditional as because it was being carried by those, whether bourgeois or socialist, who 'appeared to bring nothing but trouble'.[30] These suggestions do not imply denial of or disrespect for the autonomous cultural achievements of the labouring poor and the working class. Rather, they illuminate the limits of cultural autonomy, the political complexities of its relation to bourgeois culture, and the nature and extent of bourgeois hegemony.

Hobsbawm's writing on economic history exemplifies the kind of 'history of society' he is talking about. His great work on the Industrial Revolution in relation to the French Revolution especially stands out since he has developed his thesis of a dual revolution at adequate length. But for just that reason we might consider instead his pioneering work on the general crisis of the seventeenth century, which had to be compressed and which superficially appears a more strictly economic history.[31] In fact, it cannot be understood solely or even primarily as a contribution to economic history, narrowly defined, although it is that too. It analyses the roots of a crisis of society as a whole in the political economy of a declining feudalism and an emergent but as yet precariously perched capitalism, but it also invites consideration of the many-faceted organism to which it gave rise.

Hobsbawm risks a narrower reading by occasionally falling into ambiguous phrasing. Thus he opens his seminal essay: 'The European economy passed through a "general crisis" during the seventeenth century, the last phase of the general transition from a feudal to a capitalist economy.'[32] As the essay quickly makes clear, an essentially feudal society as a whole, not merely the economy, was in crisis. The very term 'general crisis' echoes Lenin's *Imperialism*, in which the crisis of world capitalism appears as the social crisis of a mode of production and, as such, as pre-eminently political.

Hobsbawm uses 'general' in two separate but related ways: to refer to the crisis of feudal society as a whole – a crisis that had roots in the economy but that manifested itself as a crisis of class rule; and to refer to the international crisis of the economy – a crisis primarily of the commercial market sector and, therefore, most dangerously, of the emergent capitalist sector. Had the international economic crisis occurred under ordinary feudal conditions, as it did during the fourteenth century, the end, as Hobsbawm suggests, would probably have been a retreat toward local, petty production and the strangling of the capitalist sector. The promising growth of capitalist production and capital accumulation that marked the sixteenth century would probably have proven one more false start. That it did not testifies to the extent and depth of the prior capitalist advance, most notably in England, and underscores the paradox to which Hobsbawm draws attention: 'Capitalism can only develop in an economy which is already substantially capitalist, for in any which is not, the capitalist forces will tend to adapt themselves to the prevailing economy and society, and will therefore not be sufficiently revolutionary.'[33]

Hobsbawm here makes two of his most striking theoretical contributions: first, he extends Marx's critique of merchant capital by uncovering the analogous role of the large-scale industrial capital that accompanied attempts like Colbert's to force the pace of industrialization without revolutionizing the social structure. Thereby he gives precise historical significance to his discussion of the 'paradox' of early capitalist development. This insight has yet to be exploited adequately by Marxist historians and was even resisted by Dobb.

Second, Hobsbawm presents what was to become one of his principal themes – the probability that the consolidation of capitalism, its survival and expansion as a social system after the squelching of many previous promising starts, required the conquest of the whole as yet thin and fragile world market by the bourgeoisie of a single nation-state or two at most. These intimately related theses provide essential ingredients for an understanding of the Industrial Revolution, which alone could have made the triumph of the capitalist mode of production irreversible.

The breakthrough occurred in England, in which, alone among the countries of adequate territorial extent and political consolidation, the decisive divorce of labour from the land and means of production had already taken place. Hobsbawm here follows Marx directly, in agreement with an impressive group of Marxist, and not only Marxist, historians. His specific contribution comes in his strong emphasis on the relation of this internal 'primitive accumulation' to the development of a world market and, more specifically, the founding of a new colonial system based most decisively on plantation slave labour.

Along the way he somewhat perversely credits Paul Sweezy with having been sounder than Dobb and more faithful to Marx's own analysis of the role of the world market in the transition from feudalism to capitalism.[34] Let us grant that Dobb, as well as Takahashi, Hilton, and others, may not have done full justice to the role of the world market in their generally correct emphasis on the internal transformation of the productive forces of English society. The burden of Hobsbawm's argument supports their main thesis while warning against one-sidedness, for he insists that the conquest and creation of those necessary markets required a firm base in a society that had undergone the internal transformation of labour-power into a commodity:

> The really headlong and limitless prospects of expansion which encouraged, and indeed compelled, technical revolution were probably most easily achieved in the export markets, though it is doubtful whether any country not possessed of a developed home market could, in the seventeenth and eighteenth centuries, have been in a position to seize export opportunities.[35]

Hobsbawm goes well beyond a delineation of an economic crisis in the commercial sector. He presents, in general and with particular reference to the old colonial system, a series of interlocking reference points that together account for the origins and results of the general social crisis: (1) the seigneurial origins of early colonialism; (2) the parasitic role of merchant capital both in that colonialism and in the national monarchies that spawned it; (3) the effects of the specifically commercial, international economic crisis on seigneurial society – that is, the contradictory role of commerce in those countries in which it had become wedded to a bourgeois social system capable of riding out the economic crisis and of feasting off the adversity of its seigneurial rivals.

Hobsbawm's analysis points well beyond the economy, which itself has been presented in its fullest social aspect. Its economic history, with a split focus on changes in both the forces and relations of production, draws attention to the nature of the contending classes, not merely to their economic interests, and to the class basis of state and society. Hobsbawm, in his work on the nineteenth century, can explore these themes in depth; here he must settle for probes and hints about the relation of economic developments to state formation, military history, and social and ideological coherence or breakdown.

The inherent theoretical advances extend in several directions. Nothing, for example, could appear so pointless as an attempt to build a Marxist interpretation of modern imperialism without due attention to Hobsbawm's theoretically rich history of capitalism. Here, however, we shall have to settle for the bearing of his work on some selected problems: war, the state, and social revolution.

Marx, Engels, and Lenin, took war seriously as a potential agent for social revolution. Today, many leftwing historians, Marxist and other, recoil from a positive view of war as an instrument of revolutionary policy, although they normally approve of and often support at some personal risk revolutionary civil and guerrilla wars in the Third World. For we live in a nuclear age in which the stakes have been raised to an unacceptable level that could attract only the most lunatic of fanatics.

Marx and Engels, as internationalists, viewed war as a way to radicalize politics, specifically a way to destroy the poisonous, counter-revolutionary power of tsarist Russia.[36] If the revolution was to be, in Hobsbawm's paraphrase, 'essentially an international phenomenon, and not simply an aggregate of national transformations', then war would likely have to provide the catalyst. Hobsbawm argues, for example, that before 1789 only a few regions displayed 'the purely domestic conditions for a major transfer of power'. International rivalry, in his words, 'made the situation explosive', and war put the rickety old regimes to a test they could no longer readily pass. Old-style war plunged the old regimes into crisis, and new-style war of a kind attendant upon the radical victory in France carried social revolution with it.[37] (For, notwithstanding tactically useful pronouncements aimed at children and fools, revolutions can be exported and generally have been.)

Hobsbawm insists upon facing reality without celebrating it – upon facing what even Marx and Engels often slighted: the tragedy inherent in human progress. With a touch of satire he characterizes the policy of the Girondists, 'bellicose abroad and moderate at home', as 'utterly impossible'.[38] He prefers, as any Marxist would, the policy of the Mountain, but he files a grim and appropriate caveat: 'In the course of its crisis the young French Republic discovered or invented total war... How appalling the implications of this discovery are has only become clear in our own historic epoch.'[39]

Yet the question resurfaces in sombre new form: if war has provided a principal setting for the generation and spread of social revolution, do revolutionary prospects remain in a world that eliminates great wars and severely circumscribes small ones? No one has answered this question, but Hobsbawm provides the kind of historical analysis without which no sound answer may ever be expected. And together with the extraordinary contributions to the history and political economy of imperialism scattered throughout his work, it establishes a basis for fresh political thinking.

An implicit critique and development of the Marxist theory of the state lies embedded in Hobsbawm's writings. In an essay 'Marx, Engels and Politics' in *The History of Marxism*, which he edited, he defends Marx and Engels against the charge that they reduced the state to a mere 'general staff of the ruling class'. But, typically, having dispensed with that mechanical reading, he proceeds to a constructive critique of his own, which simultaneously illuminates political history and lays firm historical floorboards for socialist politics.

He notes that Marx and Engels numbered among the functions of the bourgeois state 'the regulation of the conflict between the private interests of the bourgeois individuals and the public interest of the system'.[40] For Marx and Engels the essence of the state was concentrated political power, understood as the official expression of the relation of class forces; hence, they regarded the state as destined to wither away after the socialist revolution, which would abolish class antagonisms. But, as Hobsbawm observes, they also came to see, especially in the wake of 1848 and the rise of Louis Napoleon, that the state could achieve a considerable measure of independence even from the 'ruling' class, the interests of which it objectively serves most readily. The state emerges as a kind of reciprocal insurance policy for members of the bourgeoisie, not only against other classes that might threaten the foundation of bourgeois property, but against splits and antagonistic interests within the class. The state acts positively to prevent social disintegration and cannot be reduced to a mere vehicle of class repression.

Hobsbawm's reflections on the English Revolution of the 1640s and his studies of the great French Revolution and the revolutions of 1830 and 1848 centre upon the decisive role of the conquest of state power in the transformation of social systems, while they avoid narrow interpretations of the relation of the state to the class it most directly serves. Perhaps his most direct statement comes in *The Age of Capital*, in which he hesitates to call the bourgeoisie a 'ruling' class: 'What it did exercise was hegemony, and what it increasingly determined was policy.'[41] Similarly, the critical support he gives elsewhere to the common Marxist emphasis on the English Revolution of the 1640s as an essentially bourgeois revolution – or, as he would probably prefer, as a revolution that forged the modern bourgeoisie – implicitly recognizes the state as a terrain of class struggle, not a mere reflex of class interest, and as a political centre with considerable autonomy and yet ultimately compelled to act primarily in the interests of the propertied class.

Hobsbawm's historical appraisals inform, and have doubtless been informed by, his studies of and participation in contemporary politics. In this respect his work serves as a model for those who would ground practical politics in historical experience without imprisoning themselves in some metahistorical inevitability and for those who would bring to their historical studies the benefit of political experience without falling into presentism and ideological distortion. To illustrate, consider Part 4 of *Revolutionaries* ('Soldiers and Guerrillas'). He argues that the revolutions in the Third World, and even the non-revolutionary changes impelled by the exigencies of worldwide decolonization, have been creating the constituent social classes much more readily than vice versa. Most of the Third World has not achieved political independence by social revolution or under the pressure of mass movements: 'Much of it did not even contain the initial bases for a modern state, and indeed, as in so much of Africa, the main function of the new state apparatus was as a mechanism for the production of a national bourgeoisie or ruling class, which previously barely existed.'[42]

Hobsbawm was writing in 1967, when the Left in Europe and the United States was at the height of its romance with the Third World. I refer not to its sympathy and sometimes heroic support, which were altogether to its credit, but to its wild fantasies about the transformative consequences of Third World struggles for Western societies. Serious consideration of Hobsbawm's critique might well have prevented countless broken hearts and much widespread disillusionment. Amidst the extraordinary outpouring of hosannas for our Third World saviours, few of whom seem to have been naive enough to feel honoured, Hobsbawm wrote: 'A large part of the globe has been turned into the contemporary equivalent of the old banana republics of Latin America, and is likely to remain in this unhappy situation for a considerable time to come.'[43]

In 'Marx, Engels, and Politics' Hobsbawm summarizes the contributions to the Marxist theory of the state that lie scattered in his histories. Marx and Engels believed in the eventual withering away of the state, but they forcefully insisted upon the necessity of a transitional proletarian power and of a not-so-transitional centralization of planning and authority. Hobsbawm dismisses semantic games that solve all problems by declaring that the revolutionary and post-revolutionary authority, which no one has yet figured out how to dispense with, does not constitute a state. For the mere 'administration of things', by any other name, continues to look just wonderful to those who regard state power as necessary to the running of modern society.

The mere 'administration of things' becomes more than a semantic device, Hobsbawm argues, 'only on certain very optimistic assumptions', most notably a simplification of administrative technique in accordance with Lenin's ideal of every cook being competent to govern. Since to most observers the reverse has been happening and seems likely to continue to happen, Marx and Engels left a 'puzzling and uncertain' legacy.[44] If, however, the state cannot wither away, will it not, under conditions of unprecedented economic concentration, become ever more powerful, bureaucratic, dictatorial, and above all divorced from the class in the name of which it rules? Hobsbawm is certainly not the first to raise these questions, which have been debated among Marxists with increasing ferocity. But he has grounded his critique in historical experience and has demonstrated the continued vitality of historical materialism, and especially of the role of the forces of production, which has been disappearing from Marxist discussion, most seriously from Marxist history, with appalling results.

Hobsbawm firmly rejects the once more fashionable game of trying to turn Marx into a social democrat. With a sure hand he traces the views of Marx and Engels on revolution and makes clear that they expected it to be bloody even as they hoped that democracy would lead to socialist majorities and that the bourgeoisie would have to assume responsibility for any violence that followed. If they, especially Engels, deserve criticism, it is for having underestimated the integrative power of the bourgeois political process. For: 'The growth of mass social-democratic parties did not lead to some form of confrontation but to some form of integration of the movement into the existing system...'[45]

Hobsbawm's work on the nineteenth century goes far toward explaining the failure of proletarian revolution in the West and, for that matter, explaining the shift of social revolution to Russia, China, and the Third World during the twentieth century. Hence the added significance of war. World War I led to revolution in Russia; World War II led to revolution or, rather, to the victory of a protracted revolution in China, as well as to the revolutionary transformation of Eastern Europe. World War III offers poorer prospects. The Western proletariat has long disappointed communist revolutionaries and shows no signs of changing course. By time-honoured criteria it is a numerically declining class that may well have lost whatever opportunity it had to fulfil the destiny Marx assigned to it. And Hobsbawm sees little revolutionary potential in the classes and strata that are replacing it. As he asks about Britain, 'How far can any party be functionally revolutionary in a country in which a classical revolution is simply not on the agenda, and which lacks even a living tradition of past revolution?'[46] France has that living tradition, but the French Communist Party, no less than the Italian Communist Party, today faces the same problem of how to organize a classic proletarian revolution in a country with a diminishing proportion of classic proletarians.

If Hobsbawm's historical and political analyses do not provide solutions to these problems, they do dispose of false solutions and dispel much nonsense. Nothing in his work gives comfort to those who would beat an easy retreat to social democracy, which has a perfect record for not establishing socialism in every country in which it has taken power and which, for all the attention to the crimes of the communists, has had its own bloody record of killing millions of people in the colonies without even the excuse of building or protecting any kind of socialism. Not that Hobsbawm opposes current social-democratic politics or an alliance of communists with social democrats. As he recognizes, no other politics makes much sense for the Western Left today. But he warns against illusions of a socialist outcome from what amounts to a holding operation. And he does not provide much comfort to those who blame the failures of the Left on the great schism that accompanied the formation of the Third International. He disposes of that notion, which has become popular in the United States, by recalling that the movements which did not split – such as the British and Austrian – ended in the same kind of reformism as those which did.[47]

Consideration of the overriding problems of the twentieth-century socialist and communist movements compels reconsideration of historical materialism and of Hobsbawm's contribution to it. A dangerous tension pervades Marx's work and reappears in Hobsbawm's, where, however, it yields more positive results. Most Marxists, possibly including Hobsbawm, may gag on my formulation, which I am sure Marx would have gagged on: nothing in Marx's interpretation of history or his critique of political economy supports the philosophy of humanity superimposed upon it. According to Marx, communist man and woman will overcome the division of labour and thereby develop their full potential as rounded human beings. They will be liberated from repression and will realize their highest human nature, which by a wonderful stroke of luck will turn out to be unselfish, loving, good.

Marx's reply to the Christian theologians' assertion of original sin, which projects destructive elements in human nature, like the reply of most Marxists to Freud's secular version, amounts to little more than a demand for proof. The reply will not do. Those who take the dimmer view of human nature have the whole historical record on their side and can reasonably insist that the burden of proof must fall upon their critics. Freud, for his part, postulated the individual as a discretely biological and historical product of a world in which he or she could not avoid – indeed was only a specific case of – the internalization of the inescapable and ultimately irreconcilable conflict between the self and society.

Marx nowhere provides even the rudiments of a scientific psychology that would point to other conclusions. In replying to all such arguments he normally contents himself with nasty but unenlightening accusations of libel against the human race. His projections about a new communist man and woman rest on his assertion that technological progress under communism would overcome the hated division of labour. The assertion never had much to recommend it, and appears less plausible with each passing day. Lenin enthusiastically but unwisely based his idea of the withering away of the state on Marx's assertion; Stalin, who had studied theology and proved himself a master psychologist, knew better, however repulsive some of the uses to which he put his knowledge.

The inherent tension between an essentially idealist philosophy of humanity and a materialist interpretation of history did not disappear as Marx grew older. The mature Marx fortunately held the damage to a minimum, but he never repudiated his early beliefs, which have continued to influence Marxist thought and action. To the end he claimed for himself, or at any rate Engels claimed for him, the discovery of the historical law according to which capitalism would give way to socialism. Bourgeois apologists might whine that the communists have carried out a self-fulfilling prophecy rather than proving the validity of a historical law. But for once the burden of proof falls on them.

Marxists face a different problem: the socialism we are getting does not conform to preconceived notions, let alone preferences, and shows little tendency to pass into communism. Nor is Stalinism—'that hypertrophy of the bureaucratic dictatorial state', as Hobsbawm calls it – the main issue. Rather, as he insists, the end of Stalinism, or of its worst excesses, threw the main issue into stark relief: 'The main objective of that country [the USSR], rapid economic growth, technological and scientific development, national security, etc. had no special connections with socialism, democracy or freedom.'[48] Socialism, in effect, had become the means used by underdeveloped countries to catch up with the developed. Hobsbawm does not deny the socialist character of such countries, although he hints at a willingness to keep that question open. I see no point in keeping it open. If, in accordance with Marx's interpretation of history, we understand the transition from capitalism to socialism as the transition from one mode of production to another, then we need not be surprised to find socialism compatible with a variety of political systems and social goals – to find it another, if more promising, terrain of struggle for other goals.

Hobsbawm clarifies these questions, even as he expresses displeasure at some of the answers his history leads us toward. It should be enough to recall his scepticism about the withering away of the state, especially if we recall that Lenin, duly following Marx, felt compelled to base that fantasy on the disappearance of the division of labour and the strange notion that, in the absence of exploitation, people would internalize what looks suspiciously like Max Weber's Protestant work ethic.[49] Recall, too, Hobsbawm's suggestion that classes represent only a special case of relations of production. For if so, then we must reject the dogma that the end of exploitation will necessarily result in the end of oppression. The position of women in the existing socialist countries, and its prospects in those socialist countries we imagine and struggle for, should drive the point home, although the continuing difficulties with race, ethnicity, and nationality must also be taken into account.

Hobsbawm offers a learned and theoretically first-rate treatment of 'the principle of nationality', 'nationalism', and 'nation-building', which appears with special clarity and empirical grounding in *The Age of Revolution* and *The Age of Capital*. (Would that he may yet treat as seriously the problem of gender in historical process.) From his many-sided effort I can here extract only one strain. He demonstrates, with cold precision, the consequences of the failure of the Springtime of the Peoples in 1848, among which was the unfolding of an 'age of capital' that simultaneously produced an integrated world economy and a flourishing of nation-states. Elsewhere he analyses the failure of the world revolution in our century and the striking success of socialist national revolutions. The disturbing implications for the development of socialism require comment. In his essay 'Lenin and the Aristocracy of Labour', Hobsbawm singles out the widening division between the advanced, not merely the imperialist, countries and the 'proletarian nations' of the Third World.[50] That widening division takes on special meaning when understood in the context of Hobsbawm's theoretical extrapolations from his historical studies of social classes, state power, and the uneven development of capitalism. At the least, we have been armed against any facile expectations of an internationalist, socialist solution and have been prepared to expect bitter struggles that cut sharply across class lines on a world scale.

Yet Hobsbawm too sometimes seems suspended between Marx's philosophy of humanity, which claims his heart, and his thoroughly unsentimental reading of history: 'The strength of the Marxist belief in the triumph of the free development of all men depends not on the strength of Marx's hope for it, but on the assumed correctness of the analysis that this is indeed where historical development eventually leads mankind.'[51] Hobsbawm trenchantly observes that the emancipation of human beings from their natural conditions of production has been a process of 'individualization'.[52] But then:

> Marx's vision is thus a marvellously unifying force. His model of social and economic development...can be presented as the unfolding of the logical possibilities latent in a few elementary and almost axiomatic statements about the nature of man – a dialectical working out of the contradictions of labour/property, and the division of labour. It is a model of facts, but, seen from a slightly different angle, the *same* model provides us with value judgments.[53]

These appealing remarks reveal a sensibility and worldview that explain Hobsbawm's Marxist 'orthodoxy' – he is no kind of revisionist – and his freedom from dogmatism. They also invoke a myth of formidable political consequences. It is fair to ask him: is it true that 'progress' and 'process' are related in the way implied here? Again we may invoke Hobsbawm's own scepticism about overcoming the division of labour, about the withering away of the state, about the projected end of oppression with the end of specifically class exploitation, about any number of other pieties: for that scepticism calls into question Marx's utopian vision of communism that lies just beneath the surface of these remarks.

Hobsbawm might do well to recall one of his own more important observations, written more than a decade later, on progress and process: 'There is a danger in supporting "historically progressive achievements" irrespective of who carries them out, except of course *ex post facto*.'[54] Consider Hobsbawm's distinction between reformists and revolutionaries in the world of his primitive rebels: 'Reformists wish to create a society in which policemen will not be arbitrary and judges at the mercy of landlords and merchants; revolutionaries, though also in sympathy with these aims, a society in which there will be no policemen and judges in the present sense, let alone landlords and merchants.'[55] Hobsbawm's delineation of viewpoints is historically sound, but since he identifies with revolutionaries, not reformists, more is at stake than historical judgment.

He does not leave the matter there: 'Every man who is not a Dr Pangloss and every social movement undergoes the pull both of reformism and revolutionism with varying strength at different times.'[56] He adds, with a characteristic psychological insight that contrasts sharply with his formal disdain for the uses of psychology in history: 'The hope of a really good and perfect society haunts even those who have resigned themselves to the impossibility of changing either the "world" or "human nature," and merely hope for lesser reforms and the correction of abuses.'[57] A turbulent decade later he writes in a similar vein that a utopian streak exists in everyone but that 'it is when the relatively modest expectations of everyday life look as though they cannot be achieved without revolutions, that individuals become revolutionaries.'[58] From his early work through his late, in one form or another, he stands by the judgment made in *Bandits*: 'Men can live without justice, and generally must, but they cannot live without hope.' Thus he applauds Ernst Bloch for insisting that, in Hobsbawm's paraphrase, 'hope and the building of the earthly paradise are man's fate.'[58]

Hobsbawm is neither a sentimentalist, nor a utopian, nor a romantic, however much he might resist my attempt to assimilate him to a Marxism that has room for St Thomas Aquinas as well as Sigmund Freud. Hobsbawm observes in *Primitive Rebels* that all revolutionary movements 'by definition' have a millenarian streak since they call for a 'complete and radical change in the world'.[60] As a result, revolutionaries of all kinds 'feel a sense of almost physical pain at the realization that the coming of Socialism will not eliminate *all* grief and sadness, unhappy love affairs or mourning, and will not solve or make soluble *all* problems...'[61] Here and throughout his work he is describing and analysing with admirable insight and precision the psychology as well as the bedrock ideology of revolutionaries; demonstrating the centrality of some form of utopianism to the revolutionary temperament; presenting the history of the modern world with a clarity that exposes the limits of revolutionary action and undermines utopian illusions; and insisting on a 'principle of hope' that renders the behaviour of revolutionaries rational and indispensable to the struggle against exploitation and oppression. As he says, 'Utopianism is probably a necessary social device for generating the superhuman efforts without which no major revolution is achieved.'[62]

The tension in Hobsbawm's thought in a sense runs deeper than that in Marx's, for he sees, as Marx could not, the large element of myth in Marxism itself. Much of his work can profitably be read as a successful effort to separate science from myth while revealing the uses to which the myth has been put. With unembarrassed partisanship Hobsbawm portrays the achievements of revolutionaries, past and present, without denying that their heads have often been full of romantic nonsense and that their professed aims have generally fallen by the wayside once the victory of the revolution has been secured. Although Hobsbawm, with reason and experience on his side, says that revolutionary action probably requires utopianism, and although he generously translates utopianism into one kind of hope, he does not say that the content of any of the ever-present utopianisms has much intrinsic value or is likely to prevail in the building of socialism. He shows throughout his histories that the world revolutionaries get invariably ranges far from the world they thought they would get.

The tension in Marx's thought therefore reappears in Hobsbawm's but largely purged of its most serious weaknesses. Here it encourages a history free of wishful thinking and ideological superimposition. The fundamental concepts of class and class struggle undergo constant development rather than serving as frozen categories; yet they are never surrendered to subjectivist confusions with class consciousness. The centrality of the struggle for the social surplus throughout history emerges as embedded in political economy but without capitulation to Marx's more rigid and doubtful formulations. Hobsbawm's scepticism about the labour theory of value, for example, does not lead him away from Marx's insights into the relation of social classes to the struggle for the surplus; it invites a superior economic formulation that can provide the basis for a more satisfactory political analysis.

Revolution appears as the 'locomotive' of history, and force as the 'midwife' of social change, but neither acquires metaphysical and metahistorical properties that require their discovery, not to say invention, in historical periods or historical conjunctures at which the evidence cannot sustain them. Locomotives and midwives are not confused with the historical process itself and are not invoked as *dei ex-machinae*. In particular, the implications of the thesis that revolutionary struggles forge hegemonic classes even more readily than vice versa establishes the validity of Marx's primary insights into the historical process on the basis of empirical evidence and in defiance of rigid formulas. Hobsbawm's deep probing into revolutionaries' complex psychology and into the unintended effects of revolutionary action strips away myth and does not confuse admiration and even approval with the defence of ideological daydreaming. Ironically, Hobsbawm's work, which rejects Max Weber's neo-

Kantian 'ethical neutrality in the social sciences' and all such attempts to achieve an impossible objectivity, ends by advancing as close as humanly possible to that qualified objectivity without which the writing of history must turn into ideological swindling.

The political implications of this sweeping of ideological rubbish out of the writing of Marxist history cannot be overestimated. Today, capitalism is plunging into a multi-tiered social crisis that includes another secular economic crisis and offers its enemies new and perhaps unprecedented opportunities. Yet socialism, which has conquered much of the world and continues to advance outside the West, is also plunging into a social crisis of a new and largely unforeseen type. The threat of nuclear war hovers over us, and with it the probable end of war as a carrier of revolution in the West and perhaps, as time goes by, in the Third World as well. For lifting the threat of nuclear war may well compel the forging of a world balance of power that will reduce drastically the possibilities for local or regional wars and even revolutionary civil wars. In short, if we are to avoid a nuclear holocaust, we shall probably have to reconcile ourselves to a transition to socialism as protracted, complex, and indirect as the transition to capitalism in those countries that remained with one foot in feudalism in the period after the French Revolution.

Hobsbawm's sober assessment of the reasons for the failure of the working class of the West to make its prescribed revolution, his pregnant thesis of classes as a special case of social relations of production, and his appreciative but qualified conclusions about the uses of revolution, in its Leninist sense, in historical change do not pretend to add up to a political programme. But they do enable us to analyse the problems of the transition to socialism and the role of the traditional working class under both capitalism and socialism in a manner that demonstrates the efficacy, indeed the superiority, of Marxism while they free us from our time-honoured, deeply internalized, and increasingly debilitating myths. Politically informed yet anti-presentist history emerges from Hobsbawm's work as necessary to a sound, historically informed politics.

Hobsbawm's stature and influence as a historian who, by example more than advocacy, leads us toward that 'history of society' we must have, will grow steadily and need not detain us. Beyond that lies his demonstration, which provides a guide to the development of historical materialism and to a reassessment of socialist politics, that history is a pre-eminently political matter in the sense that politics, broadly understood, has ever lain at the core of society; that politics, shorn of ideological special pleading and presentism, must inform all historical research; and that a contemporary politics not grounded in an understanding of historical reality has no future. To those who ask how a Marxist, and a communist at that, can write great and 'objective' history, we need only reply with the dictum of the medieval scholastics: existence proves possibility.

For the rest, in establishing, with maximum empirical specificity, the relation of theory and political commitment to the writing of history, in developing Marxist thought without distorting the past and present, especially our own movement's past and present, in transforming a grim historical record into a weapon to realize, rather than an excuse to abandon, the viable ideals of our movement, Hobsbawm has earned from us the tribute I once recall having heard paid Sean O'Casey: when my nice efforts and those of my contemporaries have long been forgotten, he will be remembered as the man who refused to run away.

NOTES

1 Eric J. Hobsbawm, Preface to E. J. Hobsbawm (ed.), *The History of Marxism*, Vol. I. *Marxism in Marx's Day* (Bloomington, Ind. 1982), p. xii.
2 Hobsbawm, 'The Structure of Capital', in E.J. Hobsbawm, *Revolutionaries* (New York 1973), p. 149; Hobsbawm, 'Introduction to Karl Marx', in E.J. Hobsbawm, *Pre-Capitalist Economic Formations* (New York 1964), p. 10.
3 Hobsbawm, 'From Feudalism to Capitalism', in Rodney Hilton *et al.*, *The Transition from Feudalism to Capitalism* (London 1978), p. 160.
4 *Ibid.*, p. 160, original emphasis.
5 Hobsbawm, 'Class Consciousness in History', in István Mészaros (ed.), *Aspects of Class Consciousness* (London 1971), pp. 5–21.
6 *Ibid.*, p. 6.
7 *Ibid.*, p. 6.
8 *Ibid.*, p. 7.
9 *Ibid.*, p. 9. See his important qualification on the 'high aristocracies'.
10 *Ibid.*, p. 11.
11 Hobsbawm, 'Class Consciousness in History', p. 14, Original emphasis.
12 *Ibid.*, p. 14.
13 *Ibid.*, p. 17, original emphasis.
14 Hobsbawm, Introduction to Marx, *Pre-Capitalist Economic Formations*, p. 11, original emphasis.
15 *Ibid.*, p. 11.
16 Hobsbawm, 'From Social History to the History of Society', *Daedalus* (Winter 1971), 20–45.
17 I cannot here discuss the specific contributions to Marxist theory or to intellectual history that may be found in the appropriate chapters of *The Age of Revolution, 1789–1848* (New York 1962), and *The Age of Capital, 1848–1875* (London 1975). Suffice it to say that in the chapters on science he has much to offer to the debate among Marxists, as well as others, over 'internal' and 'social' causation. In general, he demonstrates both the value and the limits of J.D. Bernal's social interpretation. Hobsbawm's achievement may be measured against the clashing of viewpoints in, e.g., S. Lilley, (ed.), *Essays in the Social History of Science* (Copenhagen 1953).

18 Hobsbawm, *Age of Capital*, pp. 2–3.
19 *Ibid.*, p. 21.
20 E.J. Hobsbawm, *Labouring Men: Studies in the History of Labour* (London 1968), p. 28.
21 Hobsbawm, 'History and the Dark Satanic Mills', in *Labouring Men*, p. 138.
22 E.J. Hobsbawm and George Rudé, *Captain Swing* (New York 1968), p. 91.
23 E.J. Hobsbawm, *Bandits* (London 1969), p. 53; see also *Primitive Rebels: Studies in the Archaic Forms of Social Movement in the 19th and 20th Centuries* (New York 1959).
24 See, e.g., Hobsbawm, *Age of Capital*, pp. 223ff.
25 E.J. Hobsbawm, *Industry and Empire* (New York 1968), Ch. 14.
26 E.J. Hobsbawm, 'Karl Marx and the British Labour Movement', in *Revolutionaries*, p. 97; see also *Industry and Empire*, p. 5.
27 Hobsbawm, 'Karl Marx and the British Labour Movement', in *Revolutionaries*, p. 102.
28 E.J. Hobsbawm, 'Religion and the Rise of Socialism', *Marxist Perspectives* 1 (Spring 1978), p. 20.
29 *Ibid.*, p. 22.
30 *Ibid.*, p. 23.
31 E.J. Hobsbawm, 'The Crisis of the Seventeenth Century', in Trevor Aston (ed.), *Crisis in Europe, 1560–1660* (Garden City, NY 1967), pp. 5–62; Hobsbawm, 'The Seventeenth Century in the Development of Capitalism', *Science and Society* 24 (Spring 1960), pp. 97–112.
32 Hobsbawm, 'Crisis of the Seventeenth Century', p. 5.
33 Hobsbawm, 'Seventeenth Century in the Development of Capitalism', p. 152. He develops this theme in several of his books, but for a superb brief treatment see his introductory chapter, 'Agricultural England', in *Captain Swing*.
34 Hobsbawm, Introduction to Marx, *Pre-Capitalist Economic Formations*, p. 46.
35 Hobsbawm, 'Crisis of the Seventeenth Century', p. 53.
36 See Hobsbawm, 'Marx, Engels and Politics', in Hobsbawm (ed.), *History of Marxism*, pp. 252ff.
37 Hobsbawm, *Age of Revolution*, p. 24.
38 *Ibid.*, p. 66.
39 *Ibid.*, p. 67.
40 Hobsbawm, 'Marx, Engels and Politics', p. 229.
41 Hobsbawm, *Age of Capital*, p. 249.
42 Hobsbawm, *Revolutionaries*, p. 187.
43 *Ibid.*, p. 191.
44 Hobsbawm, 'Marx, Engels and Politics', p. 232.
45 *Ibid.*, p. 244.
46 Hobsbawm, 'Radicalism and Revolution in Britain', in *Revolutionaries*, p. 13.
47 Hobsbawm, 'French Communism', in *Revolutionaries*, pp. 222–3.
48 Hobsbawm, 'Reflections on Anarchism', in *Revolutionaries*, p. 85.
49 In addition to the familiar *State and Revolution*, see his *Philosophical Notebooks*.
50 Hobsbawm, *Revolutionaries*, esp. p. 126.
51 Hobsbawm, Introduction to Marx, *Pre-Capitalist Economic Formations*, p. 12.

52 *Ibid.*, p. 14.
53 *Ibid.*, p. 16, original emphasis.
54 Hobsbawm, 'Marx, Engels and Politics', p. 246.
55 Hobsbawm, *Primitive Rebels*, p. 11.
56 *Ibid.*, p. 11.
57 *Ibid.*, p. 12.
58 Hobsbawm, 'Intellectuals and the Class Struggle', in *Revolutionaries*, p. 247.
59 Hobsbawm, The Principle of Hope', in *Revolutionaries*, p. 141.
60 Hobsbawm, *Primitive Rebels*, p. 57.
61 *Ibid.*, p. 60, original emphasis.
62 *Ibid.*, pp. 60–1.

ACKNOWLEDGMENTS

I am indebted to Stanley L. Engerman and Elizabeth Fox – Genovese for their criticism and suggestions.

2

Working class and sociability in France before 1848*

MAURICE AGULHON

For several decades now the history of the class struggle has been acknowledged as a major historical field; the working-class movement and socialism are well established chapters of political and social history, and of history in general.

The history of everyday life, on the other hand, has never attained this legitimacy. Either it receives a brief mention in some appendix to an economic history ('changes in material conditions and their effects') or, alternatively, it is consigned to 'the footnotes of history' written by the amateur documenters of local tradition and peculiarities, or to retrospective ethnology; this is not to say that the latter, generally written by ethnologists themselves, is lacking in authority, but its use of the concept 'traditional way of life' all too often denies us useful chronological detail.[1]

However, there is one area in which 'l'histoire événementielle' and the history of the everyday are not inevitably divorced from each other: that is the history of the working classes. Historians who specialize in the working-class movement are generally sympathizers with it, if they are not already active campaigners in it; they are therefore bound to support the premise that the movement was the campaign of an entire class, a kind of collective entity which it is possible to describe and to analyse; a class which people must be made to recognize as such by drawing attention to the special features which set it apart from society as a whole. This in itself provides a strong reason for attempting to describe the class both as a whole and in all its aspects. There is another, even simpler, reason: the workers asserted themselves through revolt, principally because their everyday life was intolerable; the study of their life experience is therefore an essential part of any research into the causes of their collective action.

Whatever one thinks of these reasons, it would seem undeniable that historians of the working-class movement are well represented at the forefront of another movement which has persuaded historians to look more closely at material

*Translated by Suzanne Jones.

drawn from everyday life, from folklore and ethnography.[2] This development is well known or at least has been anticipated and there is no need to comment any further here on the relationship between the political avant-garde and its epistemological counterpart.

I would merely wish to point out that the study proposed in the following pages touches upon an area of research which is already well documented – that of the history of working-class life in France in the first half of the nineteenth century, which is the period in which the 'working-class movement' emerged.

The theme of this study – *Sociability*, by which I mean the peculiar aptitude for living within the group and consolidating these groups by the forming of voluntary associations – is by no means original. The worker's very particular circumstances inevitably draw him closer to those in the same position whom he meets in his locality or at his place of work; association is a natural consequence of this, if nature can be said to enter into it;[3] and it is his circumstances which drive the worker, weak and impoverished as he is, to protest to those who are much stronger. The 'unity is strength' concept is by now, of course, familiar. In attempting to compare association in everyday life and association for the purposes of the struggle I will not be the first to have tackled the subject. I hope that the development of this study will, nonetheless, be productive.

It should perhaps be said at this point, in order to establish the general orientation of this chapter at the start, that in France between 1800 and 1848 the phenomenon of association was a crucial development, not only in terms of the history of the working class; this, as we have already seen, it certainly was, as working-class gregariousness developed into fraternity and, finally, into militancy, particularly after 1830 when the workers came to advocate association not just as the means of mutual assistance but also as the means of autonomous production, which, by being collective, would be fair to every worker; association in the form of the co-operative was to be one of the fundamental ideas of the worker socialism of 1848.

There was also at this time a strong trend towards association in bourgeois society, one could say, or in society as a whole. I drew attention to this fact in a paper which I wrote several years ago.[4] Bourgeois individualism, it should be pointed out, never prevented the bourgeois from using the association as a means of appropriating the finer things of life in the cheapest and most convenient way, whether this took the form of cultural pursuits or the services and material comforts offered by the English-style club. Equally, bourgeois liberalism had need of channels of dialogue in order to get its parliamentary and electoral policies introduced and make them effective. Thus there was a definite movement in enlightened France towards the formation of associations, and this despite the suspicion with which the notion of association was viewed for almost a century by the post-Napoleonic state. For this was a state which had been rendered obsessively wary, on its left by a haunting fear of the Jacobin Club and on its right by the spectre of the congregations. So there could be said to exist a conflict between an associationist civilian society and an anti-associationist state. This conflict endured throughout the century, leaving behind archives stacked with the most detailed records of the surveillance of associations.[5] It is also partly through this surveillance of the *cercles* and bourgeois societies that new information has sometimes come to us, chance detail which unintentionally sheds light on certain aspects of working-class associationism.

However there was a considerable difference between the sociability of the upper classes and the sociability of the working class (or lower orders in general). Any upper-class association, whether it was of an informal nature (simple gatherings of *habitués*) or a formal one (with its own statute and written laws) had its own fixed meeting place. This place was its own property and one of its assets. Thus there was no great difficulty in the rich meeting together. The informal sociability of salon society took place, obviously, in the salons of the great aristocratic or bourgeois suites. The formal sociability of the male *cercle* took place in premises which were rented or purchased at the members' expense, this being an expense which they could easily afford. The worker, on the other hand, was very poor and lived in very cramped conditions.

So the first questions we should ask in studying working-class sociability are concerned with its possible locations. These will form the headings under which we will analyse in turn the various informal means of socializing before dealing with the organized associations.

The typology of working-class sociability

The locations of informal sociability: the workshop
The place of work could also be a place to meet and converse. When we talk about the setting for the social evenings of the past, this is not restricted to the classical gathering of peasant families in the main room of the farmhouse or in the cowshed; but we must also remember the neighbourhood gatherings in the workshop of the artisan, perhaps a shoemaker who worked late by lamplight.[6] However, this was not the most characteristic practice in areas where there was a concentration of the proletariat. The proletarian Joseph Benoît takes us into a typical workers' environment, the Lyons textile workshops, when he describes communist propaganda being promoted around 1840.

> Discussions and public speeches also played a large part in this constant propaganda. Meetings held outside in the woods or meadows surrounding Lyons in the summer and in the workshops in winter built on the work which the books had begun...

> Imagine twenty or thirty people of all ages and both sexes who are gathered in a weaver's workshop, sitting in any suitable place they have been able to find between the looms, and this assembly visible only by the uncertain light given off by one or two worker's lamps...
>
> At other times these meetings took place in the workshop of a folder, a hugh room for all that and one which could hold a greater number of listeners...[7]

In other trades conversation in the workshop on topics other than work would be stimulated by an established custom: in the tailoring trade fellow workers would take it in turns to read aloud to amuse their workmates as they sewed.[8]

This practice of sociability in the workshop itself, of which we most often have records when it was of a subversive nature, but which evidently grew up spontaneously as a matter of routine, presupposed the consent of the workshop foreman or the toleration of the relevant overseer. The shop-floor regulations of the modern-day large factory were to attempt to suppress this practice but in so doing were to attest to its existence. In any case, from the writings of Norbert Truquin, another worker who lived in the 1840s, we are left in no doubt as to one thing; according to him, the worker who was most badly off, 'although he appears to be the freest' was the one who worked from home:

> to escape from his isolation which wore him down he would seek out company at the tavern; here he would find out about the latest prices given for making up clothes and terms of work; he would have a drink and a song and then return to his squalid dwelling. In the factories, on the other hand, the workshops were heated, adequately ventilated and well-lit; there was order and cleanliness; the worker had companionship. At this time overseers were more concerned with quality than quantity. Wages were ten francs a week, sometimes as much as twenty: people paid the prices without quibbling. In the absence of the overseers stories were told and plays acted out; there would be mock sermons from an improvised pulpit; the time passed merrily.[9]

Locations of informal sociability: the chambrée

If it was natural to gather together in the workplace, when it was tolerated at all, it was even more natural to meet in the place where the worker returned at night to sleep. How was this possible in the overcrowded dwellings families lived in? It was possible for young single men or migrant workers from rural areas temporarily separated from their families who lived in dormitory arrangements commonly known as the 'chambrée'. This may have been an attic fitted out by the owner of the factory in proximity to the workshops or equally a room in an ordinary lodging-house, usually over a tavern.[10] The word 'chambrée' in the sense of dormitory or of a group of men housed in a dormitory has come into twentieth-century usage through its use in the military world. In the nineteenth century it was just as commonly used to refer to workers as to soldiers,[11] and was associated with sociability quite as much as it was with sleep; for joiners 'the life of the "*chambrée*", with its evenings in the taverns, promoted comradeship'.[12]

Nor was this phenomenon limited to Paris, Lyons and Marseilles. From an unpublished study of the beginnings of the workers' movement in Cette (now Sète, Hérault)[13] it is evident that a massive strike made a considerable impression at the time: the gendarmes discover that a workers' committee known as 'La Chambre' is behind it and that La Chambre co-ordinates the activities of a vast number of 'sections' or *chambrées*. In other words the strikers had organized themselves from the natural base of the collective dwelling-place. Inevitably the term *chambrée* was gradually to take on the connotation of a base for the workers' struggle and worker propaganda.

This enables us to understand why, in Provence before and after 1848, the forces of law and order and the bourgeois would so often wrongly refer to the *chambrettes*, or small peasant and villager *cercles*, as *chambrées*.[14] These Provençal *chambrettes* were a humbler version of the *cercle* ('*chambre*' in Provence), being the *cercles* (*chambres*) of the *petites gens* (ordinary people), hence the diminutive. These were not in fact *chambrées*, as people did not sleep there, but would come and spend the evening and return to their families. However, as a lot of drinking, game-playing and discussion went on in them, their activities were regarded with as much suspicion as were the workers' gatherings. Thus, despite its incorrectness, and due to a partial homophony, the term '*chambrée*', taken from the vocabulary of the French worker, slipped into usage, overlaying the dialect term of the peasants.

Here we have yet more proof, if any were needed, that the workers' *chambrée* was undoubtedly seen as a centre of active sociability, or, expressed differently, that it acted as a common bond between the workers, which could be renewed frequently and habitually. Informal sociability was not, then, restricted to the tavern. But we must now come to it, as its importance is obvious.

Locations of informal sociability: taverns and outdoor cafés

In texts from bourgeois and administrative sources the descriptions of the tavern and of the worker's frequenting it are so numerous as to leave one with the impression that nothing further needs to be said on the subject. What we can do is to try and make some clarifications, or, more accurately, some distinctions. Which taverns were important? Where were they situated? When did people go to them? Who did they meet in them?[15]

First of all, why did people go to the tavern? To escape the family with its responsibilities and duties? This was the god-fearing version of worker immorality. The tavern, the embodiment of vice, turned the man away from the family, the cradle of virtue. Those who championed the workers played this down without completely denying it and now began to retort that the evil did not lie with the natural inclinations of the workers. Flora Tristan, whose devoutness was matched only by her powers of observation, saw the family rather as the source of unhappiness and discord and the tavern as an (inadequate) form of reparation: she argued that society was so organized that the ordinary wife, legally a minor, either with no independent means or paid less than a man, and almost always less well educated, was almost inevitably looked down upon and maltreated by her husband; the majority of worker marriages were unhappy; and this is where the tavern came in; but the fault lay with higher powers.[16] We find another, completely different, but none the less complementary, argument in *L'Atelier*: the idea of wine being a food, an essential tonic, went unquestioned. It is a fact that at this time it was not customary, and was probably not possible, to buy wine cheaply and in small quantities at the grocer's to drink at home. It was only at the vintner's establishment that the worker could drink 'his sort of wine' and, *L'Atelier* proceeds logically, 'It is hardly the place of those who have every comfort to upbraid us for now and then drinking some wine, when their table runs over with wine and there is no stinting at any meal'.[17] So, for this reason, the worker went to the tavern. He went for a bit of entertainment, he drank some wine, he also joined in discussions. It was hardly the worker's fault if the tavern was the only permissible meeting place. As Flora Tristan points out: 'The situation at the moment is that the tavern is the workers' TEMPLE [*sic*], it is the only place where he is able to go. He certainly does not believe in the church; he understands nothing of the theatre,' and on top of this, she goes on, the government, fearing the political implications, forbade him to organize meetings for the purposes of reading, education or discussion. This is an important point and we will return to it.

But all this did not inevitably exclude the family, at least not as completely as has sometimes been alleged. In fact the indirect accounts which we have just looked at refer exclusively and specifically to the 'vintner' whose cramped premises were always situated in the middle of the town; the worker would stop off there on his way from home to workshop and at the end of the day after leaving the workshop on his way home. The common rhetoric of condemnation was directed solely at this practice. Naturally the sinful worker would be tempted to linger rather than return to his children, squandering with his companions the money which he should be taking back to his waiting wife. However, the antithesis of this – the family outing – also occurred: the worker did sometimes take his wife and children out walking. This would be on a Sunday when people were not in the habit of crowding into the nearest vintner's, and there was time to go out into the country (in Paris, to the open-air cafés of the *barrières* – areas lying directly beyond the city toll gates), where the bars usually sold cheaper wine as they were not subject to the city toll, and provided an open area or yard for dancing or playing bowls.[18] Naturally the single worker would take along a regular or temporary girl-friend. Now, the bad workers could not be distinguished from the good workers according to whether they went in for drinking bouts at the vintner's or outings to the country, as if they were two separate categories! Rather, it is possible to make out a common but refined sociability[19] with a dualist pattern which could be schematized in the following way:

Vintner	Open-air café
Town centre	Outside the town
More or less daily	Weekly (on Sundays)
(during the week)	
Men on their own	Families[20]

This may help us to shed some light on a rather curious observation by Michelet in his *Journal*, whose elliptical nature renders it obscure. He notes that at a mass in Vascueil in June 1849 there are only women. 'Where are the men? At the café. A sorry temple indeed which, it is true, puts one in touch with the centre of things, but which breaks up the family and isolates the women. Even the tavern was better than this, remarked Noël.'[21]

So what was being criticized here must have been the newly fashionable bourgeois-style café. This was relatively well appointed and one could read the newspaper (this is what is meant by 'putting one in touch with the centre of things') and be distracted for a bit too long by the new attractions (which would be bound to include billiards). Was it true to say, then, that people spent less time at the old tavern, which was truly a place for the ordinary people (an institution which people were beginning to refer to in the past tense) than they now spent at the café? Was it a case of a few drinks during the week, and Sundays with the family? If we interpret these lines of Michelet's in this way they further reinforce the dualist view of workers' leisure time which we have just outlined.

We need only add to this outline two important pieces of information. The establishment of the vintner (in the town and frequented by men) was not just the scene of the every-day encounter, it was also the place where the 'Saint-Lundi' was spent, whenever this profane and subversive abstention from employment was practised. Nor was the open-air café of the *barrière* merely the scene of the tranquil delights of the average Sunday. It could also at times be the rallying place of striking workers; when a whole guild was in dispute no vintner's in town would be large enough to hold all those taking part and they would go out to the outskirts to find a place with more space and where they would perhaps be less closely observed.[22]

However, we can be sure of one thing – that the same workers were able to participate in the two elements of the system. Engels, for example, bears witness to this in a text where the ethnographic evidence is all the more valuable for being given involuntarily, since this account in the letter which we quote from is supplied for purely political purposes; it concerns worker joiners of the Faubourg St Antoine in Paris in the year 1846, who meet every week to hold discussions: 'There are between twelve and twenty of them' [We now learn that these were men and the meetings did not take place on Sundays]... 'What they hear in these weekly meetings is studied in depth on Sundays in the assemblies of the 'barrière' to which come Peter and Paul [i.e. literally anyone] with wives and children.'[23]

Finally, it is worth pointing out that this double duality (what happens during the week as against what happens on Sundays, men together as against men with their families) strangely agrees with what observers of the time present as the characteristic behaviour pattern of the bourgeois and merchants of the large towns of the Midi.[24] During the week the merchants of Bordeaux and Marseilles would only leave their work to go and seek out their associates at the *cercle*; but on Sundays they devoted themselves to their families and would spend the day with them at their country houses on the outskirts of town. These were the ways of the time and, like every 'modern way', had a tendency to be copied from class to class. We will come back to this point later on.

Formal associations: trade guilds and mutual associations

It is only natural that we should know more about the organized associations of the period, and in greater detail, than we do about the informal groupings of every-day sociability. There is no need to give an explanation of the guild, since this has been done in every book on the period. On the other hand, there has been all too little written on the dissident Société de l'Union des Travailleurs du Tour de France (society of journeymen) which grew out of a crisis which developed in Toulon in July 1830 and which was instituted in Lyons in 1832.[25] It would seem to have been active principally in the ironworking trades, whereas the old guilds remained typical of the building and woodworking trades. Both these associations were based on the attainment of vocational skills and the quest for improvement was one of their main objectives. The worker who joined them did so in the context of his trade.

In this respect the different sections of the guild and the Société de l'Union were only subdivisions of the association which grouped together workers of a particular trade. The most usual and widespread form of association under the July Monarchy was undoubtedly the Société de Bienfaisance or Société de Secours Mutuels, the English equivalent being the Friendly Society.[26] Formed in the context of a specific trade, these had statutes which provided for the payment of an entry fee and monthly subscriptions in exchange for which the society met the costs of illness or accidents to its members. For obvious reasons the conditions of this material assistance were given the greatest prominence in the statutes – it is essential to be precise and specific in these matters – but, underlying this assistance was an undeniable sense of moral obligation and spiritual solidarity. Workers were expected to be good-living and principled and to look on each other as brothers; the whole society would be expected to accompany the funeral procession of a dead comrade, as if to symbolize his membership of a larger family.[27]

We know the usual problems which arose with the Sociétés de Secours

Mutuels. First, in their relations with the Catholic Church: it would seem that many of these societies continued the pluri-secular tradition of the corporative *confrèries* (brotherhoods) – the preserving of the saint's name as its title and the obligatory annual mass on the day of the patron saint attest to it in themselves.[28] Secondly, in their relations with the employers (referred to as '*les maîtres*'): these were various and variable, and, depending on the particular period, region or trade, could range from the closest collaboration (with the owners making some payment to the fund and belonging to the society as honorary members) to modern-style confrontation (with the society acting as a vital link in the organization of a strike and administering a strike fund).[29] And, finally, in their relations with the state: these varied from vague toleration under the Restoration (when anything traditional and Christian was looked kindly upon) to hostile suspicion in the first years of the July Monarchy, entering a new phase of toleration, and even encouragement, in the 1840s. Under Guizot it was considered that an institution which accustomed the worker to thrift and foresight, moderation and morality and which alleviated to some extent the awful suffering endured during periods of unemployment, had benefits which outweighed the drawbacks.

We know also that the phenomenon was spreading. More and more 'mutual societies' were appearing and, as their reputation grew, there was a tendency for societies to be set up linking specific groups of workers in neighbouring communities, when, we may suppose, no group in the locality was wealthy enough to start up on its own.[30] What is less well known is that, by reason of this very popularity, these vocational societies were coming to assume wider responsibilities in the worker's life, extending to the general sociability of his leisure time. After all, the 'home' of the guild members was the inn, with a main room providing all the comforts of the tavern and a dormitory to act as *chambrée*. The rites of the guild were taken seriously but such was its repertoire of songs that meetings would sometimes end in gay and expansive mood, by no means overshadowed by the gravity of the initiation ritual. Agricol Perdiguier did not give the impression in his *Mémoires* that these young people were exactly morose.

In his accounts of Marseilles at this time Victor Gelu expressly refers to the Société de Bienfaisance de St Laurent as a place where 'one could find both pleasant and useful things. On Sundays and saints' days people would bring their families. It was always crowded. There was drinking, laughter, songs and dancing – here they still performed the old circular dance, the "Pont des Olivettes". There were also crude theatrical turns.'[31] For these entertainments the society must have had its own premises. In view of the outlay and the legal status required to own a building it was likely that this normally consisted of the back room of a tavern or the yard of an open-air café rented from the tavern-owner or even lent by him.

As we see, it would be fair to assume that, at the level of everyday contact, the differences between habitual informal sociability which was not organized and what went on in associations as such were not so very great.

Formal associations: choral societies and 'goguettes'

This last observation leads us naturally to another type of association, the singing society. The following account shows us the sort of thing that went on in one tavern-like establishment, which was apparently operating barely within the law and had also been making too much noise at night. To these circumstances we owe this description in a police report:

> This Master Picot, who is a tobacco-seller, also sells drinks in his establishment, where he receives during the day, particularly on Mondays, and even during the better part of the nights, a number of customers comprising students and young men employed in the printing works. Among the latter we should draw attention to Master Collin, a compositor working for Monsieur Didot. Master Collin is the coryphaeus, as it were, of these meetings. He composes songs appropriate to the occasion and the guests all sing them. It was also this Collin who, after the debates on the law controlling the press, had certain pieces of writing circulated in the printing shops. He is the author of *La Corbierade*.[32]

As we see, this is no more than a 'regular' tavern, frequented by young people from the colleges and typographic workers. There was singing, as there was anywhere in those days after a drink or two. But, at the same time, it was not far from being a *goguette* on the one hand, and on the other a 'cell' of the liberal party and virtually republican.

The *goguettes* were a kind of popular singing society and a larger version of the fashionable bourgeois Bacchic societies, the prototype of which was the famous 'Le Caveau', according to contemporary accounts of local custom, culture and even sometimes politics.[33] They were in fact the stimulus for the great vogue of amateur song-writing; each member of the society – for the *goguette* was a proper society, with its own name, rules, premises, office and regular meeting day – would in turn compose a song, sing it and then have everyone else sing it.[34] Among these amateurs there naturally emerged a few expert, semi-professional writers whose names have endured. The movement really grew up in the wake of the celebrated Béranger.[35] And here we should mention the ideology associated with it, which was broadly the ideology of Béranger himself and of the liberalism of 1830: patriotic, anti-clerical, epicurean. Indeed *L'Atelier* had reason to condemn the *goguette* for giving much greater prominence in its repertoire to the key ideas of the July regime and to the joys of earthly pleasures than to social comment and the hardships endured by the people. It saw them as tainted by the authorities' complacent attitude towards them and, in the final analysis, regarded them as more petty bourgeois than proletarian. However, the effective sociology of these groups cannot be determined on the basis of their ideological leanings.

If *L'Atelier* did seem somewhat over-preoccupied with these associations it was because it knew very well that the *goguette*, petit bourgeois in style and 'popular' in the wider sense, held a great attraction for 'the innocent worker, deprived of pleasures' and because it feared that he would be corrupted by the influence of songs which were either conformist or immoral (meaning sensual, waggish or bacchic). All contemporary writers agree on this much: the *goguette* was an association which was genuinely 'popular' or *ouvrière* (from the point of view of the upper orders at this time the two words were virtually synonymous) and the songs sung at them had either bawdy or serious (liberal–patriot) overtones but never 'populist' or social ones. Even the *Revue des Deux Mondes* was to confirm the fears of *L'Atelier* by stating quite frankly that the literary output of the *goguettes* was indeed uneven but two points were worth considering – that the *goguettes* attested to 'a concern with artistic pleasures in the working classes' and 'one can say that the song, however mediocre, is an improvement on communist tracts'.[36]

It was this way of thinking, according to *L'Atelier*, that explained why the authorities tolerated them. A moral (meaning socially aware) and critical *goguette* would soon have been banned, its argument went, but what harm would it do, except to the vintner, to ban them anyway? Fathers would come to know the pleasures of the hearth and young people could go to classes or to libraries in the evenings... Apart from the fact that Paris was hardly studded with public libraries, it is fair to suppose that many workers would have preferred to have had a song with a bit of company in congenial surroundings. It should be said that similar practices went on in the provinces on a smaller scale, as one would expect; Victor Gelu, bakery worker and tavern singer, gives us some examples in his recollections of contemporary Marseilles.[37]

We will dwell no longer on the *goguettes* as we are not interested in the song as such here, but in the established fact that workers did sometimes join together and form societies, not only for the very important purpose of corporate mutual assistance but also for a cultural purpose. A number of choral societies were also in existence around 1848, but although their members were sometimes drawn from the working classes it would seem that none of these groups originated in them.[38] It is equally interesting to note an observation in the papers of Charles de Rémusat, an interior minister of the time, that in 1840 virtually nothing remained of the revolutionary 'secret societies' following the failure of the attempted coup by the 'Saisons', except for the Société des Travailleurs and the Société des Babouvistes, which were quite strong, and two weaker ones, the Société des Montagnards and the Société des Jacobins. The last, consisting mainly of casters and turners, would meet to sing and discuss together.[39]

Thirty years later, had our minister re-read this, a revolutionary cell where they sang would have struck him as very strange. I would be inclined to think that it would seem less curious if it were looked at the other way around; it is my view that this group of friends must first have come together as a society for conversation and song and later turned militant as one body. For it is known that at this time many conversions took place on the scale of the group and the notion that an association should cater exclusively for a particular professional specialization or particular objective had not yet taken hold.[40]

However, singing, be it combined with refreshment or not, was only one form of leisure activity. Would the worker in 1840 have had access to other forms or to societies with a number of different leisure possibilities? It would seem that he had.

Formal associations: the 'cercle' and the society

As we have already pointed out, the bourgeoisie of the time, by setting up their own *cercle*, were given access to premises where they could spend some time in every-day drinking, smoking, chatting, reading newspapers and engaging in pastimes such as billiards, cards, chess, dominoes and other 'society games'. All these things it was already possible to do in the cafés. But at the café there was a chance of being disturbed by strangers and casual trade whereas with the *cercle* you knew exactly whom you were likely to meet and you could rely on an atmosphere of discretion. Despite the complexities involved in organizing such an establishment with its own rules, financing and management, the *cercle* arrangement was preferred to that of the café.[41]

Where this bourgeois practice was well established it was regarded with envy and it was inevitably imitated after a fashion. The *cercle* which one came across outside the bourgeois setting was, however, quite rare and would often be pointed out as a curiosity or anomaly. In Bordeaux, a great centre of the *cercle* (which was also now and then given the English name 'club', without too much regard for the Jacobin connotations of the term in France), 'there are as many "clubs" as there are in Geneva. They tell me there are even "clubs" for the servants, to the extent of there being one for the non-coaching servants and one for the coaching servants.'[42] In regions such as Lower Provence the imitation of the bourgeois *cercle* (the *chambre*) extended even to the peasants in the villages (the *chambrette*).[43] But the coaching servants of Bordeaux and the peasants of the Var were, if anything, exceptions. It was above all among the artisans, who could only just be classified as petit bourgeois and would perhaps be better described as an upper stratum of the working people, that the creation of bourgeois-style *cercles* really caught on,[44] to the extent that the authorities were made to think seriously about all its implications.[45]

It was inevitable that from here the idea was to be introduced to the working class proper, the wage-earning manual workers, if only as a result of the occasional invitation to the *cercle* of the *maître*.[46] And then again, although texts exist giving explicit proof of imitation among the working class, is it always necessary to find models for this imitation? All that was needed for a group of regulars at a certain bar to become an exclusive association was a communal decision to do this. Whether or not its statutes were subsequently drawn up in the proper manner, the transformation had taken place. The following police statement concerning a dubious tavern, Au rendez-vous de la Rade, 4 barrière de Rochechouart, run by a Master Hugot, vintner and caterer, was written in Paris as early as 1822:

> We know that on Monday of every week fifteen to twenty individuals, some old soldiers, some jewellery or printing workers, meet at his establishment... This periodical society pays 16 francs a meeting to Master Hugot for the use of a room and no one is admitted unless he is a member or is introduced by a member... It would be useless to attempt to penetrate this tavern if one had not been initiated.[47]

This tavern with its select, reserved and exclusive entry was no longer a tavern as such, since the tavern was a business and existed to serve the public. The group of people which had decided to establish itself as a group there (at least on Mondays) was no longer a product of the informal sociability of the tavern; it already had the structure of an association, even if its statutes were rudimentary (and, what is more, illegal, because it had not been declared or authorized).

It is important to recognize that, in the context of worker associations, the *cercle*, with its functions of straightforward sociability and varied leisure activities, if not tacit political activity, must be seen as quite distinct from the mutual associations and guild sections with their strictly vocational basis and the singing societies with their cultural identification. But was this all?

Formal associations: the secret society?

In studying the groups which spearheaded the movement of voluntary association, ought we to devote some space to the modern, revolutionary phenomenon of the organization formed to fight for a political cause (a fight which, in the days when people were denied the right to vote, could hardly be carried on in any way other than through action)? It is hard to see why nowadays people fail to use their vote when the worker confrontations at the *barricades* between July 1830 and February 1848 (particularly June 1832, April 1834, and May 1839) are so well known. However, what we are concerned with here is an examination of working-class sociability, and we are venturing somewhat out of our field. The republican secret society in the Carbonarist or Babouvist tradition, or the republican society which had been forced into becoming a secret society through repression (with names such as 'Droits de l'Homme', 'Amis du Peuple') was a society which spanned several classes, even if workers sometimes represented a considerable proportion of the membership.[48] Its officers were more likely to be drawn from the bourgeois or petit bourgeois than from the proletariat. We do hear of sections composed entirely of workers but the most plausible explanation would nonetheless be that they had originally been 'ordinary' workers' societies (i.e. corporative or social) which had as a group become politically active without really being aware of a change in status or purpose. 'Les Amis de l'ABC'who met at the Corinthe tavern, immortalized by Victor Hugo in *Les Misérables*, were a group of students with a few workers but it was the students who were the organizers.[49]

During the 1840s, following the failure of the workers' revolts and the feeling of disappointment which they left, there evolved among the working classes something approaching a doctrine of non-violence. This was expressed in *Le Chant des Ouvriers* written by Pierre Dupont in 1846:

A chaque fois que par torrents
notre sang coule par le monde
c'est toujours pour quelque tyran
que cette rosée est féconde.
Epargnons le dorénavant
l'Amour est plus fort que la guerre,
en attendant qu'un meilleur vent
souffle du ciel... ou de la terre.

Each time our blood rains down
Wherever in the world
This terrible dew falls
In the cause of some tyrant
Let us spare our children this strife
Love is stronger than war
Until the day when we feel a new wind
On our faces, out of heaven... or off the earth.[50]

This idea was common to the moderates of the workshop and the zealous, intransigent Flora Tristan. There were actually two elements to it: non-violence set against the violence of revolt and *ouvrierisme* set against the Jacobin fighting spirit of the petit bourgeois. The idea of the peaceful way, during this short period of the 1840s, was more typically proletarian than the philosophy of the barricades. 'Socialism', as this peaceful alternative often called itself, was more readily identifiable with the worker class than was neo-Jacobin communism.[51] This did not prevent some workers belonging to secret societies, but the original worker societies, which renounced the use of force (and which did not yet have the vote) argued that the chief virtue of association should be its concern with the workers. Association for them meant two things – one, the idea of joining forces to undertake production (nowadays known as the co-operative system), and the other, the idea of reinforcing existing links for a better and more instructive communal life, the idea of local worker unity, which is deserving of more attention. However, we cannot discuss typology without discussing the dynamics of working-class sociability. What led up to these aspirations in the working class?

The dynamics of working-class sociability

The association as model and objective

Informal sociability has existed since ancient times, probably since the beginning of time. Already at the start of the nineteenth century fraternal consciousness among those plying the same trade and a more or less rudimentary organization of mutual support had been in existence for at least three centuries. So, too, had the tavern; the experience of the pleasures of wine and song had perhaps been around for even longer. The association, on the other hand, was at this time a fairly new development. The activities of the 'Chambres littéraires', the 'Sociétés de lecture', the 'Casino', and others, in eighteenth-century France, important though they were, can be regarded as discrete and strictly limited to the aristocratic and bourgeois elites of the towns.

It was not until after the Revolution that people saw the full potential of social co-operation (going on to produce endless variations on the popular 'club' and 'society'). The population at large woke up to the fact that there was a state and along with it laws, prohibitions and procedures; to the fact that there was such a thing as politics and (in increasing numbers) newspapers to comment on it and other people in France to react to it. The growth (we will not use the word birth) of the voluntary, organized, defined association, operating in clear view of the state, was characteristic of the first half of the nineteenth century in France. The Revolution bequeathed us *le club*; the imperial period was to revive another model.

At the beginning of his memoirs Canler, a policeman, talks about his youth. In 1816 he joins the Paris police where he meets up with some former soldiers who, like him, are doing the job to earn their living but who underneath still maintain allegiance to the Emperor. Recognized as a friend, he is invited, after careful approaches have been made, to share a meal which they have together every month (on the day they get their pay) in the private room of the owner of a café. At the end of the meal his hosts reveal that they are in fact loyal supporters of the Emperor and solemnly drink to the health of the newcomer and to the return of Napoleon. 'My friends', said the President,

> the new comrade that we have with us today in our little society has proved himself sufficiently. He was a child of the army who marched behind the banner of Napoleon through all his changing fortunes and carried out his duties faithfully right up to the time when 'the army of the Loire' was disbanded. So let us drink to his health and make him welcome here![52]

This was well and truly a 'reception', however summary the rite involved. Here we are glimpsing the moment of transition (or the intermediary state) between the basic group and the society with its own rites of initiation, a faint echo of the masonic-Carbonarist model. The tremendous growth of freemasonry under the Empire had undoubtedly contributed to the popularization of this model, and not only in the military world. Under the Empire in 1811 the mayor of Saint Rémy declared to the grand inquiry into associations that there existed a *cercle bourgeois*, etc., and 'we also have a *chambrée* of 5 workers who call themselves freemasons, although I would say that their number never reaches 20. They have no statute, no politics, no literature, no religion. The whole thing revolves around a few jars of wine.'[53]

Here again, we have a group of friends who are brought together by a need for entertainment and at the same time, one may suppose, by their ideological inclinations, and who play at being a secret society; who claim to have adopted this model because the model is considered attractive and prestigious. However, the masonic model was soon to fade from public consciousness. The association around 1830 usually took the form of the *cercle*, and the *cercle*, for reasons which we have already explained, was predominantly a bourgeois group. However this bourgeoisie was itself undergoing a process of change and enlightenment. As changes occurred in the bourgeois way of life a far greater number of ordinary Frenchmen could expect to be influenced by them.

The nascent (or, here again, would it be wiser to say growing?) working class also experienced, at first from the outside, the vogue of the *cercle* in the same way as it had glimpsed the masonic fashion.[54] The consequences of this perception need to be looked at carefully in order the better to understand why, on the basis of an innate (informal) sociability, which by definition extended to the whole class, an increasing number of associations grew up which were often 'formalized' natural groupings. They could perhaps have started in a minor key – not seriously, 'playing at being an association', as it were, almost with an element of parody. This would seem to explain a strange story which Victor Gelu recounts.[55] The scene is Marseilles in 1836, where the author gets to know the Guinguette [open-air café] de l'Ascension, 15 Boulevard de la Paix. The regulars are older men in their fifties,

> a hive of great friends, all merry as larks, although almost all are older men, many old soldiers, who all meet fraternally under the singular denomination of 'Société des Frères Endormis' [Sleeping Brothers], drinking, eating, laughing, wagering jars of wine over hands of piquet and singing lustily every night with spirit that could never be matched at any social gathering.

There was no statute, except in so far as they named the merriest of them *président pour rire* and they marked what they called 'St Napoleon's Day' (August 15th) with a banquet, like the good old soldiers they were. They adopt

Victor Gelu, who is much younger than they are but whose talent as a songwriter impresses them: Gelu writes,

> First of all I drew up for them the rules of the society, which were half-humorous, half-serious, and in which there were frequent references to the great Emperor. Then, for St Napoleon's Day, I wrote a hymn in verse in honour of this demi-god of the veterans of the Old Guard. At the same time I composed a canticle to fraternity entitled 'Les Endormis' to be sung at all their ceremonial functions.

This was not all. At the time our chronicler was writing, twenty years later (1856), 'the few surviving, less alert and gay, but still faithfully attending their meetings, still sing the "canticle"' but 'they have now set themselves up as a regular "société de bienfaisance"'.

These people were living under an authoritarian Empire when, as everyone knew, the authorities disapproved and were suspicious of any sort of meeting and tolerated only the mutual associations authorized in the decree of 1852. Under Louis Philippe things were more easy going and there was much mimicry of the *cercle*. However, the group based on friendship continued to be the most important. Apart from the fact that they were, for the most part, old soldiers of the Empire, it would be interesting to know with which occupation we should associate these 'sleepers'. I say this because we presume they belong to the working classes and this idea is strengthened by the fact that they were evidently scarcely literate; otherwise they would hardly have waited until they had adopted a young baker's lad, who was educated and a good rhymester, before being able to enter into the bourgeois game of the society with its own statutes.

In other similar instances we can sometimes detect the presence of a member of the petit bourgeois among the working men, acting as their instrument or perhaps even their initiator. The Cercle des Ouvriers de Nuits (Côte d'Or) comprised several dozen artisans, a dozen vine-growers ... a doctor, a veterinary surgeon and a teacher. Surely it would have been one of these defectors from the bourgeoisie who would have 'lent his pen' to the uneducated classes, and perhaps not just to make fun of the gentlemen's *cercle*. As it happens, we do not know and we can say no more.

On a more serious note the *cercle* was imitated *for its comforts*. Why in 1841 did the foremen of the silk factory workshops at Lyons found their own *cercle*?[56] Article 1 of their statutes suggests their reasons were professional, utilitarian and mutualist: 'Foremen of silk workshops have founded a *cercle* with the aim of drawing together all the information and knowledge necessary in their profession and supporting each other with help and advice in all aspects of their private lives.' A corporative association then? But after reading through articles on administration, elections and subscriptions we find article 19 which states that

'The premises of the *cercle* shall be at the Croix Rousse. They shall comprise a hall where refreshments are to be available and a reading room, which shall be constantly at the disposal of the members' and the remaining statutes set out the details.

The long evolution from trade confraternity to professional trade-unionism had evidently begun and during the 1840s the *cercle* became involved in this process; it was the modern arrangement of the day, giving besides benefits of fraternity the material comforts of a collective home that could only be procured through association. The café too could provide these but less pleasantly and conveniently.

The *cercle* may have been the fashionable institution and one ensuring the greatest comfort, but above all it was an essentially bourgeois arrangement and the workers were finally moved to demand it for themselves out of a concern for *equality* and an awareness of class *dignity*. We do not know if this was the motive of the artisans and the vignerons' de Nuits in setting up their *cercles* but it was certainly the motive of the revolutionary workers of the Toulon arsenal whose story has been told elsewhere.[57] Their request to create a 'Cercle de l'Union Ouvrière' was explicit in its reasoning: why not us?

It is a fact that through the convention of the *cercles*, for which the government liberally accorded the necessary authorization, the right of association was in practice accorded to the bourgeoisie. Why not, then, to the working people also? As students of Flora Tristan, as we have said, the Toulon workers were applying the explicit watchword which she had given in her little book *L'Union Ouvrière* even before she had embarked upon her tour of France.[58] Few writers of the 1840s observed working-class sociability with such precision as this extraordinary woman. She gives us a realistic view of everyday socializing, the *chambrée*, the tavern – she was well acquainted with the guilds, the associations, the mutual societies – which she called upon to federate – the secret societies, which she disapproved of (because the campaigns they planned were always for the benefit of bourgeois Jacobins who were too interested in political gain and not enough in social improvement), the *goguettes* – which she also disapproved of (those songs were 'a farrago of meaningless nonsense with not one useful message'); she was also familiar with the workers' reading societies, at least as an ideal concept and, as far as she was concerned, as a definite programme to be implemented; she called on the workers to form their own and it is possible that this call was sometimes acted upon.

In short, the *cercle* was a bourgeois preserve and the workers wanted it for themselves; this was one of the generally under-appreciated issues in the class struggle of the 1840s. Even a journal of such moderate socialism as *L'Atelier* perceived this in exposing the injustice of the authorities' bias in these matters. In its number of October 1844 it prints two different episodes which are very interesting to compare. In Paris, a *cercle* of young bourgeois revellers known as the 'Cercle de la Tour de Nesle', which was not even registered, had become the site of orgies. Following a case of rape the police were forced to intervene, but the courts were so indulgent towards them that they did not even mention the fact that the association was unauthorized in their bill of indictment. At this same time the police in Lyons were carrying out arrests of workers whose only crime had been to set up a reading society. According to *L'Atelier*,

> Certain workers of Lyons, quite justifiably convinced that any material improvement in the lot of the working people must be linked to improvement of the mind, have formed an association whose sole purpose it is to give people the chance to read together the books, pamphlets and journals which have been written on social organization – and they are treated as conspirators.

So the serious-minded worker was denied the same right which was accorded to the debauched bourgeois – the right to meet in the framework of the *cercle*. This was evidently primarily a social issue.

The ideal concept of the *cercle*, to the supporters of the working class and to the educated workers, from the point of view of socialism one might say, looked forward, then, to the Maison du Peuple (in the writings of Flora Tristan it was also to have something of the function of a *Bourse du Travail* – but is this not thinking along the same lines anyway?). It is to be a place where the worker can satisfy his need for social contact without being dependent on the tavern or its outbuildings; a place where, thanks to the economic possibilities opened up by association, he is able to enjoy comforts[59] which his miserable dwelling can never afford him; a place where he can educate himself, with access to a library. Sociability – Comfort – Culture. This explains why the *cercle* was incorporated into the Phalansterian model! The *cercle* was definitely not a Fourierist concept in itself any more than central heating was, but how could those who preached a better life for everyone afford to pass it by? This is how a character in the *Juif errant* describes the main room of the communal home of the workers in the society of the future:

> During the winter at the end of the day this room could be used as a place where the workers could meet or pass some time in company if they preferred to spend the evening together rather than return to where they lived or to their families. In this huge room, kept nicely warm by the stove and brightly lit by gas-lamps, some would read, others would play cards, others would chat or get on with small pieces of work.[60]

Fourierism was to disappear but the idea of the Maison du Peuple, a meeting place specifically for the working people, was to take hold.

In 1848 there was still a long way to go and the working-class movement imagined more than it was capable of achieving. The bourgeois, however, were not unaware of the problem and there were even those who, against the general tide of opinion, saw some advantages in the idea of *cercles* for the workers. They would be morally beneficial, first because it was plainly humane and Christian to allow the worker his pleasant evenings and Sundays as well; and then because morality was thought to come more easily to the man who read and educated himself than to the illiterate who was governed by his instincts; and finally because the *cercle* would act as a rival to the tavern and in the *cercle* there was no drunkenness and one could not fall in with the wrong sort of people.

On the basis of these principles the Baron de Gérando[61], one of the most well-known of the bourgeois philanthropists, was to draw up an ideal of the working-class *cercle* which differed little from the vision of the Fourierists and the 'atelieristes'. It would be a centre for leisure activities, well equipped (with a garden for outdoor games, billiard tables, a room for society games, etc.), within the framework of a club; people would be able to drink there – otherwise they would prefer the tavern – but there would be no way of gaining access without a membership card. In short it had all the benefits of the tavern plus comfort and less promiscuity. Reading was given less importance in the Gérando model than in the socialist model. On the other hand Gérando appreciated the consideration that should be given to such activities as group singing. The bourgeois model differed mainly on the subject of financing. Gérando would have made it the responsibility of the employers in the pattern of the well-known Alsatian paternalism; failing this, the responsibility of the Church; failing this, even the responsibility of the municipalities. However, the point was that the working class should have its *cercles*.

In fact it did not get them, because the prevailing opinion in the ruling classes and, as we have seen, in the ranks of the authorities, was that for all their advantages there would be the major drawback that the workers' *cercles* would undoubtedly act as propaganda centres. Villermé, a man with a record as a philanthropist equal to that of Gérando, prefaced his ideas with the retort:

> Imagine workers' residences where, as some of the handbills say, [about the residence at Rochechouart] the tenants, mainly single men, have a large communal room which gives them a warm place to go in the winter and, what is more, serves as a meeting place for the other workers of the district. Would we not be right to fear that, particularly in Paris, these would become places where rioting and sedition were encouraged and the more so because the participants in these meetings would have every opportunity to see each other, to conspire with each other and to plot behind their doors with the police helpless to stop them?[62]

As for the iniquitous tavern, at least it had the virtue of being penetrable by police informants...

The bourgeois were to spend a long time debating which sort of worker was the most dangerous – the one who was untutored, coarse, immoral and prone to rebel (Gérando's opinion) or the one who was cultured, made wiser, informed and consequently critical (Villermé's opinion). It was the first opinion, the more liberal in principle, which gave rise to some great civilizing efforts such as the *loi*

Guizot of 1833 on primary education. The second, more traditional, opinion kept the authorities determined to obstruct any attempt by the people to organize, which in practice meant that they were left with the original options of their hovels or the bar. The facts, after all, seemed to bear out the opinions of those who would repress the workers: political awareness came through the channels of sociability and the association.

The association as vehicle

Evidence that working-class sociability was often overlaid with a spirit of social criticism and struggle has already been indirectly provided in the first part of this study. It has often been through reports or personal accounts of a political origin or content that we have indirectly acquired important clues to ethnographical phenomena. It might be through a text by Engels on the assemblies of the *barrières* where they discussed communism, which workers and their families attended in huge numbers; or a text by the weaver Joseph Benoît on the talk that went on in the workshop, where communism was also an important topic of discussion; or texts of the authorities of the Restoration period which take us into the *chambrées* or the 'exclusive taverns' suspected of harbouring undesirable elements. The same Lyons workers which Joseph Benoît wrote about reappear with surprisingly similar features in the writings of Charles de Rémusat. The former minister is recording an account which Wolowski, the academician, economist and professor at the Ecole Nationale des Arts et Métiers, has given him, having carried out some sort of personal survey in Lyons. The year is 1847. He finds the workers

> established in definite groups with no formal membership but meeting regularly in the same cafés, rooms or *chambrées* which offered reading, conversation and refreshment. Here they would listen to readings which were always taken from literature exalting democracy or speeches made by comrades who were fine speakers. Sometimes there would be general discussion of questions raised by these communications[63]

So it was sometimes possible, with a bit of ingenuity and discretion, to set up small literary *cercles* without authorization (what other interpretation can be placed on 'rooms or *chambrées* which offered reading, conversation and refreshment'?), but at these there was no talking for the sake of it – it was talking in order to learn, and learning to improve one's lot.

It is clear then that social and political debate took place in the established locations and institutions of working-class sociability, because this was convenient, because it was discreet (at least anywhere but in the tavern) and also to exploit a trait which we have already touched upon: these simple men who looked upon each other as brothers were prone to group reactions and once an idea took hold it was not long before it was accepted by all.

This was my reply to the astonishment which I earlier presumed that Rémusat would have felt on rediscovering his statement about the Jacobin workers who sang; might it not rather have been a case of workers who sang together (normal sociability) and who at a given time took to Jacobinism (politicization)? This idea was already present in police reports of the time of the Restoration. We can take as an example the case of the Café de la Redoute, 39 rue Grenelle St Honoré:[64]

> It is kept by a master Remiot who runs a *pension* accommodating around twenty people. Meetings take place in a room on the ground floor at the back of the courtyard; they are attended only by the lodgers themselves ... It would be true to say that this house at no. 39 is a cesspit of revolutionaries ... here they sing songs composed by Béranger; they quite openly express their hatred of the government.[65]

It would appear that sociability's natural grouping (these lodgers with the same landlord) and the suspected political cell, where Béranger songs are sung and members of the government are slated, are basically the same. The twentieth century was never to afford such homogeneities. In the nineteenth century there were predictable groupings; workers could be divided into clearly honogeneous groups based on habitat, entertainment or common sentiments. We are made aware of this in these remarks by Victor Hugo's republican character Enjolras. It is Paris in May 1832, and Enjolras is talking:

> In the 'barrière du Maine' there is a group of masons, painters and practitioners in the sculpture workshops. They are basically enthusiastic but tend to blow hot and cold. For some time now I have been wondering what is the matter with them. They are letting themselves be distracted. Their ardour is cooling. They spend their time playing dominoes. They need to be given a stern talking to urgently. They meet at Richefeu's place. They can be found there between midday and one o'clock.[66]

He eventually goes there: 'One o'clock was striking on the Vaugirard church clock when Enjolras arrived at Richefeu's smoke den.' His mission was of course to be successful. But it is the same sociability grouping which, depending on the circumstances, abandons dominoes for guns and guns for dominoes.

Conclusion

I make no claim to having rewritten the considerable body of history of French working-class consciousness during the years from the start of the century up to 1848. It is the history of the beginnings of a new *consciousness* and consequently, following a well-recognized logic, of efforts towards *organization*.

The subject of organization merits a whole volume of description and analysis in itself. What I have tried to do in this chapter is to indicate general guidelines for research and consideration without suggesting that this is the only way to approach the subject; what is certain is that it should not be neglected, even if it is thought of as being of minor importance. The importance of the *economic factor* has long been recognized. It ensured that the working class grew and concentrated together in the same way as industry itself and that phases of worker agitation would always coincide with particular recurring economic circumstances. Nor can we fail to appreciate the *political* element, which W. Sewell has treated in a brilliant study.[67] The year 1830 is not just the starting point for the theory of the ownership of capital (because it was at this time that the landed gentry first became separated from the power centre), but it is also the year which saw a true revolution out of which came experiment, an ideological upheaval enabling the old trades to see themselves in terms of the association, the workers to see themselves as 'the people', and accordingly, enabling the trades to conceive of the people as the association of associations. Quite a convincing dialectic had emerged, the demonstrable result of four years (1830–4) of equally intense struggle and thought.

The data we have used concentrate more on the unexceptional years of the 20s and the 40s. Important developments were taking place during these years just the same, albeit on a different scale and attracting less attention; developments in what we might call the *cultural* sphere, for want of a better adjective. My contention is that consciousness and organization in the society of the worker was not only dependent upon what took place in the economic sphere and the political sphere but also to some extent on the evolution of social patterns of behaviour among the workers themselves[68] as well as among the bourgeois and petty bourgeois. Credit must be given where credit is due: the link which I have ventured to establish between the bourgeois practice of association and the workers' aspiration to association had been made earlier by Flora Tristan and I have done no more than consolidate and systematize the intuition of this amazingly foresighted woman.

Association – the term is always made the catchword for the events of 1848. But it has other implications: association replacing the isolation which steadily drove the workers into the hands of the employers with a united labour force of co-operative workers, dispensing with the employer – in modern terms, the idea of socialist worker-management; association broadening trade identity into class identity by increasing awareness of the fraternity of trades, or the development of class consciousness which has been reassessed by Sewell; and then there is association in relation to the Civil and Penal Codes of the time, in other words, in terms of 'society'. And this is no less important. We can see by looking at the great trade union organizations today how a general (national) confederation pulls together the whole range of trades and professions (in the case of France the *fédérations de syndicats*) as well as the whole range of geographical groupings (in the case of France, association at local, *Département* and regional levels). The very fabric of these last is formed from the basic union of workers who share the same workplace, who know one another, who are likely to have faced the same setbacks. This union is no less vital. And this was an idea which made its mark between 1830 and 1848.

NOTES

1 For further points on this subject see my article 'Les Chambrées en Basse Provence: Histoire et Ethnologie', *Revue Historique* 498 (April–June 1971), pp. 339, 367.

2 As Eric Hobsbawm has done in so much of his work. Another outstanding example of the advancement of British scholarship in this area is the classic work by E.P. Thompson, *The Making of the English Working Class* (London 1963). For the French contribution in this area see J. Droz, *Histoire générale du Socialisme* (Paris 1972), Vol. I, *Des Origines à 1875*. For more recent contributions see *Le Mouvement Social* (Paris, quarterly).

3 As early as 1856 in his *Histoire des Paysans* the Republican Eugène Bonnemère brought out the primitiveness and barbarity of rural existence by contrasting it with the usual companionable existence of the worker in the towns. 'The workers are brought together by the workshop and most also belong to some modest society which brings them together in their leisure time. He works in company, he relaxes and enjoys himself in company…' *Histoire des paysans depuis la fin du Moyen Age jusqu'à nos jours* (Paris 1856) p. 429.

4 *Le Cercle dans la France bourgeoise (1800–1848): étude d'une mutation de sociabilité*, Ser. 'Cahiers des Annales', 36 (Paris 1977).

5 French National Archives under various sub-headings of the sub-series F7 following the inventory drawn up by J. Chaumié. References for the major surveys are given in M. Agulhon, *Le Cercle dans la France bourgeoise*. Principal sources are drawn from the archives of the *Département*, ser. M. It should be pointed out that the archives of the Préfecture de Police are very incomplete in parts for the period prior to 1871.

6 Examples for Provence can be found in Frédéric Mistral, *Mes origines – mémoires et récits* (Paris 1906).

7 Joseph Benoît, *Confessions d'un prolétaire* (Paris 1968), p. 74.

8 Manuscript thesis by M. Akashi on the tailors of Paris, edited by Michelle Perrot (Paris 1978). The quotation is taken from p. 58.

9 Norbert Truquin, *Mémoires et aventures d'un prolétaire à travers la révolution* (Paris 1977), pp. 50–1.

10 The tenants who made up the *chambrée* naturally patronized the tavern, with the advantage that if they chose to stay up late drinking and playing cards in their quarters they were able to carry on later than police regulations permitted for the clientèle of the tavern. The police were concerned about this. At least this is the impression we get from two texts dating from 1822 and 1824 with reference to Paris, one concerning workers, the other concerning students. *Le Livre Noir de Messieurs Delavau et Franchet* (Paris 1829), Vol. III, pp. 407–8 and Vol. IV, p. 29.

11 We can produce numerous examples: Truquin, *Mémoires*, p. 55 (masons in Paris, *c.* 1840); A. Perdiguier, *Mémoire d'un compagnon*, posthumously published and

appearing in several editions this century. I am quoting from the pocket edition (UGE, Paris), p. 86.

With reference to the worker joiners of Marseilles, *c.* 1825: M. Nadaud, *Mémoire de Léonard, ancien garçon maçon* (Paris 1976 edition), *passim.*

With reference to masons in Paris between 1830 and 1848, a police report ('order and concord reign in the *'chambrées'* of the workers' quarters') quoted by Bertier de Sauvigny in 'Les Ouvriers d'Industrie à Paris sous la Restauration', *Bull. Soc. Hist. Moderne*, supplement to *Revue d'Histoire Moderne et Contemporaine*, 1 (1976), p. 27.

12 Statement by Perdiguier quoted by Remy Gossez in *Les Ouvriers de Paris* (Paris 1968).

13 Michèle Querol, Master's dissertation, edited by G. Cholvy and M. Agulhon, (Univ. Paul Valéry, Montpellier, 1971).

14 See M. Agulhon, *Pénitents et francmaçons de l'ancienne Provence* (Paris 1968), *La Vie sociale en Provence intérieure au lendemain de la Révolution* (Paris 1971), *La République au village* (Paris 1970); and Lucienne Roubin, *Chambrettes des provençaux* (Paris 1973); also Agulhon, 'Les Chambrées en Basse Provence'.

15 *Mémoires de Canler, ancien chef du service de sûreté* (Paris *c.* 1860) are crammed with information on the bars frequented by the working people in Paris at the time of the Restoration and the July Monarchy. *Cabaret* (translated in the text as 'tavern') is the name most commonly given to establishments of this type. *Estaminet* is rarer. *Guinguette* (translated in the text as 'open-air café') is only used for establishments with larger premises, hence situated at the very edge of the city, just beyond the toll-gates. However, there were also taverns in the *barrières* and the villages (Belleville, Grenelle, etc.) Canler never uses the term *cabaretier* to refer to the tavern proprietor but the term *marchand de vin* from *Mannezingue* in argot. The *marchand de vin* provided drink and also food. Many taverns also acted as eating-houses, with waiter service. It was also possible to eat in the open-air cafés, the most usual dish being veal and green salad (p. 251). Moreover, the *marchand de vin* sometimes acquired along with the tavern a residential lodging house so that he was a landlord too. Sometimes he would also have individual rooms to let, which could be used for a private meal or for a couple staying the night. If the *marchand de vin* was connected with the underworld, that is to say if he habitually gave shelter to thieves, his tavern would be known as a *tapis franc*. Canler's accounts are obviously mainly concerned with that (seemingly quite large) section of tavern landlords who made a habit of harbouring professional criminals and delinquents.

16 Flora Tristan, *L'Union Ouvrière* (Paris 1967 reprint), pp. 55–6. She also notes, confirming the point made earlier, that it was normal to find unmarried workers in the taverns who slept in the *chambrées* (especially, it would be fair to suppose, if the *chambrée* was in the vintner's house).

17 Article in *Variétés* of 30 April 1843 on the *Faubourg St Antoine*. Its argument is that the worker may well be revolutionary but this does not make him despicable; he has a strong and morally upright character; the drunk and debauched are in the minority. The real working people do not go drinking at the tavern more than once a week. On the consumption of wine I am indebted to A. Audiganne, *Les Populations ouvrières de la France*, Vol. I (Paris 1860), pp. 134–5. In 1852 the municipality of Rheims was to encourage coopers to produce special small barrels so that the workers could buy their wine retail and would have no need to go to the tavern.

18 For a classic period description see 'Barrière de la Villette' in *Les Français peints par eux-mêmes, Encyclopédie morale du XIXe siècle* (Paris 1840–42), Vol. 9.

19 A short analysis for Marseilles is given in a Master's dissertation by J. Estrangin, 'Marseille sous la Monarchie de Juillet' (Univ. de Provence, 1970), p. 146. For Paris see de Sauvigny, *Les Ouvriers d'industrie*, p. 31.

20 The outline above would be further complicated by taking into account the seasonal variable. The joiners of Chartres would spend Sundays either at the tavern all together drinking and singing (mainly, in the winter, can we surmise?) or in the country at 'the Assemblies and village celebrations' (in the summer months?), where there was dancing and female company to be found. (A. Perdiguier, *Mémoire d'un compagnon*, pp. 206–8). It should not be overlooked that there were also taverns in the *barrières*.

21 J. Michelet, *Journal* (Paris 1959), Vol. 1, p. 607. This extract is considerably clarified in the light of analyses of the café made in Agulhon, *Le Cercle*.

22 I have given an example of this in *Une Ville ouvrière au temps du socialisme utopique: Toulon de 1815 à 1851* (Paris and The Hague 1970) in the chapter dealing with the great dock strike of 1845.

23 Letter of Engels addressed to the communist Correspondance Committee in Brussels; taken from Marx–Engels *Correspondance* (Paris 1971), Vol. I, p. 407. A curiously similar observation is made by Victor Hugo in *Les Misérables* with reference to the taverns of the Rue de Charonne in the spring of 1832. 'At this particular time the atmosphere is politically charged, there is a constant feeling of excitement, meetings are taking place at 8 o'clock, 10 o'clock, always the same with men and women crammed into the room to hear' (pp. 884–5). He does not mention if these meetings took place on a Sunday.

24 Notably Stendhal in *Les Mémoires d'un touriste*, posthumous publication, 3 vols. (Paris 1932) and Michelet in *Journal*. For further consideration of this point see Agulhon, *Le Cercle, passim*.

25 Although I drew some attention to it in *Une Ville ouvrière*, in the chapter on 1830 and *passim*.

26 Emile Laurent, *Le Paupérisme et les associations de prévoyance – nouvelles études sur les sociétés de secours mutuels*, 2 vols. (Paris 1865) and since then an entire historiography. In the context of Paris specifically see Remy Gossez, *Les Ouvriers de Paris*. Even more importantly, in the context of Lyons, J. Gaumont, *L'Histoire générale de la coopération*, 2 vols. (Paris 1924); P. Ansart, *Naissance de l'anarchisme, esquisse*, a sociological explanation of *Proudhonisme* (Paris 1970) and Y. Lequin, *Les Ouvriers de la région lyonnaise 1848–1914* (Lyons 1977), Vol. 2, pp. 181–95.

27 For an accurate and entertaining example of this see 'L'Histoire de la société des ouvriers tonneliers à Cette', *L'Atelier* (31 March 1850). This history, written in 1850, does not give us the details of the origins of this group. The manuscript was discovered by M. Querol in the National Archives. Numerous society statutes can be located in the Archives Départementales, classified either under series M (police, general administration) which I have already mentioned for associations in general, or under series X (dealing with assistance).

28 Another archaic hangover was the practice of supervising the hiring out for work of its members, with each member given priority in strict rotation during the times when the usual employer did not have work for everyone. We know this commonly happened

among the dock hands of Marseilles but it also operated among the boatmen of Clamecy on the River Yonne who all belonged to the Confrérie de St Nicholas (from *L'Association* of April 1841 quoted by J.C. Martinet in *Clamecy et ses flotteurs* (La Charité sur Loire 1975), pp. 108–9). This was a traditional practice, then, denied by the more recent dogmas of the right to work and free competition. It had not, therefore, originated in the nineteenth century and was only perpetuated by the respect accorded to an ancient tradition and force of habit.

29 In periods of exceptional strike activity the Sociétés de Résistance would join forces with the corporative societies. There is a good study of this phenomenon in Paris of the 1830s by Alain Faure, 'Mouvements populaires et mouvement ouvrier à Paris (1830–1834)' in *Le Mouvement social* (July–Sept. 1974).

30 See the long list of '*Associations professionnelles ouvrières*' from the Office du Travail national survey (Paris 1900).

31 Victor Gelu, *Marseille au XIXe siècle*, ed. P. Guiral, L. Gaillard and J. Reboul (Paris 1971), p. 156. He also describes (p. 185) a Société de Bienfaisance of coopers which met in the harbour area of Arenc, where they also performed amateur dramatics.

32 Le Livre Noir, Vol. IV, p. 178. The report is dated 12 June 1827, from the district of St Germain d'Auxerrois. The name of Didot (later Didot-Bottin, Firmin Didot, etc.) is still associated with printing. Note the allusion to Mondays. The law which would have had the effect of restricting the freedom of the press was known as the *loi de Justice et d'Amour*; it was defeated in 1826. Corbière was minister of the interior, in the Villele government, in the reign of Charles X.

33 Arthur Dinaux, *Les Sociétés badines, bachiques, littéraires et chantantes, leur histoire et leurs travaux* (Paris 1867). Pierre Brochon dedicates an entire volume of *Les Classiques du peuple* (Editions Sociales) to the few great republican writer/singers of the *goguettes*.

34 There is a contemporary description, '*Le Goguettier*', in *Les Français peints par eux-mêmes*, Vol. IV. (This very long article, attributed to a certain Berthaud, is the source for the article entitled '*Goguette*' in the Larousse *Grand dictionnaire universel du XIXe siècle*.) See also *L'Atelier* for May, August, and October 1844.

35 Jean Touchard, *La Gloire de Béranger* (Paris 1968).

36 Charles Louandré in *L'Atelier* for 1846, 2nd quarter, p. 537. The famous review itself dedicated a survey to the general phenomenon of association.

37 *Marseille au XIXe siècle*, pp. 221–2, 227. See also p. 253 (although this actually resembles more closely a *cercle*), and pp. 256–7, describing a place in the suburbs which belongs to a masonic lodge and every Sunday is transformed into the venue for singing evenings open to the uninitiated.

38 A brief reference in *L'Atelier* of 30 June 1850.

39 Charles de Rémusat, *Mémoires de ma vie*, Vol. III (Paris 1954), p. 391.

40 This phenomenon was found even in the bourgeois milieu: many of the republican 'secret societies', active in the provinces in the early 1830s, on closer examination turn out to be *cercles* which had become politicized. (See Agulhon, *Le Cercle*.)

41 *Ibid., passim.*

42 Stendhal, *Mémoires d'un touriste*, Vol. III, p. 24.

43 Agulhon, *Pénitents et francmaçons* and *La République au village*. See also Gelu, *Marseille au XIXe siècle*, p. 166. The idea of the social practices of the different classes

being analogous is a common one for Provence at this time. If we take the example of gambling (card games for money), 'the rich apply themselves with the same obsessive frenzy as the working men in their *"chambrées"'*, wrote *La Sentinelle*, a Toulon journal, in its edition of 22 February 1846. (*Chambrée* is used here in the sense of *chambrette*, as explained earlier.)

44 The dossier on the cercle des Ouvriers de Nuits (Côte d'Or), created in September 1842, is instructive here. These *ouvriers* are actually artisans, mainly coopers, and some vine-growers. There are some *petits bourgeois* mixed in with them. They have 'established this *"Cercle"* in order to imitate that founded by the foremost inhabitants of this town', which the prefect had authorized in February 1841. French National Archives (hereather FNA), F7 12236, *dossier Nuits, cercle des ouvriers, Préfet à Ministre* (14 September 1842). This little sub-series of the FNA which contains only fragments of a national survey, gives the names of more, analogous, societies at Bressuire, Montbéliard, Munster (where it was known as *le Second Casino* – the first obviously being the bourgeois society), Lyons, etc.

45 The prefect of the Côte d'Or assesses them in the following way, before deciding in favour of authorization:

> An association of this type generally gives us cause for concern because of the sort of people who organize them, because of the influence which a few impassioned, skilful men can have on undiscerning minds and because of the kind of journals they subscribe to. I might add that the *cercle* affords opportunities for spending to men that have need of all their resources to provide for the upkeep and the future of their families, but one could reply to this last consideration that the majority of these individuals would cease going to the café and the tavern once they began to attend the *cercle*. (FNA F7 12236, *dossier Nuits, cercle des ouviers, Préfet à Ministre*, 14 September 1842.)

46 Perdiguier, *Mémoires d'un compagnon*, p. 88. 'On Sundays we [the journeymen carpenters] would sometimes go with Portalès [his current employer] to have a game of bowls or cards in the garden which he had outside the town, where a society of *maîtres* regularly met. There was much gaiety and singing was the order of the day.'

47 *Le Livre Noir*, Vol. II, p. 418. This notion of the 'exclusive café' – the *cercle* formed through reserving an exclusive right to use a certain café by a contract, formal or otherwise, with its proprietor, has been dealt with in *Le Cercle*. For another example of this phenomenon in a popular milieu see FNA F7 3092 *Feuille de travail du 21 Octobre 1813* (concerning a Brussels tavern).

48 See J. Tchernoff, *Le Parti républicain sous la Monarchie de Juillet* (Paris, 1901); G. Weill, *Histoire du parti républicain en France de 1814 à 1870* (Paris 1928); and J. Valette (ed.), *1848 Les Utopistes sociaux* (Paris 1981).

49 *Les Misérables*, La Pléiade edition, pp. 686–700.

50 Pierre Dupont, *Chants et chansons*, 2 vols. (Paris 1850).

51 The following passage, obviously biased but none the less of value, is by de Rémusat, minister of the interior (*Mémoires de ma vie*, Vol. III, p. 421). at the time of the strikes of spring1830:

However, although some workers outside the trades which had gone on strike, with a known affiliation to political societies, had taken the field and were blowing on the fire started by the coalitions, one could see in these societies the stamp of economic socialism but very few symptoms of the passions which fuel insurrections. We know that at some workers' meetings offers of co-operation from Republican groups were, after deliberation, turned down.

52 *Mémoires de Canler*, pp. 26–7. Canler, a soldier's son, eventually became a soldier himself; subsequently he had been a worker for several months before joining the police. His colleagues, former non-commissioned officers, must, like him, have been of working-class origin.

53 St Rémy (Bouches du Rhône) Municipal Archives, transcript of a letter from the mayor to the sub-prefect, 2 March 1811 – a document recorded by our friend Marcel Bonnet, secretary at the *mairie* and historian of this little town.

54 The word 'fashion' will perhaps seem a little deprecatory but contemporary accounts exist which testify to this 'craze' which spread through the uninitiated world in the last years of the Empire, giving rise to a whole pseudo-masonic movement. The situation in Toulon is described in *Les Cahiers de Letuaire* (Toulon 1925).

55 *Marseille au XIXe Siècle*, pp. 228–9.

56 FNA F7 12.237, dossier for Lyons, *Cercle des Chefs d'Atelier*.

57 Agulhon, *Une Ville ouvrière*.

58 Tristan, *L'Union ouvrière*, pp. 8, 15, 55–6, 73, 111, 118.

59 Comfort, it will be ascertained from the texts which I will quote, did not only mean access to billiards and dominoes, it meant the very basic amenities of warmth and light.

60 Eugène Sue (1845) quoted in Michel Ragon, *Histoire de l'architecture et de l'urbanisme moderne* (Paris 1971), Vol. I, p. 80. Jules Duval, another independent Fourierist, was in 1847 considering founding a corporative journal and making the reception rooms of its premises available for meetings of a new *cercle* which would be open on Sundays for workers 'whom it would be aimed at particularly as it would attempt to provide for their needs and their fancies, the pleasures of elegant society which until now have been reserved for the rich'. Eugène Sue, *Le Juif errant* (Paris 1845), quoted by Jacques Valette in his unpublished thesis on Jules Duval, Univ. de Paris I, 1975, Vol. I, p. 274.

61 'Popular recreations considered as one of the most effective means of diverting the workers away from the taverns', extract from *Annales de la Charité*, Nov. 1857 (offprint, Bibliothèque Nationale, Paris).

62 'Sur les Cités Ouvrières', *Annales d'hygiène publique et de médecine légale*, 43, 2, 1850, quoted from the work of Murard and Zylberman, 'Le Petit Travailleur infatigable', *Recherches*, no. 25, August 1976.

63 *Mémoires de ma vie*, Vol. IV, pp. 165–6. The whole page is referred to as it is of great interest for its revelations on the worker mentality and also that of the authorities.

64 *Le Livre Noir*, Vol. II, p. 355.

65 This is January 1823, the time of the ultra-royalist Restoration. Béranger is at this time a genuine subversive. It is not until after 1830, with the advent of a regime which is

officially recognized as liberal and secular, that Béranger and all his disciples in the *goguettes* are considered as conformist and bourgeois, at least from the socialist point of view.

66 *Les Misérables*, p. 896. According to Canler's memoirs (p. 307) Richefeu was in the *barrière* Montparnasse.

67 In his book *Work and Revolution in France* and in 'La Confraternité des prolétaires: conscience de classe sous la monarchie de Juillet', *Annales ESC*, July–Aug. 1981, pp. 650–71.

68 In his article from *Mouvement Social*, pp. 63, 64, Alain Faure sees in the custom of holding strike meetings in the *barrières* the vestiges of an old idea common in the guilds that at these times the town should be abandoned, expressed by making it out of bounds or boycotting it. I would be inclined to think that this is a bit too subtle and it would be simpler to attribute it simply to habit and practical considerations of space.

3

Men and women in the Parisian garment trades: discussions of family and work in the 1830s and 1840s

JOAN WALLACH SCOTT

Studies of the working-class movement in nineteenth-century France have established the fundamental role of skilled workers who drew on craft traditions in their efforts to resist proletarianization. Artisans offered association, a co-operative organization of production which regulated economic relationships, as an alternative to the ruthless competition which for them characterized the advent of industrial capitalism. *Fraternité* was the watchword of asso-ciationalism and it referred to a brotherhood of craftsmen as the basis for a new set of productive relationships. The traditional rules of the pre-industrial *atelier* were incorporated into a new vision of the *atelier social*.

An important aspect of the artisan's critique of capitalism dealt with the impact of the reorganization of work and the pressures of wage labour on the family and especially on women. In the 1830s and 40s a variety of images of the family recurred in the literature of protest as artisans – male and female – justified demands for higher wages or attacked the cupidity of the bourgeoisie, as they illustrated the depths of their poverty or raised their glasses to toast a future new society. Utopian socialists, too, made the family a central theme of their writings whether, like Fourier and the Saint-Simonians, they experimented with the forms of family organization or, like Cabet, promised qualitative improvements in the happiness of traditional couples and their children. The organization of labour and association were only two of the dominant themes in this period of working-class protest; the family was an equally important and interrelated third.

What was the significance of the artisans' discussion of the family during the 1830s and 40s? What was its relationship to demands for an equitable organization of labour? Did it, like the idea of the *atelier social*, incorporate traditional notions into demands for a more just and equitable set of arrangements in the future? These questions lead inevitably from the realms of economy and household to gender. How did ideas about appropriate activities for men and women inform the artisan's critique of capitalism? Was there a

67

single vision shared by women and men? Did longstanding popular beliefs about male and female space provide a critical standard against which capitalist organization was assessed? What was the relationship between these beliefs and bourgeois definitions of family and gender?

These questions presuppose an integration of analyses usually carried out separately. Historians of the labour movement have focused almost exclusively on the links between the conditions of work of male artisans and the organization and ideology of working-class protest.[1] A few have extended their investigations to female artisans, exploring the processes that moved skilled women to collective action or addressing questions about whether wage labour improved or worsened women's status.[2] Historians of the family have examined changes in household structure and the economic ties of family members inferring ideas and strategies without, however, examining what people said.[3] In contrast, those who analyse theories of the family articulated by, for example, a Fourier, Proudhon or Cabet sometimes characterize the social and economic experiences of their followers in misleadingly schematic terms.[4] Historians of women have addressed gender largely in terms of female experience and perception, providing an important corrective for our appreciation of a long neglected subject. Their studies treat topics that are not always comparable to studies of male workers and the labour movement but they have expanded the terrain of labour history to include cultural conceptions of gender.[5]

The most obvious way to attempt an integration of these diverse approaches is at the level of the case study. We need to examine ideas about family and gender in detailed and specific contexts, in the manner of the case studies from which generalizations were eventually drawn about the relationship between protest movements and changes in the organization of skilled trades. We need not only to broaden our subject from labouring men to labouring women and labouring families, but to extend our scope beyond a single causal factor. If we are to get at the interrelationships between economic, ideological and cultural influences in working-class politics, perhaps the place to begin is with strategies for change elaborated by various trades. By listening to the discourse as it deals not only with work processes but with family and the roles of men and women, we may at once complete our picture of the origins and meaning of early nineteenth-century working-class protest and also alter our understanding of it.

This chapter is a first attempt to merge what up to now have been, for me, two separate bodies of inquiry – one into labour history, the other the history of women; the one focusing on work and protest, the other on gender and work. It looks at the way ideas about family and gender figure in the elaboration of general analyses of capitalism and specific strategies for the reform of trade conditions. And it seeks to compare the approaches to work, family, and gender of women and men.

I have focused on the garment trades in the 1830s and 40s because they included both skilled women and men and because they offer a case study of skilled workers in transition. The garment trades employed the greatest number of Parisian workers during this period (some 90,000 as compared to the next largest, building trades, which employed 41,000 in 1847).[6] Skilled workers dominated the custom-made tailoring and dressmaking trades even though a major transformation of the organization of work had begun with the growth of the ready-made clothing industry (*confection*). As they resisted new commercial and manufacturing practices and fought to preserve the integrity of their craft, garment workers were at the forefront of working-class protest movements. Tailors organized massive strikes in the 1830s and 40s, embraced Cabet's Icarian movement, pioneered in the development of co-operative producers' associations and swelled the crowds in the revolution of 1848.[7] Dressmakers and seamstresses responded to the Saint-Simonian gospel, outnumbering other categories of the movement's working-class disciples and producing a newspaper during 1832–4, *La Tribune des Femmes*, edited entirely by and written for working women. Like their male counterparts, the skilled seamstresses organized producer co-operatives and won contracts from the revolutionary government in 1848.[8] Their leaders joined the chorus of male voices proposing co-operative and socialist alternatives to the inequities of the social order, but they added their own feminist verses, thus complicating and sometimes departing from the dominant themes.

The garment trades permit a comparison of the experiences and views of male and female workers who produced a rich and varied literature on the issues of work, women and family. The chance to compare the discussions of male and female skilled workers seems particularly important since a central aspect of the transformation of garment making involved increasingly minute divisions of labour and the employment of large numbers of unskilled workers, many of them women, whose sewing at home for low piece-rates created devastating competition for skilled tailors and seamstresses. It is possible to compare the views of the skilled men and women on the immediate issue of how to control and eliminate the competition and on the more general question of the suitability of wage-earning activity for women. On this general question, of course, the discussion was not unique to the garment trades. In defining and formulating their positions, tailors and seamstresses adapted, incorporated, added to and reacted to the ideas of others – artisans in various trades, social theorists, republican politicians and bourgeois moralists. Nevertheless, a case study of the use of these ideas by a group of workers within a specific context offers a double advantage: it illuminates structures and experiences within the trade itself and it deepens our understanding of the meaning of the larger cultural discourse.

It must be emphasized that this chapter focuses not on structures, but on discourse. It is a first probe into a study which will eventually consider more evidence about work processes and household organization, as well as about other trades. As a first step, however, it seemed worthwhile gathering evidence which demonstrated how gender and family were perceived in discussions about work.

During the early months of 1848, in the spring-time of the Revolution, workers and employers convened at the Luxembourg Palace under the leadership of Louis Blanc to hammer out a new organization of labour. The commission of tailors divided almost immediately between employers and workers in bitter disagreement over the question of the location of work. Skilled tailors insisted that all work be performed at the shop, while employers argued that some home-based production was a vital aspect of the trade's prosperity. According to the tailors, the shop was the only place where work could be divided 'in a regular and equitable manner' and where skilled workers could be trained who would 'produce that superior elegance which brings honour to French industry'.[9] The employers disagreed, maintaining that the household of the home-worker was 'the first step of the enterprise'. Not only would the elimination of these workers interfere with the training of apprentices, there also would be grave moral consequences. For by ending home-based work, the tailors would break 'the bonds of the family', separating a father from his wife and children, thus violating 'the sacred rights of humanity'.[10] The tailors refused to accept this depiction of home-work, replying that it undermined rather then enforced morality. It was far better, they said, for everyone if 'the household separated for the day' and each family member went to work 'as if he were still a worker'.[11]

The Luxembourg Commission disbanded before the tailors' dispute could be resolved. It nonetheless exposed the major problem which for more than a decade had plagued tailors and which would continue to trouble them for at least another 20 years. As is evident from the debate, the location of work was the link between the organization of labour and the family. While employers argued that the proximity of family members and their shared labour engendered affection and morality, the tailors insisted that the quality of family relationships depended on the independent status of artisans and their consequent economic well-being. These were synonymous with work in the *atelier*.

The tailor's preference for the shop was an endorsement of a mode of production that for years had characterized their trade. Indeed the statutes of the corporation of Parisian tailors in the eighteenth century stipulated that 'all work must be done in the shop, and nothing outside, so that each person can practice his craft and live by his work'.[12] Until the late 1820s most Parisian tailors worked in shops (the number of employees varied from 2 to 15 or 20) owned by masters, who themselves were skilled workers. Although ideally every journeyman could one day become a master, demographic and economic conditions had diminished those possibilities during the eighteenth century.[13] Tailors worked in a master's shop which might be either an independent establishment or some rooms adjoining the master's family lodgings. In either case, the arrangement was not a household mode of production to which all family members contributed labour. The master's wife might lend a hand in the busy season, or sew buttons and hems throughout the year; the basic unit of production was not, however, the family, but a team of skilled male workers whose livelihood depended on their wages. Unlike rural households which farmed or engaged in cottage industry or alternated between these activities, the households of Paris's skilled craftsmen depended on the wages of their members. Husbands practised a trade, wives had jobs of their own pursued full-time or episodically, either as skilled craftswomen, unskilled labourers or market women.[14] The sharp differentiation of occupations by gender that characterized all work meant that even if wives of skilled tailors were employed in the garment trades, the location of their work and the nature of their tasks would be different.

Tailoring was a seasonal trade, intensely busy in spring and autumn, slack for several months in winter and summer. Although masters relied on a corps of skilled, shop-based workers, they also needed a supplementary labour force to sew seams and finish garments in the busy season. For this they depended on women, working at home for piece-rates and on *appièceurs*, men who might come to the shop when summoned or who worked at home, usually with their families, but sometimes supervising a group of unskilled hands. The *appièceurs* may have evolved from eighteenth-century *chambrelans*, failed masters, inept journeymen or foreigners whose exclusion from guilds forced them to ply their trade clandestinely from their homes for humiliating prices.[15] Whatever their origins, they provided the necessary elasticity in the tailoring labour force and they were the only section of the trade whose families were organized in a household mode of production. In contrast to the tailors, the *appièceurs* were not well paid, their employment was precarious; indeed, they usually contracted with more than one shop and took on tremendous work loads in order to earn enough to subsist through the year. The household-based production of the *appièceur* was an exploited and marginal adjunct to the skilled tailoring craft, as was the home-based work of individual women. In the hierarchy of the trade the *atelier* was equated with skill and with an entirely male workforce. Household production, in contrast, was clearly inferior in status, skill and wages and it involved a sexually mixed workforce.

The garment industry had its ups and downs during the early nineteenth century, expanding between 1800 and 1825, a period one historian has deemed its 'golden age'[16] By the late 1820s, the prosperity of small shops began to be eclipsed by competition among themselves and by the extended operations of large cloth merchants producing ready-made garments for men. Unlike custom tailoring, which responded to the demands of individual clients, the ready-made industry mass-produced goods in standardized sizes. Skilled cutters prepared parts of a garment in shops and the pieces were assembled by women (who usually did trousers and vests) and men (who did jackets and coats) sewing in their homes. The finished garments were returned to the merchants who either sold them in large shops or sent salesmen off with them to markets and fairs. Some of the first ready-made garments were workers' clothes, since manufacturers assumed that for this kind of garment, high quality was of less importance than a low price.[17]

The manufacture of ready-made goods had enormous advantage over custom tailoring. Cloth could be purchased in bulk and there was far less wasted material. Garments could be produced year round since manufacture did not depend on individual orders. Of course, as ready-made manufacturers expanded their operations for the middle-class market, they had to wait to see what styles were being offered for the next season. But in slow periods, they could produce practical items such as work clothes, the styles of which did not change from year to year. The *confectionneurs* had better credit resources, more capital at their disposal, lower overheads and lower labour costs than did small custom tailors. A large pool of potential workers was always available and their circumstances – of poverty and isolation – mitigated against collective or individual demands for higher piece-rates. In fact, piece-rates tended to drop during the slack seasons because, in addition to the men and women who regularly served the *confectionneurs*, skilled tailors also were willing to take on piece-work until orders picked up at the shop.

Between 1830 and 1848 the ready-made garment industry steadily encroached on the custom market. By 1847, *confection* accounted for over one-third of total sales of men's clothing (by 1860, it had captured half the market).[18] The proportion of the market is somewhat misleading, however, for there were about 200 large manufacturers compared to some 3,000 custom tailors.[19] While most ready-made garment merchants earned 50,000 to 200,000 francs a year, the master tailor eked out an average annually of 2,500 francs.[20]

As they tried to meet the competition from *confection* by reducing or maintaining wage levels, masters faced intense strike activity by their journeymen. In 1833 and 1834, and again in the early 1840s, waves of strikes hit custom tailor shops all over France, usually timed for the height of the busy season.[21] Journeymen managed to win some short-run concessions in the form of higher wages, but in the long run they raised labour costs beyond what many small tailors could afford. The combination of competition from *confection* and labour protest from journeymen intensified in the 1840s. Some tailors went bankrupt. A few with reputations for very high quality work had enough clients who continued to support them. Still others began to cut labour costs by reducing the number of their skilled shop-workers and turning instead to home-workers. (According to the Paris Chamber of Commerce inquiry of 1847, slightly more than half of all men working for custom tailors were located in shops.)[22] Some masters became subcontractors and transformed their workrooms into sweatshops; journeymen joined the ranks of *appièceurs* and sought jobs from other custom tailors as well as from ready-made garment manufacturers.[23] The combined effect of these strategies was gradually to depopulate the workshops and swell the ranks of home-based labourers with former skilled workers. These men, referred to as *patrons appièceurs* in the Chamber of Commerce inquiry, either worked alone or, more frequently, supervised family members in a collective enterprise.[24]

The impact of capitalist practices on tailoring in the 1830s and 40s was to expand the number of people engaged in a household mode of production and drive increasing numbers of skilled workers into it. The exploited, marginal part of the trade grew, pulling into its ranks those who had once disdained it. The Parisian tailor, described by Le Play in 1856 as a debauched and dissolute worker, represented the transformation. His father, a master tailor, had run a large shop, employing 17 or 18 journeymen. The tailor had been trained to succeed his father, but times grew hard and he ended up on his own, doing piecework when he could get it, assisted only by his mistress [25] For skilled tailors and their families, proletarianization meant not a move from household to factory production, but a move from the workshop of one's master to one's own household. (The *appièceur* was the proletarianized tailor.) In this situation, income depended not on the wage contributions of individuals, but on marshalling the labour of family members in a common productive enterprise. The transformation involved both a loss for the tailor of the independence which followed from the collective strength of his craft and impoverishment for him and his family.[26]

Strikes and protest movements in this period came from shop-based, skilled tailors organized to resist proletarianization. They insisted that the workshop be the site of all garment production and they deplored the nefarious consequences for their trade and their families of the conflation of home and workshop in the practice of *travail à domicile*. Christopher Johnson has detailed the stages of tailor protest in the 1830s and 40s [27] Initially, the journeymen defined their employers as the source of all problems and they struck repeatedly to demand increased wages. They resented the masters' attempts to lower rates in the shop and they insisted that values of co-operation and association ought to replace the prevailing selfishness. The Parisian tailors formed mutual aid societies which they parlayed into organizations to support strikes and, in October 1833, they set up a co-operative workshop to provide jobs for the unemployed and to exemplify the equality between master and journeymen they sought in the trade as a whole.

Protest and demands for reform focused on the shop where, planning and acting in concert, tailors could exercise some control over conditions and enforce standard rates of pay. During the October 1833 strike, journeymen visited some *appièceurs* and tried to persuade them not to work for a master whose shop was on strike.[28] There are not many details about the success of this effort, but it could not have had a lasting effect. The *appièceurs* were in no position to organize since their ability to get business depended on their acceptance of low piece-rates and indeed to compete with their colleagues by working for lower piece-rates than others a master might hire. While shop-based tailors enforced pay scales within and across shops, the *appièceur* – by virtue of his dependent position – undercut those scales and accepted payments that varied from week to week and job to job. The position of the *appièceur* was antithetical to collective regulation; indeed he undermined it.

Tailors in the 1840s quite rightly located the origin of their problem in the reorganization of garment making itself and neither in the substitution of women for men in the process of production, nor in the depressing effect of women's wages on men's. The transformation of men's positions was what bothered them, for as skilled workers fell into the ranks of *appièceurs*, they became the competitors of those left in the shops, agents of the deterioration of their own craft. This was the meaning of the bitter phrase the tailors used to denounce capitalist competition: '*La concurrence qui nous font étrangers à notre état.*'

During the Revolution of 1848, tailors willingly engaged in activities with small masters to win back business for the custom trades and guarantee employment for skilled workers. Even if the work they did adopted the new divisions of labour and even if some home-workers were used in the process, as they were when *Le Travail: l'Association Fraternelle et Egalitaire des Tailleurs* won government contracts to produce National Guard uniforms, the fact that pay scales for all jobs were enforced by those who ran the workshop prevented the ruinous competition which prevailed in the so-called free market.[29]

> The *atelier*, well organized, where reciprocal obligations are conscientiously observed, prevents the drawbacks we have cited. The *atelier* has other advantages ... for the prosperity of the trade and the well-being of its workers, that is the power in all seasons, according to needs and circumstances, to divide work in a fair and equitable way.[30]

The unacceptable alternative was an organization based on household production. Above all the system did not lend itself to regulation. In February 1848, the revolutionary government exempted family workshops from a proposed law on women's and children's work because legislators objected to the inspection of private households.[31] Not only might privacy be violated, but the common interest of the work unit made it impossible to assign responsibility (to the head of the household, for example) for enforcing the law. If the government refused to regulate the family workshop, members of the trade certainly could not. The lack of regulation permitted extraordinary self-exploitation by family members, the only means of earning their subsistence.

Tailor delegates to the London Exposition of 1862 offered details of this exploitation as they bitterly dissented from the claims of a large clothing manufacturer that home-based work increased the 'homeloving habits' of workers' families.[32] These claims, they said, were 'completely contrary to reality':

> No, the practice of the labourer working at home has not improved his lot; no, children are not better cared for and watched over by their parents; no, shared labour does not soften temperaments; on the contrary it sours them more and more... In order to live, a worker toils 16 to 18 hours a day; there are even households where work never stops... While the wife rests, the husband does his share and prepares his wife's tasks; when he finishes or rather succumbs to exhaustion, the wife gets up and the husband takes her place... How can a woman in these deplorable circumstances moralize and raise her children decently, when before their eyes are discord and disagreement between father and mother, caused primarily by the suffering and forced labour to which parents are condemned?

Tailors' wives had no time for domestic tasks and they endured joyless existences; working 'without compensation' their lives were 'even sadder than their husbands'. 'When consulted it is rare to find the wife of a tailor who does not curse her fate.'[33]

The solution for the skilled tailors involved a clear separation between home and work. The separation of male and female space did not, however, carry with it a division of roles between husband and wife that excluded women from wage-earning activity. The dictum of the *femme ménagère* was absent from the tailors' rhetoric though it had already been articulated by other craftsmen, such as printers.[34] Wives, it is true, were expected to care for children and the household, but their activity was not limited to the domestic realm. Nor was work performed at home thought to be necessarily bad for women. Indeed, according to the document cited above, the sorry situation of the tailor's wife came from the fact that she was not compensated for her work. In a cruel inversion of customary arrangements the husband became the exploiter of his wife. Not only did he fail to contribute to her support, he made it impossible for her to earn her own share of the family wage. The explicit objection to the household mode of production was not that it violated separate types of male and female activity, but that it robbed family members of a certain self-determination and control over their activities. In addition, it corrupted relationships among family members, disrupting a harmony that was assumed otherwise to characterize family life.

To be sure, there were also an implicit set of meanings in the defence of the *atelier*. If work were located at the shop, it would be performed almost entirely by skilled men; the number of women sewing at home would be reduced. In addition, economic deterioration and deskilling were equated with a move from male space (the shop) to female space (the household). To the extent that definitions of maleness were associated with skilled labour and skilled labour with a location separate from the household, the protection of the workshop invoked notions of gender that were hierarchical and spatially distinct. These notions, moreover, were so universally understood that they did not need explicit articulation. Yet it seems worth noting which principles were included and which excluded as justifications for trade strategies. The tailors' discussions of the family lack specificity either about household organization or the activities of men and women. References to the family serve rather as a foil for considerations of the conditions of work. Capitalist practices are seen as disturbing a pre-existing division of male and female space, of realms in which different kinds of activity took place. But the divisions did not extend to the exclusion of women from wage-earning. At this stage in their discussion of economic and social reform, tailors as a group did not adopt a strategy or endorse a social vision which equated women solely with domesticity and men with work for pay.

As the tailors sought implementation of a new organization of labour in 1848, skilled seamstresses petitioned the republican government for support of their own plans. These were not substantially different in form and ideology from the associations proliferating among other skilled craftsmen (though they were numerically far fewer). They shared an emphasis on co-operation and self-regulation and a desire to end the disorder created by capitalist competition. Although seamstresses petitioned for workshops and, indeed, established several associations of their own, the location of work was never as central an issue for them as for the tailors. Work at home was acceptable as long as it neither gave rise to subcontracting nor paid rates below a uniform schedule. Far more important were the wages a seamstress earned, for these were the key to her integrity and independence, whether she was single or married. The variations in the programme put forward by seamstresses and tailors followed from a somewhat different set of conditions in the female sector of the garment industry and they reflected the different self-definitions and experiences of working women as compared to working men.

The structure of the female sewing trades did not exactly parallel tailoring. Hierarchies of skill did prevail and skilled mistresses trained apprentices and supervised workers in their shops. But the number and scale of these establishments tended to be small.[35] While in tailoring, economic pressures discouraged a proliferation of new businesses and increased the numbers of skilled journeymen working for a master, in dressmaking skilled married women were not usually shop employees. The location of work in the female garment trades was dependent less on skill than on marital status. Most women worked in shops only while young and single. When they married, the few trained dressmakers (*couturières*) with enough capital set up a shop, but most opened a neighbourhood 'business' which they ran entirely on their own, or took on occasional piece-work from a former employer. Even in 1847, a far larger percentage of dressmakers did most work entirely on their own than did tailors. (The comparative figures are 75 and 50 per cent.)[36] Seamstresses (*lingères*), a far larger category of female needleworkers, followed similar patterns, although many more became piece-workers after marriage because they lacked the distinctive skills of dressmakers.

Beyond a corps of skilled workers, both dressmaking and *lingerie* drew, as did tailoring, on a large pool of women with rudimentary sewing skills who did piece-work at home. The difference between these women and the skilled married women was not the location of work, but the independent status and remuneration their skills could command. Recognition for these skills came in the form of neighbourhood reputation or because a woman maintained her connection to a former employer after she had left the shop. Needless to say, the system did not always recognize skill and reward it fairly and many a skilled seamstress surely joined the ranks of poorly paid piece-workers once she had married and/or left the shop. Nonetheless, those married dressmakers and seamstresses who did succeed combined their craft and household activities and contributed an important sum to the family purse.[37]

These arrangements, while convenient for the women, tended to undercut craft solidarity. Skilled craftswomen were, to a large extent, self-employed and dispersed throughout the city and, in the nineteenth century, they were no longer united by formal membership in guilds. In the shops, the relationship between workers and mistresses was not a simple employee–employer tie (as it was for journeymen tailors and their masters); for the shopgirls were young and still in training, dependent for their vocational education on the mistress. Journeymen tailors grouped in shops spent their adult lives earning wages by supplying skills upon which the master depended. Aspirant dressmakers or seamstresses earned a wage while they also acquired skills and their stay in the shop was presumed to be temporary. Not some inherent female docility, but the structure of their craft, discouraged a tradition of collective action among female garment workers – at least in the early years of the nineteenth century. When a protest did emerge in 1848 in the context of the Revolution, the absence of a longstanding craft tradition contributed to the differences in the composition, size and impact of the women's movement.[38] The women's associations were smaller and weaker than the tailors', but also more heterogeneous, for the skilled craftswomen sought the widest possible bases of support. They articulated grievances and proposed reforms designed to mobilize women garment workers in Paris, whatever the levels of their skills. Women's activities were regularly reported in *La Voix des Femmes*, a 'socialist and political' newspaper which appeared from 20 March to 20 June 1848. Edited by feminist Eugénie Niboyet, *La Voix des Femmes* is the only source for this period that consistently documents women's organizations, their leaders' speeches, and the activities of women workers.

Ready-made manufacture was introduced in *lingerie* sooner than in dressmaking, where considerations of style and custom fit discouraged mass production.

Nonetheless, by the 1840s *confectionneurs* began to offer competition to all but the most exclusive dressmaking shops. As in tailoring, the organization of production involved cutting pieces of garments in a shop and then contracting them out for sewing. But in the ladies' garment trade the consequences of new procedure differed from those in tailoring. First, there was a transfer of the ownership and control of production from women to men. The intrusion of capitalism in this industry was synonymous with male power. Second, there was a proliferation of larger shops run by older women who were, in effect, subcontractors. They hired as many young women as could fit in the premises, gave them perfunctory instruction and paid them a piece-rate for their labour. Since the manufacturers paid the subcontractors by the piece, their gain depended on paying girls as low a rate as possible. And traditional competition from prisons and convents – with their unpaid labourers – intensified, depressing piece-rates further. In effect, the shopgirls were sweated piece-workers with no prospect of becoming skilled craftswomen. Still, a position in a shop seems to have been preferable to work on one's own. From all accounts the *femmes isolées* were the most miserable of figures.[39] An increase in their numbers was another consequence of *confection*. As the numbers of home-based workers soared, the distinction between the skilled and unskilled was obliterated. Independent seamstresses and dressmakers with clientele of modest means were the first to lose their customers to the ready-made market. These women tried to make up for their loss by taking on piece-work. But since piece-rates were very low they found they worked many more hours and still earned less. Daughters, sisters and elderly grandparents might be called upon to help a mother finish her sewing jobs, but it was rare that a husband contributed his labour. If in tailoring skilled workers complained that new conditions forced husbands to exploit their wives, in the women's needle trades skilled workers described extraordinary levels of self-exploitation and deprivation of their services to the rest of their family.[40]

In the ladies' garment industry, as in tailoring, the proletarianization of skilled sewing trades drove artisans into an expanded mass of the unskilled. It undercut the ability of a seamstress to earn her share of the family wage and forced her to spend more time in menial work. For single women, proletarianization meant relinquishing craft aspirations and an increased vulnerability to the dictates of subcontractors and the fluctuations of the market. For married women it meant a loss of control of their time, relentless subjection to wage earning, always with insufficient reward. For both married and single women low piece-rates were the issue, not the location of work. Thus seamstresses told Louis Blanc in 1848 that they were dissatisfied with the 12 sous a shirt paid them in the national workshops. On 15 April, two columns of women marched from a workshop to the Luxembourg Palace to demand either a daily wage or a rate of 1 franc a shirt. Their petition rejected the existing rate as humiliating, since it amounted to no more than a dole: 'What women want,' they told Blanc, 'is not organized charity, it is properly compensated work.'[41]

Among the deputation and, indeed, among the women's associations in this period, there were a variety of proposals about where and how work should be done. One seamstress suggested to Blanc that married women be allowed to take work home instead of sitting in the workshops. If the 'appropriate rate' were paid and the amount given out controlled, regulation of the trade would be achieved and 'households will not suffer'.[42] Others suggested that the state open crèches and national restaurants so families would prosper while women exercised their 'right to work'.[43] For these women social reorganization meant simultaneous attention to conditions of work and the family. One detailed plan called for the establishment of training centres for seamstresses in each *arrondisement* of Paris. Mothers could either leave their children in a crèche near the shop (for no charge) or, if their skills were such that they needed no supervision, they could take their work home.[44] In the co-operative enterprises set up by dressmakers and seamstresses in June and October 1848, everyone earned a daily wage; night work, if necessary in the busy season, was paid overtime. The hours for those in the shop were set from 8 a.m. to 6 p.m. 'so that women can take care of their homes and eat with their families'.[45] Single women sought alternatives to living and working alone by forming co-operative communities. One group announced its existence by marching to the Place Vendôme in March 1848 and unfurling a banner on which was written 'Vésuviennes'. In their new quarters they contributed to a common fund, shared meals and lodging and received a weekly allowance. Here, collective living arrangements were part of a vision of social reorganization aimed at 'ameliorating the lot' of working women.[46]

The seamstresses who articulated and implemented the demands of their craft insisted that women be entirely in charge of their own working affairs. They bitterly resented the fact that a man, one Duclerc, headed the Commission of Women's National Workshops on which their elected representatives sat. And they attributed the intolerably low piece-rates set by the government to male misunderstanding of their needs. Desirée Gay, a delegate to the women's commission from the 2nd *arrondissement*, denounced the entire set up as a 'deception ... despotism under a new name ... a mystification perpetrated by men to rid themselves of women' and their complaints.[47] In contrast to the government sponsored workshops, the seamstresses' producer associations were run entirely by women, who insisted on setting all policy independent of male interference. The Association Fraternelle des Ouvrières Lingères (the name suggests the androgynous conception of *fraternité* in the period) returned a government subvention it had won because the terms of support prevented their paying workers a high enough daily wage.[48]

In part, of course, the insistence on female control was simply a reiteration of the demand for the artisans' control of their own trades. Male and female craftsworkers endorsed the call to organize by *corps d'état* first and then into larger representative organizations. Both sexes also shared the disillusionment in the government's national workshops which ended up providing subsistence for unemployed workers instead of reorganizing the economy. In addition, however, the women were acutely aware of the fact that inequities of power followed male/female lines. Men had replaced women as organizers and owners of the sewing trades; men elected government representatives who enacted policies which ignored the special needs and interests of women workers. In June 1848, men in the government explicitly outlawed political meetings for women. Male workers endorsed schemes which furthered co-operation and association among themselves, but did not extend those concepts to women's work or to the relations between women and men. As she attacked the inadequacy of government measures to provide work for seamstresses, Desirée Gay insisted that women have a hand in formulating policy. Women must be admitted to men's meetings, she argued,

> so that women and men can enlighten one another and agree on their common interests, so that it cannot be said that association disunited those whom God united and so that in the future we wish to create [there will not be] two separate camps, with men in one and women in the other.[49]

For these remarks, Gay was removed by the end of April from her position as delegate to the commission of women's national workshops by the minister of labour – confirmation to her and her followers of the government's unwillingness to take women into account and of the need, therefore, to unite all women in a movement for the reform of laws which denied them family, social and political power.[50] The seamstresses' version of a social republic was one in which women could obtain divorce, control their own wages, refuse the domination of a 'selfish husband' and care for their children and households as well as enjoy the 'right to work'. 'Women ought to work ... it is better for women to have a trade than a dowry.... If men and women both furnish the means of existence, they will help one another and be united.'[51] A few women spoke of 'breaking the chains which attach us to the walls of the household', but most did not define the problem as one of ending domestic confinement. Equality was a matter of rights and most women sought relief in a new organization of work which extended men's definition of that term into the realm of the family and the state:

> Emancipated in the family and the state, mistresses of ourselves, we will be so much more painstaking in the fulfillment of our responsibilities.[52]

> The working woman will contribute her share to her family income and we, who have demanded the right to work for all, will dare also to believe in equality, the religious and fraternal expression of the two sexes.[53]

These ideas drew inspiration from Saint-Simonianism, particularly from the experience of a small group of working-class women who were followers of the movement in the early 1830s. Desirée Gay was among the group, which consisted primarily of young Parisian seamstresses like herself. The women concluded by 1832 that fulfilling Enfantin's goal of the emancipation of women required establishing an exclusively female organization devoted to 'expanding educational and work opportunities for women and reforming the family law provisions of the Civil Code'.[54] They rejected male leadership and, indeed, in their newspaper dropped their surnames when signing letters and articles. This was an expression of their intention in their personal lives as well as in society to rid themselves of exploitation by husbands, lovers, male Saint-Simonians, as well as the institutions and laws of the patriarchal state. The creation of completely emancipated womanhood, they argued, required the immediate experience by women of the greatest measure of liberation. Only women, organized on their own, could achieve that end.

It is important to note that these feminist themes were woven into Saint-Simonian theory by working women, who articulated the interconnection between their economic and social problems, family and work, gender and politics. In 1848, as in 1832, the voices of the Saint-Simonian minority provided insight into the experiences of working women. Skilled seamstresses drew on a sense of independence and professional competence as they spoke in the name of their craft and organized associations to preserve it. But the concerns they expressed and the solutions they proposed extended to all working women. Control of the labour market in the women's needle trades ultimately required regulation of piece-rates across the industry, so uniform piece-rates or day wages had to cover all categories of work. The choice of this strategy, rather than of workshops consisting exclusively of skilled workers, recognized the need for flexibility in the location of women's work. The family dimension of working women's self-definition – whether they were daughters, wives or mothers – informed the craftswomen's reform proposals and led them to speak in the name of all working women for a social reorganization that would reconcile wage earning and household work.

Tailors advocated for themselves a separation of home and workplace, while seamstresses assumed an inextricable connection between their work and family responsibilities. The seamstresses' conception of gender shared with the tailors the idea of some separation between male and female space and different male and female responsibilities, but the women explicity rejected hierarchical ideas and practices which denied the equal value of their labour and their right to political representation. (Indeed, they discovered in 1848 an inextricable connection between the reform of women's working conditions and the need for access to political power.) Despite the differences between them, tailors and seamstresses had similar approaches to the question of whether or not women should work. Although both groups associated women with domesticity neither defined it as an exclusive role which contradicted the ability or suitability of women for work. Several conclusions are suggested by this observation. First, the assumption of both men and women in the skilled sectors of the garment trades was that wage earning was not the sole preserve of the male sex. Second, although some craft groups and theorists like Proudhon had proposed removing women from the workforce, this strategy did not win universal endorsement among artisans, at least not by 1848. Third, the vision of a harmonious and co-operative society espoused by the tailors and seamstresses in their associations did not adopt bourgeois ideas which, in this period, insisted that a woman's place and all her activities ought to be exclusively domestic.

The proposals devised by tailors and seamstresses for reform of their trades, of course, addressed existing conditions. Women were not encroaching directly on skilled tailoring, so tailors did not seek to remove them from the workforce. Skilled seamstresses and dressmakers wanted to protect their trades which, under the best conditions, could be combined with domestic responsibilities. And the families of these workers depended more often than not on the earnings of husband and wife. But the proposals were not only a reflection of material conditions. As they formulated trade strategies, tailors and seamstresses incorporated longstanding gender distinctions which conceived of separate male and female spaces, associated women with domestic roles (whatever else they also did) and were hierarchical. Ideas about gender, however, were by themselves diffuse and susceptible to a variety of interpretations. The same general notions of male and female space and different roles for the sexes were inherent in the bourgeois ideology of domesticity, although its conclusions differed in important ways from those of the tailors and seamstresses. The artisans' construction, the definitions on which their strategies were based, seem to be drawn from the writings of social theorists critical of early nineteenth-century capitalism. Although the specific proposals of these writers differed greatly, they used certain images of women and the family in a similar way. In contrast to bourgeois writers such as Dr Villermé and his associates at the Académie des Sciences Morales et Politiques, who stressed the family as an institution which would provide the morality and fulfilment absent in the economic order,[55] the utopian socialist theorists used the family more abstractly, as a projection of human fulfilment, a complete alternative to capitalist alienation.

As tailors and seamstresses read working-class newspapers, debated plans for reform and (especially in the revolutionary days of 1848) joined political organizations, their craft concerns merged into and drew upon a larger discourse which had at its centre a critique of capitalism formulated in terms of common images. Those images recurred and resonated and perhaps even shaped the trade strategies. Tailors and seamstresses were exposed to these images repeatedly whether they followed Cabet and read his *Le Populaire*, attended Saint-Simonian lectures or republican banquets, read *La Voix des Femmes*, or even if they only listened to street songs and followed the fate of a heroine in a serialized melodrama in the working-class press. The images were standard, generalized ones in the culture of the period, but the meaning they were meant to convey was acquired in the heat of political dialogue and debate. Utopian socialists formed their images in critical counterpoint to bourgeois ideas in order to reveal the hypocrisy of bourgeois values and the bankruptcy of the capitalist economic and social order.

The images assumed differences between men and women, not spatially, or in terms of work, but temperamentally and in terms of emotional qualities. For seamstress Jeanne Deroin, for example, Christ's mother embodied the loving, maternal, innocent and devoted traits of the female character: 'Woman must fulfil ... her mission of sacrifice and devotion. She acts because she loves. Love of humanity is eternal love.'[56] In a marriage, women were the affective members of the partnership, providing love and warmth. Theirs was a specific feminine contribution not only to their families, but to social regeneration. Thus women in 1848 demanded their rights in these terms: 'We ask not to be good citizens, but citizenesses. If we demand our rights it is as women that we do so ... in the name of our sacred family obligations, of the tender services of the mother.'[57] Cabet described the loving qualities of women in a glorious romantic vision which also stressed their distinctive contribution, but he assumed as well that femininity did not contradict participation in productive activity. In Icaria, he wrote, all women will work 'in workshops and practise the trade of their choice; but their work will be moderate, the workday short'.[58]

Woman was synonymous with love and with the emotional bonds of the family. What she actually did with her time was less important than what she represented. Women represented human feeling. The destruction of that feeling was depicted by the downfall of a young girl. The symbol of the ultimate impact of capitalist exploitation was the working-class daughter, a seamstress, who faced the impossible choice of starving to death because her earnings were insufficient to support her or becoming a prostitute. 'Misery or shame' were different sides of the same coin: the destruction of a young innocent by greed and lust. Wrote Cabet of the 'daughter of the proletariat': 'She must work for her family to survive but under conditions in which she is brutalized, loses her beauty and health, and is threatened constantly by the plague of libertinage.'[59]

There is no question that this was a real dilemma for working-class girls. When Parent-Duchâtelet studied Parisian prostitutes in 1836 he described many of them as unemployed seamstresses who earned a living in the street when no work could be found in the shop.[60] The Chamber of Commerce survey of 1847 referred to needlewomen who 'find in loose living a supplement to their resources and finish by belonging only nominally to the trade they once practised'.[61] And the seamstresses themselves, in 1848, endorsed national workshops as a way to keep their colleagues off the streets.[62] In addition, accounts by young women themselves repeatedly talk of sexual vulnerability. Walking home from work in the evening brought fear of attack by a man; living alone, unprotected, made a girl prey for men of all kinds who knocked at her door and demanded sexual favours [63]

Yet the description of this reality provided the occasion for articulating a more complicated message. The accounts of tragedies involving young girls assumed the quality of folk tales or morality plays with a similar plot line and one of the two possible outcomes.[64] The theme of the destruction of innocence by rape or death was a stark physical metaphor for capitalism's impact on the working class. By defiling or destroying a young female life, the 'social order' attacked not only the existing generation but its progenitors – the future mothers of working-class children. In addition, the tragedy of the young seamstress involved a perversion of all that was natural and human. Purity and innocence were synonymous with female virginity. Prostitution represented the antithesis not only of virginity, but its natural loss, for woman sold for money what ought to have been given for love.

In the most shocking rendition of one of these tales, a young girl, the sole support of her family when her artisan father loses his job, in desperation becomes a prostitute. One night she approaches a man who turns out to be her father. Her only recourse, the only way to preserve her innocence after this incident, is suicide.[65] What makes the story so awful is that against her will and by force of circumstances a young girl becomes her own antithesis: innocence becomes promiscuity, familial devotion almost leads to incest, the natural becomes the unnatural, culminating in the ultimate alienation of taking her own life. The choice of a female to represent capitalism's victim resonated with cultural images for virginity and purity and for women's subordination and subjection to domination. Workers were to capitalists what women were to men.

The symbol of the destroyed seamstress addressed not only a working-class audience, but the bourgeoisie as well. For it consciously played on the middle-class idealizations of young womanhood, contrasting working-class 'reality' with bourgeois ideals. The working-class reality was attributed to bourgeois egoism, but the appeal in the 1830s and 40s was to a cross-class co-operative reorganization of the social order. Many social theorists believed, with Louis Blanc, that once the consequences of capitalist competition had been revealed, the bourgeoisie would be persuaded to help change the system. The female image provided common ground and a shared meaning from which were derived different conclusions in the political debates of the period.

In a similar way general references to the family offered ironic commentaries on the bourgeois view. If the downfall of the seamstress daughter stood for the alienation of workers under capitalism, the working-class family embodied a positive alternative for emotional fulfilment. The image of the family was not intended as a description of social reality, nor as a prescription for the restructuring of gender roles. It was an idealized vision of happiness and love projected as the opposite of the bourgeois family. While the cash nexus embodied in dowry and inheritance dominated bourgeois family relationships, the alternative *communauté* was based on nothing more than affection.[66] And while bourgeois moralists offered plans to encourage legal marriage and family life among the working class, the utopian theorists attacked the plans as empty and impossible to fulful under capitalism.

At a banquet in 1848, citizen Legre, a tailor, rose to toast the family. He followed two other workers whose toasts played on the bourgeois themes of property and order.[67] They hailed those two ideas, but inverted their customary meaning. Work was equated with property and the toast to property became an endorsement of the artisans' inalienable right to work. Order was redefined as co-operation and association, a new harmony which would replace the disorder sown by capitalist competition. Legre raised his glass 'to the human family, based on love and not money . . . [in which] solidarity replaced individualism'. The so-called defenders of the family, he went on, were charlatans; they were debauched and their daughters and wives sold themselves in return for luxury. The true friends of the family were not speculators, but those who, 'mocked by the old society, nonetheless sought in the bosom of the family the refreshing balm of love to heal their wounds'.[68] The family in this vision was not an organizational structure, but a fulfilling human experience, the collective happiness of utopian socialism which reconciled differences and harmonized opposites (as exemplified by the union of man and woman: 'The social individual is the man and the woman. Without their union nothing is complete, moral, durable, or possible').[69]

Unlike bourgeois notions that offered a sharp division of labour between men and women which corresponded to a spatial division and which would permit the coexistence of aggression and love, competition and association, the artisan vision of the family was the basis for a total transformation of human relationships in the new social order.[70] The family projected in the artisans' organic vision could not coexist with capitalism; it was meant as its critical antithesis. For tailors and dressmakers in 1848, the symbol of the distressed seamstress and the emotional fulfilment embodied in the family articulated the misery of life and a dream of its opposite. To offer specific proposals about the organization of the family or to endorse a role for women exclusively concerned with domesticity would have been to accept the bourgeois view that the family could somehow exist apart from and indeed resolve capitalism's alienating effect. The utopian socialist vision accepted no such possibility; rather it insisted that families under capitalism could not be happy, that until French society was transformed no institution could realize the fulfilment depicted in idealized visions of the family.

The invocation of notions of gender which assigned separate space and different qualities to men and women did not necessarily imply a social or political strategy of the *femme ménagère* in the 1830s and 40s. That argument emerged only later, in a different economic, political and ideological context. At the end of the 1860s and especially in the 1870s a more literal reading of the plight of the seamstress would suggest the need for male economic and sexual protection. A connection was also made between the realization of love in the family (conceived of as an institution *within* capitalist society) and the location of the activities of women. At national congresses, representatives of craft organizations debated and then adopted the goal of the *femme ménagère* or the *femme au foyer*. There were, of course, groups who dissented and repudiated the idea, but they were in the minority. Tailors and seamstresses endorsed the majority position. While the statutes of the trade union of dressmakers in 1873 sought better working conditions and higher pay, they also included a clear preference for wives and mothers not to have to work at all. And Parisian tailors in the 1870s prohibited women from speaking at meetings of their co-operatives.[71]

Workers in the 1870s advocated the exclusion of women from the workforce as a solution both to economic and 'moral' problems: women would be eliminated as a source of competition in many trades and the *femme ménagère* would reflect and ensure the harmony and prosperity of families. In addition, the family would be preserved as a 'terrain of struggle' for educating children and supporting labour's political efforts to realize the 'social republic'.[72] In the proposals that emerged, preservation of the sexual division of labour became a goal of the workers' movement, and the realms of family and work were treated distinctly. Programmes for economic reform inspired by Proudhonist or Marxist ideas were more specific and ultimately less radical on the question of family and gender organization than those which drew on utopian socialist images of the family in 1848.

In the 1890s, images of the family abounded in the rhetoric of socialist municipal leaders, as they likened the Hôtels de Ville under their leadership to the worker's *foyer*. While acknowledging that workers were still subject to capitalist domination in the economic realm, the socialists depicted the municipalities as political havens which, like the families of individuals, comforted and protected their members.[73] Despite their insistence that the municipalities were a step in the direction of revolution, the socialists' images of the family suggest what Gareth Stedman Jones has labelled in another context the 'culture of consolation'.[74]

A full examination of the discussions of family and work in these later periods is beyond the scope of this essay. It seems important, however, to mention them for they provide striking contrast to the organic, utopian vision of 1848. The strategies of the *femme au foyer* in the 1870s and the family metaphors used in the 1890s were not the result of the inherent logic either of traditional or bourgeois ideas about women and the family employed in the 1830s and 40s. Indeed, it is the *differences* in usage and meaning that demand explanation. As in the period we have examined here, the language of the 1870s drew its meaning from specific historical contexts. The images themselves provide important keys to those contexts and to the social experience of those using them, but only if they are understood in terms of that experience.

Discussions of the family and of women's roles were integral to workers' considerations of the economy, even when they adopted a strategy which endorsed a separation of male and female spheres. Analysis of those discussions provides an important insight not simply into supplementary concerns of nineteenth-century French workers, but into the central structural and ideological issues of any period. Gender relationships and family structures were as 'economic' and 'political' as were relations of production and the organization of work. The labour historian who ignores that fact misunderstands the concerns and experiences of the working women and men of the past.

NOTES

1 See for example B. Moss, *The Origins of the French Labor Movement 1830–1914: The Socialism of Skilled Workers* (Berkeley 1976); William H. Sewell, Jr., *Work and Revolution in France: The Language of Labor from the Old Regime to 1848* (Cambridge 1980); Robert J. Bezucha, *The Lyon Uprising of 1834: Social and Political Conflict in a 19th-Century City* (Cambridge, Mass. 1974); Joan W. Scott, *The Glassworkers of Carmaux: French Craftsmen and Political Action in a 19th Century City* (Cambridge, Mass. 1974); Charles Tilly and Lynn Lees, 'Le Peuple de juin 1848', *Annales ESC*, 29 (Sept.–Oct. 1974), pp. 1061–91. French studies tend to be more comprehensive, including material on family. See for example, M. Agulhon, *Une Ville ouvrière au temps du socialisme utopique: Toulon de 1815 à 1851* (Paris and The Hague 1970); Yves Lequin, *Les Ouvriers de la région lyonnaise (1848–1914)*, 2 vols. (Lyon 1977); Rolande Trempé, *Les Mineurs de Carmaux 1848–1914*, 2 vols. (Paris 1971).

2 See for example the articles in 'Travaux de femmes, dans la France du XIXᵉ siècle', special issue of *Le Mouvement Social*, no. 105 (Oct.–Dec. 1978), *présentation de Michelle Perrot*. See also Louise Tilly and Joan Scott, *Women, Work and Family* (New York 1978); Louise Tilly, 'Paths of Proletarianization: Organization of Production, Sexual Division of Labor, and Women's Collective Action', *Signs*, 7, no. 2 (Winter 1981), pp. 400–17; Michelle Perrot, *Les Ouvriers en Grève: France 1871–1890*, 2 vols. (Paris 1974), pp. 318–30; N.Z. Davis, 'Women in the Crafts in 16th-Century Lyon', *Feminist Studies*, 8, no. 1 (Spring 1982), pp. 47–80.

3 An example of this approach is George J. Sheridan, jr., 'Household and Craft in an

Industrializing Economy: The Case of the Silk Weavers of Lyons', in J. Merriman (ed.), *Consciousness and Class Experience in 19th Century Europe* (New York 1979), pp. 107–28.

4 Thus, for example, Louis Devance argues that artisans preferred the patriarchal family models advocated by Cabet and Proudhon to those offered by Fourier and the Saint-Simonians because they sought the same control over domestic conditions they were intent on preserving at work. 'To be his own master, at work and in private life, was the profound aspiration of the worker. The model of the bourgeois family lent itself to that completely.' L. Devance, 'Femme, famille, travail et morale sexuelle dans l'idéologie de 1848', in *Mythes et représentations de la femme au XIXᵉ siècle* (Paris 1976), p. 99. Jacques Donzelot, *La Police des familles* (Paris 1978) argues that reformers imposed their models on working-class families in order better to control them. Neither author examines specific conditions of artisan families in the early nineteenth century, nor the terms in which skilled workers discussed the position of their families while they also demanded control over their trades. On the other hand, Christopher Johnson, *Utopian Communism in France: Cabet and the Icarian Movement* (Ithaca 1974) provides careful detail of the social bases of Cabet's movement.

5 The articles in C. Dufrancatel *et al.*, *L'Histoire sans qualités* (Paris 1979) exemplify this approach, as do the articles by Michelle Perrot and others cited in n. 71. Perrot's discussion in 'L'Éloge de la ménagère' tends to stress the enduring aspects of ideas of male and female. We need to examine changes in the meaning and implementation of these ideas as well. An invaluable source on the entire subject of working women is Madeleine Guilbert, *Les Fonctions des femmes dans l'industrie* (Paris and The Hague 1966).

6 Georges Duveau, *La Vie ouvrière en France sous le Second Empire* (Paris 1946), p. 211.

7 Christopher Johnson, 'Economic Change and Artisan Discontent: The Tailors' History, 1800–1848', in Roger Price (ed.), *Revolution and Reaction: 1848 and the Second French Republic* (London 1975), pp. 87–114; Johnson, *Utopian Communism*, pp. 156–7, 183, 200–1; J.P. Aguet, *Les Grèves sous la Monarchie de Juillet, 1830–1847* (Geneva 1954); Direction du Travail, *Les Associations professionnelles ouvrières*, Vol. II (Paris n.d.), pp. 601–67; Octave Festy, 'Dix années de l'histoire Corporative des ouvriers tailleurs d'habits (1830–1840)', *Revue d'Histoire des Doctrines Economiques et Sociales* (1912), pp. 166–99.

8 Remi Gossez, *Les Ouvriers de Paris: l'organisation, 1848–1851* (Roche-sur-Yon 1967), p. 172; Henriette Vanier, *La Mode et ses métiers: frivolités et luttes des classes, 1830–1870* (Paris 1960), pp. 75–90, 107–24; Mäite Albistur and Daniel Armogathe, *Histoire du féminisme français*, Vol. II (Paris 1977), pp. 455–64; Claire Moses, 'Saint-Simonian Men/Saint-Simonian Women: The Transformation of Feminist Thought in 1830s France', *J. of Mod. Hist.* 54, no. 2 (June 1982), pp. 240–67; Lydia Elhadad, 'Femmes prénommées: les prolétaires saint-simoniennes rédactrices de "La Femme libre", 1832–1834', *Les Révoltes Logiques*, no. 4 (Winter 1977), pp. 63–88 and no. 5 (Spring – Summer 1977), pp. 29–60; Laure Adler, *A l'aube du féminisme: les premières journalistes (1830–1850)* (Paris 1979); Susan Hellerstein, 'Journalism as a Political Tool: The St-Simonian Working-Class Feminist Movement' Honours thesis (Brown University, 1981); Sebastien Charléty, *Essai sur l'histoire de St-Simonisme* (Paris

1896). The Saint-Simonian women's newspaper had a number of titles: *La Femme libre, La Femme d'avenir, La Femme nouvelle, Apostolat des femmes*. I have followed Claire Moses' usage to minimize confusion (Moses, 'Saint-Simonian Men/Women', p. 252, n. 27).

9 *Journal des Tailleurs* (15 Sept. 1848), p. 175.

10 *Ibid.* (16 Mar. 1848), p. 48.

11 *Ibid.* (16 Aug. 1848), p. 132.

12 Pierre Vidal, *Histoire de la corporation des tailleurs d'habits, pourpointeurs-chaussetiers de la ville de Paris* (Paris 1923), p. 50.

13 'Délégations ouvrières à l'éxposition universelle de Londres en 1862' (Paris 1863), *Rapport des délégués tailleurs*, p. 6.

14 George Rudé, 'La Population ouvrière parisienne de 1789 à 1791', *Annales Historiques de la Révolution Française*, 39, no. 187 (January–March 1967), pp. 15–33; Léon Cahen, 'La Population parisienne au milieu du XVIIIᵉ siècle', *La Revue de Paris*, 16, no. 17 (1919), pp. 148–70; J. Kaplow, *The Names of Kings: The Parisian Laboring Poor in the Eighteenth Century* (New York 1972); François Furet, 'Pour une définition des classes inférieures à l'époque moderne', *Annales ESC* 18 (1963), pp. 462, 466; Maurice Garden, *Lyon et les lyonnais au XVIIIᵉ siècle* (Paris 1970); Tilly and Scott, *Women, Work and Family*, ch. 3; Olwen Hufton, 'Women and the Family Economy in Eighteenth-Century France', *French Hist. Stud.* 9 (Spring 1975), pp. 1–22; See also Darlene Levy, Harriet Applewhite, and Mary Johnson, *Women in Revolutionary Paris, 1789–1795* (Urbana, Illinois 1979).

15 Kaplow, *The Names of Kings*, p. 36; Cahen, 'La Population parisienne', pp. 154–5. I have used the spelling of *appièceur* given in the Chamber of Commerce inquiry. Robert's dictionary gives it as *apièceur* and says that the use of the word as a noun first appeared in 1836.

16 C. Johnson, 'Patterns of Proletarianization: Parisian Tailors and Lodève Woolen Workers', in John Merriman (ed.), *Consciousness and Class Experience in Nineteenth-Century Europe* (New York 1979), p. 68. Evidence of expansion is available in numerous manuals written during the period, for example, by Compaing and Dartmann. See the correspondence in French National Archives (FNA), F12 2388.

17 Le Vicomte Georges Avenel, *Le Mécanisme de la vie moderne* (Paris 1896), pp. 31–2; *A Propos du centenaire de la belle jardinière* (Paris 1924); Pierre Parisot described his operations to the minister of agriculture and commerce, 11 July 1848, FNA F12 2337–8.

18 Johnson, 'Economic Change and Artisan Discontent', p. 95; Michael Kirby, 'Changing Structure in the Parisian Tailoring Trades, 1830–1867', Masters thesis (University of North Carolina, Chapel Hill, 1979), pp. 28, 36; Chambre de Commerce de Paris, *Statistique de l'industrie à Paris, 1860* (Paris 1864), p. 313.

19 Chambre de Commerce de Paris, *Statistique de l'industrie à Paris résultant de l'enquête faite... pour les années 1847–48*, 2 vols. (Paris 1851); vol. II, pp. 293, 294, 298.

20 Johnson, 'Economic Change and Artisan Discontent', p. 96.

21 Aguet, *Les Grèves*, pp. 75–90, 130–9, 169, 239, 240, 241; *Associations Professionnelles Ouvrières*, Vol. II, pp. 601–5.

22 Chambre de Commerce, *Statistique 1847–1848*, Vol. II, pp. 293–7.

23 Some of these journeymen were former strikers who defied stubborn masters by going

over to *confection*. In part, the measure was a temporary means of making money until a strike ended; in part, it seems to have represented an attempt – ironic and fruitless – to insist on the skilled worker's self-determination, autonomy and independence. See *Rapport des délégués tailleurs* (1862), p. 19.

24 Chambre de Commerce, *Statistique 1847–1848*, Vol. II, pp. 66, 285, 293, 297.

25 Frédéric Le Play, *Les Ouvriers européens*, Vol. VI (Paris 1878), chap. 8, 'Tailleur d'habits de Paris (1856)', pp. 388–441.

26 By examining the category of *appièceur* in the Chamber of Commerce report we can document the situation of former skilled tailors, driven from shop to home-based production. The 1847 report listed 3,393 *appièceurs*, a tenfold increase since 1830. (By 1860, the number has soared to 12,000.) Of the 3,393, only 24 employed more than 10 workers; another 418 supervised from 2 to 10 employees. These were the bona fide subcontractors and they accounted for 13% of the total. Of the remaining 2,951, 706 worked entirely alone, while 2,245 toiled *en famille*, assisted by a 'wife, daughter or other relative'. The average daily earnings of the *appièceurs* (who, like all home workers were paid piece-rates) were 3 fr. 03, lower than either the wages of a skilled journeyman (3 fr. 86) or a worker producing exclusively for the ready-made trades (3 fr. 26). See Chambre de Commerce, *Statistique 1847–1848*, Vol. II, pp. 289–90, 302; Johnson, 'Economic Change and Artisan Discontent', p. 99; Chambre de Commerce, *Statistique 1860*, p. 310. See also Albert Aftalion, *Le Développement de la fabrique à domicile dans les industries de l'habillement* (Paris 1906), p. 6.

27 Johnson, 'Economic Change and Artisan Discontent', pp. 103–9.

28 Aguet, *Les Grèves*, p. 77. See also: Vanier, *La Mode et ses métiers*, pp. 63–70; FNA CC 585 (1833–1834); R. Grignon, *Réflexions d'un ouvrier tailleur sur la misère des ouvriers en général* (Paris 1833).

29 FNA, C 930 C2394; Chambre de Commerce, *Statistique 1847–1848*, Vol. II, p. 74; FNA, C 930 dos. 5 (23 April 1848); Bibliothèque Historique de la Ville de Paris, Papiers E. Cabet, Folio 372; Tacheux, 'Aux membres composant la commission des ouvriers tailleurs' (1848); Gillard, *Revue anécdotique des association ouvrières* (Paris 1850), quoted in Jacques Rancière, *La Nuit des prolétaires* (Paris 1981), p. 310. See also André Cochut, *Les Associations ouvrières: histoire et théorie des tentatives de réorganisation industrielle opérée depuis la Révolution de 1848* (Paris 1851), p. 43 and Vanier, *La Mode et ses métiers*, pp. 117–19.

30 *Journal des Tailleurs* (15 Sept. 1848), p. 175.

31 Charles. Dupin, *Discussion du projet de loi sur le travail des enfants, des adolescents, des filles et des femmes* (Paris 1848), p. 27.

32 Lemann, confectionneur, *De l'industrie des vêtements confectionnés en France* (Paris 1857), pp. 34–5.

33 *Rapport des délégués tailleurs* (1862), pp. 20–1. See also FNA C2257 dos. 4772, 'Petition des tailleurs d'habits à l'Assemblée Nationale' (1848); and FNA C2394 dos. 683 (Paris, 3, Oct. 1849), Letter from Gautier, *tailleur*, to the national representatives.

34 See, for example, the letter of the printer and Proudhonian Louis Vasbenter to Flora Tristan written in 1843, 'La vie de la femme est la vie du ménage, la vie domestique, la vie intérieure.' Alain Faure and Jacques Rancière, *La Parole ouvrière 1830–1851* (Paris 1976), p. 199. See also the comment in *L'Atelier*, cited in Vanier, *La Mode et ses métiers*, p. 78.

35 This may have originated with the statute of 1675 that granted women the right to make women's clothing, but also limited the number of apprentices each dressmaker trained to one at a time. J. Barbaret, *Monographies professionnelles*, Vol. V, no. 5, 'Les Couturières' (Paris 1890), pp. 260–1. Gaston Worth, *La Couture et la confection des vêtements de femme* (Paris 1895), p. 9. On the history of the corporation of *couturières* see G. Levasnier, *Papiers de famille professionnelle, l'ancien communauté des couturières de Paris et le syndicat actuel de l'auguille 1675–1895* (Blois 1896).

36 Chambre de Commerce, *Statistique 1847–1848*, Vol. II, pp. 249, 293.

37 On the organization of *couture* and *lingerie* see Barbaret, *Monographies professionnelles*, Vol. V, pp. 260ff. Chambre de Commerce, *Statistique 1847–1848*; Vanier, *La Mode et ses métiers*, pp. 75–90; Aftalion. *La Fabrique à domicile, passim*; A. Parmentier, *Les Métiers et leur histoire* (Paris 1908), 'Tailleurs et couturières', pp. 45–51. Husbands of dressmakers were usually craftsmen in the city. There seems to be no particular type of worker who married seamstresses and dressmakers more frequently than any other.

38 Not much is known about shared craft traditions among skilled women workers in the nineteenth century. It is likely, however, that the trade organization which flourished in 1848 took its inspiration less from the history and structure of the crafts than from the revolutionary circumstances and from models of association and co-operation developed by craftsmen.

39 Barbaret, *Monographies professionnelles*, Vol. V, p. 266; Chambre de Commerce, *Statistique 1847–1848*, Vol. II, p. 66; *La Voix des Femmes*, 3 April 1848; Alfred Picard, *Exposition Internationale de 1900 à Paris: le bilan d'un siècle 1801–1900* (Paris 1906), Vol. IV, pp. 412–16.

40 *La Voix des Femmes*, 15 April 1848.

41 *Ibid.*, 14 April 1848.

42 'No one makes the soup, there is no dinner for our husbands, there is nothing for ourselves; is that happiness?' *La Voix des Femmes*, 15 April 1848.

43 *La Voix des Femmes*, 22 Mar., 31 Mar., 15 April 1848.

44 *Ibid.*, 21 April 1848.

45 Vanier, *La Mode et ses métiers*, p. 114.

46 *La Voix des Femmes*, 28 Mar. 1848.

47 Vanier, *La Mode et ses métiers*, p. 112; *La Voix des Femmes*, 18 April 1848; Gossez, *Les Ouvriers de Paris*, pp. 170–1.

48 Vanier, *La Mode et ses métiers*, pp. 115–16; Octave Festy, *Procès verbaux du conseil d'encouragement pour les associations ouvrières, juillet 1848–Oct 1849* (Paris 1917), pp. 96, 106–7: Julie Daubie, *La Femme pauvre au XIXe siècle* (Paris 1866), pp. 47–8.

49 *La Voix des Femmes*, 18 April 1848.

50 *Ibid.*, see the statute of L'Association Fraternelle des Démocrates-Socialistes des Deux Sexes (Paris 1848). For a discussion of feminist themes among English garment workers and for important contrasts with this chapter, see Barbara Taylor, '"The Men are as Bad as Their Masters", Socialism, Feminism and Sexual Antagonism in the London Tailoring Trade in the Early 1830s', *Feminist Studies*, 5, no. 1 (Spring 1979), pp. 27–40.

51 *La Voix des Femmes*, 26 April 1848; 30 May 1848.

52 *Ibid.*, 29 April 1848.

53 *Ibid.*, 1–4 June 1848.
54 Moses, 'Saint-Simonian Men/Women', p. 25. See also Lydia Elhadad, 'Femmes prénommées', and Adler, *A l'aube du féminisme*.
55 Louis Réné Villermé, *Tableau de l'état physique et moral des ouvriers employés dans les manufactures de coton, de laine et de soie*, 2 vols. (Paris 1840); Honoré Antoine Frégier, *Des classes dangereuses dans la population des grandes villes et des moyens de les rendre meilleures*, 2 vols. (Paris 1840). On the Academy itself see Ernest Seillière, *Une académie à l'époque romantique* (Paris 1926). See also Hilde Rigaudias-Weiss, *Les Enquêtes ouvrières en France entre 1830 et 1848* (Paris 1936). Recent studies which discuss reformers' views of the working class family are Louis Chevalier, *Classes laborieuses et classes dangereuses à Paris pendant la première moitié du XIXe siècle* (Paris 1958) and Jacques Donzelot, *La Police des familles.* Donzelot writes about reformers and their policies with no attention to the working-class participation in or reaction to the discourse. My study will ultimately expand on this point, introducing more of the reformers' arguments so they can be contrasted fully with the utopian socialists I refer to.
56 *La Voix des Femmes*, 28 Mar. 1848.
57 *La Voix des Femmes*, 10, 11 April 1848.
58 E. Cabet, *La Femme* (Paris 1841), p. 19.
59 Cited in Johnson, *Utopian Communism*, p. 90.
60 A. J. B. Parent-Duchâtelet, *De la prostitution dans la ville de Paris* (Paris 1836), pp. 73–5, 93–4.
61 Chambre de Commerce, *Statistique 1847–48*, Vol. II, p. 66.
62 *La Voix des Femmes*, 21 April 1848.
63 Suzanne Voilquin, *Souvenirs d'une fille du peuple* (Paris 1978), pp. 94–97.
64 An example of the genre as sentimental melodrama is in *Le Populaire*, February to May 1847. An important discussion of working-class reactions to melodrama is Martha Vicinus, '"Helpless and Unfriended": Nineteenth-Century Domestic Melodrama', *New Literary Hist.*, 13 (1981–2), pp. 127–43.
65 Johnson, *Utopian Communism*, p. 85.
66 It is interesting to note in this connection that when workers wrote marriage contracts they tended to opt for the *communauté des biens*, the sharing of possessions, rather than the dotal regime or any other arrangement.
67 Faure and Rancière, *La Parole ouvrière*, pp. 384–94.
68 *Ibid.*, pp. 394–5.
69 *La Voix des Femmes*, 26 Mar. 1848.
70 Bourgeois notions of the time assigned women an exclusively domestic role; some, like Villermé, were appalled at the fact that women worked away from home. Madeleine Guilbert suggests, however, that the issue of women working outside the home did not become a general one for bourgeois moralists until the second half of the nineteenth century. That may be another reason for its absence from discourse critical of and directly attacking the moralists' views. See Guilbert, *Les Fonctions des femmes*, p. 40.
71 Barbaret, *Monographies professionnelles*, Vol. V, pp. 274–5; see also J. Rancière and Patrice Vauday, 'En allant à l'expo: l'ouvrier, sa femme et les machines', *Les Révoltes Logiques*, no. 1 (Winter 1975), pp. 5–22, and on tailors, p. 16; M. Perrot, 'L'Éloge de la ménagère dans le discours des ouvriers français au XIXe siècle', *Mythes et*

représentations de la femme au XIXe siècle; Christiane Dufrancatel, 'La Femme imaginaire des hommes: politique, idéologie et imaginaire dans le mouvement ouvrier', in Dufrancatel *et al.*, *L'Histoire sans qualités*, pp. 157–86; Dufrancatel, 'Les Amants de la liberté? Stratégies de femme, luttes républicaines, luttes ouvrières', *Les Révoltes Logiques* no. 5 (Spring – Summer 1977), p. 76.

72 Perrot, 'L'Éloge de la ménagère', p. 118.
73 J. W. Scott, 'Mayors versus Police Chiefs: Socialist Municipalities Confront the French State', in J. Merriman (ed.), *Nineteenth-Century French Cities* (London 1982); R. Pierreuse, 'L'Ouvrier Roubaisien et la propagande politique 1890–1900', *Revue du Nord* 51 (April – June 1969), p. 260.
74 G. S. Jones, 'Working-Class Culture and Working-Class Politics in London, 1870–1900: Notes on the Remaking of a Working Class', *J. of Soc. Hist.*, 7, no. 4 (Summer 1974), p. 499.

ACKNOWLEDGMENTS

I would like to thank the following friends and colleagues for comments and criticism: Donald M. Scott, Charles Sowerwine, Judy Coffin, Sherry Ortner, Martha Vicinus, and Daryl Hafter. Christopher Johnson's excellent studies of tailors in the 1830s and 40s made my work easier and I am grateful for it. My greatest debt is to Natalie Zemon Davis who, at an early stage in my research asked me where the female voices were. That was the question that made all the difference.

4

Craft traditions and the labour movement in nineteenth-century Germany

JÜRGEN KOCKA

Handwerker and *Arbeiter*: distinct topics of historical research

German labour historians have long been aware of the great importance which the traditional *Handwerk* (craft system) and the *Handwerker* (craftsmen, artisans) had for the rise of the labour movement (*Arbeiterbewegung*) and the emergence of a class of workers (*Arbeiter*) in nineteenth-century Germany. It has generally been known that, in the 1830s and 1840s, the friendly societies (*Kassen*), workers' education clubs (*Arbeiterbildungsvereine*), and early radical organizations like the 'Communist League' recruited their membership largely from *Handwerksgesellen*, that is, journeymen or young artisans trained according to craft rules and working in dependent positions (for wages) in usually small and medium-sized shops: occupations such as tailors and shoemakers, carpenters, masons, book printers.

The first mass movement of German workers, the Allgemeine Deutsche Arbeiterverbrüderung (founded in 1848, with some 18,000 members all over Germany in 1850, and later suppressed by the authorities) was led by the journeyman typesetter Stephan Born, and clearly dominated by artisans, for the most part journeymen but with some small masters as well; it was not an exclusive organization, however, and tried to appeal to unskilled labourers and semi-skilled domestic workers. When unions were founded in 1848–9, and again in the 1860s, they mainly recruited journeymen and workers with an artisan background, on a craft-specific basis, although not explicitly excluding less skilled workers from their ranks. In the strike wave of 1869 to 1873 journeymen were over-represented among the strikers, though factory workers and miners already accounted for some half of the participants. Journeymen and artisans were also the decisive group in the early socialist labour parties: in Lassalle's Allgemeiner Deutscher Arbeiterverein (ADAV) of 1863, in Bebel's and Liebknecht's Sozialdemokratische Arbeiterpartei (SDAP) of 1869, and in the Sozialistische Arbeiterpartei Deutschlands (SAP), which was formed in Gotha in 1875, and which united both of these earlier parties.[1]

However, in spite of these perceptions of the close relation between craft tradition and emerging working class, historical research on German workers and on artisans/craftsmen has been strongly shaped by the conviction that there was a deep gulf, an important qualitative difference between the history of the craft system and craft traditions on the one hand, and the emergence of a working class and a labour movement on the other. *Handwerksgeschichte* (history of the crafts and the craftsmen) and *Arbeitergeschichte* (workers' and labour history) have usually been separate and relatively independent fields of study in Germany. A short note on semantics may be necessary to make this understandable. The definition has of course changed over time, and it is still not without ambiguities, but since the last third of the nineteenth century the concept *Handwerk* has usually referred to those units of production (*Betriebe*) (excluding raw material production but including some services like repair work) which are of small or medium size, whose members (including the 'master') do skilled manual work without much mechanization. The contrasting concept is *Industrie* or *Fabrik*, referring to manufacturing units on a larger scale, using machines and an advanced division of labour (including a strict division between management and employees, as well as a division between skill groups). There has always been a legal difference between *Handwerk* and *Industrie*, and it persists to the present day. It originated in the corporate world of the early modern period, and it clearly weakened, as did the corporate tradition, in the course of the nineteenth century. But it did not disappear altogether, and it was partly reinforced in response to the political pressures of *Handwerk* organizations striving for legal protection, tax privileges and some control over the labour market. In Germany and other parts of central Europe, *Handwerk* and *Industrie* have been organized in different associations, chambers and interest groups. This distinction has fundamentally structured the political rhetoric, social protests and the dominant images of social reality. While it may be difficult, particularly nowadays, to decide whether a specific unit belongs to *Handwerk* or *Industrie*, the distinction between these two categories continues to have a legal, political, and social meaning, if to a decreasing extent. *Handwerker* refers mainly to those persons who work in *Handwerk* units, but particularly to the self-employed. Since the second third of the nineteenth century at least, there has been a tendency towards equating *Handwerker* with *Handwerksmeister* (master-artisan), while those who were employed in those units were specified as *Handwerksgesellen* (journeymen) and *Lehrlinge* (apprentices).[2]

It is not easy to find an exact English equivalent for the German word *Handwerk* – neither 'craft' nor 'artisan' exactly fit. Similarly, the translation of *Arbeiter* is not without difficulties. The word has always had different meanings at the same period of time, depending on who used it and in what context. While *Handwerker* was increasingly reserved for self-employed craftsmen, the concept of *Arbeiter* had a complementary, reversed career. It was increasingly reserved for those who worked with their hands for wages. In a broad sense it tended to include all those manual workers in employed positions, including the journeymen in craft-shops, once they had lost their specific corporate status. But one frequently speaks – with respect to the nineteenth and early twentieth centuries – of *Gesellen und Arbeiter*, and in this case *Arbeiter* refers to those working for wages in larger units of work, in factories and the like. It is important to note that both in its broader and its narrower meaning, *Arbeiter* includes both skilled and unskilled persons, those with an artisan qualification and those without. The distinction between *Handwerker* and *Arbeiter*, it must be stressed, is not a distinction of skill and qualification, but partly of class, and partly of type of business unit (craft-shop versus factory and the like). 'Artisans and workers' may not therefore always be the right translation of *Handwerker und Arbeiter*.[3]

The historians of *Handwerk* have investigated its economic performance, especially under the challenge of capitalist industrialization, which had often been expected (by Marx and by conservative economists alike, as well as by many spokesmen for craft organizations fighting for state protection) to destroy the *Handwerk* and the 'old Mittelstand', but which had in reality much more differentiated effects. The role of master artisans and journeymen in the Revolution of 1848–9 has attracted some attention. Historians concerned with the second part of the nineteenth and the early twentieth century have explored the development of the interest organizations of master artisans (*Handwerkerbewegung*) and their partly conservative, partly populist role in society and politics. As to the earlier period (the eighteenth and first half of the nineteenth centuries) research has concentrated on the legal, economic, and social conditions of master artisans and journeymen, their education and culture, including their emphasis on 'honour' (*Ehrbarkeit*) and their generally noncompetitive values. We know more in general about the guilds of this period than about the journeymen brotherhoods, which were in the eighteenth century relatively autonomous units within the master-dominated guilds. They fulfilled a variety of functions for the journeymen, who were usually young and single, and frequently travelling. They provided support when journeymen arrived and departed, and housing at the hostel (*Herberge*) for a limited period. They influenced the placing of new arrivals. They defended journeymen's economic and social interests *vis-à-vis* individual masters, the guild and the town authorities. They provided insurance and pay in case of sickness, accidents and death. They had a limited jurisdictional competence, serving as courts for journeymen with grievances. They took part in the examination and initiation of apprentices becoming journeymen. They had many social functions and represented the journeymen in public, often alongside the masters, on feast-days and parades at church services and other occasions, appearing specifically as distinct crafts. They led strikes and boycotts which were numerous in the eighteenth century, and which have recently been studied. In contrast, the details and regional differentiations of the processes of de-corporation since the late eighteenth century are less well known. The policies of the absolutist states and particularly the reforms of the early nineteenth century, population pressures and the rise of capitalism severely weakened the guilds and frequently damaged the brotherhoods. The destruction of the corporate order was a protracted process, however, and elements of the guild system and remnants of corporate law continued to exist until the 1860s, particularly in Hamburg, Hanover, and in the south German states.[4]

Working-class and labour history have largely developed apart from *Handwerksgeschichte*. This is particularly true for those writing in a Marxist tradition. Marx shared with many of his German contemporaries the impression that the factory lay at the centre of industrialization, and he became convinced that the factory proletariat would be the core of the emerging working class in social and political terms as well. The relatively fast breakthrough of the factory system within German industrialization seemed to support this view. In this tradition many working-class and labour historians have regarded both master artisans and journeymen as mere transitory phenomena on the periphery, in spite of their large numbers in the nineteenth century. This is why they did not get major attention, though they were not totally excluded. They were, for example, drawn into the arguments when explanations were needed for the fact that the emerging working class was not as radical as theoretically expected.[5]

Non-Marxist writers have shown more interest in the gradual transition from *Handwerker* to *Arbeiter* in the course of nineteenth-century commercialization and industrialization. This transition proceeded mainly along two paths. On the one hand, journeymen (*Gesellen*) were slowly transformed into skilled industrial workers (*Lohnarbeiter*). In this respect historians have been interested in the slow destruction of the guild system; journeymen moving out of their masters' households; changing work conditions and changing methods of payment; moving back and forth between craft-shop and factory; increasing proportions of married journeymen, and increasing intermarriage between journeymen or artisans and other working-class groups. On the other hand, there was the gradual transition from the status of a (small) master artisan to the status of a (skilled) industrial worker. In this respect, historians have started to discuss the increasing dependence of tailors and shoemakers, carpenters and other craftsmen, who were formally self-employed and perhaps small employers themselves, upon merchants and putting-out entrepreneurs, and upon department stores and factories. Much has been said about domestic workers (*Heimarbeiter*), particularly in textiles, who combined a formally independent (self-employed) status with real dependence on merchants; they can be regarded as a stage of transition between *Handwerker* and *Arbeiter* in the full sense of the word. But, in general, the interest and attention of non-Marxist labour historians has still centred on industrial workers in larger units, above all on factory workers.[6]

This belief in a fundamental divide and tension between the craft tradition and the formation of a working class has particularly influenced the older works on the history of the socialist or social–democratic labour parties, their programmes, ideologies and politics. It has been stressed, and not without justification, that those parties directed their opposition not only against the emerging capitalist system and the bourgeoisie, but also, and quite emphatically, against any restoration of the traditional craft system with its corporate elements, such as was demanded by many master artisans and their organizations. Indeed, such demands sometimes came, if in a different form, from the spokesmen of journeymen before, during, and after 1848. In fact, both during 1848–9 and again from the 1860s onward, the rising social-democratic and socialist labour movement did not present itself as a primarily defensive movement of protest against industrialization and modernization as such, but as a progressive movement of emancipation that was deeply critical of the social and political relations in which industrialization occurred. The spokesmen for these early parties explicitly attacked craft and artisan traditions and loyalties among journeymen and (skilled) industrial workers because they correctly recognized that such traditions and loyalties were strictly craft-specific, particularistic and narrow, and that as such they stood in the path of the broad and comprehensive class solidarity which they were trying to promote. They felt that journeymen and artisans were defending their craft pride and work autonomy against not only the prerogatives and attacks of management, but also, as a form of privilege and exclusiveness, against fellow workers, in particular the unskilled and women. In this sense they tried to overcome craft traditions in order to create a class-based labour movement. Most of those who have written about the history of the labour movement shared that view.[7]

The dominant views are more ambiguous with respect to early trade-union history. After all, it cannot be denied that until the 1890s at least most unionized workers belonged to craft- or trade-specific organizations: book printers and typesetters, shoemakers, tailors, masons and so on, in a way comparable to the eighteenth-century journeymen and their brotherhoods. The numerous accounts of individual unions which were written by non-professional historians, frequently by former union officials, in the first part of the twentieth century, often opened with a chapter on the pre-history of the particular association dating back into the corporate period, particularly the eighteenth century. Had the modern unions indeed grown out of pre-industrial journeymen brotherhoods and craft traditions, as Lujo Brentano thought with respect to the English trade unions?

In the same way that the Webbs rejected Brentano's view, so later historians of the German unions have stressed the discontinuity between the journeymen brotherhoods of the early modern period and the trade unions of the 1860s and later. For a long time it became the dominant view that the unions of the 1860s were largely influenced and partly created by political parties, that is the Liberals and the Social Democrats, above all after 1868 when the parties suddenly interested themselves in unionization. One knew that the brotherhoods had been strong and aggressive in the eighteenth century, but one also knew that the absolutist governments had fought the autonomy of those brotherhoods in a long and ultimately successful struggle. In the territories occupied by the French in the 1790s and 1800s – but also in Prussia and in other German states – brotherhoods were dissolved or crippled by government repression in the first years of the nineteenth century, in the period of politically motivated prosecutions of the 1830s and 1840s, and again in the reactionary period of the 1850s. Journeymen organizations which survived or which were founded anew after 1820 were restricted to specific functions, particularly sickness insurance and funeral benefits. Consequently there just could not have been much continuity between journeymen brotherhoods and early unions, as these latter were founded in 1848–9 and again in the 1860s.[8]

The literature justifiably stressed what was new about the unions when compared to the traditional journeymen brotherhoods: proximity to political parties; a rhetoric of fundamental opposition and criticism of the system; independence from comprehensive, master-dominated guilds of which most brotherhoods had been but a semi-autonomous part; and voluntary membership of workers without strict entrance examination. In addition, any systematic comparison with the English trade unions would have shown that the German organizations were less inclined – or maybe less able – to stress craft exclusiveness. Guild-type labour market controls (e.g. union-controlled apprenticeship rules, the rejection of non-apprenticed colleagues, control of access to and dismissal from the shop-floor, closed shop and union shop) have not played a large role in either the aims or the daily work of the German unions. Nor has the fight against dilution, or the defence of traditional and dignified work rules against innovation. Furthermore, compared with the English trade unions, the German organizations seem to have been more comprehensive. The association of book printers and typesetters, for example, organized within one union different specializations which, in England, were represented by 14 distinct specialist unions. It seems that some German craft unions were in reality 'compound craft unions' from an early stage, with strong elements of 'amalgamated craft unions'. There also were early attempts to build bridges across craftlines and form rudimentary industrial unions, such as the metalworkers' unions and woodworkers' unions. While most unions concentrated on skilled workers, there were early attempts to organize the unskilled as well. And while early attempts at forming a union of unions (1869, 1872 and 1874) failed, there was another attempt to form a cartel of unions in 1878, an attempt which had to be interrupted because of renewed government suppression. In other words, there was much that distinguished the unions of the 1860s and 1870s from the traditional journeymen brotherhoods.[9] Consequently there was much justification for the dominant view stressing the gap between *Handwerk* tradition and the early working-class movements.

The changing view: continuity stressed

More recently, however, the dominant views have started to change. One observes a renewed interest in the eighteenth and nineteenth century history of the crafts, of master-artisans and journeymen, of their culture, customs and 'moral economy'. Historians seem to have become less certain of what to judge 'modern' or 'progressive', what 'traditional' or 'backward looking'. Influenced by a new mood of cultural criticism, ecological anxieties and disenchantment with modern industrialism, historians, mostly of a younger generation, have started to become more sensitive to the losses and damages brought about by industrialization and modernization. Older traditions, which had tried for a while to 'resist' change, but then got lost, have now become interesting again.[10] This changing mood indirectly contributed to a new view of the world of the old crafts, and to a changing perspective on the relationship between crafts and working-class history. Recent findings on French and English working-class history are encouraging similar research on Germany. Bernard Moss and William Sewell, for example, have demonstrated for France how closely related craft traditions and early socialism could be, in terms of ideology, semantics, and social basis. They have shown how pre-capitalist, corporate values and orientations influenced the expectations of journeymen and workers in the first half of the nineteenth century. They have argued that those corporate cultures, values and vocabularies became mixed with the egalitarian ideological heritage of the Revolution, and became compatible with, and conducive to, certain socialist criticisms of capitalism expressed within the early French labour movement with its stress on co-operative schemes.[11]

East of the River Rhine things were probably not quite the same. In the first place, the egalitarian rhetoric of a victorious revolution was not available to the same extent. In the second place, most German states and territories saw strong remnants of the old guild structure survive until the 1860s, in varying forms and to different degrees (least so in Prussia). These were rules which regulated access to position in the crafts by establishing residence requirements and providing for master-dominated examinations; laws which clearly distinguished between masters, journeymen, and apprentices in terms of economic power, social standing and influence within the changing guilds; master-dominated labour-market regulations; various instruments, by which both master organizations and communal authorities could try to control the journeymen, their hostels and their collective actions.[12] All this seems to be in strong contrast to both France and England. Against this background of survival of corporate rules which usually gave privileges to the masters, it is understandable that the German journeymen's admiration for the corporate order was limited. While the restoration of a modified guild system was advocated by many master organizations in 1848–9 and again in the 1860s, most spokesmen for journeymen took a more cautious, though frequently ambiguous stand. Given the long survival of corporate institutions and their close identification with the masters' side, the anti-corporate rhetoric of the early labour movement makes a lot of sense.[13]

Nevertheless, the proposition that there was a close relationship between the corporate anti-capitalist tradition on the one hand, and the socialist vision of the emerging labour movement on the other may prove just as fruitful in understanding the German case. It might lead to a fresh assessment of the co-operative schemes in the early labour movement (*Produktionsgenossenschaften, Assoziationen*). They have not traditionally been taken very seriously by labour historians. In the light of the programme and ideologies of late nineteenth- and twentieth-century socialism they have been regarded as the signs of immaturity and as lacking in theoretical clarity. They have frequently been seen as liberal alternatives to socialism.[14] But in reality *Genossenschaft* ideas were strong from the 1840s to the 1870s. They could form part of a radical programme for social reform as propagated by the Arbeiterverbrüderung in 1848–9, and they proved attractive to the printers', tobacco workers', tailors' and shoemakers' unions in the 1860s and 1870s. They were quite different from the co-operative plans of liberals like Schulze-Delitzsch. It cannot be denied that most attempts to set up co-operative schemes by workers proved unstable and short-lived due to superior competition and internal difficulties. But they seem to have struck a chord with threatened small masters, journeymen and skilled workers alike, by promising 'organization of work' which would help to avoid fully developed wage labour, and retain certain elements of artisanal independence, though in a collective and non-individualistic way. Here, the quest for the maintenance of craft traditions and artisanal independence in a modified form proved to be compatible with radical and socialist visions.[15]

Karl Marx was no admirer of de-centralized co-operative schemes, although he conceded that they might have limited value as instruments of transition between a private property-based economy and socialism.[16] He was of course never a critic of modern large-scale industry as such, and he never advocated the return to craft-like systems of production. He believed in technological progress and in the advancement of men's control over nature as prerequisites of an eventual human emancipation in a socialist or communist system. At first glance it does not seem easy to find a close and positive relation between Marx and the *Handwerk* tradition. But one may argue nevertheless that the basic ideas of Marx – his opposition to capitalism and to alienated work, his distrust in the 'invisible hand' of the market, and his criticism of a rather autonomous, self-regulating economic sphere that was not controlled by moral judgments or political decisions but followed a market-oriented logic of its own – reflect pre-capitalist criteria and the ideals of non-alienated, non-segmented, self-controlled work without subordination to the market; ideals, in effect, of a 'moral economy' turned political. Perhaps it was this mixture of forward-looking acceptance of modernization and the desire for revolution on the one hand, and the preservation of basic pre-capitalist orientations on the other which helps to explain (among other things) why Marxist ideas could become popular among journeymen-workers in the labour movement, at first in the 1840s, but especially from the 1870s.

This may sound speculative and hard to prove. The close relation between *Handwerk* traditions and early working-class history can be more solidly established with respect to early trade-union history. Here, recent research has started to set new emphases. Ulrich Engelhardt's painstaking research has shown that the unions of the 1860s and 70s were much less created and influenced by political parties than is conventionally held.[17] Consequently, there is new interest in earlier organizations from which the unions may have developed.

In several cases – and there are probably more to be found – local craft unions grew directly out of previously existing journeymen organizations, which had survived in spite of the de-corporation policies and repressive actions of most German governments, and in spite of the pressures from the rising market economy and the growing population. This has recently been shown in relation to Hamburg, where corporate institutions survived with the official support of the city government until 1865. Here one finds direct continuity between self-governing journeymen brotherhoods (with self-administered funds) and the post-corporate unions of the second part of the 1860s (with self-controlled strike funds, open through craft-specific membership, and frequently with affiliations to the socialist party).[18]

Such direct continuity was certainly exceptional. In other parts of Germany, especially in Prussia, the old journeymen brotherhoods had been dissolved or deprived of autonomy and functions. On the one hand, however, detailed local studies suggest that police power was not always very effective in repressing such clubs and organizations. And on the other hand it is known that the governments, after crushing the old brotherhoods, soon found it necessary again to tolerate functionally restricted and supervised journeymen organizations which could serve as friendly societies and offer insurance services for sick and travelling journeymen; in other words to fulfil the tasks which the government was not able to take over. From the 1840s, indeed, the Prussian government even encouraged the formation of new journeymen organizations for insurance purposes (*Gesellenkassen, Handwerkskassen*). Once in existence, such friendly societies may not always have restricted themselves to their official purposes. When meeting in their hostels for collecting subscriptions (*Auflage*), they would talk about other matters. They were interested in controlling the funds themselves. Local and regional differences were great, and as yet under-researched, but it is clear that in many places and in many crafts journeymen organizations existed in the 1850s and 1860s, although usually with very limited functions, dependent on master organizations and supervised by local authorities. They were different from the old brotherhoods, and frequently (perhaps mostly) they were created anew after 1820. With these limited powers and functions, they did not easily lend themselves to being directly transformed in the 1860s, into dynamic craft unions with the power to strike. In fact, they reportedly sometimes impeded the foundation of such new post-corporate organizations. But in other cases they proved to be helpful. They provided communication, meeting places (*Herbergen*), lists of addresses, and craft-based cohesion, all of which could be used by activists and organizers in establishing a strike committee or a local union. In this sense the early unions could build on previous organizations, which they would in due course try to absorb. From this point of view one understands why the early unions – in contrast to the official view of Lassalle, but in accordance with the convictions of Bebel and Liebknecht – had to have insurance schemes and similar services that were traditionally offered by journeymen organizations.[19]

There is a different line of argument stressing the connection between the late history of the old crafts and the early history of the new working class and its movements, quite separate from the question of institutional continuity. It is an argument very familiar to English readers, but one which has not really been central to the German debate until recently: that the conflict between an artisan 'moral economy' and capitalist modernization was a source of anger and protest that fuelled the early labour movement.

One could show in detail – though it still needs to be done – that the traditional corporate master – journeymen relationship was gradually transformed into a capitalist employer – employee relationship. This was a protracted process, but by the late 1860s the free labour contract had become the rule, and the last remnants of corporate laws had been largely destroyed. Traditional non-market practices of placing newly arrived journeymen in shops, or of getting them on the road again if there were no openings broke down, particularly in the reforms of the beginning of the century, in the crisis years of the 1830s and 1840s (high unemployment), and finally in the industrialization boom of the late 1860s and early 1870s. Some local authorities had tried to continue setting prices and wage rates in a few trades, particularly the building trades, but these attempts were increasingly overwhelmed by market pressures and ultimately abandoned. Fluctuations of wages increased and so did the differentials between the incomes of journeymen and masters, at least in the cases which have been studied. Journeymen increasingly moved out of their masters' households, becoming lodgers elsewhere or founding households of their own. This meant, among other things, that journeymen became more and more dependent on the market, for the monetary element in their wages jumped from about 40 or 50 per cent to 100 per cent. Factory production with its specific time discipline and far-reaching division of labour proceeded and involved a growing number of journeymen who worked in these settings either intermittently or on leaving the small craft-shop altogether. Even in the craft-shop, the atmosphere changed when it was faced with greater market competition. In several trades – textile trades, tailoring, shoemaking, joinery and others – the craft-shops became dependent on putting-out merchants, and factories – an unavoidable and degrading experience shared by masters and men.[20]

No doubt many of them experienced these changes – the rise of the market principle, the capitalist transformation of the journeyman – master relationship, increasing division of labour, the rise of the factory, the destruction of corporate laws and customs – as a challenge, as degradation, and as a threat to their rights and expectations which were still often oriented towards a pre-capitalist 'moral economy'. Market-determined wages and prices contradicted their non-acquisitive and non-competitive assumptions about 'just' wages and prices. Journeymen experienced it as a violation of their pride and a break of their standards, even as morally wrong, when their employers, under the pressure of competition, adopted new production and sales techniques, when the division of labour advanced, and small machines were adopted, when they suddenly had to work closely together with unskilled helpers, when costs became more important than quality, and time-consciousness grew at the cost of traditional customs, when masters and local authorities stepped up their century-old attacks on Saint Monday, and particularly when they had to change over to work in the newly built factories. Under new conditions, old customs changed their meaning or were misunderstood. For instance, to ask for a 'gift' (*Geschenk, Zeichen*) had been normal and respectable for the travelling journeymen, for centuries. But the same behaviour could now easily be regarded as begging, and the young small-town journeyman could be prosecuted for it when he came to a large city where guild rules and customs had been largely forgotten. His reaction would be dismay and anger.[21]

In other words, it was not only, perhaps not even primarily, the conflict between labour and capital, as Marx thought and the labour leaders said, which produced those challenges, frictions, frustrations and propensity to protest out of which the early working-class movements grew, but also, perhaps more importantly, the conflict between traditional culture and capitalist modernization. The experience of this basic conflict was not limited to journeymen but partly shared by small masters. Whether such frustrations and potential were translated into open protests, collective actions and organizations, depended on many factors; but here too artisan traditions proved helpful. Even where formalized organizations did not exist, or existed no longer, journeymen of the same trade had often maintained contact with each other that reached far beyond local boundaries. They shared trade-specific symbols and rites, transmitted from one generation to the next. Similar qualifications and work experiences meant an additional bond on which they based much of their awareness and sense of identity. These were resources which facilitated common action and organization when journeymen were challenged by new developments.

Such an argument forms one part[22] of the explanation of why journeymen and at times small masters were the main supporters of the early working-class associations, clubs, friendly societies, unions, parties and strikes, and why some journeymen seem to have been more strongly represented than others. Some categories are rarely mentioned in the sources. On the one hand were the bakers, butchers, barbers and so on, whose work and lives had changed very little, and most of whom were still integrated into their masters' households. On the other hand were those crafts which were quickly fragmented, reduced, degraded or destroyed by industrialization (spinners, some categories of weavers, certain leather and woodworking trades) and which did not play a large role, either. Artisans of this type were probably too poor and too powerless, and quickly lost the resources (stable common experiences, pride, communication, financial support from colleagues) which would have facilitated both protest and organization. Rather, it is the printers and cigar-makers, tailors and shoemakers, joiners, carpenters and masons who are most frequently mentioned in the sources on early friendly societies, clubs, protests, strikes, unions and parties. These were large categories, mostly urban crafts which had a good deal of continuity and stability, usually guild traditions (except the special case of the cigar-makers), real cohesion and relatively good bargaining power. These were the groups which had come into close contact with the technical and commercial changes associated with industrialization and had experienced most strongly the resulting challenge to their position. They usually worked in relatively large, market-oriented units (building and printing, cigar-makers), or they worked in trades which were increasingly challenged by merchant capitalist and factory competition (tailors, shoemakers, carpenters). Some of them probably had had the experience of working in a factory for a time, before returning to a craft-shop. Artisans of this type usually lived outside the households of their employers. They were far advanced in the process of transformation from traditional journeyman (or small master) to skilled wage-earner, but they still retained much of what traditionally bound the trade together, and could use this as a basis for protest and organization.[23]

Here, then, is the positive contribution of the craft tradition to the early labour movement that has been recently stressed. To sum up: pre-capitalist, artisan values and notions of solidarity may have facilitated the rise of a socialist criticism of competitive capitalism. There was some continuity, usually indirect, between journeymen organizations and the early unions. Artisan cultures, ways of life, standards of work and loyalties – under challenge but not yet destroyed – played a positive role in the rise of a general working-class consciousness and in the rise of the early labour movement.

The early German labour movement: defensive protest or movement for emancipation?

Considerations and arguments such as these bring the history of the crafts and the history of the early working class close together. Furthermore, such considerations and arguments tend to modify the conventional view of the early labour movement. Historians have traditionally stressed a discontinuity between the *Handwerker* tradition and the labour movement; they correspondingly portrayed the labour movement as an essentially brand new, progressive, forward-looking movement of emancipation, whether revolutionary or not. Incidentally, this coincides with the view the labour movement has held of itself, in both its social democratic and communist wings (not withstanding deep differences in other respects). In this perspective early working-class protests were directed neither against the destruction of an old world nor against modernization, but rather against domination and exploitation by capitalists, the bourgeoisie, and, to a certain extent, the state. In contrast to this, an emphasis on the continuity between *Handwerk* traditions and the early labour movement tends to emphasize the defensive aspects of this movement, its protests against and resistance to modernization. In this view the 'contradiction' between capital and labour need not of course be ignored, but it is not a central issue. This perspective was never very influential among the leaders and spokesmen, the press and the iconography of the German labour movement. It fits well, however, with the present mood of some historians, social scientists and intellectuals who tend to feel that capitalist industrialization and the rise of the modern, increasingly bureaucratic state – Max Weber's rise of Western 'rationalization' – were by and large more a loss than a gain.[24]

Such questions are too broad to be discussed here, but this new approach has real merits in terms of our view of the early labour movement. The bringing together of craft history and workers' history allows both fields to apply new questions and to find new answers. In this way our understanding of the early labour movement develops. It was probably both a forward-looking movement for emancipation and a defensive movement of protest, in respect of which this second aspect has received too little attention in the movement's sense of itself and in the bulk of the literature.[25] But one must take care not to exaggerate this new perspective, particularly with regard to the German case. There were many tensions and discontinuities between the *Handwerk* tradition and the early labour movement, which may be approached through summarizing and developing three of the preceding arguments:

1. The craft-specific, skill-conscious, and exclusive nature of artisan loyalties were indeed major obstacles hindering the emergence of a comprehensive working-class consciousness and labour movement. So were the craft-specific ties between masters and men. Neither the early labour leaders nor the literature were wrong about that.[26] In this respect the labour movement could not build upon the previous *Handwerk* traditions but had to break with them.

2. Remnants of the guild system certainly survived in most German states until the 1860s, in other words right into the middle of the Industrial Revolution – in contrast to France and Britain. But they survived in a very unbalanced, class-biased way. They survived better on the side of the masters than on that of the journeymen. The master-dominated guilds had lost many of their previous functions in the course of the early nineteenth-century anti-feudal reforms; but they regained some of them in the subsequent decades, and in most German states the law granted them special privileges until the 1850s or 1860s. They usually controlled the apprenticeship system, they influenced the admission of new masters to the specific local craft, and they frequently controlled the journeymen's friendly societies, to the extent that these existed at all. They influenced the local labour exchanges and the placing of journeymen in jobs. The laws clearly distinguished between *Handwerk* and *Industrie*, and within the *Handwerk* they sharply differentiated along the class line between *Meister* and *Gesellen*, between master and men. In comparison with the masters' guilds the journeymen organizations displayed less continuity. The politics of the absolutist states had hit them harder, for in contrast to the guilds they had received much less political and administrative support. Consequently, demographic pressures, the rise of the market economy, the impact of extended underemployment and crises, and structural changes in the system of work had all weakened them much more thoroughly than the politically buttressed master guilds. These may well be the sources of a major difference between the experiences of Germany and of England and France. In Germany, it was not the journeymen but the master artisans and their surviving guild-type organizations who were the main bearers of corporate continuity, and the main supporters of its maintenance or restitution.

As a result, when the journeymen and workers organized they could not simply build on corporate traditions. They even had to turn against them, at least in part, since they had survived in a form heavily biased in favour of the masters and to the disadvantage of the men. From the perspective of the journeymen, the restrictive elements of the old order survived much better than its protective ones. To them, the gradual destruction of the old order was not only a threat but also a promise. The gradual dissolution of the living-in system, the removal of corporate barriers against opening up one's own business, the abandonment of privileges the masters had secured for their sons, and the liberation of the journeymen's friendly societies from the masters' domination can serve as cases in point. While most journeymen and workers were no admirers of the emerging system of capitalism, they were no staunch defenders of the old order, as it existed, either. It is understandable that the emerging German labour movement had both an anti-capitalistic and an anti-corporate thrust.

3. Compared with older journeymen movements the emerging labour movement of the 1860s and 1870s had many new and different elements. One piece of evidence will illustrate this point, although it cannot be analysed in any exhaustive fashion.

I have compared 259 cases of eighteenth-century journeymen strikes (*Aufstände*) in Nürnberg, Bremen, Frankfurt, Hamburg, Stuttgart, Munich and Berlin (mainly between 1780 and 1805) with about 1,150 strikes of industrial workers (including strikes of journeymen in small craft-shops and of artisans/workers in factories) in the German Reich between 1871 and 1878.[27] It is interesting to note that contemporaries apparently felt that the work stoppages of the 1860s and 1870s were something new. This is indicated by the language they used. Instead of the old expression *Aufstand*, normally applied to journeymen actions in the late eighteenth and early nineteenth centuries, they added to the words *Arbeitseinstellung* and *Feiern* the English expression 'strike', imported to Germany in the 1840s and becoming more common in the 1860s and 1870s. There seems to have been an awareness of something qualitatively different in comparison with the past. What was this difference?

The old journeymen protests and the strikes of the Industrial Revolution did not differ in the sense that the former were less 'rational' than the latter. One cannot, for example, establish that the eighteenth-century journeymen usually struck under poor business conditions and in periods of increasing hardship (with, consequently, little chance of success), whereas the workers of the 1870s usually walked out when the order books were full and the prospects of winning good. Nor is there any evidence for assuming that the eighteenth-century journeymen's actions were more spontaneous and less planned than the strikes of the 1870s. The eighteenth-century protests were supported by organization, namely journeymen brotherhoods, at least as frequently as the strikes of the 1870s were supported by unions and parties. The proportion of strikes that were successful from the strikers' point of view was not larger in the 1870s than in the late eighteenth century; the conflicts that ended in compromise became more frequent. (Every third to fourth strike in the 1870s ended this way.) In both samples the success of strikes varied strongly, being closely related to business conditions in the later period, whereas around 1800 it was related not just to business conditions but to other factors as well, such as government policies.[28]

It is sometimes assumed that the old journeymen boycotts were restricted to specific localities, whereas strikes of a later period were more geographically extended, partly due to the expansion of labour markets.[29] Our sources do not support this assumption. The large majority of the 1,150 strikes of the 1870s remained restricted to particular localities; supra-local (regional or even national) extension is documented in 54 cases only. (In every third case, however, information on this issue is lacking.) Certainly, there were many cases of financial support and expressions of loyalty by workers and organizations from other places, regions and countries, but one must not forget that this was equally true in the case of eighteenth-century journeymen. In every tenth case of our eighteenth-century sample, support by journeymen from other towns and regions is documented (usually in the form of other places joining the boycott declared by their colleagues against the specific guild or the town in general). In every fourth to fifth case striking journeymen left a town, and when they arrived at other places they expected solidarity from their colleagues.

There were, on the other hand, many differences, most of them less important in the present context. In the 1870s strikes were longer, bigger and certainly more frequent than in the eighteenth century. Journeymen strikes had been short before 1800: 42 per cent lasted only one day, 79 per cent took one week or less, and only 7 per cent lasted longer than four weeks. In the 1870s only 8 per cent lasted just one day and only 32 per cent took one week or less. But 34 per cent lasted longer than four weeks. Journeymen strikes had been small: 25 per cent involved up to 20 participants and only 31 per cent involved 100 persons and more. In the 1870s, only 12 per cent of the strikes had 20 participants or fewer, but 55 per cent had 100 or more. While eighteenth-century journeymen resorted to some sort of violence in every fifth or sixth strike, this proportion was much smaller in the 1870s. Military forces intervened in 7 per cent of the journeymen strikes, but only in 2 per cent of the strikes in the 1870s. Strikers were arrested in every fourth case in the eighteenth century, but only in 6 per cent of the cases in the 1870s. Compared with the eighteenth century, governments were less a target of the strikes of the 1870s, and less involved in them. This had probably still been different throughout the first half of the century and into the 1850s. The forms of protest had also changed in many respects. Hostels and parades were less important in the 1870s; leaving the city and waiting for the employers' concessions in an inn outside the walls had become rare; this is understandable since the strikers of the 1870s were usually no longer resident in the house of their employers, and a much larger proportion of them had families of their own compared with the striking journeymen of the eighteenth century who were mostly young and unmarried.

Here I want to stress two other differences. First, the social composition of the conflicting parties changed. On the one hand there was a slight increase in the co-operation of journeymen/workers across skill and craft lines. Only in 2 per cent of the cases had journeymen of different crafts struck together in the eighteenth century; by the 1870s, however, this percentage had risen to 10 per cent (20 per cent of the factory workers' and 6 per cent of the journeymen's strikes). In the eighteenth century support for strikers from other crafts is documented in 13 per cent of the cases. In the 1870s, however, every third strike was supported by one or several labour organizations, most of which were affiliated to or had some connection with the socialist parties or the First International, that is to say with labour organizations with an inter-craft basis. On the other hand, while at least 16 per cent of the eighteenth-century journeymen strikes had been supported by self-employed masters and their organizations, support for strikers by employers had dramatically declined by the 1870s to less than 1 per cent. This is very understandable, since the strikes of the 1870s concentrated much more exclusively than those of the eighteenth century on issues which were by necessity controversial between those who employed and those who were employed: on conflicts of distribution (wages, hours) in the first place, and, less important, on conflicts of authority. In contrast, issues of honour, life-style and guild privileges, with respect to which journeymen and masters might share interests and opinions, had lost their previous predominance. While the strikes of the 1870s still displayed a very high (though declining) degree of fragmentation along craft lines, they were clearly structured by the line of distinction between employers and workers, in contrast to before 1800. In both respects, but particularly in the second one, the strikes of the 1870s were more clearly structured according to class criteria than were those of the eighteenth century.

Second, the aims of the strikes in the 1870s were different from those in the late eighteenth century. This is a difficult question since the declared strike aims as documented in the sources were presumably not always identical with the real motives of the strikers, and, particularly in the eighteenth century, even the documented strike aims had many dimensions and are hard to categorize. Nevertheless, if one categorizes strikes by declared aims and central issues the following results emerge. Some 30 per cent of the eighteenth-century journeymen strikes were exclusively or dominantly concerned with violations of corporate custom and 'honour', without a recognizable relation to economic issues (for instance strikes on the grounds that a master had touched a dead animal). Twenty-three per cent of the cases dealt primarily with economic issues like wages, fines and the provision of daily consumption, less than 10 per cent with problems of working conditions (hours, Saint Monday, dismissals), 20 per cent primarily with problems of guild regulations of the labour market (such as employment of women or numbers of apprentices per master), and less than 20 per cent with problems of journeymen's corporate autonomy (for example, in regulating finances on their own). But in all issues and controversies questions of 'honour' and custom were additionally involved. In contrast, questions of honour and custom played a rather small role among the manifest aims of the strikes in the 1870s although they may have been among their more hidden motivations. Clearly, the strikers of the 1870s were more preoccupied with market-related issues, which had become more separable from issues of honour, custom and life-style than they had been in the eighteenth century. Workers struck to improve or defend wages in 76 per cent of the cases; they were concerned with questions of working hours (27 per cent) and other working conditions (9 per cent, including problems of job control and supervision); they fought for union rights (7 per cent) and they were concerned with a form of wage payments, such as the question of piece-rates (4 per cent).[30]

In the context of the present argument, the following contrast is of special relevance. When eighteenth-century journeymen left their work, they usually did so in response to some event or condition which they perceived as a violation of their traditional rights, customs and symbols, as a challenge to their corporate dignity and standing, as an attack on their norms and their ideal of a 'moral economy'. Economic interests and demands did play an important role, but they were presented and justified within the framework of largely non-economic, multi-dimensional claims, and usually in defensive terms. In contrast, at least eight out of every ten strikes in the boom of 1869–73 had an offensive character (for better pay, to improve work conditions and so on), and, indeed, real wages went up and work hours shortened during those years. Even in the subsequent down-swing every second strike was an offensive one, as far as one can see. While defensive attitudes and rhetorical claims based on the violation of traditional rights and customs were certainly effective in the 1870s, particularly with journeymen, this was no longer the dominant mood. To judge from the demands of the strikers and the aims of the organizations which frequently supported them, there was, more often than not, the quest for improvement and progress, the hope to get more, the desire to participate in what was correctly perceived as a process of overall growth and rising wealth, the struggle for rights never possessed before, which were claimed by stressing the general ideals of equality and emancipation, the rights of citizens and human beings. There had been a clear change from re-active and defensive to pro-active and offensive protests.[31] At what point of time between 1800 and the 1870s this change occurred is not quite clear. But it was certainly a gradual change with the year 1848–9 playing an accelerating role.

These last two points of difference seem to warn against exaggerating the continuity between *Handwerk* and working-class history. There were new qualities to the labour movement of the Industrial Revolution. As the strike analysis suggests, the early labour movement was not primarily a movement of defensive protest against threatening innovation and change, but, to a remarkable extent, a movement of emancipation that fought not so much against progress as for a fair share of its rewards.

NOTES

1 As an overview, J. Kocka, *Lohnarbeit und Klassenbildung. Arbeiter und Arbeiterbewegung in Deutschland 1800–1875* (Berlin 1983); Kocka, 'Problems of

Working-Class Formation in Germany. The Early Years (1800–1875)', in I. Katznelson and A. Zolberg (eds.), *Working-Class Formation: Nineteenth-Century Patterns in Western Europe and the United States* (forthcoming).

2 W. Abel *et al.*, *Handwerksgeschichte in neuer Sicht* (Göttingen 1978); W. Fischer, *Handwerksrecht und Handwerkswirtschaft um 1800* (Berlin 1955); Fischer, *Wirtschaft und Gesellschaft im Zeitalter der Industrialisierung* (Göttingen 1972), pp. 285–357; K.H. Kaufhold, *Das Handwerk der Stadt Hildesheim im 18 Jahrhundert* (Göttingen 1980); S. Volkov, *The Rise of Popular Antimodernism in Germany: the Urban Master Artisans, 1873–1896* (Princeton 1978); H.A. Winkler, *Mittelstand, Demokratie und Nationalsozialismus. Die politische Entwicklung von Handwerk und Kleinhandel in der Weimarer Republik* (Köln 1972).

3 E.J. Hobsbawm, 'Soziale Ungleichheit und Klassenstrukturen in England: Die Arbeiterklasse', H.-U. Wehler (ed.), *Klassen in der europäischen Sozialgeschichte* (Göttingen 1979), p. 59; W. Conze, 'Arbeiter', in O. Brunner *et al.* (eds.), *Geschichtliche Grundbegriffe: Historisches Lexikon zur politisch-sozialen Sprache in Deutschland*, Vol. I (Stuttgart 1972), pp. 216–42.

4 See n. 2, and M. Stürmer (ed.), *Herbst des Alten Handwerks. Zur Sozialgeschichte des 18 Jahrhunderts* (Munich 1979); J. Bergmann, *Das Berliner Handwerk in den Frühphasen der Industrialisierung* (Berlin 1973); H. Bopp, *Die Entwicklung des deutschen Handwerksgesellentums im 19 Jahrhundert* (Paderborn 1932); K. Schwarz, *Die Lage der Handwerksgesellen in Bremen während des 18 Jahrhunderts* (Bremen 1975); J. Jeschke, *Gewerberecht und Handwerkswirtschaft des Königreichs Hannover im Übergang 1815–1866* (Göttingen 1977); A. Griessinger, *Das symbolische Kapital der Ehre: Streikbewegungen und kollektives Bewusstsein deutscher Handwerksgesellen im 18 Jahrhundert* (Frankfurt 1981).

5 But see the modifications in E. Engelberg, 'Zur Forschung über Entstehung, Struktur und Entwicklung des Proletariats', *Beiträge zur Geschichte der Arbeiterbewegung*, 20 (1978), pp. 362–9; H. Zwahr, 'Zur Genesis der deutschen Arbeiterklasse. Stadiale und regionale Entwicklungsformen des deutschen Proletariats im Vergleich', in *Zur Entstehung des Proletariats: Untersuchungen zu den Vorformen, der Entwicklung, der Lage und der Struktur der Arbeiterklasse bis zum 19 Jahrhundert* (Magdeburg 1980), pp. 25–49.

6 On *Gesellen* see n. 4, particularly the work by Bergmann. On domestic workers, cf. R. Braun, *Industrialisierung und Volksleben: Veränderungen der Lebensformen unter Einwirkung der verlagsindustriellen Heimarbeit in einem ländlichen Industriegebiet (Zürcher Oberland) vor 1800* (Erlenbach-Zürich 1960, 2nd ed. Göttingen 1979); Braun, *Sozialer und Kultureller Wandel in einem ländlichen Industriegebiet (Zürcher Oberland) unter Einwirkung des Maschinen- und Fabrikwesens im 19 und 20 Jahrhundert* (Erlenbach-Zürich 1965); B. Schöne, *Kultur und Lebensweise Lausitzer Bandweber (1750–1850)* (Berlin 1977); still indispensable is the material in: A. Thun, *Die Industrie am Niederrhein und ihre Arbeiter* (2 pts.) (Leipzig 1879). Cf. of course the recent debate on proto-industrialization, esp. P. Kriedte *et al.*, *Industrialization before Industrialization: Rural Industry in the Genesis of Capitalism* (Cambridge 1982). Three recent monographs on workers in centralized work-places: R. Vetterli, *Industriearbeit, Arbeiterbewusstsein und gewerkschaftliche Organization: Dargestellt am Beispiel der Georg Fischer AG (1890–1930)* (Göttingen 1978); H. Schomerus, *Die*

114 Jürgen Kocka

Arbeiter der Maschinenfabrik Esslingen (Stuttgart 1977); K. Tenfelde, *Sozialgeschichte der Bergarbeiterschaft an der Ruhr im 19 Jahrhundert* (Bonn 1977); the representative sample of present research on nineteenth-century workers in the conference volumes: W. Conze and U. Engelhardt (eds.), *Arbeiter im Industrialisierungsprozess: Herkunft, Lage und Verhalten* (Stuttgart 1979); Conze and Engelhardt (eds.), *Arbeiterexistenz im 19 Jahrhundert: Lebensstandard und Lebensgestaltung deutscher Arbeiter und Handwerker* (Stuttgart 1981).

7 Institut für Marxismus–Leninismus beim Zentralkomitee der SED, *Geschichte der deutschen Arbeiterbewegung in 15 Kapiteln* (Berlin 1966); H. Grebing, *Geschichte der deutschen Arbeiterbewegung. Ein Überblick* (Munich 1966) (two widely read standard histories in East and in West Germany).

8 On the brotherhoods and their dissolution: Griessinger, *Das symbolische Kapital*; G. Schmoller, 'Das brandenburgisch-preussische Innungswesen von 1640–1806, hauptsächlich die Reform unter Friedrich Wilhelm I', in *Forschungen zur brandenburgisch-preussischen Geschichte*, Vol. I (Leizpig 1888), pp. 57–109, 325–83; B. Schönlank and G. Schanz, 'Die Gesellenverbände in Deutschland', *Handwörterbuch der Staatswissenschaften*, Vol. IX, 3rd edn (Jena 1909), pp. 662–73; K. Bücher, 'Frankfurter Buchbinder-Ordnungen vom 16 bis zum 19 Jahrhundert', *Archiv für Frankfurter Geschichte und Kunst*, 3rd ser., 1 (Frankfurt 1888), pp. 224–92; W. Reininghaus, 'Die Gesellenladen und Unterstützungskassen der Fabrikarbeiter bis 1870 in der Grafschaft Mark', *Der Märker*, 29 (Altena 1980), pp. 46–55; U. Frevert, 'Krankheit als politisches Problem 1770–1880 (Göttingen 1984), Chap. 3.

9 G. Beier, *Schwarze Kunst und Klassenkampf: Geschichte der Industriegewerkschaft Druck und Papier und ihrer Vorläufer seit dem Beginn der modernen Arbeiterbewegung*, Vol. I (Frankfurt 1966), pp. 34–5; H. Bürger, *Die Hamburger Gewerkschaften und ihre Kämpfe von 1865–1980* (Hamburg 1899), pp. 79, 111–2; U. Engelhardt, *'Nur vereinigt sind wir stark': die Anfänge der deutschen Gewerkschaftsbewegung*, Vol. II (Stuttgart 1977), pp. 757ff, 802ff; H. Müller, *Die Organisationen der Lithographen, Steindrucker und verwandten Berufe*, Vol. I (Berlin repr. 1978), pp. 120–31, 255–75, 289–302, 347–58, 397ff. A recent survey: H. Beier, 'Gewerkschaften, I: Geschichte', *Handwörterbuch der Wirtschaftswissenschaft*, Vol. 9 (Stuttgart 1981), pp. 641–59.

10 J. Kocka, 'Klassen oder Kultur? Durchbrüche und Sackgassen in der Arbeitergeschichte', *Merkur: Deutsche Zeitschrift für europäisches Denken*, 36 (Stuttgart 1982), pp. 955–65.

11 B.H. Moss, *The Origins of the French Labor Movement 1830–1914: the Socialism of Skilled Workers* (Berkeley 1976); W.H. Sewell, jr., *Work and Revolution in France. The Language of Labor from the Old Regime to 1848* (Cambridge 1980).

12 On Hanover with its surviving corporate structure see Jeschke, *Gewerberecht und Handwerkswirtschaft*; in contrast the Berlin situation was less structured by surviving corporate principles; Bergmann, *Das Berliner Handwerk*.

13 P.H. Noyes, *Organization and Revolution: Working-class Associations in the German Revolution of 1848–1849* (Princeton 1966); U. Engelhardt, 'Gewerkschaftliches Organisationsverhalten in der ersten Industrialisierungsphase', in Conze and Engelhardt (eds.), *Arbeiter im Industrialisierungsprozess*, pp. 372–402.

14 From different points of view: W. Conze, 'Möglichkeiten und Grenzen der liberalen

Arbeiterbewegung in Deutschland. Das Beispiel Schulze-Delitzsch', in *Sitzungsberichte der Heidelberger Akademie der Wissenschaften: Philosophisch-historische Klasse 1962* (Heidelberg 1965), pp. 5–28; reprinted in H.J. Varain (ed.), *Interessenverbände in Deutschland* (Cologne 1973), pp. 85–102. Autorenkollektiv, *Bürgerliche und kleinbürgerliche Sozialismus – Konzeptionen (1848–1917)*. German edn by W. Krause (Berlin 1976) (Russian edn. Moscow, 1974), esp. pp. 8, 10.

15 The best survey: C. Eisenberg, 'Theorie und Praxis der Produktivgenossenschaften in der deutschen Arbeiterbewegung der 1860er und frühen 1870er Jahre' (University of Bielefeld, State examination, 1980).

16 The different statements by Marx and Engels on *Genossenschaften* are documented and analysed in K. Kühne, *Marxismus und Gemeinwirtschaft* (Cologne 1978).

17 Engelhardt '"*Nur vereinigt sind wir stark*"'. But see the modifications in J. Breuilly's review in *Social History*, 4 (1979), pp. 393–7.

18 A. Herzig, 'Kontinuität und Wandel der politischen und sozialen Vorstellungen Hamburger Handwerker (1790–1870)', paper for the conference 'Handwerkerschaft und Industrialisierung', Bad Homburg, 18–20 Nov. 1982. The numerous papers for this conference, again organized by Conze and Engelhardt, displayed a renewed interest in the history of the crafts and in the relationship between craft and labour history. The papers will be published by Klett-Cotta (Stuttgart 1984).

19 This can be most clearly studied with respect to the organizations of the book printers and typesetters. W. Krahl, *Der Verband der Deutschen Buchdrucker: Fünfzig Jahre deutsche gewerkschaftliche Arbeit mit einer Vorgeschichte*, Vol. I (Berlin 1916). Continuity in the case of Berlin joiners is demonstrated in D. H. Müller, 'Binnenstruktur und Selbstverständnis der "Gesellenschaft" der Berliner Zimmerer im Übergang von der handwerklichen zur gewerkschaftlichen Interessenvertretung', conference paper, Bad Homburg, 18–20 Nov. 1982.

20 R. Boch, 'Was macht aus Arbeit industrielle Lohn–"Arbeit"? Arbeitsbedingungen und-fertigkeiten im Prozess der Kapitalisierung: Die Solinger Schneidewarenfabrikation 1850–1920', *Sozialwissenschaftliche Informationen*, 9 (Stuttgart 1980), pp. 61–66; J. Ehmer, *Familienstruktur und Arbeitsorganisation im frühindustriellen Wien* (Vienna 1980), pp. 74–89; F. Lenger, 'Aspekte der wirtschaftlichen und sozialen Lage der städtischen Handwerker um die Mitte des 19 Jahrhundert. Am Beispiel Düsseldorfs'. Conference paper, Bad Homburg, 18–20 Nov. 1982.

21 Illustrations in G. M. Hofmann (ed.), *Biedermeier auf Walze: Aufzeichnungen und Briefe des Handwerksburschen Johann Eberhard Dewald, 1836–1838* (Berlin 1936), p. 170. A most interesting case study on North German shipbuilders, artisans experiencing the rationalization of work in growing shipyards, is M. Cattaruzza, 'Handwerker und Fabriksystem: die Hamburger und Bremer Schiffszimmerer in den Anfängen der grossbetrieblichen Werftindustrie', conference paper, Bad Homburg, 18–20 Nov. 1982.

22 Other parts of the explanation must refer to the relatively good bargaining power of these occupations in the labour market.

23 H. Berndt, 'Die auf Grund des Sozialistengesetzes zwischen 1881 und 1890 Ausgewiesenen aus Leipzig und Umgegend. Eine Studie zur sozialen Struktur der deutschen Arbeiterklasse und Arbeiterbewegung' (Humboldt University, Berlin, Ph.D. thesis, 1972), pp. 399–419; Zwahr, 'Zur Genesis', pp. 42–3; R. Stadelmann and

W. Fischer, *Die Bildungswelt des deutschen Handwerks um 1800* (Berlin 1955), p. 189; J. Bergmann in *Die frühsozialistischen Bünde in der Geschichte der deutschen Arbeiterbewegung* (Berlin 1975), p. 147; H. Zwahr, *Zur Konstituierung des Proletariats als Klasse: Strukturuntersuchung über das Leipziger Proletariat während der industriellen Revolution* (Berlin 1978), p. 322.

24 D. Peukert, 'Arbeiteralltag-Mode oder Methode?', in H. Haumann (ed.), *Arbeiteralltag in Stadt und Land* (Argument-Sonderband AS 94) (Berlin 1982), pp. 8–39, 26–32; Kocka, 'Klassen oder Kultur?', pp. 962–4.

25 In this context historians seem to have rediscovered the role small masters played, for a limited period of time, in the early labour movement. Good evidence on Berlin tailors in W. Renzsch, *Handwerker und Lohnarbeiter in der frühen Arbeiterbewegung: zur sozialen Basis von Gewerkschaften und Sozialdemokratie im Reichsgründungsjahrzehnt* (Göttingen 1980), pp. 70–107. Renzsch also shows how strikes had the effect of dividing journeymen and small masters.

26 This is sometimes overlooked by those new labour historians who sympathize with the old craft tradition and criticize the socialist labour movement for not honouring, but disciplining them.

27 The eighteenth-century sample is from the unpublished data collected mainly from town archives by A. Griessinger (Konstanz) for his work quoted in n. 4. The data on the strikes of the 1870s seem to be nearly exhaustive, collected from: D. Milles, *Tabellarische Übersicht der Streiks and Aussperrungen im Deutschen Reich von Januar 1876 bis Dezember 1882*, mimeo (Constance); L. Machtan's figures on 1871–5 are expected to be published in *Streiks und Aussperrungen im deutschen Kaiserreich 1871–1875: eine sozialgeschichtliche Dokumentation* and *Arbeiterbewegung in der Konjunktur des Klassenkampfs: zwei Fallstudien zur Sozialgeschichte des Streiks im frühen Kaiserreich* (Frankfurt). I am most grateful to these three authors for having made available to me their unpublished material, and to Bernd Uhlmannsieck who has helped to classify, process and analyse the data. See his unpublished thesis, 'Handwerksgesellen-Ausrtände und Arbeiterstreiks in Deutschland vom späten 18. Jahrhundert bis zum Ende der ersten Industrialisierungsphase' (Bielefeld 1981). Equally good data are still lacking for the period 1805–70. Preliminary figures are found in E. Todt and H. Radandt, *Zur Frühgeschichte der deutschen Gewerkschaftsbewegung 1800–1849* (Berlin 1950), esp. pp. 68–79, 200–7; E. Todt, *Die gewerkschaftliche Betätigung in Deutschland von 1850–1859* (Berlin 1950), pp. 104–18, 98–100; W. Steglich, 'Eine Streiktabelle für Deutschland 1864–1880', *Jahrbuch für Wirtschaftsgeschichte* 1960, Part II, pp. 247–82; *Deutsches Handelsblatt: Wochenblatt für Handelspolitik und Volkswirtschaft*, 3 (1873), pp. 46–52; U. Engelhardt, 'Zur Entwicklung der Streikbewegungen in der ersten Industrialisierungsphase und zur Funktion von Streiks bei der Konstituierung der Gewerkschaftsbewegung in Deutschland', *Internationale Korrespondenz zur Geschichte der deutschen Arbeiterbewegung*, 15 (1979), pp. 547–68, 549. A good summary in K. Tenfelde and H. Volkmann (eds.), *Streik: zur Geschichte des Arbeitskampfes in Deutschland während der Industrialisierung* (Munich 1981), pp. 287–303 (with the available quantitative data 1848, 1869, 1871 to 1931). U. Engelhardt is preparing strike lists for the period between 1848 and 1870.

28 Results would certainly be different if one included crowd riots and early industrial protests of a Luddite type, which are excluded from this analysis. Consequently, our findings do not really contradict the 'received thesis' stressing the different timing (with respect to the cycle), the different degree of spontaneity, and the different chances of success of pre-industrial protests and industrial strikes. E.J. Hobsbawm, 'Economic Fluctuations and Some Social Movements since 1800' (1952), in *Labouring Men: Studies in the History of Labour* (London 1968), pp. 126–57, 130–3. From a German perspective it is surprising that journeymen strikes are rather neglected in general discussions of changing patterns of protest in the eighteenth and early nineteenth century; for example, D. Geary, *European Labour Protest 1848 to 1939* (London 1981), pp. 25–37 (on pre-industrial and early industrial protests).

29 For example, in the editors' introduction to Tenfelde and Volkmann (eds.), *Streik*, p. 18.

30 In the sample of the 1870s each strike could be counted in several categories at the same time if it displayed more than one type of aim. In the eighteenth-century sample each case was counted only once according to its dominant type of aim.

31 C. Tilly, 'Hauptformen kollektiver Aktion in West-Europe 1500–1975', *Geschichte und Gesellschaft*, 3 (1977), pp. 153–63, esp. pp. 157–8. Engelhardt ('Zur Entwicklung der Streikbewegungen', pp. 551–2) notes this change as well, but perhaps over-emphasizes the 1860s as the period of change between more defensive and more offensive actions.

5

Structures of subordination in nineteenth-century British industry

RICHARD PRICE

Historically, British social relations in production have posed a peculiarly obstinate set of problems for employers and latterly the state. Indeed, the persistent tendency of the British working class to erect informal structures at the workplace that resist and impede capitalist domination of the labour process might be seen as a distinctive national peculiarity. The historical nature of this tradition of workplace organization, the often long antecedents of (for example) restrictive practices, and the interaction between the informal history of industrial relations and wider labour history at the level of union organization, employer strategies and state policy all suggest the inadequacy of regarding these phenomena as the product of spontaneous economism.[1] The tendency for empirical discussion to focus around the formation of particular trade-union government structures, incomplete bargaining systems, and the transmission of craft restrictions to the unskilled, useful though these individual studies may be, bear more towards the symptoms of this peculiarity than its causes. These characteristics reinforce reluctance to treat the tradition of workplace organization with the degree of seriousness accorded to the historic origins of other forms of labour organization. But just as, say, the structure of union government is recognized to be grounded in past history, so the same is surely true of the tradition of workplace action. Both have contained important consequences for the recent history of industrial relations, but of the two it is arguably the latter that remains sorely in need of some broader historical and conceptual framework. In particular, it is necessary to ask what it was in the historical development of social relations in the labour process that permitted this peculiarity to emerge and (episodically) to thrive in Britain.

The historical study of the labour process has tended to emphasize the technical categories that contribute to its forms and structures. Whilst the importance of such elements as market forces hardly needs to be explained, it should not be forgotten that it is the search for authority that integrates the various aspects of the process.[2] Since this is so, the extent to which that search can be realized will be conditioned not merely by technical procedures but also by the extent to which those forces are able to modify, or are themselves modified by, the prior history and traditions of productive relations. The particular configuration of the strategies of dominance and resistance that result will be a function of the accommodation that can be reached between previous traditions and practices and present needs. Different industries and countries will experience distinct forms of that accommodation – which is a major reason why the same technology and capitalist structures are capable of generating very different relations in production.[3] Although the labour process techniques of capital flow generally in a common direction, the specificity of their form and of their relation to working-class action will be determined by the previous dimensions of productive relations.

In their treatment of the nature of change in the labour process historians have generally failed to recognize this dynamic, reducing it instead to a schematic economism. The problem goes back to Marx, who used the categories of 'formal' and 'real' subordination to distinguish different stages in the development of the capitalist labour process and tied each to a particular historical period. Formal subordination applied to the period of manufacture and real subordination to the period of modern industry. The key distinction turned on the extent to which execution of work lay within labour's discretion and the types of surplus value that were extracted in consequence. Under formal subordination, labour was tied to its employer solely by the wage relationship and, as a consequence, additional surplus value could be secured only by extending the working day. The utilization of science and technology allowed the capitalist to intervene directly in the labour process, secure surplus value through controlling the intensity of work and replace labour by machinery as the governing unity of the labour process.[4]

Whilst these concepts are extremely useful, Marx's tendency to reduce them to a purely economic level and to regard them as absolute needs to be modified. As the history of eighteenth-century labour shows formal subordination cannot be divorced from the social sanctions deployed through institutions such as the law and the rituals of paternal reciprocity which were necessary to supplement the technical control exercised through the market supremacy of capital. In addition, the technology associated with real subordination did not achieve the destruction of skill but rather its re-composition, which left workers viable bases from which to retain or create certain forms of protection in the labour process. For this reason real subordination is not merely an impersonal force, but an active strategy which can seldom be put into operation through technology alone and, indeed, may be expressed by structures which by-pass technological change.[5]

Finally, and for our purposes most critically, Marx did not adequately address the relationship between formal and real subordination and, in particular, the process of transition from the one to the other. He associated that transition quite simply with the inherent logic of capitalist industrialization; but the protracted, uneven and fractured nature of the industrializing process immediately suggests the inadequacies of this formulation.[6]

This, we may suggest, is of especial significance for Britain because the transition to industrialization was slower there than almost anywhere else. For about one hundred years Britain was indisputably an industrial capitalist nation both in its social structure and in its economic mainsprings, but one in which authority in the production process was secured within the framework of formal subordination. In consequence, the peculiarity of British social relations in production was forged by the entrenchment of traditions of resistance at the workplace which stood at odds with the implications of modern industry. Not until the end of the nineteenth century did formal subordination reach its limits as a means of securing industrial discipline and productivity. But real subordination could not merely then take over with the new technological or organizational arrangements of the second Industrial Revolution. The constraints of the past – in particular, the strong traditions of resistance at the workplace – ensured that real subordination could be a viable strategy only through a reformulated formal subordination. This occurred most significantly – though not exclusively – through the agency of the procedural instruments of collective agreements. Real subordination thus emerged out of contradictions within the prior tradition of social relations which continued to suffuse its character.

It is increasingly recognized that a significant fact about the Industrial Revolution was its technical incompleteness. Mechanization was limited essentially to the two sectors of cotton spinning and engineering; but even here large units of production created in their wake numerous smaller ones which remained the typical place of work. Similarly, mechanization itself spawned and depended upon a vastly expanded hand labour sector, both skilled and sweated, even in cotton textiles. In short, industrial capitalism mobilized wage labour on an unprecedented scale but organized and exploited it through traditional modes and methods.[7] The tendency to exaggerate the symmetry of industrialization was present from the beginning. Both Marx and Ure accepted the premise that mechanization combined with capitalist control over the division of labour was sufficient automatically to achieve subordination. They tended to assume that the substitution of 'mechanical science for hand skill' and the replacement of skilled labour by 'mere overlookers of machines' was already an accomplished fact. That this would occur immediately was a commonplace expectation amongst political economists and some employers in the 1830s. But the self-acting mule did not replace the hand mule until the 1860s and in both spinning and engineering the division of labour was recomposed in such a way as to allow skilled workers to transpose 'craft' skills and control onto the new structures of work.[8]

Indeed, the division of labour remained the main method by which employers endeavoured to control the execution of work, just as during the period of manufacture. Adam Smith's assumption that 'the greatest improvement in the productive powers of labour... seem to have been the effects of the division of labour' and his subordination of machine development to the division of labour was accepted by political economists well into the 1830s. The shift within political economy towards emphasizing the machine as the source of capital formation only began when the Industrial Revolution was almost complete. Although this implied a changing conception of the importance of superintendence, political economists contributed very little concerning the means whereby control over the productive process was to be implemented, because moving power itself was assumed to be an automatic guarantor. Throughout the period of industrialization and beyond, control over the division of labour continued to be the main aim of employer authority and their practical alternative to mechanization as the source of productivity.[9] Adam Smith's pin factory remained the model for capital's drive to integrate and co-ordinate production. The principal impediment to the full and free development of the division of labour, however, lay in the restrictions upon the labour supply imposed by the laws and practices of apprenticeship regulation. The crucial battles of the early nineteenth century revolved around this issue. The campaign for repeal of the Statute of Apprentices was initiated by the engineering employers of London (assuming for the first time their role as spokesmen for the rest of the employing class) eager to establish a new division of labour. In the 1820s the defeat of London tailors and shoemakers on the apprenticeship issue effectively ended their attempt to defend a handicraft division of labour. The destruction of the Grand National Consolidated Trades Union in the early 1830s allowed employers in the non-mechanized trades to rely upon a sweated toil to secure subordination.[10]

Within the work process itself, however, the central problem of discipline remained as it had been under the putting-out system: control over time. Frequent recourse to the law had failed to resolve this problem and mechanized factory production was seen by Ure at least as an inevitable stimulant to 'industrious habits'. But the realization of a capitalist definition of time required close regulation of behaviour both within and without the factory walls. A major part of Wedgewood's task was to combat the fairs, wakes, and drinking sprees indulged in by his potters. Elaborate rule books, systems of fines, lengthy contracts of employment (common in the factories until the 1840s) joined with the broader social attack upon pre-industrial culture to meet this problem. The uneasy compromise reached within the textile factories in the late 1840s did not extend to other sectors of labour. Until the 1870s, the major struggles of labour revolved around hours of work; Saint Monday remained a cultural force until the 1860s. The resistance to systematic overtime common to all skilled trades rested upon the notion that overtime lay within the men's sphere of authority. It reflected the continuing power of 'pre-industrial' concepts of independence well into the last third of the nineteenth century.[11] Conflict and trade union organization were stimulated as the logic of the market impinged upon custom. The most protracted strike in the Birmingham building trades in the 1830s was over the contractors' refusal to pay allowance money for beer – an issue capable of mobilizing the London shipwrights as late as 1856. Relationships were altered by a vast extension of traditional modes of exploitation rather than by creating thoroughly new relations in production. The expansion of such methods as the truck system in the coal, iron, railway and building industries suggests that this was the typical pattern.[12]

Since the denial of 'custom' was the central issue, the failure of proletarian ideology adequately to reflect the concealed shape of industrial capitalism is hardly surprising. The focus upon unequal exchange as opposed to unequal distribution, the interesting failure to separate politics and economics as classical political economy was beginning to do, the identification of middlemen, 'old corruption' and the tax structure as central parts of the radical critique, all revealed the fractured reality of social relations in production rather than the inadequacies of working-class consciousness.[13] Independence remained the key concept of a heightened, more unitary working-class consciousness precisely because it retained a certain viability at the point of production; the central threats to its survival flowed from loss of control over the division of labour, the market supply, and time. This was particularly true for the 'labour aristocracy' whose status was defined by their social, political and craft independence. Their ability to translate craft control and autonomy into the age of industrial capitalism reflected the ambiguous effects of the machine division of labour in the mechanized industries of cotton spinning and metals and the absence of this division in other trades such as building and shoemaking. Thus, independence in the eighteenth-century sense could be re-defined into autonomous regulation whose expansion in the mid-nineteenth century seems to have been a general feature of labour's experience.[14] The singular strength of the British aristocracy of labour lay in the fact that it did not represent a modern class formation, but a more ambiguous structure, able to define itself in more than economic terms because artisan notions of independence concerning running the machines, determining output and maintaining internal workshop discipline, remained viable foci for worker autonomy.[15]

Throughout the early and mid-nineteenth century the limited and fractured impact of mechanization ensured that the character of relations in production demonstrated fundamental continuities with the period of manufacture. Actual subordination remained formal rather than real. Perhaps the most suggestive, though negative, illustration of this was the notable failure of the Industrial Revolution to create new theories of managerial ideology or new structures of supervision. Past experience had taught the risks of delegating authority; direct oversight combined with profound suspicion of innovative interference (which in its turn reflected the delicate balance between order and authority in the factories) determined managerial attitudes towards supervision.[16] Indeed, this was reinforced by the fact that the central problem of discipline was correctly perceived as one of acculturating the unruly plebian culture of domestic workers. A more general social and moral reform was the key to the installation of industrious habits. The main energies of the early industrial pioneers were directed towards this end. When Boulton and Watt reorganized their labour process in 1800, for example, it was to combat the social freedom that an unrestrained control over time allowed the men. Just as Arkwright, Wedgewood and Robert Owen had deployed extensive and carefully tailored paternal structures to reform their workers, so Lord Londonderry constructed schools in every village to meet the challenge of unionization in the 1840s. The techniques and methods of moral reform were at one with the paternal structures of discipline within the factory itself where a face-to-face relationship was reinforced by various efforts to deflect responsibility for output onto the workforce itself. Robert Owen instituted a system of monitors, Boulton and Watt used the more common method of piece-work, to ensure that their workers made best use of their time; Wedgewood cultivated a fearsome reputation to keep productive efficiency high.[17] The importance attached to force of personality reflected the dependence of employer control upon hierarchical obedience; but since constant attendance by the employer was impossible, the evocation of paternal relationships was an extremely important strategy of subordination.

Paternal rhetoric and ideology were invigorated by industrialization because it created the necessity and the opportunity to re-create (as Cobbett put it) those 'chains of connection between rich and poor' that were endangered by economic progress. Nobody wanted to bring back the feudal system, intoned Arthur Helps, but 'there is the same need for protection and countenance on one side, and for reverence and attachment on the other'. He went on to recommend the 'parental relation' as the 'best model on which to form the duties of the employer to the employed'. But the hierarchy of obedience could only be legitimized if it was surrounded by the rituals of reciprocity and, in their different ways, early factory masters reconstructed the ambiance of paternal obligation in their schools, dwellings, libraries, festivals and prizes. Arkwright gave cows to his best workmen. These practices carried over into the second and third generation of industrialists and it has been suggested that the internalization of this bastardized paternalism through the family assured real subordination.[18]

It would be a mistake to ignore the significance of this paternal culture; it seems more reasonable to argue that the rituals of reciprocity resulted from the *absence* of alternative techniques of labor process subordination. These structures of paternalism were neither continuous nor universal but tended to be produced when subordination needed to be affirmed or when it had fractured and needed to be restored. The most ambitious attempts to create the milieu of familial loyalty were made in those places where tyrannical discipline was strictly enforced. 'Good feeling' and 'sympathy' were paralleled by compulsory renting, political victimization, fines and the direct authority of the overlooker. In these ways 'discipline in the mill and firm control over the labour process' was typically maintained, but they were methods that remained external to the labour process. In addition, these forms of paternalism possessed indefinable limits. Once these were reached, the formal nature of subordination was revealed in the employers' conception of industrial conflicts as struggles for authority. Strikes were treated as symptoms of the pathology of ignorance, strikers tended to be treated as wayward children. Not until the 1870s did industrial conflicts begin to be conceptualized as economistic struggles for rewards. Similarly, collective negotiation was generally rejected because it would destroy the myth of an individual relationship between masters and men. Paternal reciprocity was a delicate and complicated matter that was bargained and negotiated through symbolic rituals like the excursion to Blackpool, or the banquet and ball given by the first Blackburn employer to grant the 10 per cent wage increase in 1853, who received in return silver candelabra from his men; both occasions were part of the bidding between employers 'not merely for the labour services, but also for the loyalty and affection of their operatives'.[19]

When the paternal structure broke down, only industrial warfare could decide upon what terms it should be re-established, for there were no internal procedures available to restore hegemony. the central characteristic of formal subordination was that it depended upon sanctions and systems outside the workplace to maintain its legitimacy. In the eighteenth century this function was performed principally by the law whose role in the class hegemony of that period is now receiving serious attention. Concerning relations in production, the law provided a frequently invoked regulatory framework and compensation for the absence of employer control over work execution. Until the 1870s, the character of labour law remained fundamentally continuous with its eighteenth-century antecedents. The Act of 1825 lay firmly within that earlier tradition both in the nature of its statutory definitions and in the close relationship it maintained between statutes and cases. Earlier statutes had proscribed combinations in particular trades; the legislation of 1825 generalized that prohibition. Similarly, following earlier Acts regulating outworkers, it explicitly endorsed the subordinate status of workers by confirming the authority of the employer over the management and regulation of his business. The one innovation, of allowing action on wages and conditions of work, provided this was not linked to organization, had been anticipated by the Act of 1799. Indeed, as the history of eighteenth-century legislation revealed and as the genesis of the 1825 Act suggested, this formulation of legal relations was necessary precisely because relations in production remained so problematic. Huskisson pointed out that the necessity to repeal the more permissive Act of 1824 lay in 'that assumption of control on the part of the workmen in the conduct of any business or manufacture which is utterly incompatible with the necessary authority of the master at whose risk and by whose capital it is carried on'.[20]

The continuity of the law is most strongly evident in the fact that the statutes themselves closely restricted the possibilities of industrial action. Case law between 1825 and 1875 consisted largely of applying the negative implications of the statutes and contained virtually no precedents for the possibility of peaceful action. The legality of action on wages and hours was obviated by extending the definition of conspiracy in restraint of trade – a trend begun in the eighteenth century. Hence Stephen's remark in the 1880s that 'no part of the whole story is so remarkable as the part played by the judges in defining and ... creating the offence of conspiracy'. Before 1825, such offences had been limited by specific Acts to specific trades. The effect of the repeal of the combination laws was to generalize and extend this penalty.[21] Thus, until the 1870s, statute law remained broad enough to encompass both criminal combinations and violations of the statutory prohibition on industrial action.

The precise extent of the use of the law as an agent of industrial discipline in the mid-nineteenth century requires investigation. One authority has noted how 'strikes in the mid-Victorian generation led more directly to legal cases than had the many silent struggles of the first half of the century'. In some countries there were over 10,000 Master and Servant cases per year in the late 1850s and early 1860s. Contrary to the usual assumption, it is highly probable that the Master and Servant Law reached well beyond the non-factory trades, and was used extensively to prosecute absenteeism, enforce fines, punish individual acts of ill-discipline and to break strikes in all industries.[22] The end of this style of legal intervention came when the legislation of the 1870s transformed Master and Servant into Employer and Workman and separated the limit of industrial action from the legal existence of trade unions. Once the statutes neither restrained institutional presence (the possibility of industrial action) nor expressed the formal subordination of workmen to employers, the relationship between statutes and cases was reversed. With the removal of the offence of conspiracy to combine and the legalization of all types of industrial action outside molestation, it became the province of case law to define the limits of the statutes. This is shown by the pattern of labour law from 1875–1971. Case law developed particularly important initiatives at those periods (for example, the 1890s and 1960s) when tensions at the workplace required authority relations to be defined. The periodic intervention of liberalizing statutes to redress the balance of case law decisions reflected the persistence of a restrictive case law which had been integrated into the acts of 1871 and 1875 through the definitions of coercion and molestation.[23]

The demise of statutory expression of formal subordination reflected and reinforced that wider shift in the late nineteenth century to a more organized stage of social and class relations. But for over a century industrial capitalism had expanded and secured its hegemony largely through archaic economic and social formations. At work, reliance upon formal subordination permitted the transposition of pre-industrial notions of independence, especially by strategically placed skilled workers who transplanted traditions of resistance to capitalist control at the workplace. Until the later part of the century their presence posed no particular problem for British capitalism due to its general market supremacy. However, once the necessity arose to assert a real subordination of labour the obstacles presented by these traditions became of fundamental importance in determining not only the course of industrial conflict but also the shape and forms assumed by strategies of real subordination. Productive relations could not be re-cast without confronting the reality of these traditions; they could not be beaten into submission. Nor could they be outflanked by a thoroughly new Taylorist division of labour; pre-existing investment in productive techniques made it less feasible to ignore them and to reconstruct a new labour process as Henry Ford was able to do. Thus, the effort to impose real subordination was far more constrained by the presence of the past than it was elsewhere; real subordination was more problematic and complicated and its particular strategies were conditioned, formed and modified to take account of the firmly embedded traditions of resistance to capitalist control of the labour process.

The emergence of a strategy of real subordination occurred as the 'Great Depression' imposed both internal and external imperatives for a more demanding efficiency of production. The prolonged nature of the depression and its key elements – falling prices and profits combined with rising real wages and interest rates – could only be resolved by enhanced competitiveness. Thus, the initial response, facilitated by widespread unemployment, was to cut labour costs by increasing exploitation through traditional methods such as expanding piece-work and working hours. After the 1880s, however, the combined pressures of competition and labour militancy placed a premium on improving the techniques of production either through the application of newly available technology or the more effective operation of older methods. Both of these pointed towards a pervasive restructuring of the labour process and moved the question of intensified work to a general level of experience. These developments were complicated (and to a certain extent disguised) by the absence of a predominating new technological division of labour or even a rationalized reorganisation of production. Within the same industry old and new methods worked unsystematically together.[24] But in contrast to the early nineteenth century the expansion of exploitative methods soon exposed the limits of formal subordination and undermined its efficacy to govern productive relations. The process by which these limits were reached and real subordination emerged from the prior traditions of productive relations assumed three broad routes, which may be distinguished primarily by the degree of balance between the inherent demands of new techniques and the more effective operation of traditional methods.

The first category may be defined as one in which the intrinsic demands of new technology and methods implied a disruption of formal relations in production. Social factors were by no means irrelevant; the relative success of engineers in resisting the new division of labour in the 1890s demanded a re-thinking of social relations which led directly into the struggle of 1898, the collective agreement procedure and (as our prime example of this category) the premium bonus system. However, even without the opposition such methods were bound to meet, they could not successfully operate without a rearrangement of social relations in production. Premium bonus was designed to side-step the restriction of production which ordinary piece-work allowed and also to avoid the direct control required if day work was used to reduce labour costs. It aimed to restore individual competition by providing a bonus for the time saved over time allowed for a particular job. It should be noted that the emphasis in British premium schemes relied less on the crude Taylorist division of labour and more on the mystification of wages calculation whose computation was possible only with access to all job and time cards and rate tables. The aim of this sophistication was to encroach upon the discretionary sphere of 'setting up time', which in the non-standardized work that characterized British engineering occupied up to five times the run time and provided the key area of worker control. But the system was not a self-acting intrusion into the autonomy of worker time: 'if the men made a lot of money they did not come in before breakfast and possibly not on Monday morning'. It was constantly stressed, therefore, that the key to success was to remove discretion in wage bargaining away from the men and foremen into a specialized rate-fixing department where mathematical formulas would sever the worker-determined link between time and effort.[25] Thus, a more extensive apparatus of bureaucratic control was required to remove the mutuality which piece-work implied over time-keeping, job breakdown and rate determination and to define those matters as subject to managerially controlled scientific analysis. The intrusion of management mushroomed. Greater productivity required the employer to 'do all in his power to help his men do their best' by providing proper tools in a separate tool room with strict rules on their distribution and use. Wherever the system was introduced it 'brought management into touch at once with the methods employed in the workshop and their results in detail'.[26]

The premium bonus system was not alone in entailing bureaucratic intervention in the labour process. The traditional discretionary power of the men and foremen over cutting speeds ensured restrictive practices which could partially be countered by a central supply of lubricant, speed tables, and speed and feed men. But the invention of high-speed steel and its infiltration of Britain in the 1890s made it imperative that worker discretion over speed and cut be displaced by a scientific planning department. In its turn, this required a more formalized hierarchy to ensure that standards were achieved and kept. Thus, the more precise definition of the foreman's role (a feature wider than this sector alone) was achieved by separating them more fully from the work through the provision of offices, where they may 'never under any circumstances be out of sight of [their] men' and subjecting them to a new hierarchy of white-collar route clerks, instruction card men and time and cost clerks, whom one manual described as the 'shop disciplinarians'.[27]

In the utilization and application of science to the labour process, in the increasing specialization of supervisory function and in the prime emphasis that came to be placed on the necessary bureaucratic apparatus of control within the factory, these kinds of structural-technical forces most neatly reflect the original definition of 'real subordination'. But these types of development were far from typical of the process of changing social relations even in engineering. The mid-Victorian labour process was more usually disrupted by intensifying older methods of exploitation, adding a new item of technology or a new variation in organization. The main effect of changes of this kind was to threaten to downgrade traditional skills by speed-up or the creation of new classes of worker. In engineering, for example, the expansion of piece-work occurred where repetition work was dominant and premium bonus unnecessary; the expanded use of handymen on machine manning actually completed a process begun in the 1840s which had been halted by worker resistance. In spinning, the increased use of lower-quality yarn implied a speeded-up work process and reduced status; the newly acquired occupational identity of cardroom workers was being challenged by the attempt to add extra duties to their work and so reduce them again to jobbing general labourers.[28] In printing, the linotype machine did not require a reconstructed hierarchy of authority and in boot and shoe making the mechanization of lasting and the trend towards factory production went hand in hand with the expansion of traditional methods of intensification. In these sectors the problem was how to modify the pre-existing structure of social relations without impairing their effectiveness in achieving productivity. As long as the authority of an employer could secure compliance, the purely technical alterations themselves did not demand the transcending of formal subordination. Thus, we tend to see employer efforts to control the labour process manifested by such traditional means as the method of wages payment and the assertion of control over them. But it proved impossible to contain the expansion of such methods within the limits of traditional relations in production because the restrictive traditions of the workers effectively impeded their productivity potential. In this sector, the limits to formal subordination were reached through a process of socio-structural change where the necessity to alter social relations was not inherent in the techniques themselves but rather in the effort to impose them through traditional modes of exploitation.

The relationship of the linotype to employer control over execution, for example, lay not so much in the machine itself but in the restrictions that the men tried to impose on its mode of operation. To work the linotype to its fullest advantage required employers to secure improved control over time. Initially, employers tended to demand long-term contracts whilst in later years there was a distinct tendency to erect tighter rules on time-keeping. Similarly, employer control of overtime formed a central issue in all the negotiations of the period. It was a telling illustration of printers' traditional power at the workplace that the first introduction of the linotype had been made on very advantageous conditions. Employers were willing to accept piece wages and the placing of apprenticed compositors on the machine as the price of guaranteeing its smooth introduction. But these concessions generated enormous wages and effective restriction of production, enforced by the men's refusal to allow machines to be fitted with automatic counters.[29] The problem was accentuated by the autonomy of local union branches who engaged in successful leap-frogging claims. At the local level, employers were led explicitly to insist on their right to manage; but at the national level, the market structure of printing (which confined questions of productivity to the time of production rather than its cost), the lack of an imperative to full-scale rationalization, and the superior technical expertise of the men, all combined to deter employers from full-scale confrontation with the union. National collective agreements provided the only means of mitigating the local power of the men and the only feasible road to altering relations in production to end the traditional exclusion of employers from the determination of the conditions of work. Similarly, the pressures of unemployment, the spread of piece-work, and the threats of linotype employers to secure an alternative labour supply through training schools were all working to make the men receptive to the idea of mutual negotiation.[30]

Thus, from the beginning, the linotype employers (which meant mainly those in the newspaper sector) moved to end autonomous regulation by subjecting those issues which restricted efficient working to collective agreement and establishing the authority of central negotiations over local conditions. Their successes in 1896 and 1898 were limited and not until 1911 did they gain a moratorium on hours agitation, the right to measure output and the supremacy of a national conciliation board over the rights of local units to call strikes. The relevance of this strategy to managerial authority was revealed most clearly in Scotland where since 1900 employer attempts to secure mutual negotiation had foundered on the principles of autonomous regulation and rank and file sovereignty. A particularly restrictive set of rules in 1912 inspired employers to present a united front, demand an end to formal subordination and extend negotiation beyond wages and hours into areas traditionally the authority of the men:

> This is the first time in the history of the association that a demand has been made on the part of the employers for a say in the framing of these rules. Of course, the rate of wages paid and the hours constituting a normal day's work have been invariably fixed by mutual agreement, but in regard to such other rules as have been introduced, until now these have gone unchallenged.

By 1913, of course, the possibility of maintaining a viable justification for autonomous regulation had long since passed. Pressured very heavily by the National Federation of Printing and Kindred Trades (which played the role of honest broker), the Scottish union ultimately agreed to inclusive bargaining.[31]

Boot and shoe employers faced similar problems. In this industry, the labour process power of the men was less solidly entrenched than in printing and the imperative to organizational changes in the form of a fully developed factory division of labour was considerably greater. Nevertheless, the conflicts in the industry revolved essentially around the same issue of how to counter the constraints imposed by the men on the modified forces of production. One answer was to disperse the productive process into the non-unionized areas of the Midland villages or the East End of London. The 1880s saw a marked increase in basket working and sweat shops in these locations. But this was effectively countered by union organizers chasing after the work, by the militancy of the better-class workers in London and by the competitive pressures of the mass market which made centralized production a virtual necessity. But this development immediately raised the question of control over time, which workers had traditionally secured through the negotiation of complicated piece-rate scales. In no other industry, it was claimed, was so much time lost by walking about and other manifestations of worker control over the pace of working. In the early 1890s the Midland employers were obliged to launch a general attack upon such social customs as the autumn race meetings and the spring militia training period.[32]

The inability to fit the demands of the new techniques into the existing structure of authority relations was further illustrated by the successful resistance of the men to the spread of the team system – a truly Taylorist subdivision of labour – which made it desirable to switch from piece-work to day wage and to hire boy labour. Although the union dropped its opposition to day wages in 1888, employer efforts to secure a smooth reorganization of production were impeded by intensifying restriction of output in the early 1890s. By 1894, for example, branch control of overtime was official policy and in Leicester restriction of output was scientifically managed by committees which calculated how much should be produced under the prevailing day system.[33] By the middle nineties the inability of employers to secure the necessary degree of subordination was manifest. The conciliation and arbitration system erected in 1892 was of no help. Many of its local boards had been destroyed by the refusal of the men to abide by their decisions. The right of the union to bring any issue before the Board together with the requirement that awards be based on custom and practice reinforced the obstructive power of the men. Equally, collective organization was too strongly entrenched to destroy and potentially too advantageous to be ignored. The consensus within the manufacturers' association was that union officials had lost control of the rank and file who 'have formed an overweening estimate of their own strength'.[34] Thus, the central task was to reduce the restrictive control which militancy imposed on the forces of production through collective agreements and procedures that would legitimate employer authority. The employers' demands leading to the 1895 lock-out reflected the necessity to shift social relations from a purely formal basis to one which secured employer control over work execution; employers were to be free to make any regulation regarding the working of the factory, to have sole authority over time-keeping; either piece or day wages could be paid; machines were to be introduced wherever the employer peased; there was to be no piece-work on the new lasting machines, no restriction of output and employers were free to employ whomever they pleased. As in engineering, this authority was protected by the conciliation procedure which denied the union the right to initiate questions before the board, restricted board responsibility to hours and wages, and abolished the central arbitration board. It was ten years before the union and militancy were able to revive. Unsurprisingly, the years following 1895 saw the most rapid expansion of technical change and organization.[35]

If the extensive relative autonomy of mid-Victorian skilled labour was being broken up in sectors subjected to a variety of technical and organizational changes, by a concurrent process the limits of formal subordination were reached more purely through its own internal contradictions. This process was primarily a social dynamic from which technical or structural change were not completely absent but proceeded slowly and without contradicting the nature of productive social relations. Resistance was created and made viable by the intensification of the existing division of labour sought through the continued assertion of paternal control. Indeed, the common theme of increased exploitation in this sector was the use of traditional methods of extending the work day or imposing, through the over-stocked labour market, a sweated style of wage cutting, both of which placed hours limitation at the centre of the agenda of resistance.

The docks and gas works illustrate one variant of this process. In both cases, the expansion of traditional modes of exploitation intensified the prior division of labour, allowed a greater specialization of job function and occupational identity and shattered the mid-Victorian 'general labourer' category, to create a semi-skilled stratum able to contemplate unionized resistance. The explosion of the 'new unionism' may be seen as the conjuncture of this development with the trade cycle opportunity of 1888–92.[36] The temporary success of the new unionism in the docks and gas works signified the inadequacy of relying purely upon the internal fragmentation of labour to secure control. In both cases the restoration of employer discipline mainly took the form of revitalized formal subordination. The creation of a 'free labour' organization by the shipowners was the most ambitious expression of that process, until in 1912–20, the possibility of collective organization was at last realized.

In the gas works, control was not recreated so unambiguously. The strike wave of the late eighties killed arbitrary paternal control as a way of securing the intensification of work that had been growing since 1880. In the north of England, where the municipalities owned the gas supply, collective bargaining was fairly rapidly conceded – although not without some very fierce struggles. In London and elsewhere, however, authority relations were reconstructed by linking a profit-sharing system to obedience. Formulated by George Livesey (and by 1914 adopted by 33 other companies employing 250,000 men), this scheme required a one-year contract, prohibited union membership, specified forfeiture of bonus if strikes occurred, demanded absolute obedience to the foremen and complete authority of the employer over the deployment and distribution of labour. Increased production was achieved by investing one-half of the bonus in company stock and linking its scale to the selling price of gas. It is somewhat ironic that a system of labour control that had been tried and failed in mid-Victorian industry, and which most contemporaries felt to be too indirect to produce effective results, became the main instrument of subordination in the gas industry until the 1920s.[37] The challenges of the late eighties were a shock to the docks and the gas works because they revealed that the structural modifications necessitated by the 'Great Depression' had undermined the arbitrary exercise of paternal discipline. Elsewhere, the social contradictions of formal subordination were exposed by a more active process.

On the railways and in the slate industry, reduced profits led employers to seek greater intensity of exploitation through the aggressive assertion of paternal control which disrupted the traditional balance of social relations, stripped the mask from reciprocity and rendered paternal authority problematic.[38] With the possible exception of coal mining, the railways provided the clearest example of modern industry expanding within the context of a formal subordination of labour. Discipline was secured by an exchange between company welfarism and job security in return for militaristic obedience. This reciprocity was dictated by the demands of the time-table, the impossibility of direct supervision and the enormous contradiction that placed the productive forces almost completely in the workers' hands. No other industry, perhaps, relied so much on worker skill and responsibility. The nature of formal subordination was perfectly reflected in the isolation of the signalman in 'his' box, the possession of individual trains by their drivers, and of certain brake vans by goods guards. As Frank McKenna shows, 'bailiwicks' of autonomy were created within which 'a man could often create his own administrative system' and exercise a proprietorial job control.[39] Infringements of this autonomy undermined a structure of subordination that had been remarkably successful for 40 years.

By the late 1880s, railway companies faced the triple pressures of declining revenue, heightened capital improvements required by the state, and a diminishing flexibility of labour costs due to victorious hours strikes in the late 1880s and restrictive legislation in 1893 and 1894.[40] Cost saving efforts were, thus, displaced from the traditional control over time and towards a more efficient use of time and resources which disrupted and confounded paternal loyalty. New pay and promotion scales raised the spectre of reduced job status and security; new disciplinary procedures denied the essence of paternal fairness and reciprocity. Reclassification schemes removed the sense of security and status which so pervaded railway-worker consciousness. Experimentation with the 'trip system' of payment promised rate cutting and the creation of a class of casualized guards required to be on hand to deal with sudden surges of traffic. Signalmen were confronted with secretly determined rate scales, reduced wages and arbitrary transfers; job security was subverted by electrical systems of signalling which threatened to diminish the labour force. In 1886, the Midland Railway abolished the guaranteed week and imposed a new schedule of fines for such transgressions as allowing coal to fall from the tender or refusing to pass signals at danger. In the 1890s, the Taff Vale Railway instituted a new policy of instant dismissals and grade reductions so that 'experienced drivers have been suspended and reduced who are yet unable to discover their offence'. Work tasks were intensified by a variety of means. There was a growing tendency to adopt American-style pooling arrangements, to use larger wagons and to bring train loads more into line with engine capacity. After 1900, increased tonnage and mileage per goods train was coupled with a contraction in total volume of traffic, so that firemen not only shovelled more coal but were also less likely to achieve promotion to driver. Interlocking points increased the intensity of signal work.[41] The agglomeration of these developments in the 1890s and early 1900s and their direct relationship to the intrusion upon bailiwicks that marked the companies' search for more efficient working methods, infused them with an explosive potential.

In addition, it was widely recognized that shrinking profit margins could best be reversed by a more ordered movement of trains and a series of reforms was recommended to define duties, improve record keeping and establish more precise lines of authority. More significant, though, was the revision of the whole system of traffic management which rested upon ascertaining the general level of demand in each centre and moving empty wagons towards their location. This system was inelastic. It could not respond quickly to unforeseen fluctuations, but neither did it demand a bureaucratized managerial control. The real change in the structure of railway discipline and management came after 1900 when companies began to adopt the American practice known as the control system, which was designed to match movement of rolling stock to availability and need through a tightly centralized administration of flow and supply. Like the specialization of supervisory function in engineering, the system depended upon close bureaucratic oversight and required a strictly enforced hierarchy of obedience and accountability to the district controller: 'the essential characteristic of the control system is that orders are conveyed speedily at any moment from headquarters'.[42] At Middlesborough, for example, the traffic controller was in constant contact with all signal boxes by telephone and monitored each movement; his presence was also felt in the driver's cab by the system of plotting movement on a control board so that 'if necessary, further instruction to the guard can be issued by the controller' through the signalman. As was pointed out at the time, 'the control system is causing a revolution in railway methods of working' not so much because it demanded a new kind of obedience but more because the level of subordination required disrupted the traditional balance between domination and autonomy.[43]

The control system was consistent with the strategy pursued since the early nineties of endeavouring to secure greater efficiency on the basis of a discipline that assumed unlimited paternal authority. But these policies contradicted paternal reciprocity because they changed the rules that had previously governed social relations in production. Amongst the litany of complaints that Taff Vale railwaymen made against Ammon Beasley's intrusive style of management was that alterations in the uniforms issued to the men reduced the distinctions between grades and made everyone 'go around looking more like tramps than anything else'. More seriously, the case of signalman Ewington, which sparked the Taff Vale strike of 1900, illustrated the same contradictory tensions. In ordering Ewington to move to another box, and in refusing to respect his right to retain his 'own' box, the company had removed one of the bases upon which loyalty rested because such a refusal was not customarily defined as a breach of discipline.[44] Thus, the violence associated with the strike of 1900 was the climactic breakdown of paternal loyalty whose progression through the nineties was marked by each piece of managerial aggression being matched by a consequent strengthening of union membership. Not only was Taff Vale one of the most profitable lines in the country, it was also the most highly unionized and, given the methods Beasley had applied to turn a struggling line into a prosperous one, the relationship seems a natural partnership. One kind of reciprocity had been replaced by another.

The strikes occasioned by the guard Richardson and driver Knox cases (1912 and 1913) signified the same theme of a paternal authority undermined by its own excesses. Both involved the claim of the companies to complete obedience. The Knox case was particularly interesting because the dismissal of a man who was drunk off duty represented the assertion of a total control over habits and life acceptable 20 years before because it was seen as part of a whole system of paternal relationships. By 1912 that system had been gutted of any meaningful reciprocity.

In its place, solidarity shifted to the union and to the vaguer but no less important sense of collectivity epitomized by the all-grades movements, whose emergence in the 1890s was a clear manifestation of the demise of paternal loyalty. Certainly, by 1911, the time honoured approach of petitioning was rejected as 'degrading' and traditional upholders of isolated individualism like signalmen had emerged as the prime movers in syndicalist and all-grades action.[45] By the early 1900s, therefore, the limits to formal subordination of labour on the railways had been effectively reached, but only the North Eastern Railway tried to resolve the consequent problem of legitimacy by union recognition. Most companies followed the example of Beasley of Taff Vale, who systematically refused to allow any collective group to intervene between himself and the rights of individual petitioners. Increasingly this was a sham; the men showed growing disinterest in retaining such rights. The significance of the Taff Vale case lay precisely in the attempt to fill the void of authority that had opened up by clarifying the limits of trade-union action and responsibility – exactly the issue the statutes left undefined. Devolving a disciplinary function onto the unions contained distinct attractions for the union leaderships – Richard Bell (general secretary of ASRS) actually welcomed the judgment – but it could only work as part of a collective bargaining reward structure. The refusal of the companies to accept this consequence was less a function of ideological obstinacy and more of fear of the impact bargaining would have upon labour costs, given government control of rates. Once the government promised to revise the rates, the companies accepted collective bargaining structures, but not until they were allowed to link rate charges to labour costs did they operate the system in good faith.[46]

The conciliation system erected in 1907 and amended in 1911 cannot be seen simply as the product of union agitation and government pressure. Indeed, the scheme was instigated by Sam Fay, manager of the Great Central, its form decided in tortured discussions inside the Board of Trade, and it was presented to the unions, on twenty minutes notice, as non-negotiable. The system regenerated prior relations in production by formalizing what the companies had always been willing to grant and legalized an authority previously secured paternally. The conciliation boards were organized on a sectional basis, which reinforced the natural fragmentation of the railway workers. Union officials were excluded, the principle of direct representation preserved, and preceding any appeal traditional petitioning channels had to be utilized. Employers' authority was explicitly protected, they retained the right to interpret arbitrators' awards and the discretionary power to exclude disciplinary issues. In contrast to France, where the contemporaneous radicalization of railwaymen may be attributed to more 'political' causes, in Britain the process was rooted in changing relations of authority at the workplace.[47]

This was a common theme in these years. Whatever the precise effects upon industrial militancy, political radicalism or internal union structures, the central feature of class relations in this period is the shift from an obedience based upon hierarchy to one secured by consent through procedural structures and bargaining institutions. Technical changes in the division of labour had fractured or undermined prior traditions of social relations but were themselves inadequate to secure the necessary changes in the structure of authority. The reason for this was that the industrial capitalist labour process was far less *tabula rasa* in Britain than elsewhere and, in consequence, formal subordination continued to infuse the strategies devised to secure real subordination. Thus, whether the imperative for real subordination emerged from a new division of labour or an extension of the old, it was obliged to operate through procedures that reconstituted legal affirmations of formal subordination. The necessity to formulate the strategy of managerial intervention in this way, however, preconditioned both its success and the characteristic focus of British industrial relations on procedural rules as opposed to the substantive regulation of local bargaining (which is characteristic of Germany and the USA). That focus, dictated by the need to constrain localism, confirmed and enhanced the importance of union dominated structures of collective bargaining, but it also left open the possibilities for workplace organization to thrive. The period is also marked by the emergence of shop stewards' and workshop committees which represented the formalization of previously informal traditions of resistance in the labour process and the genesis of the modern alternative system of industrial relations.

Both official and unofficial systems are crucial to understanding the course of social relations in modern Britain, but it is the strongly entrenched unofficial system which has posed the central problem of productive relations by its fluctuating and uneven contestation of authority at the workplace. The historical lineage of this system, its complex relations with the official system, have received all too little attention. Indeed, the significant questions need to be directed beyond those limits and towards its role in the subsequent development of British capitalism. It may be argued that this aspect of working-class experience represents a legitimate historical tradition which has to be related to the failures of British capitalism effectively to re-structure, the historical character of managerial ideology and the issues and concerns of national politics.[48] Our

138   Richard Price

immediate purpose, however, has been more modestly to suggest that this feature
of labour in society derives from the specific historical development of productive
social relations in Britain since the Industrial Revolution.

NOTES

1 Richard Price, 'Re-thinking Labour History: the Importance of Work', in James
   Cronin and Jonathan Schneer (eds.), *Social Conflict and the Political Order in Modern
   Britain* (London 1981).
2 Richard Edwards, *Contested Terrain* (London 1979); Harry Braverman, *Labor and
   Monopoly Capital* (New York 1974); David Noble, 'Social Choice in Machine
   Design', *Politics and Society* 8, nos. 3–4 (1978); Richard Price, 'The Labour Process
   and Labour History', *Social History* 8, no. 1. (Jan. 1983).
3 Duncan Gallie, *In Search of the New Working Class* (Cambridge 1978), pp. 300–6,
   314–18; W. Lazonick, 'Production Relations, Labour Productivity, and Choice of
   Technique: Britain and US Cotton Spinning', *J. of Econ. Hist.* 41 (Sept. 1981).
4 Karl Marx, *Capital*, Vol. I (Moscow, repr. of 1887 English edn.), pp. 13, 329, 364,
   477–78; *Grundrisse* (New York 1973), p. 693; *Capital* (Penguin edn. 1976), 'The
   Immediate Results of the Process of Production', p. 1024.
5. Charles More, *Skill and the English Working Class* (London 1980); W. Lazonick,
   'Industrial Relations and Technical Change: the Case of the Self-acting Mule',
   Cambridge J. of Econ. 3 (September 1979); see Daniel Clawson, *Bureaucracy and the
   Labor Process* (New York 1980).
6 Patrick Joyce, *Work, Society and Politics* (Hassocks 1980), pp. 52, 61, 226; Gareth
   Stedman Jones, 'Class Struggle and Industrial Revolution', *New Left Review* 90
   (1975), pp. 49–50, 63, 65; More, *Skill and the English Working Class*, pp. 227, 235–6;
   Maxine Berg, *Technology and Toil* (London 1979), pp. 5–6.
7 V. Gatrell, 'Labour, Power and the Size of Firms in Lancashire Cotton in the Second
   Quarter of the 19th Century', *Econ. Hist. Review* 30, no. 1 (1977); R. Samuel, 'The
   Workshop of the World: Steam Power and Hand Labour in mid-Victorian Britain',
   History Workshop Journal 3 (Spring 1977), p. 15; C.K. Harley, 'British Industry
   before 1841: Evidence of Slower Growth During the Industrial Revolution', *J. Econ.
   Hist.* 42, no. 2 (June 1982).
8 Marx, *Capital*, p. 689; Andrew Ure, *The Philosophy of Manufactures* (New York repr.
   1968), pp. 20, 21, 23; Samuel, 'The Workshop of the World', p. 19; Lazonick,
   'Industrial Relations and Technical Charge'.
9 Adam Smith, *The Wealth of Nations* (New York 1937), pp. 9, 14; Maxine Berg, *The
   Machinery Question and Political Economy* (Cambridge 1980), pp. 6, 10, 14, 125–30,
   144.
10 Iowerth Prothero, *Artisans and Politics* (Folkestone 1979), pp. 58–9; John Rule, *The
    Experience of Labour in the 18th Century* (London 1980), pp. 96–97, 109–12, 114–19;
    T.K. Derry, 'The Repeal of the Apprenticeship Clauses of the Statute of Apprentices',
    Econ. Hist. Review, 1st ser., 3 (1931–2); E.P. Thompson, *The Making of the English*

Working Class (New York 1963), pp. 280–3; M.J. Haynes, 'Class and Class Conflict in the Early Nineteenth Century', *Literature and History* 5 (Spring 1977); T.M. Parsinnen and I. Prothero, 'The London Tailors' Strike of 1834 and the Collapse of the GNCTU: a Police Spy's Report', *Internat. Review of Soc. Hist.* 27, pt. 1 (1977); G.D.H. Cole, *Attempts at General Unionism* (London 1953), Chap. 15.

11 Ure, *The Philosophy of Manufactures*, p. 279; R.S. Fitton and A.P. Wadsworth, *The Strutts and the Arkwrights 1758–1830* (Manchester 1958), pp. 99–101, 233–6; Neil McKendrick, 'Josiah Wedgewood and Factory Discipline', *Hist. J.* 4, 2 (1961), pp. 38, 51; Berg, *The Machinery Question*, p. 233; Gosta Langenfeldt, *The Historic Origins of the Eight Hours' Day* (Stockholm 1954); Douglas Reid, 'The Decline of St Monday 1766–1876', *Past and Present* 71 (May 1976); Richard Price, *Masters, Unions and Men: Work Control in Building and the Rise of Labour 1830–1914* (Cambridge 1980), pp. 90–1, 112, 146–8, 150; Prothero, *Artisans and Politics*, pp. 336–7.

12 Rule, *The Experience of Labour*, pp. 195–7; Clive Behagg, 'Custom, Class and Change: the Trade Societies of Birmingham', *Soc. Hist.* 4, no. 3 (October 1979), pp. 467–9; *Webb Collection* (British Library of Political and Economic Science), E. A. Vol. 32, ff. 38–9.

13 Patricia Hollis, *The Pauper Press* (Oxford 1971), pp. 210, 244, 246–7, 286–7; Prothero, *Artisans and Politics*, pp. 336–7; Berg, *The Machinery Question*, pp. 313–14.

14 Rule, *The Experience of Labour*, pp. 201–2; Keith Burgess, *Origins of British Industrial Relations* (London 1975), pp. 38–9; Alan Fox, *The National Union of Boot and Shoe Operatives* (Oxford 1958), pp. 66–70; Price, *Masters, Unions and Men*, pp. 79–94.

15 Geoffrey Crossick, *An Artisan Elite in Victorian Society* (London 1978); Thomas Wright, *Some Habits and Customs of the Working Classes* (New York repr. 1967), pp. 103–4.

16 Cf. Germany, where a supervisory bureaucracy was created at the very beginning of the industrializing process; see Jürgen Kocka, 'Capitalism and Bureaucracy in German Industrialization before 1914', *Econ. Hist. Review* 34 no. 3 (August 1981); Sidney Pollard, *The Genesis of Modern Management* (Harmondsworth 1968), p. 35; Joyce, *Work, Society and Politics*, pp. 100–1, 162; Dennis Chapman, 'William Brown of Dundee 1791–1864: Management in a Scottish Flax Mill', *Explorations in Entrepreneurial History* 4 (1952), pp. 124–5, 129.

17 Eric Roll, *An Early Experiment in Industrial Organisation* (New York repr. 1968), pp. 186–7, 192, 201; McKendrick, 'Josiah Wedgewood and Factory Discipline', p. 39; Sidney Pollard and John Salt (eds.), *Robert Owen: Prophet of the Poor* (Lewisburg 1971), pp. 149–53; Robert Colls, '"Oh Happy Children!" Coal, Class and Education in the North East', *Past and Present* 73 (November 1976), p. 176.

18 John Seed, 'Unitarianism, Political Economy and the Antinomies of Liberal Culture in Manchester 1830–1850', *Soc. Hist.* 7, no. 1 (1982), pp. 22–5; Arthur Helps, *The Claims of Labour* (London 1846), pp. v, vi, 157; Fitton and Wadsworth, *The Strutts and the Arkwrights*; Eric Sigsworth, *Black Dyke Mills* (Liverpool 1958), p. xi; Joyce, *Work, Society and Politics*, pp. 124, 153, 180–3.

19 H.I. Dutton and J.E. King, 'The Limits of Paternalism: the Cotton Tyrants of North Lancashire, 1836–54', *Soc. Hist.* 7, no. 1 (January 1982); and by the same authors,

'*Ten Per Cent and No Surrender.*' *The Preston Strike 1853–54* (Cambridge 1982), p. 92; Price, *Masters, Unions and Men*, pp. 73–9.

20 Rule, *The Experience of Labour*, pp. 124–33; C.R. Dobson, *Masters and Journeymen: a Pre-History of Industrial Relations 1717–1800* (London 1980); A.P. Wadsworth and Julia De L. Mann, *The Cotton Trade in Industrial Lancashire 1600–1780* (New York repr. 1968), pp. 365–8, 395–9. On 1825 see John Orth, 'The British Trade Union Acts of 1824 and 1825', *Anglo-American Law Review* 5 (1976), p. 148; S. and B. Webb, *History of Trade Unionism* (London 1894), pp. 93–101. Also, R.S. Wright, *The Law of Criminal Conspiracies and Agreements* (London 1873), p. 56; Sir James Fitzjames Stephen, *A History of the Criminal Law of England*, vol. III (London 1883), p. 208.

21 Wright, *The Law of Criminal Conspiracies*, pp. 12, 45–8; Stephen, *A History of the Criminal Law*, Vol. III, pp. 209, 212–15.

22 John Orth, 'Striking Workmen Before the Courts 1859–71', unpublished paper, p. 3; Daphne Simon, 'Master and Servant', in John Saville (ed.), *Democracy and the Labour Movement* (London 1954), p. 160; *Select Committee on Master and Servant*, 1866, Vol.XIII (449), ques. 1358–66; Dutton and King, 'The Limits of Paternalism', p. 66; *Newcastle Daily Chronicle*, 14/9/1864, p. 2.

23 Thus, in the 1890s, *Allen v. Flood, Curran v. Treleaven, Trollope v. LBTF* for how the men could influence hiring practices; *Quinn v. Leathem, Lyons v. Wilkins* for the extent to which picketing constituted interference. On similar patterns in the 1960s see K.W. Wedderburn, *The Worker and the Law* (Harmondsworth 1971), pp. 323–5, 355–8, 363–8, 374–8; Stephen, *History of the Criminal Law*.

24 Keith Burgess, 'New Unionism for Old? The Amalgamated Society of Engineers in Britain 1890–1914', unpublished paper, pp. 8–9; Giovanni Arrighi, 'Towards a Theory of Capitalist Crisis', *New Left Review* 111 (Sept–Oct. 1978); Dieter Groh, 'Intensification of Work and Industrial Conflict in Germany 1896–1914', *Politics and Society* 8, nos. 3–4 (1978); Jonathan Zeitlin, 'The Labour Strategies of British Engineering Employers 1890–1914', paper for the conference 'New Unionism in Europe', Tutzing 1981, p. 6.

25 W.F. Watson, *Bedaux and Other Bonus Systems Explained* (London 1932); 'The Psychology of the Pay Envelope', *The Human Factor* 7, no. 10 (October 1937), pp. 357–8; J. Rowan, 'A Premium System Applied to Engineering Works', *Institute of Mechanical Engineers, Proceedings* (March 1903), pp. 204, 209; William Rowan Thomson, *The Rowan Premium Bonus System of Payment by Results* (Glasgow 1917), pp. 54–6. Dempster Smith and Philip Pickworth, *Engineers' Costs and Economical Workshop Production* (Manchester 1914), pp. 49, 52; Judith Merkle, *Management and Ideology* (Berkeley 1980), pp. 221–2.

26 J. Slater Lewis, *The Commercial Organisation of Factories* (London 1896); Sinclair and Frank Pearn, *Workshop Costs for Engineers and Manufacturers* (Manchester 1905); Rowan, 'A Premium System', pp. 227, 238; Thomson, *The Rowan Premium System*, pp. 15, 16, 60, 67; Amalgamated Society of Engineers, *Monthly Journal*, May 1902, p. 65; December 1902, p. 68; W.F. Watson, *The Worker and Wage Incentives* London 1934), pp. 11–12.

27 Arthur Barker, *The Management of Small Engineering Workshops* (Manchester 1899), pp. 15, 103–4, 113, 131–2; Smith and Pickworth, *Engineers' Costs*, pp. 78, 85–91; see also Alfred Williams, *Life in a Railway Factory* (London 1915), pp. 79–80, 134, 183–4,

274–6, 302; Price, *Masters, Unions and Men*, pp. 177–8; Joe Melling, 'Non-Commissioned Officers: British Employers and their Supervisory Workers 1880–1920', *Soc. Hist.* 5, no. 2 (May 1980).

28 Zeitlin, 'Labour Strategies of British Engineering Employers', pp. 4–5; Burgess, 'New Unionism for Old?', p. 10; Joyce, *Work, Society and Politics*, p. 103; Joseph White, *The Limits to Trade Union Militancy* (Connecticut 1978), pp. 112–15.

29 Sarah Gillespie, *A Hundred Years of Progress* (Glasgow 1953), pp. 110–12; *Typographical Circular*, October 1893, p. 7; September 1895, p. 7; January 1899, p. 5; June 1899, pp. 4–5; June 1911, pp. 3–7, 15; June 1912, p. 3; Typographical Association, *Extracts from Delegate Meeting, 1893* (London 1893); *Webb Collection* B, Vol. 74, ff. 33, 41.

30 Linotype Users' Association, *Monthly Circular*, May 1898, p. 2; April 1899, pp. 2–5; December 1900, pp. 1–4; May 1901, p. 8; *Typographical Circular*, May 1898; May 1900, p. 16; Ellis Howe, *The London Compositor 1785–1900* (London 1947), pp. 499–501; G.B. Diblee, 'The Printing Trades and the Crisis in British Industry', *Economic J.* 12 (March 1900); John Child, *Industrial Relations in the British Printing Industry* (London 1967), pp. 137–9, 152; A.E. Musson, *The Typographical Association* (Oxford 1954), pp. 140–3.

31 *Typographical Circular*, January 1899, p. 5; February 1899, pp. 4–5; June 1911, p. 15; Howe, *The London Compositor*, pp. 502–9, Linotype Users' Association, *Monthly Circular*, February 1900, p. 1; March 1900, p. 4; *Scottish Typographical Journal*, December 1912, pp. 463–64; August 1913, p. 147; February 1913, pp. 36, 37–55; Gillespie, *A Hundred Years of Progress*, pp. 217–18, 226.

32 Fox, *National Union of Boot and Shoe Operatives*, pp. 99–106; *Shoe and Leather Record*, 26/7/90, p. 98; 4/1/90, p. 12; 17/7/91, p. 145; Keith Brooker, 'The Northamptonshire Shoemakers' Reaction to Industrialisation', *Northamptonshire Past and Present* (1980), p. 154.

33 *Shoe and Leather Record*, 10/8/89, p. 154; 8/1/92, p. 70; 15/1/92, p. 122; 21/1/91, p. 224; 11/3/92, pp. 609–10; Fox, *National Union of Boot and Shoe Operatives*, pp. 132, 141, 201, 207, 212–213; National Union of Boot and Shoe Operatives, *Monthly Reports*, December 1890, p. 2; Ramsey Macdonald, *Socialism and Society* (New York repr. 1970), p. 52; W.B. Hoffman, 'The Late Boot War', *Econ. J.* (June 1895).

34 *Shoe and Leather Record*, 15/1/92, p. 122; Elizabeth Brunner, 'The Origins of Industrial Peace: the Case of the British Boot and Shoe Industry', *Oxford Economic Papers*, no. 1 (1949); S. and B. Webb, *Industry Democracy* (London 1913), pp. 185–91.

35 Fox, *National Union of Boot and Shoe Operatives*, pp. 221–33; National Union of Boot and Shoe Operatives, *Monthly Reports*, November 1894, p. 2; Brooker, 'The Northamptonshire Shoemakers', p. 157.

36 White, *The Limits to Trade Union Militancy*, pp. 112–15; in shipbuilding the chippers and drillers might be regarded as such a group and there is some information to suggest this in *Webb Collection*, E. A., Vol. 33, ff. 221–30. For docks and gas see E.J. Hobsbawm, 'General Labour Unions in Britain 1889–1914', 'National Unions on the Waterside', and 'British Gas Workers 1873–1914', in *Labouring Men* (London 1964); Richard Price, 'The Labour Process and the New Unionism 1880–1920', conference paper, Tutzing, 1981.

37 *Royal Commission on Labour*, 1893–94, Vol. 34 (c. 6894–ix), ques. 26926, 26969,

23839, 26835–885, Appendices 51, 52: *Journal of Gas Lighting*, 2/7/89, p. 22; 12/11/89, p. 928; 31/12/89, p. 1256; Smith and Pickworth, *Engineers' Costs*, pp. 65–6.

38 Merfyn Jones, *The North Wales Quarryman's Union 1874–1922* (Cardiff 1981).

39 Frank McKenna, *The Railway Workers 1840–1970* (London 1980), p. 40; 'Victorian Railway Workers', *History Workshop J.* 1 (Spring 1976), pp. 66–7; T.R. Gourvish, *Mark Huish and the London and North Western Railway* (Leicester 1972).

40 R.J. Irving, 'The Profitability and Performance of British Railways 1870–1914', *Econ. Hist. Review* 31 (1978); Geoffrey Alderman, 'The Railway Companies and the Growth of Trade Unionism in the late 19th and early 20th Centuries', *Hist. J.* 14 no. 1 (1971), pp. 132–3; Henry Parris, *Government and the Railways in Nineteenth-Century Britain* (London 1965), pp. 218, 223.

41 *Railway Review*, 22/3/89, p. 133; 12/7/89, p. 325; 9/9/89, p. 383; 8/22/93, p. 5; 22/12/93, p. 5; 29/12/93, p. 6; 2/2/94, p. 5; George Paish, *The British Railway Position* (London 1902), pp. 31, 239; Rowland Kenny, *Men and Rails* (London 1913), pp. 153–4; McKenna, 'Victorian Railway Workers', pp. 61, 68, 72; *Royal Commission on Railway Conciliation and Arbitration Scheme of 1907*, 1912–13, Vol. 45 (Cd. 6014), ques. 6390, 6400, 6402; *Royal Commission on Labour*, Vol. 33 (c. 6894), ques. 26517.

42 G. M'Donnell, *Railway Management, With and Without Railway Statistics* (London n.d.); *Railway News*, 15/12/00, p. 868; H.M. Hallsworth, *The Elements of Railway Operating* (privately published, n.d.), pp. 231–2, 234–5; *Railway Review* 7/3/13, p. 3; 4/7/13, p. 5.

43 Hallsworth, *Elements of Railway Operating*, pp. 324–81; *Railway Review*, 20/6/13, p. 8; 28/2/13, pp. 1–2; 7/3/13, p. 3; Philip Bagwell, *The Railwaymen* (London 1960), p. 339.

44 Kenny, *Men and Rails*, pp. 148–9; *Railway Review*, 22/9/93, p. 1; *Railway News*, 25/8/00, p. 321; McKenna, 'Victorian Railway Workers', p. 58.

45 *Railway Review* 3/11/11, p. 9, 9/9/89, p. 383; *Royal Commission on Labour*, Vol. 33 (c. 6894), ques. 26384, 28037; Bob Holton, *British Syndicalism 1900–1914* (London 1976), pp. 97–8, 104–10, 164–7.

46 *Railway Review*, 15/12/93, p. 4; H. Clegg, A. Fox and A.F. Thompson, *A History of British Trade Unions* (Oxford 1964), pp. 316–18; Alderman, 'The Railway Companies', pp. 146–8.

47 Bagwell, *The Railwaymen*, pp. 268–71; Kenny, *Men and Rails*, pp. 175, 204–5, 209, 216; *Industrial Syndicalist*, May 1911, pp. 7–14; Margot Stein, 'The Meaning of Skill: the case of French Engine-Drivers 1837–1917', *Politics and Society* 8, nos. 3–4 (1978).

48 See David Purdy, 'British Capitalism Since the War', *Marxism Today* (September and October 1976); Keith Middlemas, *Politics in Industrial Society* (London 1979); John Child, *British Management Thought* (London 1969).

6

The First of May 1890 in France: the birth of a working-class ritual*

MICHELLE PERROT

> Present-day revolutionary myths are almost pure; they make it possible to understand the activity, the feelings and the ideas of the masses as they prepare to enter upon a decisive struggle; they are not descriptions of things, but expressions of determination.
>
> Georges Sorel, *Reflections on Violence*, Introduction.

The history of the First of May 1890 – the first time May Day was celebrated by the labour movement in France and the rest of Europe – is exemplary in several ways. The demonstrations held that day were the result of a deliberate political decision, and thus illustrate an intentional and deliberate element in class formation, as the socialists sought to give political and cultural unity to the working class through the educational use of a public holiday (*une fête*), in a way which had been tested many years before during the French Revolution in its principles, its impact, and its limitations.[1] The decision to celebrate the First of May undeniably came from above, and in particular from the best organized politically of the socialist groupings, the Marxists (which in France meant the Guesdists of the Parti Ouvrier Français).[2] Hence the reservations and quarrels which marked its birth, and the objections raised by other groups (the Possibilists and the anarchists for instance) not just for sectarian reasons, but also because they opposed on principle a move which they saw as a form of manipulation of the masses. This is a debate which is still going on today.

But although the First of May was a deliberate creation, neither the timing nor the organization was arbitrary. Not only was it preceded by proposals and experiences which in some respects it crystallized – the wealth of experience of the American labour movement for instance, with which the European movement expressed broad solidarity – but also, more indirectly, it had roots in the rebellious associations which the month of May held for working people (it was a record month for strikes) and perhaps too in the more ancient village

*Translated by Sian Reynolds

tradition of Maytime and the rites of spring. The month of May carries a strong symbolic charge. Whether this was taken into account, and if so in what way and at what level of the collective consciousness or unconscious, remains to be discovered. What is more, as events turned out, this first May Day went beyond the intentions of its promoters. Already the occasion of controversy, it also became the focus of different strategies, practised for example in planning the routes of marches. Moreover the orginally specified ritual, which was both simple and rigid, was overtaken by popular forms of expression in local communities. And finally, by sparking off a wave of unexpected strikes, the event escaped from the control of its initiators, who had intended to limit it in time and to give it a fixed aim. *La mise en demeure*, the presenting of demands to the authorities, became a wider and more general expectation of change for certain workers, and these were often the most downtrodden.

In later years, socialist and trade-union education would bear fruit. A tradition would become established, with a code of practice for processions, agreed slogans, and a concern above all to assemble what is today regarded as the key to successful demonstrations – large numbers and an overwhelming evidence of consensus. But this first May Day in 1890 had all the uncertainty and unpredictability of a beginning. Of whom were the first May Day demonstrators the inheritors? What did they carry with them? What was in their minds on that fine Thursday in spring? At any rate, what did they actually say and do?[3]

The invention of the First of May

The idea of celebrating the First of May is associated with the creation of the Second International, whose first congress was held in Paris in July 1889. On Saturday 20 July, after a somewhat confused debate (during which the choice of date in particular was discussed) the following resolution, proposed by Raymond Lavigne, a Guesdist militant from Bordeaux, was passed:

> A great international demonstration will be organized on a fixed date, so that in every country and every town, on the same appointed day, the workers may simultaneously present to the authorities the demand that the working day be legally reduced to eight hours and that the other resolutions of the Paris International Congress be applied. Since a similar demonstration has already been arranged for the First of May 1890 by the American Federation of Labor, at its congress held in St Louis in December 1888, this date is adopted for the demonstration.[4]

There are some striking features about this resolution: for example that the chosen interlocutor of the workers was to be 'the public authorities', in other words the state in its various manifestations. A 'demand' was to be made to the state that social reforms be applied, foremost among them the reduction of the working day, a unifying element in the claims of the workers. A further feature is the reference to the American precedent for the choice of the First of May as the date – in preference to other possibilities (14 July, 18 March or 21 September) which were rejected as too closely tied to French political history and thus insufficiently universal for an international rendezvous. The American First of May, inaugurated in 1886 by the Knights of Labor, had already claimed victims. Violent clashes with the forces of order that day had led to nine deaths in Milwaukee and six in Chicago. The trial of the eight 'Chicago martyrs', four of whom were hanged on 11 November 1887, had made a real impact, revealed in popular newspapers and imagery.[5] Benoît Frachon, a veteran of the old working class tradition, refers to them at some length in his memoirs.[6] The vigorous American labour movement, with its spectacular strikes like that on the railroads in 1877, was relatively well-known and respected in France.[7] In a general way, at least until the turn of the century, the view of the United States held by French workers was an essentially favourable one, though we need to know more about it. They admired American technology, which had been on show at the Great Exhibitions,[8] and the wide-open spaces of America were the stuff that youthful dreams were made of. Gangs of youths in Belleville called themselves 'Apaches' (in a rather different context, it is true).[9] America was still the New World: these were the days when the *West* was red.

The political history of the First of May nevertheless remains controversial. Everyone likes to claim credit for it, even today, as can be seen in a recent book – well-documented and magnificently illustrated, it must be admitted – by André Rossel. The author, sympathetic to communist historiography, tends to minimize the importance of the anarchists and the Americans and gives greatest credit to Guesdist orthodoxy. Working-class memory is a constructed phenomenon and can still be fought over and disputed. The Guesdists undoubtedly played an important part in the story. At the 1888 congress of the Fédération Nationale des Syndicats Ouvriers (the National Federation of Workers' Trade Unions – under Guesdist control) held in Bouscat, Dormoy and Lavigne had succeeded in getting carried a proposal that formal demands (*mises en demeure* was again the expression used) be put to the public authorities in the form of petitions, in February 1889. Demonstrations of this kind did indeed take place at the appointed time in about 60 localities. But at the London Congress in the same year (6–10 November 1888), a meeting more clearly representative of trade unions since it was composed entirely of working-class delegates, the Parisian joiner Tortelier spoke in favour of an international general strike to mark the opening in 1889 of the Universal Exhibition in Paris, which would make a natural rallying-point. The workers, he argued, 'should all stop work at the same time everywhere. I propose an international general strike, to begin on the opening day of the Exhibition.'[10] The Belgian delegate Anscele proposed alternatively that a workers' demonstration should be held on the first Sunday in May 1889, 'at the same time, with the same slogans on the banners'.

In fact, the idea of an international workers' demonstration had been in the air since about 1883–4, notably in libertarian circles. Paradoxically, the idea of a general strike[11] and the practice of petitioning the authorities had originated with the French anarchists, on the occasion of the mass demonstration by the unemployed of Paris in March 1883. The choice of the First of May and the Eight Hours Campaign had originated with the American anarchists. And it was in America too that blood had first been shed, thus in a sense consecrating the day. The Guesdists were anxious above all to channel the energies of the working class towards the state, to give the movement a political, rather than a social or anti-capitalist, thrust. It was this political takeover which the anarchists sensed, resented and condemned. Over and above such quarrels about paternity, which in fact disguised real differences over strategy, stand the more interesting issues of the longer-term origins of the movement, those formative influences common to all, whether these related to specific elements or to an overall approach.

Petitions to the authorities, the eight-hour day, the First of May: do these elements have their own history? Approaches to the powers that be were not new in France – indeed they were classic tactics, particularly during periods of unemployment. Since the beginning of the nineteenth century, and more especially since 1830, processions of demonstrators had been calling on local authorities and prefects to organize relief and open new building sites, to the cry of 'Break and Work!'. During the depression of the 1880s and particularly after 1883, the unemployed had poured into the streets and surrounded town halls at the bidding of the anarchists, who began from this time to clash with the Guesdists over forms of action. The anarchists were above all concerned to expose the rich to the sight of poverty. 'Come and display your rags before the luxury of the rich. Show your poverty to these monopolists, not to make them feel sorry for you but to frighten them.' The Guesdists preferred meetings behind closed doors, from which deputations would solemnly take the resolutions formulated there as formal demands ('*mises en demeure*' was becoming the standard expression and is to be found in the call to a meeting on 7 December 1883) to the town hall and, increasingly, to the prefectures and the government, which was 'called upon' to intervene.[12] This practice of addressing the state, not only in calls for relief but also for reforms, with the route of workers' marches being planned to end at the seats of power, was no doubt the major innovation, signalling the political dimensions of this First of May. It was intended as a demonstration rather than a holday, a means of pressure rather than a mode of expression.

The second element is the campaign for the eight-hour day, the ambivalence of which sheds light on the movement. In English-speaking countries, where the organization of working hours was more advanced, this could be of immediate relevance.[13] In France, a country where long days were worked, on the agricultural pattern,[14] it could only constitute a long-term aim, except for miners, which may explain their particular concern. As a result, many groups of workers spontaneously reworded the slogan and called instead for the ten-hour day, revealing their anxiety to place their demand in the realms of the possible. But this was to overlook both the origins and the utopian dimension of the campaign. Maurice Dommanget reminds us that Denis Veiras, the author of *L'Histoire des Sévarambes*, a utopian work written in 1677,[15] imagines the ideal day as divided into three equal parts: work, pleasure and rest. One would no doubt have to go much further back to its roots in myths and in the rules of golden numbers to find the origins of this three-fold and three-functional vision of time. 'Eight hours' work.Eight hours' rest. Eight hours' leisure' – the famous 'Three Eights' which became a rallying cry from this period[16] – expressed both a quasi-structural representation of the world and the projection into the future of a harmonious and balanced society. Conveniently translatable into graphic form, the Three Eights inspired certain artists, who depicted them as landscape scenes or female symbols. Grandjouan (in *L'Assiette au Beurre*, 28 April 1906) has three female nudes, reminiscent of the Three Graces, each with a different posture and hairstyle, representing the *trois huit*. The subject has interesting possibilities for iconographical research.

The choice of the First of May was, to the French at least, more puzzling. The date does not commemorate any precise event. It might be thought of as a deliberate break with the past, a hegira marking the beginning of a new age, as so many people took it to be. But it appears that the Americans, whose initiative actually determined the date, chose this day for eminently practical reasons, mentioned by Gabriel Deville, among others.[17] In New York State, the First of May is 'Moving Day', like a quarter day in Britain, or the Feasts of St John and Michaelmas in France, a date when leases and contracts of all kinds come up for renewal; consequently it was a day when many people moved house. The original resolution proposed by Gabriel Edmonston was indeed worded rather like a lease: 'eight hours shall constitute a legal day's labour from and after 1 May 1886'.

The American militants were unconsciously linking hands with an ancient rural custom in France, which as Varagnac has shown, formed the background to the planting of *mais* ('may-trees' or maypoles erected by peasants in certain areas). 'The whole household was renewed in May: it was the hiring season, when the farmhands changed like the vegetation.'[18] Mona Ozouf has pointed out the connection between the official planting of 'trees of liberty' in 1789 and the spontaneous planting of *mais*, 'symbols of revolt, monuments of insurrection',[19] whose rebellious potential the French revolutionaries had tried to tap for their own ends. 'At the level of the unconscious at least,' she concludes after a searching investigation, 'revolutionary symbolism was less alien to peasant tradition than is sometimes suggested.'[20] The same could probably be said of the 'workers' May', which was grafted on to very ancient practices, through the unexpected mediation of the American movement. It would not after all have been the first time that folklore had provided a background for politics. It was by similar means that the republic had once won over the villages in the Var and elsewhere,[21] but the connection in this case is more tenuous, more distant, and works more by analogy. In concrete terms, as we shall see, working-class ritual was less rich. Here there were no trees of liberty, no maypoles; instead there were flags, made from fabrics that were the product of industry rather than nature. The forest now was the People, on its feet, challenging the Old World. Was there perhaps some 'transfer of sacredness' in that spring time of 1890, operating in favour of the working class, the key to the future?[22]

Nineteenth-century socialism had been much preoccupied with the need to create new rituals, to bring about 'a new alliance between politics and religion', as Abensour has shown in connection with the Saint-Simonians and Pierre Leroux,[23] who were so anxious to reconcile aesthetics and politics. The Saint-Simonians had a keen eye for the telling detail, and an aptitude for using costume, colour and gesture for symbolic scenarios. For Pierre Leroux, 'civil religion was to be the aesthetic locus where political communication would be freely exercised by means of symbols, ceremonies and feasts'.[24] Did these people formulate any precise plans for celebrating 'the feast of labour'? Criticizing the vulgar *laisser-aller* of Carnival, with its 'singular triumph' of the Fatted Ox, the Saint-Simonian journal, *Le Producteur*, had a rather different ceremony in mind.

> We believe for our part that when one day science, labour and the love of mankind are everywhere honoured, a ceremony in which crowns of laurel would be conferred on a Newton, a Pail Riquet, a Franklin, a Watt or any other benefactor of humanity would be of great interest and would unite not the delegates of a few Greek townships or the suburbs of Paris, but representatives of the whole of Europe and ambassadors from the two worlds.[25]

Those who are familiar with the writings of Étienne Cabet (1788–1856) will not be surprised at the obsessive precision with which he describes, in his utopian *Voyage en Icarie*, the festivities on 'the anniversary of Icarian regeneration': 13 June, the day of the People's uprising. Highly ritualized, these will extend over three days. On the first, 'uprising, fighting, victory'; on the second, 'funeral rites'; and finally 'dictatorship of Icar; triumph'.[26] In a chapter devoted to 'Holidays, games, pleasures and luxury', Cabet establishes the principle of a republican holiday, which he contrasts with the monarchical holidays in England and France. A committee for public holidays proposes a plan for such a holiday, which the People's Assembly then turns into a law, 'so that it is the People as a whole which has ordered and planned the holiday and consequently it is not astonishing that the People should execute what it has voluntarily undertaken to execute.'[27] The Icarians are moreover invited to compose dramatic works, from which a selection is made by a committee. Among the ceremonies, corporative processions naturally have a place. 'One sometimes sees all the workmen and women, grouped by trade, each with a different banner.'[28] It is the intention of the Icarian republic to surpass monarchy in 'fine and noble feast-days' while turning tradition to its advantage. 'There is nothing in the ancient world or the present which we have not studied, which we do not know about and which we have not profited by, keeping the good and discarding the bad.'[29] A profound desire for syncretism moved the socialist and working-class militants who slipped spontaneously or consciously into the images and vocabulary of previous times, notably those of the Christian heritage which still weighed so heavily in the last years of the nineteenth century.[30]

And yet what is so striking about the period immediately preceding the First of May is the contrast between the paucity of precise instructions and the grandiose vision conjured up. The aim was to show the strength of the proletariat by the simultaneous timing of the demonstration ('on a fixed date...at the same time ... on the same day') to give the working-class an awareness of its own existence through the carrying out of similar actions over a vast area – the 'two Worlds' – and to impress public opinion by this display. It was intended to promote 'a working population which would acquire the habit, from one end of the land to the other, of acting simultaneously and with determination', to deploy 'the imposing, imperious and irresistible force of this people of toilers rising up unanimously in the face of its masters ... to demand in a single mighty voice its right to life, well-being and the benefits of civilization'.[31] 'The Proletariat is about to do something unique in the annals of the world! Throughout the civilized nations, it will be affirming an identical principle by the same means. The workers of Saint Etienne [are] bowed under the same yoke as their brothers in Europe and America...'[32]

The weight of words and images evoked here reveals a sure sense of drama and an ability to use the mass media, indicative of a growing awareness of what Gustave Le Bon termed 'crowd psychology'.[33] But beyond these modern elements, working-class ritual was following in the paths of the most ancient religious traditions, with the communion of saints and the commemoration of sacrifice. *Doing the same thing at the same time*: this great principle of religious practice was now, by a stroke of genius, transferred to the labour movement, a new Moses leading the way to a new Promised Land. As the exaltation of a People united in a common celebration, the First of May was in fact the High Mass of the working class.

The celebration of the First of May

Preparations

As a political initiative, the decision to celebrate the First of May was immediately challenged in France by the Possibilists, some of the Blanquists[34] and the anarchists. Some were simply hostile to the authoritarian methods of

'German socialism', others were opposed, at a deeper level, to any bid by the Party to take over the trade-union and labour movement. *Le Prolétariat*, the official Possibilist newspaper, and *L'Emancipation*, a paper published in the Ardennes, the constituency of the Possibilist Jean-Baptiste Clement, condemned what they called kowtowing (*suivisme*) by the French Marxists – the Guesdists – whether to German social democracy or to Boulangism.[35] Stopping work in mid-week was arbitrary and did not correspond to customs in French workshops – where workers were in the habit of celebrating Saint Monday. They argued that the skilled workers in Paris at any rate would not follow the movement.[36] The anarchists were even more hostile: 'The demonstration on the First of May was planned by people with only one aim: to seize power and make the most of it. They tell the people to demand an eight-hour day (to fatten their idle masters for only eight hours a day, what progress!) but they want to be MPs or councillors themselves, doing nothing and getting paid for it ...'[37] However the anarchists were pragmatists enough to join the movement. 'All out on the First of May', reads another of their posters. 'The anarchists, although not in favour of the eight-hour day, which is less practical than the social revolution, have nevertheless decided to take an active part [in the demonstration].'[38] In fact, they tried to convert the First of May to their way of thinking and to impose upon it their own style – violent and direct action aimed against the capitalists. Their more populist language was, at this time, more popular.

The First of May was thus surrounded by controversy, and all the more carefully prepared for that, at least from March 1890 onwards when we find the earliest traces of active propaganda. Trade-union branches and socialist groups were mobilized, sometimes acting jointly, and within their ranks were a number of determined militants moved by the shared conviction that 'the Great Day was coming'. They contributed at grass-roots level to minimize the divergences at the top. As between ordinary militants, there was in fact little difference in the language spoken, even when it came to the subject of the general strike, which had its enthusiasts even in the ranks of the Guesdist Parti Ouvrier.[39]

In the regions where the Guesdists were well-entrenched, 'standing committees' and 'People's Leagues for the reduction of the working day' were set up, with the task of distributing propaganda, encouraging workers to take the day off and selecting the deputations to approach the authorities. Some militants tried to give the slogans a local dimension. In Thizy (Rhône), where the weavers had been virtually on strike for weeks, Durousset organized the drawing-up of what were effectively *cahiers de doléances* (lists of grievances as in 1789) to be presented to the authorities. Less elaborately, petitions were circulated for signing in the workshops. Private meetings in local cafés, and public meetings with 'guest appearances' by Parisian leaders (Jules Guesde himself contributed a massive personal effort) were stepped up towards the end of April. In the Rhône *département* for example, 15 meetings are listed as being held on Saturday 26 April, and the same number on the following day; some 70 union branches or groups were involved.[40] These were Guesdist strongholds, of course, but elsewhere, in more out of the way places, perhaps 15 workers might meet in a café to discuss what they could do. Each nucleus, whether large or small, formed a link in a network of surprisingly large compass, and one which adds up to a 'photographic' record of the potential of the labour movement at a time when it was rapidly gaining ground.

Through this network circulated the spoken and written word, which flourished to such an extent that this First of May has a modernity worthy of communications analysis.[41] The freedom of the press, introduced by the 1881 law, had made it possible for a wealth of socialist papers to spring up – ephemeral, unstable and multifarious. The rapid transmission of slogans would have been inconceivable if this press had not existed, and in this respect a comparison with the methods of communication used by the Saint-Simonians would be instructive.[42] The Marxists understood the power of the press better than anyone. On this occasion, they created a newspaper entirely devoted to preparations for the First of May: *Le Combat, organe quotidien des Travailleurs Socialistes,*[43] a first-class source for the historian on Guesdist education and propaganda methods in this context. Other papers had been envisaged (*Les Huit Heures, Le Producteur*). Posters and tracts made it possible for propaganda to be decentralized for they were less demanding of effort and more adaptable. Their spread can be seen from the many examples in the departmental archives, or the archives of the Prefecture of Police in Paris. The anarchists made particular use of them. One of their posters, '*Le père Peinard au Populo*' (Father Layabout to the People) appeared all over the place: in Le Havre and Bordeaux this led to the prosecution of some of their militants. Tracts encouraged the expression of more personal sentiments, especially when they were handwritten. Individual militants could use them to take over the official discourse and slip in their own amendments, so making their presence felt. One poster, confiscated by the police in the Rue Quincampoix in Paris, added to the Three Eights a fourth: '8 francs a day!'[44] After 1905, the more widespread use of *papillons* (printed stickers which the neo-Malthusian birth-control campaigners seem to have been the first to use) were effective instruments of spreading the word while at the same time undoubtedly standardizing the language of popular politics.[45] In the study of propaganda material, attention needs to be paid to the very texture of the medium employed.[46]

Finally, at the more modest level of workshop or factory, workers anxious to have their plant closed down, so that the First of May really could be a day off work, wrote to their employers in a variety of tones. The dyers of Lyons had a firm but respectful circular printed:

Messieurs the Master Dyers,
The Union of dye-workers in Lyon has the honour of informing you that as a result of a decision taken at a general assembly and voted unanimously, and in view of the decision taken at the international congress of Paris, you are invited to close the works on the First of May 1890.[47]

The tone was often more threatening. The Paris police archives contain a number of anonymous letters warning the bosses to close the factories or suffer reprisals:

You can lounge about in your palace, *petite mère*! We'll see that it's reduced to rubble on Thursday. You and all those who own what they have robbed from us will see what we're made of, the day after tomorrow. Hide behind your walls all you like, dynamite's not for playing games with. You have been warned. I don't give a damn for you or anything you can do.[48]

Some workers made direct threats by word of mouth. Marius Henry, a very popular militant in the Lalle mine, in the Gard, threatened the manager that he would 'blow his brains out'.[49] His dismissal led to a long strike in May.

As the First of May approached, incidents of this kind became more frequent, and as the word spread, they merged to form a general rumour, creating quite a wave of alarm. In Oullins (Rhône) a worker told the twelve-year-old son of a market gardener: 'After the First of May, we'll make the bosses and landowners cough up, your father like the rest of them.' The police inspector who reported these words also overheard his barber's wife telling customers that one worker had said to another: 'On the First of May, either we'll get the eight-hour day or the knives will be out.' A worker at Coquard's in Bourg-de-Thizy, a calm and honest man, replied to relations who were advising him to get in some food: 'No point, on the First of May, we'll know where to find what we need.'[50] In Lyons, an 'incredible' number of industrialists, bankers and shopkeepers applied to the authorities for measures of special protection, according to the prefect.[51] 'Everyone is dreading the First of May because they are frightened of outbreaks of violence such as happened at the Theatre Bellecour . . . It is said that most of the silk-mills have stored their stocks in a safe place, and two of the biggest mill-owners have already left for Geneva.'[52] In the nearby region of Thizy where the weavers had been on strike for many months, such anxiety was particularly pronounced. It was feared that large-scale demonstrations would be held; that gangs would come down from the mountain localities, with banners and *women* at their head (for women read 'furies') and would converge on a field near Pont-Trambouze which had been hired for the purpose.

The country landowners, especially those in isolated places, are in some apprehension of the damage which might be caused to their property by demonstrators, especially when the latter are returning at nightfall to their respective localities. Some of these people are literally panic-stricken, believing that there will be excesses and looting.[53]

'Truly I shudder to think what is going to happen on the First of May,' writes a police informer in Lyons.

It was certainly the case that the First of May presented a particularly alarming profile in this region, where the textile industry was in crisis and where anarchism was rife.[54] But similar waves of fear, whose detail and motives have yet to be analysed, were reported in many other places. There was, for example, something of an exodus by the bourgeoisie from Paris, a phenomenon which would be repeated every time the First of May promised to be particularly lively (in 1906 for instance, the high point of bourgeois panic and, perhaps, of the workers' hopes).[55] The scale of the precautions taken – the postponement of religious ceremonies or paydays, the compulsory closure of major public or private establishments, the preventive arrests and military preparations[56] – all contributed to the sense of imminent danger. The expectation of a day of rioting, which the anarchists did their best to promote, was undoubtedly rooted in the historical experience of the revolutionary *journées*. In spite of the Guesdists' appeal for calm, the idea of a peaceful demonstration, a working-class celebration of Labour, was not easily accepted, so closely was the image of the working class associated with violence, especially in the years after the Commune.

The events

'Shall we have a *journée*?' (*L'Eclair*, 12 April 1890)
'The People are at last coming together. This is the Great Day' (Poster, Vienne).

Without reaching tidal-wave proportions, the First of May demonstrations undoubtedly made an impact. If one bears in mind the comparatively poor communications of the time, and the lack of a central working-class organization (the Guesdist-controlled Fédération Nationale des Syndicats was a mere skeleton) one cannot fail to be surprised by the dimensions of the event. The provinces reacted more strongly than Paris. From Lille-Roubaix to Lyons and Marseilles, from Trelazé (Maine-et-Loire) to Alais, from Bordeaux to Reims, Amiens, or St Quentin – in 160 to 200 different places, the workers showed in one way or another their support for the First of May. In some *départements* – Nord, Rhône, Isère, Loire, Gard, Allier for instance – a whole string of municipalities were affected, often by direct contact or as a result of infectious propaganda emanating from one centre. But there were also demonstrations in small places or isolated factories and sites without any apparent interconnection. In Raismes (a district of Saint-Amand, in the Nord) the 250 workers of the Franco-Belgian metalworks formed a procession and set off for Anzin, trying to persuade other factories to join them. 'There had been no previous indication to warn us of this movement.'[57] In Vernon (Eure), 30 workers walked off their building site.[58] In Saint-Pavace (Sarthe), 26 workers in a small foundry seized the occasion to protest about the harsh discipline.[59] In the forests of the Nievre, at Vandenesse,

300 woodcutters demonstrated, demanding a wage-rise,[60] as did the 100 workers at a lime-quarry at Saint-Léger-des-Vignes.[61] At Bar-le-Duc (Meuse), which was usually a very quiet place, 'on the occasion of the workers' demonstrations planned for the 1 May, a strike began among the weavers at Baudot and Co.', writes the prefect. 'On 30 April, at three o'clock in the afternoon, the workers walked out of the building after a demand for a wage-rise had been turned down... A band of about fifty or sixty young people, girls and boys aged between thirteen and fifteen, ran round the town, without holding a demonstration.' On 1 May, a delegation went to the Town Hall and there was an attempt to negotiate.[62] In this case, the workers were adapting the First of May to their own needs. But it had a more general resonance, although it is not easy to identify the channel of transmission. In these early days of socialist propaganda, the role of individuals, 'agitators' who were good at communicating information and enthusiasm, was very important.[63] Formal networks (the POF, the trade unions, the anarchist groups), informal contacts through relatives, neighbours or friends, personal initiatives – all these channels of communication were combined or added to each other on the first May Day, building up a composite and differentiated geographical picture.

The same was true of professional groups. If the print-workers, railwaymen and, to a lesser degree, building-workers remained silent, few trades stood totally aside from the movement, local commitments no doubt proving stronger than professional conditioning. Foundry-workers, dyers and workers in shoe factories demonstrated alongside the glass-workers, textile-workers and miners who provided the big battalions. The same could also be said of the units of production. If in Paris the industrial suburbs (glass-works, gas-works) were more likely to be on strike than the small workshops in the city centre, it was if anything the reverse in Lyons. The handloom weavers in this region were threatened with mechanization, and were very sympathetic to the eight-hour campaign, which they interpreted as a kind of work-sharing. 'We are not afraid of being replaced by other proletarians who are out of work, since if less is being produced, our exploiters will be obliged to give work to more people,' said one speaker at a meeting in Roanne on 30 April.[64]

What is nevertheless striking is the industrial character of the demonstrations and the importance of the workplace both in the preparations for and the conduct of the First of May. In Roubaix, petitions were signed in individual spinning or weaving mills, and delegates were chosen on the same basis.[65] In Troyes, the workers arrived 'in works teams'. 'From all sides, the workers are flocking in [to the Place Saint-Nizier]. The strike has evidently been more complete than we hoped, for all the time we hear people say, "Here come the workers from such-and-such a mill to join us."'[66] The social force of the workplace was more effective than demarcation by trade. Big firms preoccupied authorities and workers alike: stoppages there were dreaded by the former and energetically sought by the latter. It was important to 'win over' Cail's at Denain, Leclerq-Dupire's in Wattrelos, Holden's of Reims, Koechlin's of Belfort, Raffin's of Roanne. Recalcitrant factories attracted demonstrators. The anarchists in particular made them the centres of action, since they were the 'fortresses' of the employers, where battle had to be joined. Hence the violence of incidents at the Jeansoulin oilworks in Marseilles or at the Brochard mill in Vienne.

As a demonstration of producers and citizens, fighting for 'protective' legislation on women's and children's labour,[67] the First of May was very much an occasion for adult males. Women and children were certainly there in the background, at meetings and some demonstrations, but they were rarely given a place in processions and were never included in deputations, although there were clear differences of approach amongst the organizers. The Guesdists, preoccupied with politics, addressed themselves to male workers. The more populist anarchists showed a great willingness to turn to women and young people: in Vienne, they even centred their campaign on them. The festive side of the First of May would be accentuated in later years; the demonstrations, still a predominantly male affair,[68] would be accompanied by 'family gatherings' embracing the nuclear family which was so strong in the working-class milieu.[69] 'Grand meeting at three o'clock. Bring your wives,' read a notice on the front of a Belgian *maison du peuple*. The frontier between public and private, exterior and interior, ran through the First of May as it did through all forms of working-class culture.[70] Women and young people did nevertheless play some part in the action, but often only by forcing themselves in, chiefly by joining in subsequent strikes or the movements which developed from the First of May.

As to the nature of the day itself (was it a strike? a holiday? a political demonstration?) and the forms it took, the unclear and sometimes hesitant vocabulary and the laconic tone of the instructions sent out, left plenty of room for interpretation and improvization. Small communities in particular seem to have taken advantage of this latitude, as they would in later years.[71] Two courses of action had been proposed to the workers. In both cases, the day was to be taken off work, and on this point there was general agreement. But the Guesdists called for a peaceful holiday – 'Go for a walk' – marked only by the deputations to the authorities, carrying petitions collected by trade or workplace. The anarchists wanted mass rallies in the street, a popular, lively and violent demonstration directed against the class enemy, the bosses and their factories, a revolt by the 'slave-labourers' against their 'slave-drivers'. The Guesdists had in mind the observance of a particular day, limited in time; the anarchists reacted against the rigidities of this somewhat military discipline and thought in terms of a movement with its own dynamic of which the day might only be the beginning.

On the whole, the Guesdist plan prevailed in the demonstrations; but the notion of their being 'only the beginning' met a widespread response, no doubt because it corresponded to popular expectation.

I have already mentioned the steps taken by the workers (in oral or written form; individual or collective; respectful or violent) to persuade the employers to close down the factories and to make Thursday 1 May not so much a strike as a day off. This was certainly a new departure, and the fact that it was so widespread is, in the circumstances, astonishing. This desire to be recognized, combined with an underlying demand for more free time, regularly surfaced either when political circumstances were favourable, or when the economic situation looked promising. An upturn was always marked by a higher incidence in strikes on demands for shorter working hours;[72] 1848 and the eleven-hour day, 1936 and the first paid holidays, 1968 and fourth week of holidays; 1981 and the fifth, with the perspective of a possible 35-hour working week, are all part of the same historical trajectory in France, expressing the constant pressure of the labour movement for a lightening of the burden and an increase in leisure-time. The symbolic unity of the working class may have been built round the exaltation of Work and the Producer, but in everyday life, the work ethic had not penetrated workers' consciousness. In the villages, women felt guilty if they were not constantly occupied, having internalized the full-time job of housewife.[73] The factory on the other hand asked too much. Real life was somewhere else. On this point, working-class resistance was remarkably strong.[74] The eight-hour day demanded in 1890 was a very popular utopia.[75]

Many people did indeed treat the day as a holiday, marked with festivities and various forms of recreation. A number of eye-witness accounts remark – with some insistence it is true, because the worst had been feared – on the relaxed and good-natured atmosphere and the happiness of the worker on this fine spring day. In Paris, 'the workers have put on their Sunday best, people stop to chat in the streets with smiling faces: "Well here we are, the First of May and we're not at work." "Of course not," the comrade replies, "it's a holiday."'[76] Some of the workers went to the parks (the *Bois* round Paris): 'The demonstration has a rural atmosphere: it is a springtime demonstration,' said the *Petit Parisien* (3 May.) Or they might invade the rich districts, the Champs-Elysées which had become the parade-ground of the privileged,[77] just as in later years the Popular Front crowds invaded the beaches which were at last within their reach, and flocked to the Côte d'Azur, the symbol of high society. Elsewhere, notably in the *département* of the Loire, subscription banquets were held in the old popular and republican tradition: in Roanne, 'in most of the spinning-mills, lists were sent round...and every subscriber had to pay 2 F in order to attend the banquet and ball which were held'.[78] In Narbonne and several places in the Aude, 'a monster punch' was held in the premises of the *chambrée* (workers' dormitory), the birthplace of the oldest forms of comradeship, as Maurice Agulhon has shown.[79] Dances were organized in many places, with all the traditional festive trappings; there were Chinese lanterns in the Saint-Savinien suburb of Troyes, and illuminations–red ones of course–in the socialist municipality of Montlucon.

La Défense des Travailleurs on 11 May 1890 printed an account of an exemplary First of May, perfectly conforming to the Guesdists model, in which a popular holiday and political initiatives were combined in an atmosphere of calm unanimity. 'A majestic sun smiled on the workers, and in the suburbs they discussed the events that might take place during the day. Most of them were in their shirtsleeves and barefoot in sandals, relaxing after a hard week's work.' At ten o'clock, everyone went to the Circus (here as elsewhere the usual venue for a public meeting) to hear the Guesdist militants Massey, Renard and Langrand speak about the dawn of a new age: 'The old world is dying, the old world is dead.' Then people brought out their picnics: 'the gardens, the bar, the café and corridors of the vast establishment were crowded; on all sides one could hear songs, cries of joy and bursts of laughter; it was like being in the Land of Make-Believe'. In the afternoon, deputations went to the subprefecture with petitions from the workshops. In the evening, it was back to the Circus for a concert, 'where everyone could sing ballads, socialist songs or comic songs, as appropriate'. Nothing was missing, least of all joy: 'Contentment and hope were imprinted on the most unprepossessing faces,' according to the journalist.

In this idyll, pleasure and politics mingled in perfect harmony. It was everything the First of May ought to be, a true workers' festival, as opposed to the 14 July, the 'so-called national' holiday of the bourgeoisie, and the target of criticism from the revolutionary Left.[80] A family holiday and a political demonstration, an extraordinary mixture of high mass and village fête, this picture of the First of May at Saint-Quentin–whether real or imaginary–is a sort of prefiguration of the present-day *Fête de l'Humanité*.[81] The perfect expression of a counter-society.

The First of May did not have this integrated character everywhere. Most of the time it simply consisted of demonstrations of varying size, combined with public meetings (the English word 'meeting', denoting size, and sometimes noise, was much used). This simple programme was based on very ancient practices of political democracy: delegates from union branches, workers' groups or popular assemblies were to present the claims of the workers to the authorities, usually in the form of petitions signed at the workplace. The workers would themselves accompany and support the delegates, either by assembling on the main squares – the site of power – or in more solemn processions through the town, following a more or less direct route from the usual assembly points – the theatre, circus, cafés, perhaps the Labour Exchange (in Marseilles for instance) – to the town-halls, prefectures or subprefectures. Sometimes interviews with the authorities had been formally requested, despite the criticisms of the anarchists.

The processions took place at various times – from ten o'clock in the morning (in Clermont-Ferrand where the deputation was a very small one) to six o'clock in the evening – in order to include workers who had been unable to have the day off (in Troyes for example). The processions themselves were fairly orderly. In front came the delegates, preceded by socialist councillors when there were any (as was the case in Marseilles, Lyons and Montlucon), next the flag-bearers (a 64-year-old worker was picked for this task in the northern mining town of Frais-Marais), then the workers, sometimes grouped by factory, whether dressed in their working clothes or their Sunday best. The nucleus of the procession was exclusively male. But it might be accompanied by a crowd of any size – 4,000 in Troyes, 6,000 in Marseilles, 12,000 in Lens, 20,000 in Lille – according to the very approximate contemporary estimates.[82] These mixed crowds, including variable numbers of women and children, were barely organized, surrounding or tagging along behind the official processions. The demonstrators sang 'patriotic and republican songs' or revolutionary ones like *La Carmagnole* and chanted '*C'est huit heures qu'il nous faut!*' ('We want the eight-hour day!') Pedron's 'Eight Hours Song', which later became a classic, was first sung in his home town of Troyes. Brass bands and drums are frequently mentioned, especially in mining areas. There were a few banners, but mostly it was flags – tricolours, very occasionally black flags (in Vienne in the Isère), but above all red ones. Everywhere – in the streets, the assembly halls, in streamers, as rosettes, buttonholes or armbands – red reigned triumphant. The red flag so hated by the authorities was unquestionably the most popular class symbol.[83] Sometimes the flags bore inscriptions: 'Eight hours' work a day'; 'First of May 1890. Social demands'; or simply 'Eight hours a day' or 'Eight hours'; one read 'Long live the Commune'. There were no placards or stickers and few slogans. Material accessories were few, and the ritual was still rather limited,[84] though we have only the terse police reports to go on, and the inspector was no anthropologist!

Journalists paid a little more attention to this kind of thing. The description printed by the *Indépendant du Centre*[85] of the demonstration at Doyet-les-Mines (Allier) is worth mentioning. At 1.45 p.m., it tells us, a procession set off, consisting of workers 'in their Sunday best', miners for the most part, carrying a red banner with the words 'Long live the Commune'. At the head marched the delegates, some in workers' smocks (Christou Thivrier, the member of parliament for the Allier was famous as *le député en blouse* because he wore his in the Assembly, out of working-class solidarity), others in jackets, but all with a red rosette pinned to their left sleeves. A crowd of children accompanied the march as it proceeded to the town hall to present the miners' petitions, before going on round the town, drawing people out of doors. Most interesting of all, behind the workers came the local conscripts, playing music on drum, bugle and hurdy-gurdy; and brandishing a tricolour flag which had previously been flown in the Hôtel Mathonière, bearing the following words: 'Workers Party [Parti Ouvrier]. Brothers, let us unite. Class of 1889.' The white stripe in the tricolour was occupied by 'a painting representing the Republic, holding a dagger in one hand and a laurel wreath in the other. Underneath, a worker in his shirt-sleeves is shaking his fist at a frightened bourgeois in a frock-coat. The dagger held by the Republic is over the head of the bourgeois, the wreath over that of the worker.' The journalist does not give further details of how the republic is represented, as if his readers could take this for granted (the history of this fascinating subject has been traced by Maurice Agulhon).[86] What is striking here is the insertion of the class struggle into the republican allegory; as if on Judgment Day the republic would, like God, reward the just and punish the wicked. The female figure of the republic would before long be adapted to represent the General Strike; and later again the Revolution.[87] It is worth noting too the classical symbols, dagger and laurel wreath, and the use of costume to denote class (the Bourgeois in frock coat, the Worker in shirt-sleeves). A systematic study would no doubt reveal other material evidence of this form of working-class expression and make it possible to trace its political, aesthetic and symbolic development.

The example of Doyet-les-Mines tells us about other things too: the inventive part played by the young, who were here well integrated into village life; the mixture of religious motifs (the tasselled banner and expressions like 'Brothers let us unite') with political formulas ('Workers' Party'); and lastly the combination of a political event with a folk event. The whole episode took place in an atmosphere of impressive unanimity: in this coalfield, in Bézenet, Monvicq, Doyet, Commentry, the strike was almost one hundred per cent. In Montlucon, it is true, only the glass-workers came out, but in all these places there were assemblies in the main square and deputations to the authorities. In Montlucon, Jean Dormoy, who was a Guesdist local councillor, accompanied the worker delegates. This founding father of the First of May had probably made a special effort in his own *département*. The Parti Ouvrier, well entrenched in this old republican region where the Left had always meant the extreme Left, had been able to mobilize and channel working-class traditions into a demonstration with a holiday atmosphere.

The First of May at Vienne (Isère): anarchist and anti-employer

The anarchists went about things rather differently. After first criticizing and condemning the Guesdist initiative, the anarchists threw themselves determinedly into preparations for the First of May and did their best to guide it into their own preferred channels: not deferential appeals to the public authorities, which they regarded as a form of acceptance of and submission to a state they challenged, but direct action on a massive scale at grass-roots level, with mobilization of the most downtrodden members of society and if necessary violent confrontation, in order to provoke a spectacular incident which would lend itself to propaganda and the affirmation of more widespread solidarity. Above all, it was to be directed against the employers, for *les Patrons, voilà l'ennemi.* Hatred for the 'exploiters' was the crucible of consciousness and the ferment of the workers' struggle.[88] Threats, whether written or delivered verbally to the manufacturers, to force them to close the factories, inflammatory tracts ('Set fire to houses, shacks, mattresses,' said a poster put up by the Italians in Marseilles),[89] and stirring speeches all heightened the tension. In Trelazé (Maine-et-Loire) where there was a strong libertarian nucleus among the slate-quarrymen, one speaker invited his audience to 'take up arms and blow up the houses of the bourgeoisie with dynamite'.[90] The First of May demonstrations, he said, should make these and the factories their target.

This was what happened at Cette, Marseilles and Vienne, where there were violent incidents. In Marseilles a band of Italian workers and young *nervis* (the name given to the youths who hung about the docks) invaded and sacked the Jeansoulin oil-works in the course of the evening. The armed forces were called in and there were 76 arrests and prosecutions, leading eventually to 46 prison sentences of between six days and three months.[91]

Vienne (Isère) a textile town in the Rhône Valley, was the scene of a full-scale riot, well-documented because of the subsequent trial.[92] It is a fairly representative example of a 'direct action' May Day. The anarchist group in Vienne consisted of 80 *compagnons*, led by Pierre Martin, known as *le Bossu* ('the Hunchback') and Toussaint Bordat, a former weaver who was banned from Lyons and had since 1887 been living in Vienne, as a newsagent and distributor of anarchist literature. In 1880, *La Révolte*, the anarchist newspaper, sold up to 150 copies there and as many as 500 when there were articles of local interest.[93] The violence at Vienne was anything but spontaneous. The arrival of Louise Michel ('the great patriot' as Pierre Martin called her) on 27 April was part of an intensive propaganda campaign aimed in particular at women and young people, the subproletariat of the weaving mills who had already engaged in some hard-fought strikes. The *appondeurs* (weavers' assistants) were aged between 12 and 16; scattered throughout the different mills, they were very mobile 'and always ready to walk out'. Tracts and posters, such as the appeal 'To the women of Vienne', which is fairly typical in its down-to-earth and very human tone,[94] or the appeal 'To the young mule-operators', were specifically addressed to these groups, spoke to them of their own situation and urged them to stand up and claim a reduction in working hours. 'We knew,' Martin later said at his trial

> that there were children working more than fourteen hours a day, who did not have a moment at midday to eat their dinner. There were women in similar conditions; we had to protest against such inhumanity, and that is why we discussed the demonstration of the First of May. For our labouring population here, it was a big achievement to get an hour off for dinner.[95]

A sixteen-year-old girl, Josephine Tavernier, confirmed during the trial that 'she had heard a call at the meeting for a wage rise and an hour off for the midday meal'. The anarchists wanted to root the First of May in the real-life situation of the workers, to make specific demands and obtain the immediate satisfaction which would strengthen the workers in the confidence that they could change their lives. As the appeal 'To the women of Vienne' splendidly puts it: 'No! No! We will not put up with this miserable state of affairs any longer. Let us lift up our heads, let us demand our rights, let us demand our place in the sun, let us dare to say to our Masters: "We are made of flesh and blood like you, and like you we ought to live a free and happy life through our labour."'

Here was a determination to make hearts beat faster and egalitarian pulses race with a sense of misery and injustice; a determination to resurrect the *sans-culotte* tradition: it was to the sound of *La Carmagnole*, the old revolutionary song, that the anarchists urged the workers, women and children in front, to march on the factories and in particular to the mill owned by Brocard, an employer hated for his harsh attitude during the 1879 strike. They seized a 43-metre length of cloth and, to cries of 'Take it, it's yours', threw it to the crowd which tore it up and took pieces home as a kind of trophy. This was a spectacular scene of collective repossession, of ritual destruction (extravagance is after all part of the substance of a holiday) and a very pictorial one with the forest of red and black flags and the joyful faces of women and children. The anarchists had a highly developed sense of spectacle, of bodily gesture, of physical participation, a capacity for integrating older forms of behaviour into a new ritual, and a recognition of symbols, all of which made these libertarians the greatest respecters of history. When the presiding magistrate asked him what the meaning was of the red and black flags, Martin replied:

> The red flag has always been the emblem rallying rebels against tyranny, against every kind of reaction. The red flag was flying during the taking of the Bastille, it flew in 1830, it was flown in 1848 by the revolutionary socialist people; and it was in the hands of the conquered soldiers of the Commune in 1871. The black flag expresses the dark social misery which asserts itself at certain times, as in 1831, when the Lyons silk-workers wrote upon it 'Let us live working or die fighting.' We are not attached to the cult of flags, but it is sometimes necessary to use them during a battle.[26]

Thus was the memory of a struggle created.

Vienne and Doyet-les-Mines offer us a contrasted pair of pictures, two different scenarios corresponding to two different strategies: the anarchist version – more populist and more violent – sought to bring about the Revolution by appealing to the poorest, most downtrodden people to revolt; the Guesdist version – much more disciplined, orderly and controlled – was based on the big battalions of the industrial proletariat, commanded by political and trade-union leaders, unified by simple slogans and looking towards the central power. On the new revolutionary stage, where so much was reminiscent of the old, the anarchists were playing the *Enragés* and the Guesdists the Jacobins.

One more feature distinguishes the two, relating to the conception of the First of May and its duration. For the Guesdists, this was to be a demonstration confined to a particular day. This disciplined version of militant action – a very modern one in fact – shocked the anarchists with their vision of the Revolution as a dynamic process starting with a general strike. For them, the First of May was just a beginning, a possible starting-point for further action, the extent and length of which would depend on the enthusiasm of the mobilized masses. In this respect, the anarchists were closer to the practices of strikers at the time. Nothing could have been more foreign to the conduct of a strike than to fix a time for it to end. Workers went on strike without any idea when they could go back to work; it was a beginning whose end no one could predict. This was the reason why many workers found it impossible to go back to work after the First of May. Like a seismic shock, it triggered off a wave of strikes inspired by a quasi-messianic hope in which the religious expectation of a Coming and the vision of a historical movement were intermingled. This aftermath is the subject of my conclusion.

The Great Day?

After this intoxicating day of festivities, 'going back to work', returning to the 'slave-drivers', to the bosses, and to the likelihood of reprisals seemed impossible. Many simply did not go. Moreover, workers who had not taken the day off on the First of May in turn joined the movement, sometimes putting forward belated claims. Others did not make any demands, but said they wanted to 'do the same as everyone else'. A wave of strikes and demonstrations unfurled from the First onward, making May 1890 a month of much unrest. Twenty-six per cent of all the strikes and 58 per cent of all the strikers of that year are accounted for by this single month (as against the May average over the period 1871–90 of 13 per cent and 19 per cent respectively). It was a wave particularly felt in the northern textile industry, in the coalfields both north and south (in particular in the Gard), and in the northern suburbs of Paris (glass-works and gas-works). The movement had different features in different sectors, but was almost always inspired by the First of May. In one sector (the Paris glass-works) there was a straightforward clash with authority; the employers wanted to get rid of the union branch which had organized the strike on the First of May, and had led the workers of Aubervilliers, Pantin, and Bas-Meudon on a march towards Paris, waving red banners.[97] Among the miners, the idea of an industry-wide strike, which had indeed been envisaged by their general congress at Jolimont in Belgium, was gaining ground – something which explains their sympathy for the First of May movement. In both the north and the south, most of the miners had demonstrated on the day itself, but if they went back quite quickly in the north, elsewhere they stayed out longer – in Saint-Eloy-les-Mines, in Ronchamp, in the Allier and the Gard, they refused to go back down the pits. In the Allais coalfield, they drew the originally reluctant silk-spinsters into the movement and the disturbances continued until July, with some of the features of a peasant rebellion, a kind of unrest which the Cévennes, home of the Camisards, had so often seen in the past. The popular Marius Henry, hero of several previous strikes, who had been dismissed for threatening the mining engineer on the First of May, was arrested but later released by the crowd, and took to the hills. He hid out in the wooded mountains behind the village of Lalle and 'there he receives newspapers and gives orders. Several strikes are in charge of his security and whenever danger threatens, he takes refuge in the abandoned mine-workings where he goes to earth like a rabbit.'[98] Clandestine meetings took place in the woods: Armandine Vernet, a young women of 32, wife of a miner and mother of five children, often spoke here, turning out to be an excellent speaker capable of moving her audience, although 'she had never drawn attention to herself before'.[99]

In the textile towns of the north, the return to work was difficult, and a number of dismissals made the situation explosive. On 3 May in Roubaix, close on 35,000 strikers marched through the streets chanting, and over the next few days the strike spread to the nearby communities: Tourcoing, Wattrelos, La Madeleine, Hellemmes, Lannoy, Roncq, Neuvilly, Lille, and more. Groups of men went round singing the weavers' old song:

> *Si n'veulent pas nous renquérir,*
> *Nous allons tout démolir.*
> (If they won't have us back,
> We will take the place apart)

The strikers were unskilled workers on modest wages with many women and young people among them, the *rattacheurs* (piecers) whose ardour and impatience were on display almost everywhere. They were particularly sensitive to the shock wave that swept the area after the First of May. Such workers had experienced it not merely as a moment of protest, but as a beginning, the dawn of a new day, a hope of things to come. *Something was going to happen* which would change their lives. Of the blanket-makers of Cours (Rhône), who had been on strike for two months, the prefect wrote in February 1890: 'If they can hold out for another two months, it is the opinion of these poor people that they will have won a brilliant victory and a radical transformation of their condition.'[100] This feeling of expectancy was noted by many observers, among the workers as well as among the bourgeoisie. The counterpart of this great working-class hope was bourgeois panic.

'Will there be a *journée*?' the papers had asked. And we do find here both the practice and the evocation of the 'revolutionary days', those moments when history suddenly moves with great speed and the world can tilt the other way. The notion of the 'Great Day', a precursor of the *'Grand Soir'*[101] was an underlying theme of the First of May. It drew on many sources, religious as well as political. Introducing the vision of 'the earthly paradise', Saint-Simon had written in 1803: 'The day will come when I will turn the earth into a paradise.'[102] The militants of the First of May took on the voices of prophets to speak of 'the right to happiness', whose regime was on the way.

The 'Great Day' was more than this. It was a vision of rapid change, of a Revolution which would happen quickly because it was inevitable – a vision widely held at this time among socialist leaders as well as among ordinary workers[103] and reiterated in the meetings on the First of May. At Trelazé, citizen Brunet, a joiner from Paris, predicted as much to his comrades in the slate-quarries, exhorting them to stop work, to march to the prefecture and demand the eight-hour day. If they did not obtain satisfaction, he advised them, as we have already seen, to 'take arms and blow up the houses of the bourgeoisie with dynamite... At last the moment of the Revolution had come, and the army would stand by and watch.'[104] His words are merely a fragment of a widely-employed discourse, one with more or less violent undertones, which one finds repeated time and again. The working-class militants were, like the prophets, 'intoxicated with the future': in short they had faith.

The idea of imminent major change pervades the end of the century. The pessimism of the ruling classes called it 'decadence' or 'catastrophe'; the optimism of the socialists called it 'Revolution'. It is not a simple matter to explain this phenomenon of social psychology in which several factors are at work. No doubt the end of the century led contemporaries to reflect on the passage of time – the whole of Proust's writing is anchored in such reflection. In the shorter term, the centenary of the French Revolution, which was celebrated with pomp, recalled to mind the changes that had affected French society and stirred its potential successors: was it not time for the *Fourth* Estate to take the stage? Was not the Great Depression of the 1880s a sign of a new age? In the First of May we see portrayed various visions of society, and as such it crystallized these many influences. It stood at the meeting-point of several traditions, and held a place in the millenarian perspective which would remain for some time to come a feature of the working-class vision of the future.

By no means all French workers shared in this hope, however. Those who stood aside from the demonstrations were unquestionably far more numerous than those who took part. The history of the First of May cannot be written – any more than can the history of the labour movement as a whole – in terms of the irresistible advance of a growing mass, or of the course of a river in full spate, swollen with the streams inevitably flowing into it from all sides. This impassioned vision has very little to do with reality. While working-class consciousness of a shared destiny does have something comparatively spontaneous about it, acceptance of an identity signalled by a unified ritual has nothing of the sort. The external political act, which in many cases claims to be creating this identity simply by proclaiming it, may be felt as an injury, an intrusion into the secret life of groups fashioned by very ancient practices, especially if attempts are made to suggest to them, indeed to force upon them, a particular mode of behaviour. And the indifference, resistance and indeed hostility which the First of May encountered has also to be recorded.

In Brittany, for example, whose trade-union history has recently been studied by Claude Geslin, the First of May was not an event which made uniform progress; it had its ups and downs and even faded from view at times, usually in connection with the political situation of the moment. The socialist and labour organizations did their best to promote it with circulars and slogans handed down from on high, that is, from Paris. But the watchwords did not correspond to local demands, and the obligatory work-stoppage was borne with impatience. Nor did a nationwide, French, ceremony really appeal to the Bretons. Some of them did nevertheless make a splendid effort to adapt it to their own way of life. In 1905, the militants of the Basse-Loire hired a steamboat – the *Basse-Indre* – which sailed, all decked in red, down the Loire from Saint-Nazaire to Nantes, at every halt taking on board workers' delegations with their banners, marking each stop like the stations of the cross – but this was a joyful occasion, in which laughter mingled with the singing of the Internationale and plenty of the local Muscadet was drunk. Was the arrival of the boat at Nantes, where a reception committee of comrades was waiting on the quayside, too disorderly? At all events, the leadership of the CGT intervened in the name of working-class respectability. 'On 1 May 1907, Griffuelhes made it clear at Saint-Nazaire that the First of May was supposed to be a day of protest, not a holiday. No more boat-trips down the Loire.'[105]

In a general sense, this necessarily ambiguous 'holiday', shot through with tensions as it was, would never have the popularity of the *Quatorze Juillet*. In some respects it reveals the comparative isolation of the working class in French society and the difficulties of building a new culture. It nevertheless remains without doubt the most complete of working-class rituals and a fascinating experiment in the creation of a symbolic event.

NOTES

1 Mona Ozouf, *La Fête revolutionnaire*, 1789–1788 (Paris 1976).
2 In May 1890, the French socialist movement was still divided among a number of groups and did not form a united party until 1905. The two largest were the Marxist Parti Ouvrier Français, led by Jules Guesde (the Guesdists); and the 'Possibilists' (Fédération des Travaileurs Socialistes de France) led by Paul Brousse, who adopted a more reformist approach. (Later in the same year the left wing of the Possibilist Party left to form the Allemanist Party.) The Blanquists, followers of the

revolutionary leader Auguste Blanqui (*d.* 1881), were a small but still influential group; and the anarchists had militants in Paris and other towns. For more details see Aaron Noland, *The Founding of the French Socialist Party, 1893–1905* (Cambridge, Mass. 1956).

3 The history of the First of May has usually been written in terms of politics and events, and historians have been more concerned to distinguish the roles played by different parties and groups than with a study of its symbolic content. The pioneer work on the subject, still indispensable, is Maurice Dommanget's *Histoire du Premier Mai* (Paris 1953); see also his *Histoire du drapeau rouge* (Paris n.d., *c.* 1966). André Rossel's *Premier Mai. Quatre-vingt-dix ans de luttes populaires dans le monde* (Paris 1977), a remarkable source of documentation and above all iconography, falls rather into the first category. The studies by Mona Ozouf and Maurice Agulhon – see in particular his *Marianne au combat* (Paris 1979) now translated as *Marianne into Battle, Republican Imagery and Symbolism in France 1789–1880* (Cambridge 1982) and the forthcoming sequel, *Marianne au pouvoir (1880 à nos jours)*—have shown how fruitful it can be to reflect on the relations between politics and symbolic form. Eric Hobsbawm has himself explored this approach in his article 'Sexe, vetements et politique', *Actes de la Recherche en Sciences Sociales* 23 (1978) and the debate is continued in no. 28 (1979). What better way is there of saluting him than to pursue a path he has himself pioneered?

   Mention should also be made of Miguel Rodriguez's current doctoral thesis, 'Premier Mai. Etude sémantique et symbolique'. On the methodology of analysing demonstrations, see the special number of *Ethnologie Française*, 'Anthropolgie dans le champ urbain', 12/2 (April–June 1982).

4 Rossel, *Premier Mai*, p. 66.

5 Jules Vallès's paper, *Le Cri du Peuple*, reported it at some length. *Canards* (broadsheets) about the 'eight Chicago martyrs' were apparently printed, since the bookseller André Jammes mentions one in his Catalogue no. 241, item 889.

6 Benoît Frachon, *Pour la CGT. Mémoire de Lutte (1902–1939)* (Paris 1981), pp. 11ff: 'Le ler Mai: de Chicago à mon village minier'. Frachon was closer to the syndicalist tradition of direct action, and refers much more specifically than Rossel to the influence of the events in Chicago. The CGT (Confédération Générale du Travail) was the central French trade-union organization.

7 E. Levasseur, *L'ouvrier américain*, 2 vols. (Paris 1898), especially Vol. I, chap. 4; M. Dommanget, *La chevalerie du travail française* (Lausanne 1967). On the French view of the American labour movement in the late nineteenth century, see M. Debouzy, 'Regards français sur les Etats-Unis: de l'observation à l'histoire', *Revue d'Etudes Americaines* 13 (February 1982).

8 Some French workers' delegates went to the Philadelphia World's Fair in 1876 and the Chicago Fair in 1893; they subsequently published reports in which they analysed the living and working conditions of the American workers, comparing them with the situation in France.

9 M. Perrot, 'Dans le Paris de la Belle Epoque: les Apaches, premières bandes de jeunes', in *Les marginaux et les exclus dans l'histoire, Cahiers Jussieu*, no. 5 (Paris 1979).

10 Rossel, *Premier Mai*, p. 48.

11 M. Perrot, *Les Ouvriers en grève (1871–1890)*, 2 vols. (Paris 1974), pp. 489ff; Dommanget, *Histoire du Premier Mai*, p. 65.

12 Perrot, *Les Ouvriers en grève*, p. 162.

13 Dommanget, *Histoire du Premier Mai*, pp. 28ff.

14 Perrot, *Les Ouvriers en grève*, pp. 283ff: 'La durée de la journée du travail et son organisation'.

15 Dommanget, *Histoire du Premier Mai*, p. 12.

16 Rossel, *Premier Mai*, p. 84 ('Manifeste du Parti Ouvrier Francais de la région du Nord') and p. 87 (*Le Combat*, 29 April 1890).

17 Dommanget, *Histoire du Premier Mai*, pp. 36–7. And May Day was of course a date traditionally celebrated in medieval and Tudor England: many rituals still survived in 1890, as some still do today.

18 Ozouf, *La Fête révolutionnaire*, p. 294.

19 *Ibid.*, p. 290, for details of the rebellious associations of the peasant *mai* or maypole.

20 *Ibid.*, p. 294.

21 M. Agulhon, *La République au village* (Paris 1970).

22 The expression is Mona Ozouf's: *La Fête révolutionnaire*, pp. 317ff; chap. 10, 'La Fête revolutionnaire: un transfert de sacralité'.

23 M. Abensour, 'L'Utopie socialiste: une nouvelle alliance de la politique et de la religion', in *Le Temps de la réflexion* 2 (1981).

24 *Ibid.*, p. 105.

25 *Le Producteur*, Vol. II (Paris 1826), p. 330. On the theme of Carnival and Revolution, see Alain Faure, *Paris Carême-Prenant. Du Carnaval à Paris au 19e siècle* (Paris 1978).

26 Étienne Cabet, *Voyage en Icarie*, 2nd edn. (Paris 1842), p. 253.

27 *Ibid.*, p. 269.

28 *Ibid.*, p. 271.

29 *Ibid.*, p. 271.

30 Perrot, *Les Ouvriers en grève*, Vol. II, p. 637.

31 Quoted by Dommanget, *Histoire du Premier Mai*, p. 67, circular by Lavigne, published in *Le Cri du Peuple*, 27 January 1889.

32 Archives Départmentales (Hereafter AD) Loire, 10 M 87, item 109 (poster captioned 'Workers' groups supporting the Demonstration').

33 S. Moscovici, *L'Age des foules. Un traité historique de psychologie des masses* (Paris 1981), pp. 144ff.

34 Protot was one of these. Cf. n. 2.

35 *Le Prolétariat*, 5 April 1890.

36 Joffrin, a leading Possibilist, predicted a fiasco: *Le Radical*, 13 April 1890.

37 Archives de la Préfecture de Police (hereafter APP), BA 41, item 464: poster dated 14 April 1890.

38 APP, BA 41, item 488, a poster issued by the anarchists of the 11th and 12th *arrondissements* of Paris.

39 On the Guesdists and the regions where they were strongest, see the standard reference work by Claude Willard, *Le Mouvement socialiste en France (1893–1905). Les Guesdistes* (Paris 1965).

40 Yves Lequin, *Les Ouvriers de la région lyonnaise (1848–1914)*, 2 vols. (Lyons 1977).

Another example is Roubaix (Nord): AD Nord, M 159/2: the local trade union had set up a committee of five members 'with the task of studying the means to be employed to bring work to a stop on 1 May'. In mid-April, the prefect passed on to the minister of the interior a whole list of meetings planned in both Lille and Roubaix. One Guesdist militant, Delory, worked himself very hard: on 13 April he was speaking at the Harmonie café, on the 14th at the Deseck, on the 15th at La Glacière, on the 19th at the Orphéon at Fives-Lille, on the 21st at the Barque, etc. There were local ward meetings every night. The crucial role played by certain militants clearly emerges here – in some respects one could almost say that the First of May was the work of a handful of men.

41 Cf. Gabriel Tarde, *L'Opinion et la foule*, which stresses the importance of communications for the functioning of mass society; and Moscovici, *L'Âge des foules*, pp. 250ff.

42 Jacques Rancière, *La Nuit des prolétaires. Archéologie du rêve ouvrier* (Paris, 1981) describes, among others, the forms of communication used by the Saint-Simonians.

43 *Le Combat*, Vol. I, no. 1, 19 March 1890; it ran until 21 December 1890. (Bibliothèque Nationale (hereafter BN), Paris, Le 2 4131).

44 APP, BA41, item 478 (reproduced in Rossel, *Premier Mai*, p. 109).

45 Miguel Rodriguez will in his thesis carry out a systematic analysis of the style and vocabulary of the *Papillon*, which provide a homogeneous corpus of material for semantic study. For many militants, the First of May campaigns would always be associated with sticking up these *papillons* or fliers. Benoît Frachon was a schoolboy in Firminy in 1906, and remembers the First of May campaign: 'Every day, we found tracts and fliers which provided us with slogans and objectives... So in order to be like the grown-ups, we had to prepare our own material, our fliers, our placards and our red flags... One slogan in particular had attracted our attention: 'Anything is possible if you want it enough: we want the eight-hour day.' We made some fliers with this wording, but there was something wrong: we could hardly call for an eight-hour day, since the school day was only six hours. That didn't matter! We made our slogan 'the four-hour day' instead, and stuck it up in all the classrooms', *Pour la CGT*, pp. 12–13.

46 As has been done by the Piero Gobetti Centre in Turin, for the collection of *bandiera* (banners) in the Museum of the Risorgimento in Turin. See the magnificent published catalogue.

47 AD Rhône, series M, file on 1 May 1890, report from the special police inspector, 29 April 1890.

48 APP, BA 41 (reproduced in Rossel, *Premier Mai*, p. 89).

49 Archives Nationales (hereafter AN), F 12, 4667, report by the gendarmerie, Bessèges, 2 May 1890.

50 AD Rhône, series M, file on 1 May 1890, special inspector to the prefect, 17 April 1890.

51 AD Rhône, *ibid.*, report by the prefect (Jules Cambon) to the minister of the interior, 1 May 1890: 'Today, all these people are breathing again.'

52 AD Rhône, *ibid.*, police report, 1 May 1890.

53 AD Rhône, *ibid.*, report from the justice of the peace, Thizy, 24 April 1890.

54 Yves Lequin, *Les Ouvriers de la région lyonnaise*, Vol. I, pp. 94ff on the economic situation; Vol. II on the anarchist movement.

55 H. Oeconomo, 'Le Premier Mai 1906 à Paris' (University of Paris VII, master's thesis, 1978).

56 *Le Dix-Neuvième Siècle*, 2 May 1890.

57 AD Nord, M 159/2, item 3, report by the gendarmerie, 2 May 1890.

58 AN BB 18, 1816, report by the gendarmerie, 30 April 1890.

59 AN, F 12, 4667, the prefect of the Sarthe to the minister of the interior, 5 May 1890.

60 AN, F 12, 4667 and *L'Indépendant de l'Allier*, 3 May 1890.

61 AN, F 12, 4667.

62 AN, F 12, 4667, prefect of the Meuse to the minister, 5 May 1890.

63 Cf. Rancière, *La Nuit des prolétaires*, Perrot, *Les Ouvriers en grève*, pp. 450–470, 'La conduite de la grève: les meneurs'.

64 AD Loire, 10 M 87, file on preparations for 1 May: report on a public meeting in Roanne, 30 April 1890. In this region, which was undergoing a crisis, the fight against unemployment was at the heart of the argument: the eight-hour day was made necessary by technological progress.

65 AD Nord, M 159/2, item 2, list of the petitions handed in to the subprefect and prefect.

66 *Le Combat*, 5 May 1890.

67 Rossel, *Premier Mai*, p. 66. Demands for the legal protection of female and child labour, which were very prominent at national level, were taken up hardly at all at local level.

68 Oeconomo, 'Le Premier Mai à Paris', particularly stresses this point. The demonstrations were more male-dominated in Paris than in the provinces, where they were attended by a wider public and therefore had a family appeal. When, in 1891, troops fired on the demonstrations in Fourmies, the victims were women and children, because they were in the front of the procession.

69 APP, BA 49, sub-file 11, on the First of May demonstrations in the Paris suburbs, carries reports of '*fêtes familiales*' described as *Fêtes du Travail* (Feasts of Labour) in Adamville, Montrouge, Boulogne-Billancourt, and Choisy-le-Roi, where they were organized by revolutionary socialist groups and (less frequently) by local union branches.

70 On this point see Hobsbawm, 'Sexe, vêtements et politique'; M. Perrot, 'Masculin/féminin dans les classes populaires urbaines au 19e siècle', unpublished paper given to the Society for French Historical Studies, March 1982, New York.

71 What we do not know is whether there was a trend towards the standardization of the forms taken by the demonstration, or on the contrary whether local initiatives and a greater diversification of the modes of expression used for the First of May became more frequent. Miguel Rodriguez's thesis will bring us more information on this point.

72 Perrot, *Les Ouvriers en grève*, Vol. I, pp. 283ff.

73 M. Garmiche-Mérit, 'Le Système buéton. Bué-en-Sancerrois (1900–1914)' (University of Paris VII, doctoral thesis *3e cycle*, 1982).

74 On resistance to work see Rancière, *La Nuit des prolétaires*; on resistance to the

factory see Michael Seidman's unpublished research on labour disputes at the time of the Popular Front.

75 Claude Geslin, 'Le Syndicalisme Ouvrier en Bretagne avant 1914' (University of Paris X-Nanterre, state doctorate, 1982) qualifies this view somewhat. In the Basse-Loire for example, the organization of work at plant level was not easily reconciled to the eight-hour day, and many workers were reticent, not to say hostile to this slogan which moreover forbade them to work any overtime.

76 *La Defense des Travailleurs de Saint-Quentin*, 4 May 1890.

77 Cf. *Le Figaro*, 3 May 1890: 'some even thought it was a joke to fall over, with great waving of the limbs and guffaws, near the most irreproachably elegant ladies in their silk dresses'. One can judge from this how 'scandalous' it was at this time to approach the luxury of the rich.

78 AD Loire, 10 M 87, item 104; item 9: there were banquets at Charlieu (45 guests); Saint-Denis (150 guests), Boishameau (15 guests), etc.

79 Maurice Agulhon, *La République au village*, has shown how formative the *chambrée* was: the traditional meeting-place for men, it became a political and trade-union headquarters – a good example of changed function. See also chapter 2 above.

80 Rosemonde Sanson, *Les 14 juillet, fête et conscience nationale, 1789–1975* (Paris 1976), esp. pp. 56ff, 'La Fête de la Bourgeoisie'.

81 The *Fête de l'Humanité* is the French Communist Party's annual fair, fund-raising event and solidarity rally, which takes place on the second weekend in September in a Paris suburb.

82 At the time, no one really knew how to measure the size of a crowd, so the figures reported vary considerably. The engineers of the *Ponts-et-Chaussées* (Highways Department) had only very recently begun to apply themselves to this question.

83 Dommanget, *Histoire du drapeau rouge*. The dropping of the red briar rose as a symbol of the First of May in the twentieth century in favour of the white lily-of-the-valley, raises the problem of a symbolic transference; in a way it denotes the shift from a revolutionary demonstration to a 'Labour Day' such as the Vichy government, for example, was happy to accept.

84 Miguel Rodriguez, in the course of his research, has discovered about two hundred different slogans on the placards carried on 1 May 1919.

85 *L'Indépendant du Centre*, 2 May 1890. On the leading role played by Jean Dormoy in the success of the First of May in the Allier département, see Dommanget, *Histoire du Premier Mai*, pp. 78ff.

86 Agulhon, *Marianne au combat*.

87 For an example of this iconographical transfer see Perrot, *Les Ouvriers en grève*, fig. 9, p. 300, illustration for *La Grève générale* (The General Strike) a revolutionary song, 1900.

88 M. Perrot, 'Le Regard de l'Autre: comment les ouvriers français voyaient leurs patrons', in M. Levy-Léboyer (ed.), *Le Patronat de la seconde industrialisation* (Paris 1979), pp. 293–307.

89 AD Bouches-du-Rhone, M 6 3405.

90 AD Maine-et-Loire, 71 M 2.

91 AN, BB 18 1816.

92 AD Isère, 75 M 2 (file containing 321 items); AN, BB 18 1816, on the Martin Affair (Vienne); *Le procès des anarchistes de Vienne devant la Cour d'Assises de l'Isère (12 août 1890)*, pamphlet (Saint-Etienne 1890).

93 AD Isère, 75 M 2, item 284.

94 This poster (from AD Isère, 75 M 2, item 187) is reproduced in M. Perrot, *Les Ouvriers en grève*, Vol. I, p. 140, fig. 2.

95 *Le Petit Dauphinois Républicain*, 9 August 1890.

96 *Le Procès des anarchistes*, pp. 33–4.

97 APP, BA 170, file on the glass-workers' strike (73 items).

98 AD Gard, 14 M 447, report from the police inspector in Bessèges, 7 May 1890. J.M. Gaillard, 'Le 1er mai 1890 dans le bassin houiller du Gard', *Le Mouvement Social*, no. 94 (January – March 1976).

99 AD Gard, 14 M 447, police file dated 3 June 1890.

100 AD Rhône, series M, file on 1890 strikes, the prefect to the minister of the interior, 22 February 1890.

101 Perrot, *Les Ouvriers en grève*, Vol. II, pp. 631–2; on the theme of *le Grand Soir* see D. Seenhuyse's extremely interesting study, 'Quelques jalons dans l'étude du thème du *Grand Soir* jusqu'en 1900', *Le Mouvement Social* 75 (April – June 1971). The author detects the first use of this expression (literally 'the Big Night' – rather than 'the Great Day', *le Grand Jour*) in 1882, during disturbances at Montceau-les-Mines, but 'we have to wait until 1892 for more reliable information: this was when the expression was officially coined'. It originated in Bohemian circles of writers and journalists in Paris. 'It was only in 1898–9 that the expression "le Grand Soir" would be used in a revolutionary sense in anarchist circles, among militants and journalists concerned with written propaganda.' The author analyses the religious and social origins of the expression and its connection with millenarianism. He estimates that the popularity of the myth among the working class was at its height between 1900 and 1920.

102 H. de Saint-Simon, *Lettres d'un habitant de Genève à ses contemporains* (1803), quoted by M. Abensour, 'L'Utopie socialiste', in *Le Temps de la Réflexion*, no. 2 p. 74.

103 On millenarianism among workers and socialists, cf. Perrot, *Les Ouvriers en grève*, pp. 630ff; and *Le Socialisme français et le pouvoir* (Paris 1966) (with Annie Kriegel); and Seenhuyse's article (see n. 101).

104 AD Maine-et-Loire, 71 M 2, item 175.

105 Claude Geslin, 'Le Syndicalisme Ouvrier en Bretagne', p. 810. This study contains much information about the local history of the First of May. Victor Griffuelhes was the general secretary of the CGT.

7

Civic rituals and patterns of resistance in Barcelona, 1890–1930

TEMMA KAPLAN

Civic rituals, including folkloric events, religious holidays, and funerals, can contribute to modern as well as traditional political life insofar as collective rites create a sense of community.[1] The content of the rituals can vary even when the forms remain the same; therefore civic rituals, which, under ordinary circumstances are used to enhance those in power, can become collective acts that create solidarity in regionalist and working-class movements, just as they did in Barcelona between 1890 and 1930.

Because ceremonies can help forge collective consciousness, debates often ensue about how rituals should take place, in what language, and with what goals. Struggles for control over collective identity can take place through holiday celebrations and use of folklore as well as in other arenas which are not usually thought of as political. This is especially true when normal civil rights are circumscribed, as they have been so often during the past century in Barcelona. Under such circumstances, cultural struggles can attain extraordinary political importance.

The industrialists and businessmen who made Catalonia the richest province of Spain lacked power in the national state and had to fight for local political control against the appointed civil governor of the province and the military captain-general, both of whom had their main headquarters in Barcelona. Conservative Catholic businessmen tried to forge popular alliances around shared Catalan culture. Artisans, shopkeepers, journalists and some professionals were attracted to more radical programmes for the reorganization of Spain into a federal republic that would provide Catalonia and other regions with control over their own schools, roads, social services, and artistic development.[2] Until after 1905, working-class groups were not attracted to movements that stressed shared Catalan values, but they had discovered in class-based rituals a way to unite the working-class community, male and female, around a sense of popular identity that was at least citywide.[3]

Civic rituals entail use of public city space to publicize certain ideas. In

Catholic countries, ritual and folklore often merge in urban celebrations so that although people in the religious and political hierarchy may lead processions for holidays such as Corpus Christi in early June, pagan figures and stock characters from popular theatre also assume their rightful place in line. The blend of sacred and profane, of conservative and politically innovative groups in a number of Barcelona's civic rituals, contributed to numerous resistance movements in that city. Political struggle came first, but once its parameters were set, civic rites could provide an arena for struggle. Between 1890 and 1926, similar rituals were used by the working class to confront local rulers, including the Church, and by Catalan patriots, including those from the popular classes, against the state.

Different kinds of rituals did, however, characterize different social groups; and the more folkloric and the less specifically historical or political, the more people they engaged. Thus the celebrations that began as religious holidays could even draw upon anti-clerical groups, just as rituals of resistance or communal funerals of protest might do. Even clergy and army officials joined in a 1905 funeral to protest against the central government's inability to protect the city against bombings. Middle-class republicans attracted some workers in rituals that commemorated heroic moments in Barcelona's history.

What united all classes in Barcelona was the use of the Catalan language, which became a rallying point for conservatives, religious, monarchist Catalan nationalists, as well as Catalan federalist republicans. Working-class groups placed less emphasis upon repression of the Catalan language, though they spoke it, than upon the violation of their civil rights, especially their right to associate in labour syndicates and their right of assembly. Periodically, in mass meetings and in political marches, they created a new working-class civic ritual to protest against indignities and the suppression of their rights as a working-class community.

Resistance to dictators, whether to Miguel Primo de Rivera, whose reign from 1923–30 was known as the 'Folkloric Dictatorship', or against Francisco Franco, between 1939 and 1975, often assumed cultural forms because repression against ordinary organization and assembly was so severe. It is a distinguishing characteristic of folklore, which both Primo de Rivera and Franco promoted, that it can be transformed to serve the interests of otherwise powerless groups. Those in power may try to establish the meaning of specific ceremonies and the characters in them, but they are not always secure against subversion. Dominant groups repress certain folkloric practices – both Primo and Franco outlawed the celebration of carnival early in their dictatorships – but the apparent pettiness of repression of holidays and language masks for historians what dictators comprehended: that politics spawned in communal rites can constitute underground political movements when all appearance of political life has been suppressed.

Four episodes in the history of Barcelona between 1890 and 1930 indicate how civic rituals became transformed to contribute under certain circumstances to new senses of community through new patterns of resistance. They include the first May Day in 1890; the 1905 funeral of two sisters killed when a bomb exploded at the flower market on the Ramblas, Barcelona's main promenade; the political funerals of Salvador Seguí and Francisco Comas, murdered by gangsters from the yellow unions that employers established in the twenties; and the counter-celebration of San Jordi Day on 23 April 1926. Dictatorial decrees to force Mass traditionally performed in Catalan to be said in Latin drove groups from throughout the city's population to practise civil disobedience by moving the sacred space from one building to another.

European leftists and labour leaders, many of whom organized the Second International Workingmen's Association, met on Bastille Day, 14 July 1889, in Paris. Among those assembled were August Bebel, Eleanor Marx, Domela Nieuwenhuis of the Netherlands, and Pablo Iglesias of Spain, who agreed with the others to call for co-ordinated popular demonstrations throughout the world for the first of May 1890. The ceremony they envisioned was designed to publicize working-class determination to win the eight-hour workday and the regulation of female and child labour. To emphasize their own ties to the revolutionary history of the international working class and to root their new effort in the past, the delegates went to the Père Lachaise cemetery where the victims of the Paris Commune were buried.[4]

Socialists and anarchists in different Spanish cities disagreed about the meaning of the demonstration and the day on which it should be celebrated. The first of May 1890 fell on a Thursday, and many socialists, such as those in Bilbao in the Basque country, decided to postpone their participation until Sunday the 4th, rather than lose a day's work on the first. Anarchists there and adherents of all parties in Barcelona agreed to organize for 1 May, but they split over how to proceed because they disagreed about the meaning of the event.

The leftists who initiated May Day in Paris wanted it to be a demonstration, not a festival; yet, so strong were the habits of civic rites, that the working class, even while they rejected the Church and the ruling classes, experienced a tropism in the direction of civic rituals. Urban demonstrations, particularly in Catholic cities such as Barcelona, invariably cover the same ground and move down the same streets to some of the same historically legitimated sacred secular spaces as Catholic processions do. Even those who adamantly rejected Catholicism could not help imitate it in creating a civic ritual.

May Day became a revolutionary international holiday, complete with anthems, banners such as the red flag which commemorated the blood spilled by the Communards and, in Barcelona, a yellow triangular ribbon. Although organizers attempted to build upon recent experience in labour mobilization, particularly during strikes, their counter-emblems drew their force from association with Catholic traditions. Even though organizers attempted to transform the old icons and cleanse them of religious references, some strongly emotional symbolic meanings seeped in.

May Day took two separate paths in 1890 Barcelona, where it was celebrated both as a festival and as a general strike. Popular newspapers began to announce the celebration in late April, and by 1 May people from the surrounding towns and outlying parts of the city of Barcelona flocked into town and filled the narrow streets of the old working-class districts near the harbour. Although some of the anarchist press insisted that May Day was a strike, railroad workers, some of whom were anarchist, stayed on the job as companies added as many carriages as locomotives could pull. Women and children joined the men, as hawkers mingled with the crowds to sell the triangular ribbons that called for the eight-hour day.[5]

The major celebration in Barcelona, organized by socialists with some republican support, drew men, women, and children from the working-class community as a whole. There was a mass meeting followed by a march and the presentation of a petition to the governor of the province, whose offices were in Barcelona. The major celebration began at the Tivoli Theatre in downtown Barcelona, where the audience heard speakers call for the eight-hour day, an end to child labour under the age of fourteen, and a six-hour day for children between the ages of fourteen and eighteen. They demanded the abolition of most night work and the prohibition of female employment where, as in the mines, the health of a woman or her unborn child might be at stake. They called for consecutive 36-hour rest periods every weekend or half-day on Saturday. They demanded that the government regulate jobs where workers' health might be endangered. Over the platform from which the speakers addressed the crowd hung the red flag inscribed with the goals: 'International workers' demonstration for the eight-hour day'.[6]

About 25,000 people marched from the Tivoli Theatre in the civic centre of Barcelona, the Plaza of Catalonia, which dominates the Ramblas. The procession, including a blue banner that called for 'Universal justice' moved down the Ramblas to Columbus Way, and north, along the harbour to the civil governor's office in the Plaza of the Palace. On this occasion, people in the balconies above the Ramblas cheered the festive demonstrators, who, though primarily working class, did not apparently appear as a threat.

When the crowd reached the governor's offices at the Plaza of the Palace near the harbour, they sent a delegation up to see him. Representatives petitioned Governor Ramón Blanco for the eight-hour day. The ritual aspects of the procedure were deferential: peaceful supplicants stood below as the governor appeared on the balcony, as if giving a political version of a blessing to the crowd, which applauded him. The parallels to religious holidays were obvious to contemporary observers, one of whom compared the first May Day to Holy Thursday before Easter.[7]

Groups among the most militant male anarchists insisted that May Day should not be a holiday, but a general strike. They drew strength from those workers who had been engaged in recent labour struggles. Trolley drivers, who had been organizing to win shorter shifts and better conditions, enthusiastically endorsed the anarchist vision of May Day as a general strike. They were not the only workers who linked their immediate grievances to a prolonged struggle beginning with May Day. They were joined by glass-workers, the ever-striking barbers, tailors, waiters, and cooks. The hatters and bakers, who, until well into the twentieth century were more militant than industrial workers were if judged by the frequency of strikes, declared their intention to stay out until they had won the eight-hour day, the ostensible goal of May Day.[8]

The militant anarchists boycotted the Tivoli Theatre meeting and the peaceful march to present a petition to the governor. Instead they met in the Carolina fields at the edge of the Tetuan Plaza at the centre of the north-eastern working-class section of Barcelona. The small group of men who attended the outdoor meeting vowed not to return to work the next day, as the milder demonstrators planned to do. The militant anarchists agreed to assemble at 9 a.m. on Saturday 3 May. From the Tetuan Plaza they moved across the rondas or boulevards that ringed the downtown working-class neighbourhoods; as they proceeded down the Ramblas the men shouted for a general strike and they met opposition. The Civil Guard, organized in the nineteenth century to capture bandits in the countryside but increasingly used as an urban army in Barcelona, occupied key civic spaces at the Plaza of St James, where the medieval gothic provincial government building, the Diputació, faced city hall, and at the Plaza of Catalonia. Troops stationed along the Ramblas stopped the march, and shouts rang out in the Plaza of Catalonia. The Civil Guard apparently had orders not to shoot, but simply to seal off escape routes and contain the demonstrators in the centre of the city, away from the governor.[9]

Although the militants were not numerous, an estimated 20,000 workers remained out on Saturday, 3 May, and stayed in the city on Sunday, 4 May. They filled the downtown areas of the Plaza of Catalonia and the Ramblas where normally on Sundays flower-sellers abounded and the cafes were filled. On this Sunday, however, the female flower-vendors, like most women, had receded from the downtown area as they often disappeared when there was fighting in the streets during trade-union struggles. The number of people in the streets caused the captain general to declare a state of siege and impose martial law.[10]

May Day became emblazoned upon the consciousness of the population of Barcelona, which continued to celebrate the day as a festival whenever it was permitted. The way this new civil ritual established itself indicates one way traditions get adapted and transformed and how consciousness can emerge even through peaceful collective action. Experiences structure the way people think about the future, and thus even ceremonial occasions can shape political thought. The elements of the first May Day, especially the political processions that took place, are so common a part of any demonstration that its meaning is often blurred. As John Berger has argued: 'A mass demonstration can be interpreted as the symbolic capturing of a capital... The demonstrators interrupt the regular life of the streets they march through or the open spaces they fill. They 'cut off' these areas, and, not yet having the power to occupy them permanently, they transform them into a temporary stage on which they dramatise the power they still lack.'[11] A peaceful communal demonstration such as the one that started at the Tivoli Theatre can have greater impact in some cases than a more violent one in which women and children are not present. Although many anarchists criticized the notion of a 'festival of labour' which May Day increasingly became after 1890, the repetitive symbolic seizure of the city by women as well as men ritually represented a world that was not divided between the social concerns of women and the political and economic concerns of men.

The working class of Barcelona adopted May Day as its principal celebration, a combination of demonstration and festival. By May Day 1891, practices that subsequently became 'traditional' had already begun to take certain ritual forms. These included the mass meetings, the march through the city, or through the sacred political spaces, and the proliferation of new emblems. In 1890 Barcelona, there were signs calling for improved working conditions, but women passed out the carnation, which quickly became the working-class flower. People watched street plays and listened to choral groups. Above the crowds, especially during the march from the Plaza of Catalonia down the Ramblas to the harbour, the tones of the republican anthem, 'Riego's Hymn', could be heard. Authorities continued to recognize the threat that, at least ritually, workers were creating their own alternative community on May Day. In a year of intense class struggle, such as 1900 when there had been a wave of strikes, the mayor banned May Day festivities. Would-be demonstrators from Barcelona organized a political pilgrimage out of the city to a hillside resort nearby. With bands playing political anthems, the crowds organized a political version of a religious pilgrimage, not to any shrine, but into the open air. They abandoned the city to go on a political picnic.[12]

The degree to which a political popular culture based on civic rituals such as May Day contributed to a class-conscious community in Barcelona worried those who preferred a regional strategy of Catalan nationalism which allegedly could bridge class differences. Spokespeople for this view portrayed the Castilians and the central government in Madrid as the principal enemy of all Catalans regardless of class. On May Day Eve, 1904, a Catalan republican warned about the divisiveness of class-based politics which enabled the government to divide Catalans along class rather than cultural lines.[13] The most radical of the Catalanist republicans wanted to replace the monarchy with a republic, and anarchists were generally attracted to any form of administration that contributed to local control. Republican holidays celebrated heroic moments in the history of Catalan resistance to Madrid, of which the most important was 11 September, the anniversary of the day in 1714 when the Catalan hero Rafael Casanova had had to submit to the triumphant Bourbons, who won the War of the Spanish Succession. As a result, Catalonia lost the aristocratic and common laws that permitted it to govern itself. Thus 11 September became Autonomy Day, to mark the hopes of Barcelona and its province for future rights to self-government.

Social disorder rocked Barcelona and intensified the significance of civic rituals in the late nineteenth and early twentieth centuries. Bombings and assassinations, often provoked by police, followed and engendered further police repression of the labour movement, especially between 1892 and 1897, between 1902 and 1906, and again from 1919 through to 1923.

Terrorists sometimes attacked generals, police, and people of the popular classes during ritual and cultural events. In 1893, for example, as the captain-general of the province reviewed his troops (a modern addition to the celebration of the Day of the Virgin of Mercy on 24 September), an anarchist, outraged by the year-long persecution of the labour movement in Barcelona and mass arrests, attempted to assassinate him. Officials were not secluded from the public in late nineteenth-century Spain as they are now, so attacks need not have taken place during civic rites. But to stage them there was to publicize the event, to gain an audience, and to desecrate the ceremony, although it also assured capture of the assassin.

The attempted assassination gave police further excuses for persecuting the working-class community by closing its newspapers and alternative schools, shutting union halls, and arresting all dissidents. In retaliation, other terrorists attacked a civic ritual of sorts–opening night at the opera. As the second act of *William Tell* began, bombs blasted the Lyceum Theatre where this major social event of the season was taking place. The escalating violence subsided for a while as the Cuban War of Independence began in 1895, and Spanish workers were conscripted for the army.

Cuban terrorists in Barcelona or the police themselves may have been responsible for the bombing, on 7 June 1896, of the Corpus Christi procession, possibly the oldest civic ritual in Barcelona. While the captain-general and the leading ecclesiastical officials of the Church in Barcelona led the procession, the six killed and the 40 wounded were almost all poor people at the rear of the procession.[14] Corpus Christi was the first rite of summer. Although the procession with rulers in the lead was a moving picture of the city's social hierarchy, the procession included allegedly historical and Biblical skits, complete with giants, ornately costumed characters made up of people standing on stilts or another's shoulders, and grotesque figures with huge papier mâché heads. They engaged in raucous, even lewd acts and gestures, giving some of the procession the air of carnival.[15]

The whole city of Barcelona felt attacked when on Sunday, 3 September 1905, a bomb went off at the flower market along the Ramblas at 1.20 in the afternoon. Pedestrians filled the narrow promenade as female flower-sellers pursued their most active weekly trade. The bomb, which was probably set by a police agent or a Cuban rebel against Spain, exploded in an outdoor urinal behind Petxina Street. The narrow street, just behind the flower market, was the site of art galleries and chocolate houses, and was regarded as one of the most picturesque streets in Barcelona. The bomb raised smoke and dust. At the moment of the explosion, people fell over one another in confusion, and blood ran in front of the Trillo watch shop where the large watch shop-sign, which served as a local landmark, had shattered along with the windows. Among those gravely injured was the wife of a colonel and his two daughters, several flower-vendors, and other young women.

The brutal attack on the most beautiful and widely frequented section of the city on a Sunday afternoon, when crowds of people were teeming in the streets, was given human dimension by the murder of two young working-class women. The explosion wounded sixty and killed four, two of whom were working-class sisters out for a stroll with their cousin, who suffered wounds. Rosita Rafa, aged 19, had lived with her 16-year-old sister Josefa and their mother as poor residents of the Gothic Quarter, a centre of artisan and working-class life, complete with its own saints and popular festivals. Rosita Rafa died of head wounds in the hospital that night. The mother, who had come to mourn one daughter, discovered the other was also dead, and went out of her mind with grief. Others wounded included flower-sellers, most of whom were too poor to re-establish their businesses right away.[16]

Following the general strike of 17–24 February 1902, during which time barricades had gone up in the city, the police detained 900 people, and again repressed working-class newspapers and cultural centres. They persecuted unions, ransacked working-class cafés and music halls, and generally made it difficult for the masses to carry on their normal social and work life. Once forced underground, the working-class movement became increasingly infiltrated by police agents. In the spring and summer of 1905, bombs were planted at the Palace of Justice and on the fashionable St Ferdinand Street, not far from the flower market. The police blamed 'anarchists', although their failure to designate any specific suspects lends credence to rumours that they themselves were responsible. Anarchists claimed that police and 'shameless separatists' once again seemed to be fanning the flames of terrorism in order to round up dissidents. Conservatives viewed social disorder as the failure of the monarchy to provide sufficient police to preserve public order, and argued that a measure of autonomy, at least the power to rule in their own area, would reduce the violence.[17]

Collective mourning through political funerals is a pattern of civic ritual that enables a community to reclaim sacred space and cleanse itself of death. The government notified the uncles of the two slain girls that the city would organize the funeral. The cortège began at the morgue on Hospital Street, just behind the Ramblas. The procession moved down the Ramblas to the Columbus monument and then proceeded to the new cemetery. The civic leaders, rather than the family, led the procession, thus demonstrating that the city itself was the chief mourner. There was a mounted escort for the luxurious hearses that carried the girls who had lain in state and on view at the hospital. Their heads crowned with flowers, they resembled Madonnas as they rested on fine white satin of the kind they probably never had close to their bodies in life.

Following the city officials and the uncles, the civil governor, the captain-general, and three other generals participated in the lead, but as the procession curled onto the Ramblas, the crowds, the vast majority of whom were poor and female, stopped the progress of the cortège. Women, many poorly dressed, cried as they passed the black-draped stalls of the flower-vendors. Balconies above the Ramblas were hung with black crêpe, and closed shops displayed signs such as the one that said, 'Closed due to the death of the innocent victims of a repugnant attack on the Ramblas of Flowers. The city of Barcelona protests.'[18]

The funeral of Salvador Seguí and his fellow victim, Francisco Comas, revealed how the working class adapted the civil ritual of a political funeral to express its opposition to the state, which in turn permitted virtual civil war to reign in Barcelona. Between 1920 and 1923, hired guns of the employer-sponsored Free Unions, anarchosyndicalists and police made ordinary life impossible in the working-class sections of Barcelona. Some have even argued that the city was deliberately destabilized to discredit the already weak parliamentary government and to prepare the way for the dictatorship of Primo de Rivera in September 1923.

Seguí, who attempted to win supporters back from armed warfare to the construction of big unions, represented a special threat because he was such an effective moderate leader. Big strikes of municipal workers indicated a higher degree of co-ordination than ever before among the workers of Barcelona. The syndicalist strategy was to organize massive general strikes to topple the government and create an egalitarian society of which the syndicates were to be the principal institutional form of management, but the employers went outside the law to stop them from trying.

Seguí, widely known as 'Sugar Boy' because of his legendary sweet tooth, was a popular local figure with deep roots in neighbourhood social life as well as in leadership of the anarcho-syndicalist movement. He had worked alongside his mother when he came to Barcelona from Aragon as she sold flowers and he sold candy in local theatres. In Barcelona, known as 'the Paris of the South', the rich cultural life of the music halls and cafés blended social life and political argument into daily life. By the period between 1905 and 1914 when Seguí and countless others among Barcelona's working-class intelligentsia gathered at the Spanish Café, republican versions of Catalan nationalism, with its demands for local autonomy, not only became a frequent topic of debate but reappeared in the guise of anarchist ideas about self-determination through direct democratic controls, an early theme in Spanish anarchism. And Seguí, who spoke Catalan, tried his hand at writing fiction as well as political arguments, although he had limited literary talents.[19]

Seguí's daily habits kept him in his own neighbourhood, the pre-eminent working-class section of Barcelona, known as District V, across the Ramblas from the Gothic Quarter. Almost every day he stopped by the St Simplicimus Street building that housed four unions and served as a hangout for anarcho-syndicalists, and then he usually spent some time at the Tostadero Café on his way home. Despite attacks on his life in 1923, he refused to change his habits or accept a guard. Between 1920 and 1922, when constitutional guarantees were restored after a state of siege brought on by warfare in the streets between members of the (yellow) Free Unions and syndicalists, Seguí was periodically detained. He was deported to a prison island, brought back, and permitted to resume his union work until he was murdered on 10 March 1923. Seguí and his friend Francisco Comas Pagés had gone to a labour meeting and stopped at the Tostadero, where Seguí played billiards with the Catalanist deputy Luis Companys. Comas and Seguí left together and walked down the street in the old industrial hub of Barcelona. As they stopped for a traffic light, gangsters from the Free Unions shot at them, killed Seguí, and fatally wounded Comas. A few weeks before the assassination, Seguí and his common-law wife and their son had been followed home, where Seguí had narrowly escaped with his life.[20]

Outrage spread through the community not only because Seguí was a voice of moderation among syndicalists and Catalan nationalist republicans, but because his death was yet another example of how unsafe daily life in the working-class neighbourhoods had become. When the Pompey Theatre, a popular music hall, had been bombed in mid-September 1920, large numbers of women had gathered at the hospital, just as they had followed the caskets of the Rafa sisters, to demonstrate their demand for civilized behaviour and safety in their own community.

A civic ritual in the form of a political funeral became essential to restore the wholeness of the community after Seguí's death. The syndicalists called for a mass protest meeting at the Plaza of Catalonia, followed by a march, but they also wanted to declare a general strike.[21] On the Sunday morning following Seguí's death, police had secretly carried the body from the morgue to the new cemetery and had buried it without his mother, wife, or children present. A commission of Barcelona's Federation of Labour Syndicates as well as leaders of the National Confederation of Labour protested against the killing and burial to Civil Governor Salvador Raventós: the government had twice stolen Seguí, once with his murder and once with his burial.

The march, scheduled for 3 o'clock in the afternoon, had various purposes. It would unite workers with the general members of an outraged civic community to assert their rights to the streets by taking them in a peaceful procession to the offices of the civil governor. There they would protest against the assassination to the official who represented the state. They made no attempt to win support from other citizens of Barcelona and called upon no civil official to stand up for them, for their struggle was with Spain, not Barcelona. They marched to the new cemetery despite the governor's prohibitions.[22]

Militant posturing characterized the behaviour of syndicalists and police as they faced each other in the Plaza of Catalonia. By 4 o'clock in the afternoon, the entire downtown area around the Plaza was filled with people who came from all over Barcelona as well as from the surrounding towns to register their opposition to the murder of Seguí. The procession moved to the Angel Gate, via the Plaza of St Anne, to the civic centre at the Plaza of St James. From there, the crowd proceeded to the governor's office near the harbour and, by this action, they symbolically reclaimed and purified the streets that assassination had profaned.

The issue of whose community had come under attack became crucial in the days that followed. As the street demonstration drew to a close at the governor's office, he attempted to join the working-class community as a victim of the tragedy. He addressed the crowd and mourned with them for the death of Seguí and the wounding of Comas. Some National Confederation of Labour (CNT) leaders joined him on the balcony and they exhorted the people below, but the local Federation of Industrial Unions, the single unions for which Seguí had planned and fought, met at their own centre at 6 o'clock and called for a general strike.

The absence of the body made the physical space from which the calls for action came extremely important. Without a body, the efficacy of the ceremonial demonstration on Seguí's behalf diminished. The indignation was there, but the rite lacked focus. The Plaza of Catalonia had become an armed camp. Women and children, who also felt Seguí's loss, did not normally congregate in union halls, and visits to the governor's offices did not seem to alleviate their sorrow.

When poor Francisco Comas died as a result of his wounds, he received, on Sunday 18 March, the burial meant for Seguí. By coincidence, this was the date republicans in Barcelona had frequently chosen to commemorate the Paris Commune although no commentators noticed this in 1923. Thousands returned to the city and thousands more flowed downtown from the industrial and artisan-inhabited suburbs. The correspondent for the Madrid daily newspaper, *El Sol*, noted that an unusually large number of women waited outside the morgue for Comas' body. Men prepared the hearse by removing the cross, and they wrapped the coffin in a red flag. Crêpe, cut flowers, and crowns were placed on the bier. At 9.45 a.m. the cortège went down the street, past the Civil Guards. About 20,000 people lined the streets. The procession passed through the Plaza of Spain where, in a modern touch, photographers waited. A group of neighbourhood people placed five bouquets of flowers on the hearse, and then the cortège wended its slow way through the working-class Sans District to the cemetery, in the suburb of the Hospitalet. When they reached the cemetery, Seguí got some recognition as the crowds burying Comas walked solemnly past Seguí's grave.[23]

Civic rituals became a means of struggle that radical Catalan separatists and anarchists employed against the dictatorship of General Miguel Primo de Rivera between 1923 and 1930. With the apparent consent of the king, Primo staged a coup on 13 September, 1923 from Barcelona. Although he was from Andalusia, Primo had become a personal friend of conservative Catalan nationalist businessmen during the time just before the coup when he had served as governor. The conservative Catalan nationalists who had organized themselves since 1901 into the Regionalist League, apart from any national Spanish party, had succeeded in 1914 in winning a semi-autonomous federation of Catalan municipalities, known as the Mancomunitat. Barcelona dominated this federation of Catalonian cities, which provided some control over local government and placed it largely in the hands of the Catalan ruling elites. Since their needs at the local level were largely cultural and philanthropic, they contributed to the well-being of a large number of Catalans through the consolidation of public libraries, research institutes, schools of agriculture and normal schools as well as hospitals and public-welfare institutions.[24] During the first days following the coup, the president of the Mancomunitat, Josep Puig i Cadafalch, welcomed Primo. He seemed to accept what his predecessor as the leader of conservative Catalan nationalism, Prat de la Riba, had argued: that Catalanism prospered under dictators who could reduce class struggle and enable culture to develop peacefully.[25]

During the first days following the coup, it appeared as if Primo would give his friends among the Catalan ruling class special privileges. Although the coup of 13 September had forbidden public assemblies, Primo not only permitted a scheduled furniture exhibition to take place in Barcelona, but he volunteered to attend himself. Therefore the 18 September decree, which made the publication of Catalan nationalist literature a crime, subject to the military jurisdiction of the Council of War, came as a special blow to Primo's conservative friends.[26] By

January 1924, Primo had suppressed the use of the Catalan language in public institutions, including the Church. Dancing the regional dance, the *sardana*, and flying the Catalan flag were both prohibited. Since newspapers had been censored from the beginning of the coup, it was difficult to convey information or to organize opposition except clandestinely.[27]

The labour movement and most leftists were prohibited from meeting, and roundups began as early as January 1924. Mediation boards of labour and management were established, but all strikes were outlawed. Except for certain members of the Socialist Labour Party (PSOE), leftists and labour organizers, including the newborn Communist Party, were driven underground or into exile. By March 1925, the leaders of the small Communist Party and the massive anarcho-syndicalist movement in Barcelona were almost all behind bars.[28]

Organization of insurrection in Spain, so often associated with anarchist strategy, had a long history among Spain's republican bourgeoisie who, beginning in 1820, had made various plans to establish a republican federation of cantons to replace the centralized state. Military insistence upon centralization has made the attack on Catalan and Basque cultural autonomy, including language, rituals, and emblems, mandatory for any military dictatorship in Spain and has persuaded moderate republicans outside Catalonia to curb Catalan freedoms in the hope of preventing an army coup.

The militant federalist republican tradition in Barcelona found expression in the twenties in the paramilitary Estat Català founded by Francesco Macià.[29] To create a Catalan state, Macià and his followers attempted invasions, assassinations, and insurrections with the goal of overthrowing the dictatorship, and they were sometimes supported by underground and exiled anarchists, who were less interested in Catalan separatism than in the destruction of the military regime.

Many of the most violent and celebrated attempts to overthrow the dictatorship by force, as well as most of the civic rituals that employed the tactic of civil disobedience, were organized by Estat Català. Conservative Catalanists, who had been willing to support the monarchy and even the dictatorship at first, lost clout. Repression of the Catalan language, music, and flag simply made reassertion of traditional Catalan rituals and folklore a radical act. The group that gained power as leaders of the Catalans were the Macià republicans, who favoured separatism rather than regionalism. 'Just as repression had strengthened the extremists in the CNT [the anarcho-syndicalists], so it gained sympathy for Macià's Republican separatism The *grande bourgeoisie* had lost control. Catalanism was now the affair of middle-class radicals and convinced Republicans.'[30]

The first San Jordi (St George) Day (23 April) and the first May Day under the dictatorship in 1924 promised to indicate how much control Primo had gained over Catalan and working-class culture. During the usual civic rite for San Jordi,

Patron Saint of Catalonia, flower-vendors moved their stalls from the Ramblas to Bishop Street, on the right-hand side of the Diputació building, where Catalonia's medieval parliament had met. By custom, Mass in Catalan, not Latin, was said in the Chapel of San Jordi, and people congregated on the Patio of Oranges just outside the chapel. Everyone, especially engaged couples and newlyweds, bought roses on Bishop Street and carried them with them to the chapel and the patio. Crowds customarily thronged the square in front and the streets around, especially Bishop Street.

Long before Mass could legally be said elsewhere in the vernacular, the Church in Barcelona had performed Mass in Catalan, especially on San Jordi's Day. But, following the coup, the general prohibition against using Catalan mandated that Castilian or Latin would be the language of the 1924 ceremony. Rumours circulated that the Diputació would not be open for the rites, but no decree to that effect appeared. Flower-sellers acted upon hearsay and boycotted their usual places in Bishop Street, and dispersed their stalls throughout the Gothic Quarter. Many people, hoping to avoid trouble, simply stayed away from the Diputació, and the crowds were thinner than normal.[31]

Uneasiness about San Jordi led to discomfort among authorities about what would happen the following week on May Day, so, on 24 April, the dictator prohibited its observance. Since groups required permits to hold meetings, various associations (unions were outlawed) requested permission to celebrate May Day as their festival. The government refused this request and 'analogous demonstrations of a political character' for fear of 'possible, although not probable, incidents which, in the present circumstances, would have to be severely repressed'.[32]

San Jordi's Day in 1925 went off without incident, and Bishop Street was filled with the usual flower-stalls and crowds. Apparently Mass in the Diputació chapel was said in Catalan. But violence had erupted during the course of the year, perhaps persuading Primo to tolerate the folkloric aspects of Catalanism, the better to repress the more violent activities of anarchists and Catalan separatists.[33] Violence had recurred that year as anarchists took vengeance upon those who were persecuting them. The hated General Severiano Martínez Anido who, as governor, had helped provoke 700 political assassinations in Catalonia between 1919 and 1923, Seguí's among them, became under Primo the minister of the interior and thus, the chief policeman in Spain. Militants were given a difficult time and, in retaliation, anarchists gunned down the city executioner of Barcelona at the end of May 1924, which action in turn led the government to round up all those they believed were anarchists, whether or not they were linked to the assassination.[34] In November 1924, anarcho-syndicalists, led to believe they might find support for a mutiny against Primo among soldiers garrisoned in Barcelona, went to the Atarazanas Armoury near the harbour. They had hoped to co-ordinate uprisings in Barcelona, Madrid, Valencia, and Zaragoza with an invasion from France, led by Buenaventura Durruti and Francisco Ascaso, but the movement fizzled out. The French police arrested anarchists on their side of the border, and, on 10 November, the Spanish authorities garroted two anarchists they named as ringleaders.[35]

A month after the peaceful 1925 celebration of San Jordi, in May 1925, an attack on the train carrying the king and queen towards Barcelona failed to take place in the Garraf tunnel south of the city. An informer tipped off police who were thus able to prevent the regicide. They traced the plans to four young conspirators, all between the ages of 17 and 20, who were members of Estat Català. Unknown to either the Garraf prisoners or the government, which kept them in isolation from the numerous leftists in prison, the anarchists and communists planned to free the young republican terrorists during a jailbreak for which they had collected weapons. A common criminal assigned to new duties discovered the arms cache and denounced the prisoners. The trial of the Garraf prisoners was set to begin on 30 April 1926, a week after San Jordi and just before May Day.[36]

Mounting repression cut off the means by which Catalanists and the working-class community could act. The government, prone to repress what it could not control, tightened its grip on Catalonia. The so-called gentle dictator of 1925, who had retreated a little to admit the importance of local customs, permitted San Jordi Day to take place as usual that year, and treated it as folklore. The intervening events, especially the stepped-up activities of Macià's separatists and anarchist exiles in France, may have persuaded the dictator to use San Jordi's Day 1926 for a showdown.

The government stipulated that Latin, not Catalan, would be the language of the Mass in the Diputació chapel, and Catalan separatists organized massive civil disobedience. Through messages passed by hand, the underground asked people to boycott the Diputació building and the Plaza of St James in front of it, and to avoid Bishop Street. Official Catalan worship of its patron saint would take place at the San Jordi chapel of the main Cathedral, not at the Diputació. People were asked to convene at the Cathedral 'in the morning and at noon to pray for Catalonia, for prisoners, for exiles, and especially for those the prosecutors had asked to be executed in connection with their attempt on the lives of the King and Queen at the Garraf Railroad Station'.[37] The handbill offered detailed instruction about how people should proceed and how a truly Catalanist ritual of resistance should take place. Civic ritual gave way to political mobilization as people were asked to buy their flowers only in front of the St Lucy entrance to the Cathedral. All flowers were supposed to be placed on the San Jordi altar inside the Cathedral. From there, people were asked to take candles to the San Just chapel, Barcelona's oldest shrine, deep in the working-class district.

With the lives of the Garraf terrorists at stake, Catalan separatists seem not to have wanted to risk a massive, potentially violent demonstration. Instead, precautions were taken to act silently and with dignity. Those who could reach the Cathedral were asked to pray for Catalonia as the bells chimed 1.45, and if they could not come downtown, to pray where they were. There seem to have been quiet observances throughout the city, and the usually crowded Bishop Street and Plaza of St James were empty. The civic ritual most dear to the Catalans could be an occasion for civil disobedience to a dictatorship that attempted to violate what was popularly regarded as a traditional cultural right.

The show of silent force through a civic rite on San Jordi Day did not prevent the court from sentencing the would-be bombers at Garraf to death, although they were very young and nothing had happened to the king and queen. Even those who opposed terrorism were outraged by the excessive sentences. A plot, the Sanjuanada, scheduled for St John's Eve, 24 June 1926, attempted to unite anarchists, clergy, monarchists, generals, separatists and even a former prime minister. The occasion, one of the most pagan of all popular holidays, celebrated the summer solstice with huge bonfires, firecrackers, and all-night celebrations, making it a cross between New Year's Eve and the Fourth of July in the United States. The plot was accidentally revealed, but those angry about growing economic disaster in Spain and the persecution of all Catalans continued to provide the grounds for opposition to Primo.[38]

The success of the civic rite of disobedience on San Jordi, followed by the Sanjuanada, raised the dictator's fears. No sooner did the anarchists Durruti and Ascaso arrive in Paris in July 1926, after their exile in Argentina, than they were accused of plotting to assassinate the king during his visit to France. The French tried them and handed down three-month sentences. Then, in August, an anarchist named Domingo Massach tried to assassinate Primo at the government centre at the Plaza of the Palace. Massach's stupid deed cost him eight years in jail.[39]

In November 1926 Macià was arrested with 50 followers of his Estat Català on the French side of the Pyrenees, just as the group was about to invade Spain. Twenty alleged supporters were arrested in Barcelona and held without evidence that they had conspired to organize an insurrection. Macià left France, and, after raising money in South America, gathered together about 100 young Catalans for another invasion. Informers denounced them, and they were tried in France, where they too received light sentences.[40] Another military plot, known as the Valencia Conspiracy, failed to materialize in 1928, and on May Day 1929, Macià called for a general strike of all Catalan patriots. May Day had become a rite for the civic community, not just for workers. By 1929, Primo had no support. At the end of the year, when he queried leading officers about the strength of their enthusiasm for him, they replied weakly. He resigned on 28 January 1930.[41]

Civic rituals, closely associated with a sense of community in cities such as Barcelona, often cut across class lines. Whether organized for religious, folkloric, or political reasons, urban pageants carried with them a measure of solidarity that surpassed the elements of ritual content. Holidays such as Corpus Christi and San Jordi attracted even anti-clerical republicans and leftists because they were popular folkloric holidays, celebrations in which the working-class community participated.

Terrorists in the nineties drew attention to their acts on a civic stage by attempting assassinations during civic rites. Police agents could play that game too, as they probably did in the bombing of the Corpus Christi procession in 1896 and in the bombing of the flower market in 1905. Even such an informal practice as the Sunday afternoon stroll down the Ramblas past the flower-stalls constituted a popular ritual that expressed some of the few joys of urban life enjoyed by the poor of Barcelona.

The folk holidays of workers and radical republican separatists were different, but both groups unconsciously recognized the importance of civic ritual for celebrating solidarity. Some anarchists might rail against May Day as a celebration of exploitation,[42] but the working-class community adopted it with glee. Yet the fact that the first May Day was celebrated differently in Paris and Barcelona indicates how significant urban traditions, including different anarchist and socialist traditions, were to structuring even such an internationalist holiday as May Day.[43]

Catalan nationalism appeared to threaten the physical integrity of Spain, and the army opposed it. The cultural content, including the civic rituals, that characterized Catalan nationalism enabled it to draw upon people across classes to create new political meanings from old ceremonial practices. The government could never be certain about the loyalties of Barcelona's ruling-class mayors, councillors, and dignitaries. Class struggle in the city was certainly intense, and the Catalan ruling class was willing to use police and hired guns to attack the working-class movement, as it did so brutally in the nineties, after the 1902 general strike, and in the period following the First World War. But from Madrid's perspective, even conservative Catholic businessmen and industrialists were not dependable, especially about cultural matters. And the Catalan ruling class wanted to rule, at least in the cities and the province, while the army simply would not permit any government to preside over 'the dismemberment' of Spain.

Catalan nationalism itself remained factionalized, and it never represented a single political ideology or a single social class. But it became a potent force against twentieth-century dictators in Spain. As a 1924 clandestine flyer in the form of an anagram asked, 'While the director [dictator] continues to prohibit our flag and language in schools and public centres, while he suppresses publications, can a thousand patriots and community groups not join together and provide an example for the masses of Catalans?'[44] Such examples were frequently found in civic rituals which built upon traditional practices to create new forms of solidarity to resist oppression.

NOTES

1 This study draws upon the works of Eric J. Hobsbawm, especially the essays in *Labouring Men: Studies in the History of Labour* (London 1964), which sparked ideas about how old traditions contribute to new forms of solidarity. Two recent works that discuss formalized civic rituals in which an oligarchy repeatedly re-enacted its power are Edward Muir's *Civic Ritual in Renaissance Venice* (Princeton 1981) and Richard C. Trexler's *Public Life in Renaissance Florence* (New York 1980). Richard Sennett's *The Fall of Public Man: The Forces Eroding Public Life and Burdening the Modern Psyche with Roles It Cannot Perform* (New York 1977) deals with the interiorization of consciousness following the decline of public life in eighteenth-century France and England. David I. Kertzer's *Comrades and Christians: Religion and Political Struggle in Communist Italy* (Cambridge 1980) provides insights about modern political appropriation of communal rituals and rites of passage.

2 There is no complete analysis of Catalan nationalism and the stages of its conservative and republican developments, but an introduction to the problem can be found in Santiago Albertí, *El Republicanism català: la restauració monàrquica* (Barcelona 1972), Claudi Ametlla, *Memòries polítiques, 1890–1917* (Barcelona 1963); Jordi Borja de Riquer, *Lliga Regionalista: la burgesia catalana i el nacionalisme (1898–1904)* (Barcelona 1977); Enric Jardí, *Puig i Cadafalch. Arquitecte, polític i historiador de l'art* (Mataró 1975); Josep María Poblet, *El moviment autonomista a Catalunya dels anys 1918–1919* (Barcelona 1970); Jordi Solé-Tura, *Catalanismo y revolución burguesa* (Madrid 1970); Josep Termes, *Anarquismo y sindicalismo en España. La Primera Internacional (1864–1881)* (Barcelona 1967); and Juan J. Trías Vejarano, *Almirall y los orígenes del catalanismo* (Madrid 1975).

3 The use of the word 'community' throughout this chapter draws upon my article 'De l'émeute à la grève de masse: conscience de classe et communauté ouvrière en Andalousie au XIXe siècle', *Mouvement Social* (Paris) 107 (April–June 1979), pp. 15–50. Arguments about how 'female consciousness' contributes to a sense of 'community' can be found in my essay, 'Female Consciousness and Collective Action: The Case of Barcelona, 1910–1918', *Signs* 7, no. 3 (1982), pp. 545–66.

4 Joaquím Ferrer, *El Primer 'ler de Maig' a Catalunya. Documents a la Reçerca* (Barcelona 1972), p. 27. Ferrer relates events in Barcelona to those of Paris in 1890 as described in Maurice Dommanget, *Histoire du Premier Mai* (Paris 1972 edn.); see especially pp. 41–2, 47–8, 104, 348. For a discussion of the development of May Day in the cultural tradition of the Left, see Georges Haupt, *La Deuxième Internationale 1889–1914; étude critique des sources. Essai bibliografique* (Paris 1964), p. 106. *El Trabajo* (Sabadell), 28 April 1899, reviews the origins of May Day in Catalonia, as does Migael Izard, *Industrialización y obrerismo* (Barcelona 1973), pp. 173–83.

5 Ferrer, *El Primer*, p. 88.

6 *El Imparcial*, 2 May 1890.

7 *El Imparcial*, 2 May 1890; Ferrer, *El Primer*, pp. 91–3.

8 *El Imparcial*, 1 May 1890.

9 Ferrer, *El Primer*, p. 103.

10 Ferrer, *El Primer*, p. 108.

11 John Berger, 'The Nature of Mass Demonstrations', *New Society* (23 May 1968), pp. 754–5.

12 'Manifestación del l° de Mayo en Barcelona', *Revista Fabril* (27 April 1900).

13 Fibló, 'Als obrers catalans', *La Tralla* (29 April 1904).

14 There is no definitive study of the terrorist waves of the nineties, but a lot of evidence appears in Helena Rotés, 'Anarquismo y terrorismo en Barcelona, 1888–1902' (Memoria de licenciatura, University of Barcelona, 1981).

15 Descriptions of the Corpus Christi festival can be found in Antonio Aragón Fernandez, *La Festividad del Corpus Christi en Barcelona* (Barcelona 1925); José Aymar y Puig, *Memorias inéditas de la procesión de Corpus* (Barcelona 1900); Aurelio Capmany, *Calendari de llegendes, costums i festes tradicionals catalans: juny, juliol, agost* (Barcelona 1978); and Clovis Eimeric (pseud. Luis Almerich), *Tradiciones, fiestas y costumbres populares de Barcelona* (Barcelona 1944), pp. 45–52. Although police arrested 400 dissidents immediately following the bombing of Corpus Christi day and held most of them for a year, they took the whole summer to bring specific charges. Meanwhile, those subjected to the reign of terror of the authorities included people who lived in common-law marriages or who failed to baptize their children. Close relatives of those charged with the 1893 attacks were also arrested. Systematic use of torture outraged European public opinion, which charged that a new Inquisition had begun in Spain.

16 'La Dinamita en Barcelona', *El Imparcial* (4, 5, 9, 11 Sept. 1905); 'Barcelona', *Diario de Barcelona* (Barcelona) (4–9 Sept. 1905).

17 Joaquín Romero Maura, 'Terrorism in Barcelona and its Impact on Spanish Politics, 1904–1909', *Past and Present* 41 (1968), pp. 130–83; and Romero Maura, *The Spanish Army and Catalonia: The Cu-Cut! Incident and the Law of Jurisdictions, 1905–1906* (Beverly Hills 1976). For an example of anarchist charges that police had planted the bombs, see 'De Barcelona', *Tierra y Libertad* (21 Sept. 1905).

18 'Después de la explosión', *El Imparcial* (6 Sept. 1905).

19 E. Salut, *Vivers de revolucionaris. Apunts històrics del districte cinquè* (Barcelona 1938) is a description of District V in the biography of Seguí. See also, Magdalena Fernández Cervantes, 'Una nueva fuente històrical sobre la formación de la ideología anarquista Barcelonesa: E. Salut y su obra *Vivers de revolucionaris*', *Convivium* 44–45, pp. 101–2.

20 There is no definitive biography of Salvador Seguí, but a useful study can be found in J.M. Huertas Clavería, *Salvador Seguí 'El noi del sucre': Materiales para una biografía* (Barcelona 1976). Research by conservative historian Colin M. Winston supports leftist charges that the employers, with the support of the governor and the police, sponsored the Free Unions. See his 'Apuntes para la historia de los sindicatos libres de Barcelona (1919–1923)', *Estudios de Historia Social* 2–3, pp. 119–40. Details about Seguí's last day can be found in 'El sabado fué a balazos', *El Sol* (12 March 1923); and 'La muerte del "Noy del sucre"', *El Sol* (15 March 1923).

21 Joan Manent i Pesas, *Records d'un sindicalista llibertari català, 1916–1943* (Paris 1976), pp. 100–1.
22 Manent, *Records*, pp. 101–2.
23 Manent, *Records*, pp. 103–4: 'Los atentados obreros. Un documento de la Confederación Nacional del Trabajo', *El Sol* (20 March 1923).
24 Josep Puig i Cadafalch, *Als Diputats de la Mancomunitat de Catalunya: en pendre posessió de la Presidència per la qual fou novament elegit*, Barcelona (12 Sept. 1919), p. 15; Jardí, *Puig i Cadafalch*, pp. 123–72; Jean Malye, 'Barcelone et l'orientation spirituelle de la Catalogne', *Revue Politique et Littéraire. Revue Bleue* 61 (Paris 1923), pp. 272–5.
25 Shlomo Ben-Ami, *The Origins of the Second Republic in Spain* (Oxford 1978), pp. 7–8; Raymond Carr, *Modern Spain 1875–1980* (Oxford 1980), pp. 107–8.
26 Santiago Alba, *L'Espagne et la dictature; bilan-prévisions – organisation de l'avenir* (Paris 1930), pp. 73–9.
27 Carr, *Modern Spain*, pp. 104–7.
28 For leftist organization up to the dictatorship, see Albert Balcells, *El Sindicalisme a Barcelona (1916–1923)* (Barcelona 1965); Gerald Meaker, *The Revolutionary Left in Spain 1914–1923* (Stanford, Cal. 1974); Manuel Núñez de Arenas, *Historia del movimiento obrero español*. Annotated by Manuel Tuñón de Lara (Barcelona 1970); and Joan del Pi, *Interpretació llibertaria del moviment obrer Català* (Toulouse(?) 1946). An important memoir about repression on the Left under the dictatorship is Albert Pérez Baró, *Els 'Felicos' Anys Vint. Memories d'un militant obrer, 1918–1929* (Palma de Mallorca 1974), pp. 185–6.
29 Federalist republicans, as early as the mid-nineteenth century, attempted to win a republic by armed struggle. For a discussion of how progressive republicans in southern Spain attempted to gain local control over their region after the 1868 revolution in Spain, see Temma Kaplan, *Anarchists of Andalusia, 1868–1903* (Princeton 1977), pp. 92–110. Treatment of republicanism in Spain and particularly in Barcelona can be found in Álvaro de Albornoz, *El Partido Republicano* (Madrid 1918), M. Gonzalez Sugranes, *La República en Barcelona* (Barcelona 1903); and C.A.M. Hennessy, *The Federal Republic in Spain: Pi y Margall and the Federal Republican Movement, 1868–1874* (Oxford 1962); Victor Kiernan, *The Revolution of 1854 in Spanish History* (Oxford 1966); Clara E. Lida and Iris M. Zavala (eds.), *La Revolución de 1868: Historia, pensamiento, literatura* (New York 1970); Jaume Miravittles, *Crítica del 6 d'octubre* (Barcelona 1935); Joaquín Romero Maura, '*La Rosa de Fuego': el obrerismo barcelonés de 1899 á 1909* (Barcelona 1975); and Joan Connelly Ullman, *The Tragic Week: a Study of Anticlericalism in Spain, 1875–1912* (Cambridge, Mass. 1968).
30 Carr, *Modern Spain*, pp. 106–7.
31 'Febus', 'Información general de tóda España. La festividad de San Jorge', *El Sol* (23 April 1924).
32 'La manifestación del Primero de Mayo, prohibida...', *El Sol* (25 April, 1924).
33 'Cataluña. Información general de toda España', *El Sol* (24 April 1925).
34 Adolfo Bueso, *Recuerdos de un cenetista. De la Semana Trágica (1909) a la Segunda República (1931)* (Barcelona 1976), p. 203.
35 Bueso, *Recuerdos*, pp. 213–14.

36 Bueso, *Recuerdos*, pp. 236–9; 244–6. For a summary of the testimony and the sentences in the Garraf trial, see 'Vista de la causa por el atentado frustrado de Garraf', *El Sol* (30 April 1926).

37 A group of 50 handbills, clippings, and letters has recently been declassified at the Instituto de Historia de la Ciudad de Barcelona (IHCB), and labelled 'Documentos clandestinos de la dictadura de Primo de Rivera'. The documents are not catalogued or annotated.

38 Manent, *Records*, p. 109; Murray Bookchin, *The Spanish Anarchists: the Heroic Years, 1868–1936* (New York 1977), pp. 210–11.

39 Bueso, *Recuerdos*, pp. 239–40; Diego Abad de Santillán, *Alfonso XIII, la II República, Francisco Franco* (Madrid 1979), p. 109.

40 Bueso, *Recuerdos*, pp. 240–1.

41 Handbill dated 1 May 1929 (IHCB); Bookchin, *The Spanish Anarchists*, pp. 211–12.

42 For two of many anarchist attacks on the concept of May Day festivities more than a decade after they had begun, see Anselmo Lorenzo, 'Fiesta del Trabajo?' *Tierra y Libertad* (27 April 1905) and Luis Castellar, 'El 1° de Mayo. Replica a los farsantes por la jornada de ocho horas', *Tierra y Libertad* (22 March 1906).

43 See chapter 6, above.

44 The anagram is a typed 3 in. × 11 in. thin sheet of paper, without annotation, in IHCB.

ACKNOWLEDGMENTS

Without Eric J. Hobsbawm, few of us would be writing the kinds of articles included in this volume and we would all know far less about political traditions, much less any other kind. My special thanks also go to Hans Medick, Joan W. Scott, and Richard C. Trexler for comments they made on earlier versions of this chapter.

8

English landed society in the nineteenth century

F.M.L. THOMPSON

It was only natural that the country which invented the railway should immediately devise three separate classes of passenger compartments, strictly segregated but each open to anyone who could pay the appropriate fare. Natural, too, that a country attached to its familiar traditions but capable of tardy recognition of social change should arrive at a two-class railway system by the interwar years, but insist on retaining the nomenclature of first and third. The final triumph of rational adaptation was only realized, of course, with nationalization, whereupon the substance of the two classes was retained but they were renamed first and second. They ought, to be sure, to have been labelled second and third, for it is hard to deny that the comfort and cossetting of true first-class travel cannot be experienced on British Rail in the Age of the Train.[1]

Here lies encapsulated the whole conventional history of the English class structure, its origins, its form, its content, its continuity, its chronology, its changes, and its confusions. England came to possess three classes, their consciousness and character forged by industrialization in a process which coincided in its fruition with the opening of the Liverpool and Manchester Railway,[2] and their composition considerably influenced by the size and source of incomes. At some time in the later nineteenth century or early twentieth century, perhaps at different times in different regions and communities, the first two classes, upper and middle, became so intermixed, intertwined, and intermarried that they effectively merged into one. It remained unclear whether what survived were best called the upper class and the working class, the middle class and the working class, the wealthy and the not-so-wealthy, the bourgeoisie and the rest, but whatever the label on the package its contents were two broad classes, with variable numbers of subsections as their ingredients.[3] To round out the picture, one should add that in pre-railway travel there were also three classes of passengers, or maybe four: those who owned their private carriages, inside and outside passengers on public conveyances, and those who went on foot. This suggests continuity across the great divide of the Industrial Revolution, which current proto-industrial fashions hint was not a great divide after all; it also suggests that industrialization may not have been the powerful motor of class formation it has often been taken for. More like an augmented orchestra giving a new arrangement of an old tune.

Like the poor, class has always been with us. As befits a country with a great international reputation for being class-ridden and class-conscious, recent years have witnessed an outpouring of works bearing upon the class structure, class conflicts, and class cultures of British industrial society. The class struggle during the Industrial Revolution, and the social stability or at least the social order which issued from it, have been documented, analysed, and categorized from left, right, and centre, in books of considerable, if variable, theoretical power as well as research content.[4] The strong tide has washed up deposits of class furniture and flotsam, albeit of a strongly descriptive nature, in the current textbooks; and the current is so powerful that all history writing has become, in some sense, social history.[5] Part of the excitement and fascination of this vast body of literature is to see the unravelling of the social and class significance of everyday behaviour, attitudes, and relationships, to encounter the class implications of what went on in the mill, the workplace, the pub, or at the fireside. Part, also, is to observe how those historians concerned primarily with the means of production and the relationships between those who supplied the factors of production on the whole discover that the new technology and organization of factory production produced new class forms; while those primarily concerned with consumption or family and community behaviour on the whole discover the survival and persistence of deep-rooted traditional customs and habits from early modern or pre-industrial times often until well into the twentieth century. And, since all good things can be divided into three parts, part is to register that preoccupation with the role and impact of manufacturing and extractive industry, and with the numerical majority of the population, has led to an understandable concentration of attention on the working class, on the life styles and struggles of working-class groups, and on the conflict relationship between the working class and the class which directly employed them.

The existence of class, whether as a set of people or a cast of mind, implies conflict, overt or implicit, as the defining and classifying experience; and conflict can only occur between opposing and antagonistic groups. The trouble with the care and attention which social historians have lavished on the working classes is that the opposing force in the class struggle has inevitably been portrayed as the employing class, the bourgeoisie. Not only has this remained something of a shadowy army, under-researched and stereotyped in terms of the supposed public face of captains of industry and capitalist employers, but also it has been assumed that the bourgeoisie defined themselves almost exclusively through conflict with the workers. Hence, on the presumption that when the chips were down everyone else in society lined up with the bourgeoisie, the attractions of arguing that Britain became a two-class society as it became an overwhelmingly industrial and urban society in which the only fundamental and irreconcilable social tensions were between working class and middle class; all else were minor frictions between subgroups which never pursued their differences to the point of threatening the social fabric, because *au fond* all other subgroups had become part and parcel of the same capitalist economy. Viewed from the bourgeois end of the telescope the reality of social, economic, and political development was never so simple and clearcut. The English, quite properly, have never felt altogether comfortable with the 'bourgeoisie'; they prefer to talk about the middle class, and it was, and remains, in the middle, sparring with, warring with, and kept in its place by an upper class which is aristocratic, was landed, and is gentrified and pseudo-landed. It is impossible to describe, let alone to understand, the British economy and society of the late twentieth century without some appreciation of its landed inheritance.

It is not simply that wealthy, hereditary landowners survive into the last quarter of the twentieth century, their ranks depleted from the golden nineteenth-century years but still far from negligible. Some few continue to be public figures of the first rank, the 6th Lord Carrington and the 14th Earl of Home (now, after vicissitudes, Lord Home of the Hirsel, a life peer) being obvious examples; others who do not aspire to public careers can still possess great local importance and influence, as the 10th Duke of Rutland recently demonstrated when it was proposed to mine coal in the Vale of Belvoir; others again, like the 5th Duke of Westminster, appear to be simply extremely wealthy. Neither is it simply that some men with industrial and commercial fortunes, no doubt a mere trickle beside the traditional flow, continue to aspire to found landed families, or at least to acquire large landed estates, although a successful popular composer like Tim Rice has steered a large slice of the proceeds of *Jesus Christ Superstar* into Oxfordshire land, while some small part of the Vestey fortune from shipping and retail butchering has gone into cobbling together four or five thousand acres in Suffolk.[6] It is rather that the landed classes, in spite of the evident shrinkage in their numbers and possessions, especially in the interwar years, have bequeathed a set of values and aspirations, a way of life, and a mentality which are the social and cultural framework of a living, and normally dominant, class. This legacy is of far greater consequence to the social, economic, and business life of the country than a mere pseudo-gentry veneer of living in 'places in the country', knowing the right people, and subscribing to *Country Life* and *Horse and Hound*. Landed society, as the Victorians knew it, certainly declined and all but expired at some stage between about 1880 and 1940; but while dying it provided for survival through reincarnation.

This is, after all, hardly surprising when one considers the inconclusive and confused result of the great struggle of the middle class, or at least of the manufacturing middle class, against the aristocracy and the landed interest, which in many ways dominated social and political life in the first half of the nineteenth century. Any articulate member of the middle class, above all of the provincial middle class, of Richard Cobden's generation would have agreed that it was the landed interest, entrenched behind privilege, patronage, and the aristocratic system, which barred the way towards free trade, free enterprise, economical administration, and that liberal and beneficent progress which would carry the productive middle class to its rightful position in the body politic of dignity and meritorious dominion. Alongside the throttling tentacles of the hereditary aristocratic monopoly, the disturbances, disorders, and insubordinations of the working classes were but an intermittent nuisance. 'The battle is still against the aristocracy,' was Cobden's cry in 1837, and he defined the class enemies, the landed interest, as 'the interest of the aristocracy and squirearchy of the country, a body constituting not a fraction of one ten-thousandth part of the entire community, as opposed to the just interest of the nation at large'.[7] And yet, when the immediate battle had apparently been won, over the chosen symbol of the Corn Laws, the landed interest remained at the pinnacle of society and in the saddle of power in such an apparently unruffled and effortless way that a generation later it still seemed likely to stay there for ever. 'The aristocracy and the landowners are overwhelmingly represented not only in the House of Lords, but in the House of Commons', Bernard Cracroft wrote on the eve of the second Reform Act.

> So vast is their traditional power, so broadly does it sit over the land, so deep and ancient are its roots, so multiplied and ramified everywhere are its tendrils, and creepers, and feelers, that the danger is never lest they should have too little, but always lest they should have too much power . . . The 1832 Reform Bill . . . has left class ascendancy quite untouched . . . nor is it likely that any extension of the suffrage or any redistribution of power will place it [political power] elsewhere. Under any Reform Bill, the same classes who wield political power now will continue to wield it . . . The parliamentary frame is kneaded together almost out of one class; it has the strength of a giant and the compactness of a dwarf.[8]

Obviously there is more than a whiff of radical and democratic defeatism and frustration behind this view. Nevertheless, as history it was substantially accurate and as prophecy not so wide of the mark as those who have supposed that Reform Acts, whether in 1867, 1885, or 1918, of themselves would usher in democracy and either cause or confirm a fundamental shift in the social basis of power. As history, if taken to refer narrowly to the broad course of political events since 1832, it was possible to explain the survival of landed predominance in purely technical and tactical terms. On the one hand, the franchise could be what it liked – no doubt it was roughly middle-class in its property-owning and property-occupying provisions – but so long as the distribution of seats between boroughs and shires, genuinely urban towns and rural areas, and the constituency boundaries, remained what they were, biased against the actual distribution of population and in favour of the countryside and its small town dependencies, then effective control of the majority of seats remained with the traditional landowners. On the other hand, so long as the politicians among the traditional landowners bent a little before the pressures of insistent opinion, and expediency, then they would succeed in trading some of their prejudices and short-term sectional interests against continued occupation of the seats, and trappings, of power. Timely concessions plus careful attention to the nuts and bolts of 'legitimate influence' might seem to be the recipe for survival.[9]

That the landed aristocracy and gentry were able to devise such a settlement of the parliamentary reform issue in 1832, make it stick until 1867, and, arguably, prolong their dominance well beyond the Second Reform Act, speaks volumes for their power and for the weakness of bourgeois forces and middle-class consciousness. It is the social and economic strength of the landed class as a class which is missed by the mechanistic explanation. And it is the subtle transformation of that class into an upper class no longer necessarily or habitually defined by the enjoyment of independent incomes from landed estates, but nevertheless an upper class thinking of itself in terms derived from traditional landed values, which is missed by views which confuse parliamentary democracy with liberal–bourgeois rule, or reduce late nineteenth-century or twentieth-century British society to a two-class dimension.

'Whoever says Industrial Revolution says cotton,' Eric Hobsbawm remarked in a memorable phrase which has steered a generation of undergraduates towards one of the hearts of industrialization.[10] In terms of the scope, novelty, and scale of new technology, new business methods, and social impact this phrase sums it all up. But it is only those who are mesmerized into thinking that cotton – and what it epitomized in textile and consumer goods industries more generally – was the only thing that was happening of any importance in economic growth, who are in the least surprised at the resilience of the landed classes, or at the astonishing wealth which they accumulated, during the early phase of the Industrial Revolution. It is perfectly true that established landowners played virtually no part in the cotton industry, in other textiles, in pottery, in the metal-working industries, or in the engineering and machine-tool industries which were largely spawned by these others in the first half of the nineteenth century. Or rather, it should be said, landowners were not conspicuous among the ranks of entrepreneurs and promoters in these activities; all of them necessarily required some land as an input, even if only for standing room, and some required more extensive land-controlled resources, clay pits or water courses perhaps. The land and property owners who controlled the favourable locations and the key real-estate assets were, presumably, not backward in obtaining their share of the new wealth.[11] Industrialization, however, was also a matter of coal and iron, and of transport; important long before Eric Hobsbawm's 'second phase of industrialism', they moved to the centre of the industrial economy in the age of railway construction.[12] Coal seams and iron ore beds belonged, in general, to the surface landowners;[13]

transport improvements, canals, harbours, docks, and railways, required large amounts of land and large amounts of capital. Moreover urban growth, in many ways a phenomenon independent of industrialization, though sharing a common link with population growth, was equally land- and capital-hungry.

It is, perhaps, unnecessary in the present context to do more than state that the processes of industrial and urban growth presented a great array of opportunities to landowners to grow rich by allowing their property resources to be used and exploited. Coal, iron, slate, gravel, clay, houses, even railway lines, these were bountiful crops to grow; and those landowners who adopted a passive, rentier, stance and allowed others to do the donkey-work and risk-taking of their cultivation enjoyed a relatively assured and trouble-free growth in incomes. The fortunate beneficiaries of such developments were, no doubt, a small minority of the entire landed class as it stood on the eve of the Industrial Revolution; the little group of the super-rich, who could afford town-palaces as well as large country houses, who could gather astounding art collections or, later in the century, run steam yachts, was but a tiny minority of this minority. Nevertheless, in the first half of the nineteenth century the top dozen or so of the super-wealthy were landed aristocrats, Grosvenors, Stuarts, Leveson-Gowers, Percys (Smithsons), Cavendishes, Russells, Montagu-Douglas-Scotts, Vanes, Lambtons, Vane-Tempest-Stewarts, and the like. One or two commoners without inherited landed wealth possibly approached these giants in terms of income; none equalled them in capital assets, and none were in the same social or political league.[14] Every one of the aristocrats in this pinnacle of wealth was amply endowed with coal, canals, or prime building land. As it happened, most of them did not adopt a passive, rentier, attitude towards the roots of their swelling fortunes, but on the contrary were among the foremost risk-takers, and through their agents among the most imaginative entrepreneurs, of their times. But even if they, and the hundreds of other landowners who profited on a less spectacular scale from industrial and urban expansion, had all been idle parasites the whole structure of society, politics, administration, education, and cultural life was geared to give predominance to families which combined great wealth with established position.

It is important to note that fortunately-located landowners had a good Industrial Revolution.[15] It is even more important to note that most of those who did well out of it did not antagonize or alienate the businessmen with whom they came in closest contact. It is perfectly true that one school of thought came to flourish among businessmen, from the 1820s onwards, which saw landowners as parasitic, viewed 'the aristocratic system' as the prime obstacle in the way of a liberal society, allied with the anti-landlord currents of political economy, and applauded Joseph Chamberlain's denunciation of

> the class ... who toil not neither do they spin; whose fortunes ... have originated by grants made in times gone by for services which courtiers rendered kings, and have since grown and increased, while they have slept, by levying an increased

share on all that other men have done by toil and labour to add to the general wealth and prosperity of the country.[16]

Such an anti-aristocratic, anti-landed, posture may indeed be seen as lying at the heart of middle-class consciousness, and the protracted tussle with the land question as the struggle which forged the English middle class. On the other hand, this was never the position of more than one fraction of businessmen; another fraction found no difficulty in getting along with aristocracy and gentry, in accepting their values as well as their economic support, and in identifying with and seeking to imitate and adopt their life-style. There are no good reasons, apart from ideological prejudices, for supposing that the one fraction rather than the other constituted the 'true' English bourgeoisie. Indeed, the main stream of recruits to the anti-landlord middle class came quite noticeably from those business and professional men who had least direct and everyday contact with landowners; the millocracy, the Brummagem men, the doctors, writers, and intellectuals. The gentrified middle class tended to come more from the heavy industry and transport side, industries closely linked to agriculture such as brewing and distilling, and the professions much mingled with land and property ownership – finance and banking, the law and the real estate professions – or, like the Church, themselves owning land (nonconformist ministers, by definition, tended to belong to the other group, although doubtless because they were non-Anglican rather than because they were landless). It would be misleading to press such a determinist line of division very far; but for what it is worth the second middle-class group probably packed more financial muscle and general economic weight than the first.[17]

While it is useful to think of the leading capitalists flowing in two broadly different streams during the formative phase of industrial society, the pro- and anti-landlord tendencies, it is necessary to remember that the pros were not simply aristocratic lackeys or toadies, spaniels fawning upon masters in the expectation of receiving crumbs from the table, victims of the aristocratic embrace lured away from their 'true' or 'objective' class identity and loyalty by some mess of pottage flavoured with 'false consciousness'. They took their route for perfectly valid reasons of self-interest when business affairs indicated that it was better to humour and co-operate with the landowners than to antagonize them; they could sympathize with or respect aristocrats who might remain disdainful of petty trade and counting-house morals while embracing grand designs of economic development; and they could aspire to some of the standards, values, comforts, and outlook of landed society without sacrificing their capacity to drive hard bargains at the detailed level where the interests of lessee and landlord, buyer and seller of property rights, conflicted. In the long run, by the mid-twentieth century, this group had transformed the traditional landed society of the late eighteenth century as much as, or more than, it had transformed them. The 7th Duke of Bedford, running Woburn as the headquarters of aristocratic Whiggism in the 1840s and 1850s, would no doubt find it hard to recognize as his descendant the showman 13th Duke, running Woburn as a fun-fair in the 1970s; but then, frugal Quaker ancestors might have equal difficulty in recognizing their descendant in Sir Anthony Tuke, past-chairman of Barclays Bank, beside his Hampshire trout stream. The two contemporaries, however, might have less trouble in recognizing themselves as members of the same class.

Whether or not landowners in general were an incubus on economic development, sucking into a sponge of conspicuous consumption via rents and royalties a surplus which could have been more productively employed if there had been no landowners at all, it is undeniable that in certain key areas great landowners provided an economic leadership that could not have come from anywhere else. In so doing a few individuals highlighted a positive, creative, role for great landowners in industrialization and urbanization, and gave solid material proof that the super-wealthy did not merely exact tribute from the rest of society. A case can no doubt be made for the key role of many individual landowners in investment, or development decisions, in infrastructures of strategic importance to particular local communities or economies. To collect particular instances, while absorbing, is laborious and not very convincing; two contrasting areas, coal-shipping facilities and resort towns, can however be selected to illustrate the point.[18]

The eighteenth-century model for the great baronial regional economies of the nineteenth century was pioneered by the Duke of Bridgewater. Much has been written about the great wealth which flowed to the Duke, and eventually to the Leveson-Gowers, from his canal; and the canal, while immensely profitable to its owners, was clearly vital to the growth and prosperity of Manchester, at least until the stranglehold on transport was broken by the Liverpool and Manchester Railway, itself financed to a critical extent by the chief canal proprietor, Lord Stafford, who recognized the wisdom of siding with the future rather than making futile attempts to keep it at bay. Much also has been written on whether the credit for the original initiative, planning, work organization, and technology-transfer should be accorded to the first (and last) Duke or to James Brindley. Be that as it may, the critical point is that no one but a great landowner was financially capable of, or foolhardy enough to become involved in, undertaking a large-scale enterprise, completely untried in the English industrial environment, of totally unknown worth. The Bridgewater Canal, in other words, required the presence of a landowner with large property assets to secure large-scale and highly risky finance (and which stood to benefit largely from the enterprise if it worked); and of a landowner whose family and social traditions included the curious blend of aristocratic panache, boldness in seizing the main chance, indifference to petty tradesmen's calculations, penchant for cutting a dash and doing things on a grand scale, and paternal sense of responsibility for dependent communities, which, when applied to the economic world, could produce feats of dazzling grandeur that were monumental follies by sensible and prudent counting-house standards.

Sometimes these feats actually worked; their perpetrators then became respected, even on occasion admired, leaders of economic progress, treasured geese who had laid precious local golden eggs.[19]

It would not be true to say that this model was endlessly repeated; nor to say that no other means existed for conceiving, financing, and managing individually lumpy projects of strategic importance in the creation of the infrastructure of the industrial economy. Other canals, obviously, were provided by joint stock enterprises, in which local landowners frequently played prominent, but not necessarily decisive, roles. Highly expensive dock and harbour constructions, similarly, were created by joint stock or municipal enterprise in London, Liverpool, or Bristol. No landowner flair or finance was needed here; the point, however, is that prudent men of capital put their money into such ventures only in conventional well established situations, where the value of 'improvements' was already well-attested by previous commercial activity. In opening up new territories with no history of trading on the grand scale, by contrast, the presence of a great landowner with sufficient vision to grasp the future potential of the region (including, naturally, his own estates in it), or sufficient wealth and commercial ignorance to be indifferent to counsels of accepted financial prudence, was indispensable. Thus, the 3rd Marquess of Londonderry created Seaham Harbour and town between 1821 and 1835, out of a small uninhabited cove, with a financial recklessness which continually alarmed his advisers and trustees who regarded the whole venture as ridiculously grandiose, but which was no doubt eased by the fact that it was his wife's fortune, that of Frances Anne Vane-Tempest, which he was pledging, and that he was able to tap a little public money through a loan from the Exchequer Loan Commissioners.[20] The ultimate success of the scheme, however, in providing a new port through which poured the coal of east Durham, from other collieries as well as Londonderry's own, vindicated his early vision that building 'a better harbour of our own than Sunderland ... will give us greater credit than in building an immense house here or in London, which would be now an entire sink of capital'.[21] With aristocratic fickleness he accomplished all three in the end: Wynyard, Co. Durham, and Holdernesse (Londonderry) House, Park Lane, were rebuilt by Benjamin and Philip Wyatt, on the grand scale, in the 1820s; Seaham Harbour began to pay off rather later.

In the west Cumberland coalfield three large landowners, the Senhouses, the Curwens, and the Earls of Lonsdale, exerted considerable influence and control over the towns and ports of Maryport, Workington, and Whitehaven from which their coals were shipped; but only in Whitehaven, through the Lonsdale interest on the Harbour Board, was the dominant landowner centrally involved in the shipping facilities.[22] Within west Cumbria it was left to Lord Burlington, later 7th Duke of Devonshire, to play the Londonderry role; from the 1840s onwards he created Barrow-in-Furness out of nothing with single-minded determination and almost single-handed. The Devonshire investments in the Furness Railway, and in

Barrow's housing, harbour, and industry, were immense, reaching over £2 million by the 1880s. The profits, in the boom years of the 1860s and 1870s, were large too; but when thereafter growth faltered and decline threatened, debt piled up on an equally impressive scale. Without the Duke there might well have been no Barrow; without Barrow, the Duke would have been a less worried and financially embarrassed man. Within his own lifetime the imprudence of pursuing the maximum development of estate resources through great ambitious schemes involving whole new towns and ports was made manifest; nevertheless, his sense of commitment to promoting the welfare of his inheritance had given birth to a complete new industrial and urban community that has managed to survive on its own.[23]

Similarly, no Bute, no Cardiff. In 1822, when the 2nd Marquess of Bute first began to think of constructing a dock, Cardiff was a minor port with 3,500 inhabitants; by the 1880s, when the 3rd Marquess's investment in the Bute Docks exceeded £2 million, Cardiff had become the premier port of the British coal trade and, with a population of 83,000, the leading town of Wales. The two developments were linked by rather more than the simple fact that the Butes owned all the important bits of land in the area. By the 1880s it was possible to float the Bute Docks as a public company, a considerable relief to the Bute family finances which could no longer bear the strain of the continually rising investment needed to keep the dock facilities expanding in line with the traffic; and which found the paltry yield on the dock capital of two or three per cent an awkward item in the estate accounts. But in the 1830s, when the first dock was building, a public company for such a speculative and long-gestation venture in such a backwater was as inconceivable as it would have been for Seaham Harbour. Either the 2nd Marquess had to be his own capitalist, or there would have been no dock. He embarked on the enterprise because he had the long-term perspective of the future ingrained in landed families, a sense of responsibility for bringing out the full capacities of his inheritance, vast landed assets to offer as security for borrowing, and an immense hinterland of coal royalties which stood to gain directly from an improved outlet to the sea. It was, indeed, the rapidly rising colliery income which made the minuscule and 'unprofitable' dock income tolerable to the Butes. Nevertheless, the concurrence of landed interests and attitudes which impelled the Butes to create the docks nurtured a very favourable developmental atmosphere; however much some Cardiff residents came to resent life in Bute town, they still did proper honour to the 2nd and 3rd Marquesses as the chief makers of their town's prosperity and importance.[24]

Finally, in a roundup of coal docks, the case of the Northumberland Docks on the Tyne is instructive. Opened in 1857, built on the Duke of Northumberland's property at the Hayhole, and with sole landward access by the Blyth and Tyne Railway which was a wayleave line paying a tonnage rent to the Duke and contracted to ship all its coals from the dock for 50 years, this was virtually as private a dock as the Bute Docks. The difference was that it was built by the Tyne Improvement Commissioners, with loans secured on the future dock dues, and the Duke contributed only £10,000 in debentures towards the total cost of over £150,000, thus neatly avoiding the fate against which his agent warned him, of becoming 'at once the Proprietor and Adventurer in a Dock Undertaking' and having 'to advance or procure by loan or otherwise (secured I presume on the Estate) an indefinite sum... and be subject to all future risques and contingencies'.[25] The Duke escaped from the undesirable position of entrepreneurial risk-taker because he was operating in a long-developed coalfield with an outstanding reputation in the London coal trade – indeed the purpose of the exercise was to turn the existing coal-spouts on the Hayhole River shore into a full-tidal collier dock – and in such a situation there was little difficulty in finding public capital to finance a well-tried construction for a well-proven traffic. Nevertheless, the presence of a Duke with large property, royalty, and wayleave interests in the region, and very considerable local and national influence, was vital for obtaining a dock at all. The trouble was that the conservancy of the Tyne rested immemorially in the hands of Newcastle Corporation, who had done so little about it that between 1816 and 1850 the width of the Tyne had shrunk from 329 to 175 feet, and its depth at low tide from 14 to 6 feet. Besides being indolent and inefficient the Corporation was much attached to the sizeable income which the conservancy produced from shipping dues, and it required much pressure from the Duke, discreet words to the Admiralty, the Tidal Harbour Commissioners, and at private bill committees, to persuade it to surrender its rights to the new body of Tyne Commissioners, one of whom was the Duke's nominee. All this was achieved with great tact 'without Your Grace taking a prominent part in a measure which cannot be otherwise than galling to the inhabitants of the most important Town in the North of England; and one which after all is and will continue to be our Metropolis and chief place of resort and consumption'. A masterpiece of smooth aristocratic politicking, which had the happy result of saving face for Newcastle while being pretty well as good for the coal and trading interests of the Tyne as it was for ducal finances.

If muck was money, with some aristocrats playing a prominent part in creating it, cleanliness, comfort, and class in proper proportions preferably beside the sea also meant money; at least one duke, Devonshire, had a brand new resort to his credit as well as an industrial town. 'The Duke can do without Eastbourne, but Eastbourne cannot do without the Duke,' it was claimed in 1878; and David Cannadine has shown how the foundation and growth of Eastbourne as a successful, high-class, exclusive resort was completely dependent on the 7th Duke of Devonshire, on the planning control inherent in his sole ownership and on his willingness to finance the necessary public utilities and amenities.[26] Some urban historians and geographers have argued that unified, mainly aristocratic, ownership was a pre-condition for the development of select, fashionable, resorts because it provided the means to exert stringent control through building leases and covenants, and the will to permit only what was genteel, seemly, and decorous.[27] The theory that the greater the unification of ownership, the higher the social tone of the resort development (or, indeed, of city and suburban residential development more generally), and that the more ownership was fragmented, the greater the likelihood of mixed, undesirable, and poor-quality development, has powerful attractions. For it would go far to explain how residential aspirations and their protection against destructive intrusions, and the life styles which went with them, attached those sections of the wealthy which desired such living conditions to the aristocratic and landed classes who could provide and protect select and secluded environments.

Unfortunately, this theory has not survived critical and empirical scrutiny. For every high-class resort, conjured out of air, beach, and cliff, which had unified ownership, another arose which did not. Eastbourne, Folkestone, Torquay, Bournemouth, Bexhill, and Southport had their Dukes of Devonshire, Earls of Radnor, Lords Haldon, Tapps-Gervis-Meyricks, Earls de la Warr, and Heskeths and Scarisbricks; but Brighton, Hastings, Worthing, Clacton, or Grange-over-Sands had no predominant landowners, no landed creators and benefactors to commemorate in statues or parks. Popular resorts for the masses might arise where ownership was fragmented, as in Blackpool or Southend; but they could also be deliberately created by the policy of a sole owner, as the Earl of Scarborough did with Skegness.[28] Some of these owners earned their place in the local pantheon as fathers of their town, through the care and money they devoted to obtaining suitably dignified and attractive housing, public buildings, services, and amenities. Others, like the Meyricks, mainly looked after their own interests, seeing that their estate was developed with large villas adapted for wintering the upper class but leaving most of the trouble and expense of equipping Bournemouth with piers, winter garden, civic orchestra, and a morally-policed beach free of vulgar hawkers and trippers to the Improvement Commissioners and later to the municipality.[29] Some unfortunates entertained expensive high-class thoughts, but bungled the execution either through misjudging the location or through incompetence. The Lancashire Fleetwoods never managed to make Fleetwood a success as a high-class holiday town; and that other Lancashire gentry family, the Cliftons, had no more than the satisfaction of not making a loss on its speculation in founding St Anne's, left the creation of Lytham on its estate entirely to a building company – although the two towns, merging into one, prospered on a high social level sustained by their golf course – and completely failed to make anything out of their large estate in Blackpool.[30]

It may be that the creation of a seaside resort from scratch, on virtually a green-field site, required such a large initial outlay on a basic infrastructure that included some specialized recreational or valetudinarian facilities as well as the normal urban foundations of roads and services, that aristocratic owners tended to be highly important, although not indispensable, agencies for starting developments and for determining their precise location, on this bay or cliff rather than that. If so, this did not prevent development or building companies, with non-landowner capital, acting as successful surrogate aristocrats by piecing together large sites out of small holdings and launching ventures that might either prosper, like Clacton under the London Steam Boat Company, or falter with honour, as did Aberystwyth in the hands of the Cambrian Railway.[31] The precise delineation of the roles of landownership, topography, and consumer taste in creating seaside resorts – or for that matter, in shaping the urban environment generally – while fascinating, is not, however, of central importance for the present argument. It is only necessary to establish that the aristocrats with fine crops of desirable villas were something more than parasites on the enterprising and productive sections of the community; and that in particular places local businessmen and local residents had good reason for believing that the local landowner was someone to be welcomed and supported as the source of welfare, not resisted and opposed as a monopolist with unacceptable values.

There was, naturally, an unacceptable face of aristocracy: the Londonderrys wore it much of the time. Frances Anne was generally held to be 'odious and overbearing', and her husband, the 3rd Marquess, was so notoriously arrogant, vain, pompous, ill-tempered, and ruthless in his resistance to combinations of miners and to public regulation of safety in mines – he denounced as 'infernal' the 1850 Bill for the inspection of mines – that it is hard to imagine that his death in 1854 was marked by the sorrowing of a whole county such as brought Northumberland to a standstill on the death of Algernon the Good in 1865.[32] Nevertheless, personally unattractive as he may have been, Londonderry was decidedly not one of Thomas Carlyle's lazy aristocrats, 'the owners of the soil of England, whose recognized function is that of handsomely consuming the rents of England, shooting the partridges of England, and as agreeable amusement... dilettante-ing in Parliament and Quarter Sessions'.[33] Whether out of self-interest alone or, as he sometimes claimed, in order to promote the prosperity of the people of County Durham, he showed that wealthy aristocrats could be extremely active, enterprising, and daring businessmen. To discover that a few aristocrats were crucial figures in the creation of coal docks or in conjuring flourishing resorts out of the sands does not, of course, suggest that all coal docks or all resorts were the creation of great landowners, nor that all great landowners were industrial or urban entrepreneurs. By the same token, to discover that some cobblers were radicals does not suggest that all radicals were cobblers or all cobblers radical; but it does suggest that contemporaries were right in thinking there was some association between the two things, strong enough not to be undermined by the appearance of a few reactionary or apolitical shoemakers. The association between economic development and property rights was sufficiently close, and the position of owners of large collections of property rights sufficiently crucial, for it to be apparent that by the 1840s there was a great deal more to be said about the landed aristocracy than that they were 'plundering your manufactures and their artisans... [and levying] their infamous bread tax upon your industry'.[34]

Some of the landed aristocracy, therefore, were not merely swept along by the tide of the Industrial Revolution to new shores of fabulous wealth without lifting a finger, but steered that tide into new-dug channels of regional prosperity, or captained the ships which navigated the ever-widening high seas. Even if this was a minority of the class, it was the key minority in fashioning an influential public image. Not the public image presented by the anti-landed bourgeoisie, and largely accepted by the early Victorian intellectuals: that referred to a feudal, agricultural, aristocracy engaged in exploiting or eliminating the 'peasantry', and was rooted in some notion of inherent conflict between agriculture and industry, country and town. But the public image entertained by that part of the business world which flushed out aristocrats as railway directors, enlisted their support of local improvements, and strove to emulate their style. Cobden himself was well aware, by 1849, that 'we are a servile, aristocracy-loving, lord-ridden people, who regard the land with as much reverence as we still do the peerage and baronetage'. By the middle years of the century he had identified, and despaired of, 'our aristocratic middle class' as a group in social and political life quite distinct from the liberal – radical bourgeoisie, a group nourishing 'the spirit of feudalism... in the midst of the antagonistic development of the age of Watt, Arkwright and Stephenson'. 'So great is [the] power and prestige [of feudalism],' he held, 'that it draws to it the support and homage of even those who are the natural leaders of the newer and better civilisation. Manufacturers and merchants as a rule seem only to desire riches that they may be enabled to prostrate themselves at the feet of feudalism.'[35]

'It remains a fair deduction from the life-patterns of such as the Arkwrights, Strutts, Crawshays, Marshalls, Wilkinsons, Wedgwoods, or Courtaulds,' Professor Coleman has reminded us, 'that social advancement was one of the most prized possessions to be bought by an English business fortune.'[36] To these might be added many more, too numerous to recount; although in the present context the Buddles, Taylors, Cooksons, Lambs, and Guests, being closely associated with the mining and commercial enterprises of Londonderry, Northumberland, and Bute, are particularly noteworthy. The advancement, of course, was sought in terms of acceptance into upper-class society, and the well-trodden route was through the acquisition of landed estates. To seek absorption into this class and milieu was not necessarily, however, to renounce all commercial origins, sever all links with the business world, and retreat into pure rural landlordism. The landed aristocracy, if it had ever been un-capitalist or anti-capitalist, had certainly gone more than half way towards embracing capitalist methods and ideals by the mid-nineteenth century; hence it is misleading to argue that the drive towards landed status, and the adoption of gentlemanly values, inevitably sapped 'the industrial spirit', turned assertive entrepreneurs who had once been high-achieving devotees of the work ethic and the profit motive into cultured unentrepreneurial gentlemen, and robbed the middle class of its cream by turning it into simple landed cheese.[37] Rather, the tendency from the business side met and mingled with the tendency from the aristocratic side, to merge and form a reshaped upper class; its core and its code were nurtured in a shared experience of public schools – to a lesser extent in the older universities – and in the concept of clubbability, institutional forces which may be regarded as autonomous even though deriving from landed and establishment origins; but its line of descent from the landed classes was clear and unmistakable, its attachment to some variant of the landed life-style unswerving.

Most mid-Victorian observers took it for granted that successful and wealthy merchants, bankers, financiers, industrialists, or professional men would seek to acquire landed estates as an essential step on the social ladder, thus continuing a process of converting new wealth into high status, via landed possessions, that stretched back to the sixteenth century and beyond.[38] This view, echoed by many historians, has recently been challenged by Dr Rubinstein, who argues that the Industrial Revolution and its consequences did not engender any large-scale movement of new men of wealth into the land, but on the contrary produced an increasing dichotomy between landed and business wealth in the nineteenth century.[39] His figures show that between two-thirds and three-quarters of the newly wealthy of the nineteenth century – those whose personalty made them millionaires or half-millionaires – made no move into land, measured by the acquisition of an estate of 2,000 acres or more. Moreover, 'considerably less than ten per cent of all Britain's greater landowners in 1883 ... were the products of business and professional wealth created after 1780', so that, if landed status is measured by the possession of a large estate, the overwhelming majority of successful businessmen cannot have turned their fortunes into land.[40] On this evidence the conventional wisdom has been routed. No more than a scrap seems to survive when an analysis of 45 individual 'new' millionaires who did acquire large estates shows that only 11 made their fortunes in manufacturing industry (including two brewers), while 21 were in banking or overseas trade, 6 in minerals, and 4 in railway contracting, thus confirming the tendency of new wealth to be divided in its affinity with the land in accordance with the type of business concerned.[41]

Before accepting that these statistics demonstrate something more than a territorial dichotomy between landed and business wealth, but a social, cultural, and class division as well, one should consider the possibility that they demonstrate a rather different phenomenon, the downgrading of the territorial stakes demanded by the landed elite for admission into the upper class. The cultural and social attraction of the gentlemanly ideal, for many if not all businessmen, is after all as widely attested as is the propagation and nurturing of that ideal by the landed classes.[42] It was of course possible for those of non-landed birth to approximate to that ideal, and gain a measure of acceptance as gentlemen, from offices in Whitehall, professional chambers, or select villas in Edgbaston, without ever putting down the smallest roots in the country. It was much easier to do, however, and on a more convincing scale, from the base of a house in the country which could provide all the facilities for country-house entertaining, riding to hounds, a spot of shooting, and local charitable works. The traditional justification of the large landed estate as the essential foundation of gentry or aristocratic status was that it supplied sufficient rentier income from the surrounding or associated tenanted land to support the style and dignity of a country-house household, the tenants and other dependants furnishing the visible evidence of the position and consequence of the landowner. From the mid-nineteenth century onwards, more easily than ever before, rentier or near-rentier incomes could be readily procured from non-landed sources, and the initiatives and experiences of leading landed aristocrats led them to acknowledge that persons with large non-landed incomes were persons of consequence. The railway did the rest, permitting frequent visits to a house in the country and severing the link between acres and status. Some, a small minority, of the new wealthy preferred to follow the traditional route by acquiring sizeable estates; they, the Strutts, Bairds, Barings, Overstones, Rothschilds, Guinnesses, or Watneys, may well have thereby elevated themselves into the top flight of a super-elite of the new wealthy, closer to the hearts and bosoms of the old landed aristocracy than their fellow business men who remained but pseudo-gentry.

The also-rans, however, cut no mean figure. Sir Julius Wernher lived in authentic, indeed over-opulent, country-house grandeur every Sunday at Luton Hoo, with 'fifty four gardeners, ten electricians, twenty or thirty house servants, and endless labourers' early in the twentieth century; yet he had purchased nothing but the mansion and its park, lived on his diamond and industrial enterprises, and in any cadastre would have appeared as a very modest or small landowner.[43] What he did on the grand scale, spending £30,000 a year on the upkeep of his country house alone, many more did in a less expensive or showy way. The house in the country, with just a few hundred acres to support it in the landscape, but not financially, was not new to the nineteenth century: wealthy London merchants had just such establishments at least from the late middle ages, in Kent, Essex, Middlesex, or Surrey. From the middle of the nineteenth century they became much more numerous, with the Thames Valley, Bagshot Sands, and Surrey Downs developing as happy hunting grounds for the London-based, and with most large provincial cities also providing a suitably attractive hinterland. Such houses might be as large as more traditional country houses, or more modest; they might be surrounded by several hundred acres of grounds, or only with the minimum acreage needed for horse paddocks and a house cow. The tendency by the closing years of the nineteenth century was for the houses to grow more compact and less servanted, and for the acreage to shrink to ornamental garden size; though in each case the surviving scale would have struck a middle-class suburbanite as enormous. Lutyens, Norman Shaw, or Lorimer were very largely employed in designing such houses.[44]

Of those millionaires whom Rubinstein found to be landless, Thomas Ismay of the White Star Line, for example, had Norman Shaw build him Dawpool in the Old English vein; and the biscuit manufacturer, Samuel Palmer, built Marlstone House in Berkshire.[45] It is difficult to be certain how many of the apparently landless millionaires were in fact small country landowners sporting the style of landed gentry with the economy of a house in the country. The only listing of the smaller landowners, the New Domesday Book of 1873, is notoriously difficult to use because of its numerous inaccuracies; and doubly hazardous when attempting name-identification. The impression is, however, that of those millionaires dying before 1899, who might reasonably be expected to have made any land purchases they were going to make in time to get recorded in 1873, while only one-third had estates of 2,000 acres or more, only one-quarter appear to have had literally no land at all; around 40 per cent, in other words, may have entered the ranks of the pseudo-gentry and possessed houses in the country.[46]

In terms of social esteem the pseudo-gentry were, obviously, not on a par with the genuine landed gentry; and it must be doubtful whether the landed aristocrats consented to mix with them as a matter of course, although they certainly came to accept many individuals from the house-in-the-country set by reason of their non-country importance and influence in the business world. Nevertheless, it is in terms of a significant, perhaps, dominant, section of the business and professional groups reaching out towards the landed life-style in this way, as well as in terms of a significant section of the established landed aristocracy reaching out towards the world of business, that the birth of the modern upper class should be seen. Continuity of forms, traditions, manners, and families is highly persistent, and the most profound economic changes do not readily displace them; it must be doubted whether the triumph of the 'entrepreneurial ideal' and the abandonment of the 'aristocratic ideal' ever occurred.[47]

NOTES

1 Traditional late Victorian or Edwardian first-class luxury can, of course, still be experienced on certain Soviet or Indian trains; but to pursue such thoughts would be to enter the controversial area of the old-fashioned class structure of communist and post-imperial societies.

2 That the formation of the working class was effectively complete by 1830 was the message of E.J. Hobsbawm, *The Age of Revolution, 1789–1848* (London 1962), pp. 200–16, and E.P. Thompson, *The Making of the English Working Class* (London 1963). More recently the completion has been postponed to the 1880s.

3 Hobsbawm in *The Age of Revolution*, and in *Industry and Empire* (London 1968), adopts a two-class model for British society, although leaving the chronology of the merging of

the landed aristocracy into the general body of the bourgeoisie a little unclear. So too does E.P. Thompson, e.g. in 'The Peculiarities of the English', *Socialist Register* (1965), pp. 315ff.

4 A few examples only can be mentioned: John Foster, *Class Struggle and the Industrial Revolution* (London 1974); Patrick Joyce, *Work, Society and Politics* (Brighton 1980); H.J. Perkin, *The Origins of Modern English Society, 1780–1880* (London 1969).

5 For instance, N. Gash, *Aristocracy and People: Britain, 1815–65* (London 1979), contains substantial descriptive sections on social classes.

6 Pers. comm. local inhabitants. The bulk of the Vestey fortunes has, of course, been spirited away outside the UK.

7 R. Cobden, *Incorporate your Borough: a Letter to the Inhabitants of Manchester* (Manchester 1837), pp. 1–2, reprinted in W.E.A. Axon, *Cobden as a Citizen* (London 1907).

8 B. Cracroft, 'The Analysis of the House of Commons...' in *Essays on Reform* (London 1867), pp. 156–65, 173–4.

9 Such a bald summary does less than rough justice to the important works of N. Gash, *Politics in the Age of Peel* (London 1953), and D.C. Moore, 'Concession or Cure...', *Historical J.* 9 (1966); 'The Other Face of Reform', *Victorian Studies* 5 (1961), and *The Politics of Deference* (Hassocks 1976).

10 Hobsbawm, *Industry and Empire*, p. 40.

11 In Stockport, for example, water rents for power supplied to cotton mills – and later in the nineteenth century simply for condensing water – were an important part of the incomes of such local landowners as Lord Vernon, T. Bradshaw Isherwood of Marple Hall, or Jesse Howard of Marple: Brady MS, Brady and Son, auctioneers, Warren Street, Stockport, Particulars of Lord Vernon's Sale, Nov. 1850; Valuation of estate of late T.B. Isherwood, lunatic, June 1896.

12 Hobsbawm, *Industry and Empire*, p. 88.

13 A coal royalty owner did not always need to be the surface owner; where coal lay under a former common or waste it was normal, on enclosure, for its ownership to be retained by the lord of the manor although the surface might be allotted to other individuals.

14 W.D. Rubinstein, 'British Millionaires, 1809–1949', *Bull. Inst. Hist. Research* 48 (1974), lists all those who left personal estates (excluding real property) at death worth £1 million or more. It is hard to see how any of those dying before 1850, being non-landed, could have enjoyed incomes from their personalty above the £50,000–£100,000 range, a range comfortably exceeded by the top aristocrats.

15 There is a useful summary account of those carried upwards by the tides of industrial and urban development by D. Spring, 'English Landowners and Nineteenth-Century Industrialism', in J.T. Ward and R.G. Wilson, (eds.), *Land and Industry* (Newton Abbot 1971).

16 Joseph Chamberlain, 30 March 1883, at Birmingham; quoted in S. Maccoby, *English Radicalism, 1853–86* (London 1938), pp. 269–70.

17 W.D. Rubinstein, 'The Victorian Middle Classes: Wealth, Occupation, and Geography', *Econ. Hist. Review*, 2nd ser., 30 (1977), supports the view that the great majority of top 'middle-class' wealth-holders came from banking, commerce, transport, and food-and-drink, rather than from manufacturing industries.

18 A number of particular instances can be found in Ward and Wilson, *Land and Industry*.

19 The Bridgewater Canal story can be most conveniently pursued in H. Malet, *Bridgewater, the Canal Duke, 1738–1803* (Manchester 1977); F.C. Mather, *After the Canal Duke* (Oxford 1970); supplemented by Eric Richards, *The Leviathan of Wealth* (London 1973).

20 R.W. Sturgess, *Aristocrat in Business: the Third Marquis of Londonderry as Coalowner and Portbuilder* (Durham 1975).

21 Marquess of Londonderry [Lord Stewart] to Lord Castlereagh, 1821, quoted in Edith, Marchioness of Londonderry, *Frances Anne* (London 1958), p. 70.

22 J.D. Marshall and John K. Walton, *The Lake Counties from 1830 to the mid-Twentieth Century* (Manchester 1981), esp. chap. 2.

23 J.D. Marshall, *Furness and the Industrial Revolution* (Barrow 1958); D. Cannadine, 'The Landowner as Millionaire: the Finances of the Dukes of Devonshire, *c*.1800–*c*.1926', *Agricultural Hist. Review* 25 (1977); D. Cannadine, *Lords and Landlords: the Aristocracy and the Towns, 1774–1967* (Leicester 1980), pp. 295–8, 322–3.

24 John Davies, *Cardiff and the Marquesses of Bute* (Cardiff 1981), esp. chap. 7.

25 Alnwick MS, Alnwick Castle, Northumberland, Business Minutes, IX, 24 Oct. 1851, pp. 64–8; and for the Northumberland Dock generally, see F.M.L. Thompson, 'The Economic and Social Background of the English Landed Interest, 1840–70' (University of Oxford D. Phil. thesis, 1956), pp. 437–50.

26 Cannadine, *Lords and Landlords*, p. 298, quoting the *Eastbourne Gazette*; and Part III, 'The Devonshires and Eastbourne'. The Duke of Northumberland gave some encouragement to Alnmouth, but had no ambitions for turning this fishing village into anything grand. He was indifferent to the development of Whitley Bay, which became the popular resort for 'his' Tyneside colliers, apart from successfully claiming a royalty on civic deck chairs pitched on the foreshore, to which he had a right as successor in title to Tynemouth Priory.

27 H. Carter, 'A Decision-Making Approach to Town Plan Analysis: A Case Study of Llandudno', in H. Carter and W.K.D. Davies (eds.), *Urban Essays: Studies in the Geography of Wales* (London 1970); H.J. Perkin, 'The "Social Tone" of Victorian Seaside Resorts in the North-West', *Northern Hist.* 11 (1975).

28 Cannadine, *Lords and Landlords*, chap. 3, and pp. 408–16.

29 R.W. Roberts, 'The Development of the Economic Functions of Urban Local Government in England and Wales, *c*.1880–1914, with special reference to Bournemouth' (University of Cambridge Ph.D. thesis, 1981). This may, however, understate the role of the Meyricks in the very early stages of Bournemouth's growth.

30 G. Rogers, 'Nineteenth-Century Lancashire Estates, Social and Economic Change, with special reference to the Clifton Estate, 1832–1916' (University of Lancaster Ph.D. thesis, 1981).

31 The fabulous gothic hotel, having become a white elephant, served agreeably as a university building: E.L. Ellis, *The University College of Wales, Aberystwyth, 1872–1972* (Cardiff 1972). After a 30-year lull another company, the Aberystwyth Improvement Company, tried again with the Royal Pier Pavilion, the Hotel Cambria, and the Cliff Railway, enjoying moderate success.

32 Robert Blake, *Disraeli* (London 1966), p. 296; Alnwick MS, Business Minutes, XXXV, 28 Feb. 1865, p. 119.

33 Thomas Carlyle, *Past and Present* (London 1888 edn.), p. 153.

34 Cobden, *Incorporate your Borough*, p. 2.

35 J. Morley, *The Life of Richard Cobden* (London 1881), pp. 518, 878; and passage quoted in M.J. Wiener, *English Culture and the Decline of the Industrial Spirit, 1850–1980* (Cambridge 1981), p. 12.

36 D.C. Coleman, 'Gentlemen and Players', *Econ. Hist. Review*, 2nd ser., 26 (1973).

37 This is the central argument of Wiener, *English Culture*.

38 A bald statement of this view is contained in the *Economist*, 16 July 1870; see also S.T. Coleridge, *On the Constitution of Church and State* (London 1839), p. 25, and Cobden in 1851, in Morley, *Life of Cobden*, p. 651.

39 W.D. Rubinstein, 'New Men of Wealth and the Purchase of Land in Nineteenth-Century Britain', *Past and Present*, 92 (1981).

40 *Ibid.*, tables 1 and 2, and p. 137.

41 Millionaires taken from Rubinstein, 'British Millionaires', and possession of a 'large landed estate' taken as an entry in J. Bateman, *The Great Landowners of Great Britain and Ireland* (London 1883 edn.), following Rubinstein, 'New Men of Wealth'. The remaining 3 of the 55 individuals were a builder, an urban landowner, and a Bengal civil servant.

42 H. Taine, *Notes on England* (London 1872: English translation, E. Hyams, 1957), pp. 142–5; Coleman, 'Gentlemen and Players'; Leonore Davidoff, *The Best Circles* (London 1973); Wiener, *English Culture* esp. chap. 2.

43 Barbara Drake and Margaret I. Cole (eds.), *Our Partnership by Beatrice Webb* (London 1948), p. 413.

44 For the development of the Ascot–Sunningdale–Virginia Water–Farnham–Wokingham districts, see M.H. Ferguson, 'Land Use, Settlements, and Society in the Bagshot Sands Region, 1840–1940' (University of Reading Ph.D. thesis, 1980). M. Girouard, *The Victorian Country House* (Oxford 1979 edn.), p. 9; M. Girouard, *Life in the English Country House* (New Haven 1978), pp. 306–10; Jill Franklin, 'The Victorian Country House', in G.E. Mingay (ed.), *The Victorian Countryside* (London 1981), vol. 2.

45 Girouard, *Victorian Country House*, pp. 76–7; Franklin, 'Victorian Country House', p. 410.

46 *Return of Owners of Land, 1873: England and Wales* (Command Papers C.1097, 2 vols. 1875); *Scotland* (C.899, 1874) (The New Domesday Book). The figures are no better than approximate, for the reasons given in the text.

47 The reference is to the major thesis of Perkin, *Origins of Modern English Society*.

9

British and European bankers, 1880–1914: an 'aristocratic bourgeoisie'?

JOSÉ HARRIS and PAT THANE

Economic history of all ideological shades has long been built around the two-fold assumption that the major event in the transition to modernity was the Industrial Revolution, and that this transition involved a fundamental shift of social and political power away from the aristocracy towards the industrial middle class. Marxian and classical economic theorists (with the exception of Adam Smith) concurred in seeing the middle class as the motor of economic change, the aristocracy as ornamental relics from a bygone age who continued to cling to personal privilege, but who had long ceased to have any wealth-creating function and were rapidly losing their hold on political power. Historians, including Eric Hobsbawm in *The Age of Revolution* and *The Age of Capital*, have broadly accepted this analysis as the salient from which to view historical developments of the past two hundred years.

These assumptions have not always gone unchallenged. In the early 1960s Anderson and Nairn questioned their application to Britain, arguing that the British bourgeoisie never attained undisputed hegemony; rather there had been a 'deliberate, systematized symbiosis' between landed aristocracy and industrial bourgeoisie, in which the aristocracy remained the undisputed senior partner.[1] Though cogently argued, the Nairn-Anderson thesis was largely unsupported by empirical evidence and made little impact on subsequent historiography. Recently, however, the role of the industrial middle class has been subjected to much more far-reaching analysis and factual scrutiny. Studies of economic elites in Britain, France, Italy and Austria-Hungary have suggested that, well into the twentieth century, the generators of greatest private wealth were not manufacturing industries but land and finance – the two last often closely interlocked and intermarried.[2] Of the greatest fortunes bequeathed in Britain between 1809 and 1939 only one was made in cotton and one in railways – supposedly the two leading sectors of the Industrial Revolution.[3] Compared with the wealth of the Duke of Westminster (largely derived from urban rents and overseas landowner-ship) or with fortunes amassed in the City of London (notoriously divorced from domestic manufacturing industry) the economic power and personal wealth of individual industrialists begins to look rather slight.[4]

In tandem with the questioning of the *economic* dominance of manufacturers (though largely independent of it) has come a similar questioning of the previously assumed *political* power of the industrial middle class. In the German Empire it has been shown that the participation of businessmen in representative politics rose in the 1880s but declined in the 1900s;[5] executive power remained firmly in the hands of an ennobled civil service and a court-based aristocracy. In Prussia the vast majority of senior local officials and police administrators continued to be drawn from the landed classes.[6] In France of the third republic, perhaps the most authentically 'middle class' of late nineteenth-century European regimes, bourgeois control of central government made surprisingly little impact on the wider, and widely varying, structure of French provincial society.[7] In Britain, the nineteenth-century Reform Acts (once celebrated in both Whig and Marxist literature as triumphs for Manchester liberalism) have been reinterpreted as subtle reassertions of aristocratic landowning power.[8] Repeal of the Corn Laws, seen by Marx in *Capital* as Manchester's death-blow to English feudalism, turns out to have been a political coup at least partly supported by and designed to favour the interests of enterprising landowners [9] Within the actual structure of government, landowners were the most numerous group in all British cabinets till 1906; and certain key sectors of the civil service (long seen as the heartland of middle-class Benthamite liberalism) remained predominantly aristocratic till 1914.[10]

Furthermore, there have been recent restatements of the Nairn-Anderson argument about the British aristocracy's long-lasting retention of all-pervasive *social* power. Martin Wiener has attributed Britain's assumed long-run economic decline to the eclipse of the industrial middle class by a powerful resurgence of aristocratic life-styles and aristocratic values – a resurgence that, he argues, began in the 1860s and has permeated all aspects of politics, culture and economic life down to the present day [11] On a more ambitious and pan-continental level, Professor Arno Mayer claims to have turned Marx on his head by reinterpreting the political, administrative and cultural history of Europe right down to the First World War as *The Persistence of the Old Régime*. Mayer concludes that the European bourgeoisie never attained either hegemony or class cohesion; that indeed 'by disavowing themselves in order to court membership in the old establishment [they] impaired their own class formation and class consciousness and accepted and prolonged their subordinate place'.[12]

If these re-evaluations are to be taken seriously, they pose certain major problems, both theoretical and empirical, for historians of modern European society. If they are correct, then they will force a total reconstruction of the conceptual framework within which 'modern' history has been written for over a hundred years. Even if they are wrong, they should at least encourage liberal,

Marxian, and 'functionalist' historians to examine more closely the kinds of assumption that they make about the mutual coherence of economic, social, and political structures.

At a theoretical level, they compel one to ask certain fundamental questions about the nature of class analysis. If both the economic significance of industrialization and the political significance of the middle class have been exaggerated, then were Marx, Ricardo *et al.* simply wrong in seeing economically defined class division as an irreducible category of social analysis? Or, were they right to emphasize class, but wrong to see it as a function of the means of production and wrong in their predictions about which class was historically predetermined to come out on top? Or, has their conceptual framework been applied too schematically to the awkward realities of history, thus ignoring Edward Thompson's advice that 'class' should be treated 'not as a thing, but a happening...a social and cultural formation...which cannot be defined abstractly or in isolation but only in terms of relationships with other classes'?[13] In other words, one should recognize that class identities and their boundaries are not static and unchanging but can ebb and flow.

Questions such as these have long been posed about conceptions of the working class: hence the proliferation of debate about such categories as peasants, the lower middle class and the labour aristocracy. But few such questions have been asked about the aristocratic and middle classes – even though at an empirical level numerous historians of the nineteenth century have found evidence of convergence and interpenetration between the two. Within this context, it seems plausible to hypothesize that neither the middle class nor the aristocracy formed a coherent class in the classic sense of the term; instead, they both contained subgroups whose interests were mutually hostile, and whose economic and political alignments were closest to other subgroups outside their own class. If the term 'labour aristocracy' has at least an heuristic value, then why not an 'aristocratic bourgeoisie' performing similar functions of (according to your viewpoint) class leadership/value transference/social control/class betrayal? Such an analysis has the advantage of fitting a variety of idiosyncratic historical and national situations that can only be tortuously accommodated within a more orthodox class analysis – situations such as the support of aristocratic 'high farmers' for Free Trade, the gulf between the City and Lancashire, the Junker-industrialist alliance in Wilhelmine Germany, and the absorption of recently ennobled Jewish finance capital into pre-1914 Hungarian latifundia.

Whilst it solves some problems, however, the affirmation of intra-class antagonisms and inter-class connections creates others – not least that of identifying what was actually happening within a specific social structure during a given historical period. Given that there are many examples in nineteenth-century Europe of aristocratic–bourgeois fusion, how should this trend be interpreted? Was it a totally new kind of historical phenomenon, or simply the acceleration of a trend that had been occurring for two millennia? Are apparent similarities between different European societies significant points of historical comparison – or simply misleading bisections of vectors travelling in opposite directions? Does it make more sense (or indeed any sense?) to talk about the 'feudalization of the bourgeoisie' or the 'embourgeoisement of the aristocracy'? Do such formulations actually explain anything about subsequent economic and political processes? To suggest an intermingling of at least parts of the aristocratic and bourgeois classes is not new. Schumpeter,[14] Mayer, Anderson, Nairn, E.P. Thompson and in this volume F.M.L. Thompson have all pointed in the same direction. But the first four all conclude that this convergence left the aristocracy in control. Was this so? Was the process, in some societies at least, a more equally balanced, two-way flow? Is it possible that the outcome was, not victory for one class or the other, nor an armed truce, but the genesis of a totally new and historically unique class formation of a kind not envisaged in the predestinarian categories of much Marxian and classical economic thought?

An initial difficulty in answering these questions lies in the definitions of aristocracy employed by Mayer, Wiener *et al.* They jointly subscribe to a list of 'aristocratic' attributes – 'cultivated style, pursuit of leisure, political service',[15] amateurism, leadership, hierarchy, attachment to the land as a source of power and status – which they assume to be 'traditional' at the beginning of the nineteenth century and essentially unchanging thereafter. There is a lack of precision about these definitions and considerable difficulty in applying them to the actual behaviour and values of hereditary landowners. Wiener in particular tends to conflate quite different interpretations of 'aristocracy', so that, for example, the arguments of Matthew Arnold in favour of an Aristotelian aristocracy of merit are cited as support for an aristocracy based on land.[16] The energetic, improving, profit-conscious landlords, developers of mineral resources, canal and port builders described by Max Weber, F.M.L. Thompson and others, are not easily described as 'amateur'. Nor is the philistinism of much of the British and Prussian aristocracy easily reconcilable with Mayer's identification of *ancien régime* aristocrats as guardians and leaders of high culture.[17] Similarly, assumptions are made about the values and practices of the bourgeoisie whose validity is by no means self-evident. Was, for example, the undoubted commitment of many of them to public service and philanthropy derived, as Mayer *et al.* assume, from a desire to emulate the aristocracy, or was it rooted quite independently in their own religious and ethical beliefs? (It is in any case by no means clear that philanthropy was a characteristic 'aristocratic' virtue.)[18] The acquisition of land by successful bourgeois is often seen as the touchstone of their desire to emulate the aristocracy; but how many of them bought how much land? And when they did so, was their purpose conscious or unconscious emulation, or something else? Were the sons of entrepreneurs indeed seduced away, in significant numbers, from hard-working business lives towards amateurism and leisure? Were the bourgeoisie as uncreative and unintellectual as Mayer believes? He ignores, after all, much of non-operatic music and most of literature and social and political thought; none of which were spheres in which aristocratic traditions or individual aristocrats were prominent in the nineteenth or early twentieth centuries.[19] What had happened to the view, common among the early nineteenth-century British bourgeoisie, that middle-class values and practices were not merely different from but inherently superior to those of a decaying aristocracy?[20]

Such questions can only be answered by looking at the actual values and practices of the bourgeoisie and aristocracy. This cannot adequately be done in the space of a single chapter. However, we propose to start by looking at a group of people whose social status and economic functions were closely enmeshed in the ambiguities outlined above: British and European merchant bankers and private financiers in the late nineteenth and early twentieth centuries. It may be instantly objected that such bankers were a small and idiosyncratic group of declining commercial significance, whose experience was in no way typical of the wider banking community, let alone that of the whole bourgeoisie. This of course is true. But they have the advantage of being a manageable and readily identifiable research group on whom to test the Wiener–Mayer thesis. They also have the advantage of being a recognized aristocracy within the bourgeoisie.[21] If they were at all successful in resisting aristocratic domination and absorption, then *a fortiori* it seems more than probable that the same must have been true of the bourgeoisie as a whole.

From the start of their history in late medieval Italy and Germany, private bankers had lived in the interstices of the European social system. Functionally they were pioneers of the development of capitalist rationality out of primitive accumulation; yet for centuries they were socially, politically and legally dependent on the princes who employed their services. They provided the finance for governments, for international trade, for infrastructural developments and for waging war. In every country they were among the richest. They acquired honours, titles, land, places at court. By the end of the nineteenth century private banking houses like Rothschilds, Barings and Hambros, and freelance financiers like de Hirsch and Ernest Cassel had the appearance of an aristocratic elite within the very heartland of modern capitalism. In the twentieth century they have figured largely in the demonology of European historical writing – on the left as the puppets or puppet-masters of capitalist imperialism, on the right as infectious carriers of the anomic cosmopolitanism that was reputedly tearing up the roots of European life. Yet their real historical role remains obscure. They appear only fleetingly in recent studies of the composition and nature of ruling elites – both Mayer and Wiener concentrating their cutting-down-to-size of the bourgeoisie on industrial rather than finance capital. Their somewhat legendary status is exemplified by J.A. Hobson's *The Evolution of Modern Capitalism*, where it was continually asserted but nowhere demonstrated that financiers, 'worked "politics"' and the coercive machinery of the State at every turn in their career'.[22] The rest of this chapter will attempt to place bankers and financiers within the aristocracy/bourgeoisie debate, by reviewing what is known about their social and political affiliations and economic power.

First, their economic position and economic power. As indicated above, a number of recent studies show that in Britain, France, Italy, Germany and Central Europe, by the 1880s leading bankers and financiers were among the wealthiest in each country, outstripping industrialists with the exception of a handful of owners of heavy industrial firms.[23] Among the ten wealthiest men in Berlin in the years prior to the outbreak of the First World War none was primarily a manufacturer, all were merchants, bankers and financiers.[24] In Britain and France financial wealth began to rival even that of the greatest landowners; and the latter were increasingly dependent upon financiers' investment advice for maximization of the incomes that were needed to support an aristocratic style of life.[25]

The possession of great wealth does not, however, necessarily imply a correspondingly dominant role within the economic system. The economic function of bankers, and their salience within different national economies, varied widely in different European countries. Relics of their original dependence on princes survived to a greater or lesser extent down to the nineteenth century. In Central and Eastern Europe most large-scale bankers were 'court bankers' until at least the 1870s – their activities being dramatically described in such works as Fritz Stern's study of Bleichröder[26] and Lion Feuchtwanger's novel *Jew Süss*. From the 1860s onwards they played an important role in financing the development of industry, railways, roads and ports in Germany, Central and Eastern Europe. The house of Warburg in Hamburg became major promoters of German shipping and shipbuilding, and marketed bonds for the imperial government in North America.[27] In France the old-style court banker formally disappeared with the revolution; but nevertheless, the most important arena for large-scale private banking, at least until the 1860s, was government finance. Major French houses were also closely involved in trade; the Hottinguer bank was for long the principal importer of cotton into France, while the Paris Rothschilds had a virtual monopoly of the rather smaller trade in tea.[28] It was in France (under the patronage of Napoleon III) that one of the major banking 'revolutions' occurred, when the Périere brothers pioneered the process of harnessing small savings to speculative industrial development, thereby transforming and almost certainly 'embourgeoisifying' French high finance.[29]

In Britain, the formal necessity for a court banker was early removed with the development of parliamentary finance, and the founding of the Bank of

England; but nevertheless, down to the twentieth century one of the major functions of successful private banking firms was the raising of public loans – initially for the British government, by the late nineteenth century for central and local authorities throughout the world. Their other major function was one that grew up as an adjunct to Britain's role in the international economy – the acceptance of bills for overseas trade. From the 1880s onwards they played a major part in financing overseas investment – a process that brought them into increasingly close contact with landowners looking for alternative investments and more substantial liquid assets during the agricultural depression. In the 1890s St Swithin's Lane, the London headquarters of the Rothschilds, housed a cluster of overseas investment companies, whose boards were largely composed of landed aristocrats and whose interests were mainly concentrated in South African mining finance.[30] With few exceptions, City of London bankers played little part in investment in British industry, the reasons for which are not entirely clear. City financiers do not appear to have refused help to British manufacturers, they were simply not asked for it. Later complaints about an 'institutional gap' are hard to substantiate in the pre-1914 period, since manufacturing firms did employ City bankers as discount houses and bill-brokers.[31] Moreover, City of London financiers as prominent as Rothschilds, Barings and Sir Ernest Cassel frequently had close contact with British manufacturing firms engaged in overseas enterprises, which they not only financed but in whose development they were actively involved both personally and through intermediaries, as in the South African mining industry. Sir Ernest Cassel took significant personal initiatives and risks in the development of iron-ore mining, steel production and railway and port building in Sweden in the 1880s and 90s, and in the building of the Assuan Dam and other enterprises in Egypt from the later 1890s. He also played an important part in the development of Egyptian agriculture and of Mexican and American railways.[32] The house of Rothschild, through its large-scale holdings in the Rio Tinto Company, pioneered the exploitation of Spanish and North American copper[33] – thus making possible the 'electrification' revolution of the 1900s. Merchant banks also provided finance for the import of essential raw materials, and for estate development and railway-building abroad, which further cheapened these imports.[34] French bankers brought railways, electricity, sugar refineries and other businesses to the Ottoman Empire, where German banks also had a growing role by 1914. The legendary Austrian financier Moritz de Hirsch crowned a career of investment and industrial development in Central Europe by building the line which carried the Orient Express.[35]

The hard-working, risk-taking involvement of bankers in such developments, which continued unabated down to 1914,[36] suggests that their working lives were very different from Wiener's description of the 'milieu of finance' as 'clean', confined to 'associating with people of one's own class in fashionable surroundings', and 'well removed from the actual processes of production'.[37] Clearly the degree of involvement in business enterprise varied with different firms and different individuals; and doubtless there were some who shared the more passive ideal of Daniel Meinertzhagen, of a capitalist economy 'living on an income of foreign investments, the land given over to sport'.[38] Economic relationships with other classes also clearly varied in different countries. However, it may be argued that, unlike the 'labour aristocracy', bankers in all European countries were by the late nineteenth century ceasing to perform archaic economic functions: on the contrary, they were adapting more successfully than other bourgeois groups to changing economic circumstances, and were innovators of the most advanced processes. This was true of old established firms as well as new ones. Therefore, in an economic sense, the analogy with a 'labour aristocracy' does not hold up. Nor, by the same token, can they be seen as buttresses of the old regime: they may have helped individual aristocrats to adapt themselves to changing circumstances, but in no sense can they be interpreted as propping up a pre-capitalist or pre-bourgeois economic system.

Banking houses were, of course, operating within and alongside the expansion of formal and informal empire, which raises the question of their role within European political systems. This is perhaps the most difficult aspect of bankers' history to interpret. An earlier generation of radical historians had no doubt about the nature of this role. Bankers and politicians 'belong to the same social world', wrote H.N. Brailsford: 'the City does not invest where investments would hamper our foreign policy: the Foreign Office will stand by the City where it has invested' – a claim which he supported with a long list of examples.[39] Similarly, to Hobson and Lenin bankers were the mediators between imperialistic governments and the growth of monopoly capitalism, while Rudolph Hilferding developed the theory of *Finanz Kapital* from the close intertwining of banks, industry and government in Austria of the 1900s. By contrast, Arno Mayer sees banking interests as usually marginal and always subordinate in European political life.

Such generalizations on either side are by their nature difficult to sustain or refute, since almost by definition *éminences grises* do not leave trails of paper behind them. Yet such empirical evidence as is available suggests that general theories about the political role of bankers need much qualification. Fritz Stern claims that the Bleichröder archives confirm empirically what Marx 'inferred analytically' about banker–politician relationships.[40] Yet on Stern's own showing they do nothing of the kind: they suggest that sheer economic weight was by no means the autonomous and dynamic variable in power politics that Marx often assumed, since Bleichröder's relationship with Bismarck was always that of a passive, subordinate, even servile, client. On the other hand, Stern's study surely refutes Mayer's claim that in a political context finance capital was as 'uncommon' as republicanism.[41] On the contrary, it was precisely the support he received from finance capital that enabled Bismarck to keep republicanism and parliamentary democracy at bay.

In a French and British context the politics of banking appear to be equally resistant to grand historical generalization. In France close collusion between Parisian bankers and the French ministry of finance meant that business interests often prevailed over political commitments.[42] In Britain the reverse was usually true, and it is not difficult to show that in a political context H.N. Brailsford was inaccurate in almost every respect. For example, he claimed that the City of London had 'boycotted' loans to Russia from the Crimean War in 1854 through to the opening of negotiations for the Anglo-Russian *entente* of 1907. In reality there had been substantial City lending to Russia, either directly or through Paris, in the 1880s and 1890s. There was some coolness amongst investors towards the Russian gold loan of 1891, largely because of the Czarist government's persecution of Jews; but it was only in 1906, when negotiations for the *entente* were in full swing, that the London Rothschilds tried (unsuccessfully) to form a bankers' ramp against Russia in revenge for the pogroms in Odessa.[43] The British Foreign Office did not 'stand by' the attempts of British bankers to invest in the Ottoman Empire, in fact quite the reverse.[44] In Egypt the Rothschilds lost the support of the British Treasury because their 'method of doing business' was insufficiently 'square-toed'.[45] In foreign affairs from the late 1890s until 1914 many senior London banking houses threw their weight behind appeasement of, and possible alliance with, imperial Germany – with, as it turned out, conspicuous lack of success.[46]

On the other hand, it is impossible to deny Brailsford's claim that City bankers and British politicians occupied 'the same social world'. From the 1870s through to the 1900s City of London private bankers were regularly used by the Treasury as unofficial economic advisers (often as a counterweight to advice tendered by the Bank of England). This unofficial advice was accompanied by regular meetings with ministers and officials at country-house parties, private dinners, London clubs.[47] Private bankers were employed by the Foreign Office as unofficial negotiators with foreign powers, largely because their channels of information were more alert and less cumbersome than those of conventional diplomacy.[48] Lord Cromer as viceroy of Egypt kept his secret service account at his family bank of Barings.[49] Successive chancellors of the exchequer fully shared the City view that the most important and fastest growing sectors of the British economy were financial services and overseas investment rather than domestic manufacturing industry – a view clearly spelt out by Sir William Harcourt in response to Lancashire demands for protection and bimetallism in 1892.[50] Prior to 1909 the only late-Victorian or Edwardian chancellor who seriously offended City opinion was George Goschen – himself an ex-partner in a London merchant-banking house, who should perhaps be seen as a poacher turned gamekeeper.[51] Goschen was indeed unusual in being one of the very few British – or other – bankers willing to enter political office at all (a characteristic which, in terms of political culture, linked bankers with the bourgeoisie rather than with the aristocracy). However, sons of such British banking dynasties as the Barings, Gibbs and Smiths did enter back-bench politics and imperial administration. In the 1890s and early 1900s there were over 200 members with financial connections in the House of Commons,[52] though those for whom detailed personal information is available seem usually to have stood for parliament *quā* landowners rather than *quā* representatives of financial interests. Prolific Victorian banking families often sent some sons into the bank, others into influential occupations which extended the range of the family's skills and contacts. For example, of the five sons of Edward Charles Baring, first Baron Revelstoke, the two eldest joined Barings' Bank and spent their careers within it. The third son, Everard, became a brigadier-general; Maurice became a diplomat; the youngest, Hugo, worked for a succession of other banks, first for Parrs', then for two of Ernest Cassel's enterprises: the National Bank of Turkey and the National Bank of Egypt. Of their three sisters, two married titled aristocrats, the third Ernest Cassel's right-hand man, Sidney Cornwallis Peel.[53]

What is known of the party political affiliations of the City of London does not simplify the issue. The City was predominantly Whig–Liberal down to the mid-1860s, returned a mixture of Liberal and Conservative MPs down to the 1880s, and then became continuously Conservative. Many prominent merchant bankers, such as the Rothschilds and the Grenfells,[54] joined the migration to Liberal Unionism in 1886. When the Conservative leader, Arthur Balfour, lost his seat in 1906 it was the member for the City, Alban Gibbs, who immediately resigned so as to provide him with a convenient by-election.[55] The hostility of the City to Lloyd George's budget of 1909 appeared finally to confirm the City–Conservative alliance.[56] Yet this alliance was more uneasy and more complex than might at first sight appear. Well into the 1900s financiers and directors of banks were strongly represented on both sides of the House of Commons. After the election of 1900 members representing 'financial interests' constituted the largest single group in all the four major party groupings – Liberal, Conservative, Liberal-Unionist and Irish-Nationalist (perhaps thereby accounting for contemporary radical fears that politics was in the grip of finance capital).[57] Most City interests continued to favour the Liberal policy of free trade rather than Conservative policies of protection; and many City opponents of Lloyd George finance were direct beneficiaries of the Liberal government's encouragement of overseas investment. Even in 1909 there was still a substantial quorum of Liberal bankers and financiers, and Lloyd George had little difficulty in finding advisers among Liberal private bankers, notably Lord Swaythling and Sir Edgar Speyer.[58] Moreover, some, at least, would have shared

Ernest Cassel's view that business was best served by party-political neutrality. Cassel emphasized his 'absolute loyalty to whatever government I happen to be serving, and if whoever happened to be in power could not be certain of that he would not give me, and I certainly would not wish, his confidence'. Cassel, who lacked the security of a base in an established City dynasty, did not sign the City's 1909 anti-budget petition and maintained close ties with leading Conservatives and Liberals.[59]

It therefore seems clear that bankers' political loyalties and attitudes to government were no less diverse than their economic activities. The very fact that the City so strongly denounced the budgetary policies of 1906–14 surely undermines the suggestion that British politics was in the pockets of a homogeneous financial bourgeoisie. On the other hand, it is undeniable that throughout the late-Victorian and Edwardian period bankers and financiers had much easier access to the ear of government than any other entrepreneurial group. It is perhaps in this context that some kind of concept equivalent to the 'labour aristocracy' seems most appropriate. It was here (at any rate in Britain) that a small financial elite may be seen to be functioning as an 'aristocratic bourgeoisie', at least partially divorced from their own class, and sharing the perspectives and interests of the class above them. If such an elite did exist, however, it is scarcely compatible with the Mayer–Wiener argument that the whole of the bourgeoisie was locked into a system of aristocratic hegemony. Moreover, bankers shared with other businessmen (and indeed with many landowners) broad acceptance of principles that did become hegemonic in the nineteenth century but which were not aristocratic in origin: principles such as free disposability of property, representative government and the rule of law.[60]

Thirdly, bankers in social and cultural life: how far did banking families exemplify either aristocratic or bourgeois modes of landownership, marriage, religion, work, leisure and high culture? 'The Rothschild clan had six palatial estates in the Paris region alone,' states Arno Mayer in support of his *ancien régime* thesis.[61] But this of course begs the whole question, since if the ownership of palatial estates is automatically equated with acceptance of aristocratic values then everything else follows. The limitations of mere landownership as a litmus test of aristocracy or of aristocratic aspiration have already been mentioned. The buying of estates by successful businessmen was not new in the nineteenth century, nor was its social meaning automatically self-evident.[62] In central and eastern Europe land long continued to be a precondition of social and political status; but in France and Britain this was much less true by the later nineteenth century. Successful bankers, like other businessmen, were buying fewer and smaller estates, and treating them as sources of leisure and pleasure and as arenas for business discussion and the making of contacts, rather than sources of status, income and power in their own right.[63] In the context of Germany it has been argued that the purchase of Junker estates was a mark of bourgeois success rather than of capitulation and that such purchase did not necessarily entail a whole package of 'aristocratic values' (even supposing that late nineteenth-century Junkers possessed such things).[64] The significance of titles and other honours, everywhere almost certainly more frequent among bankers than other businessmen, must be treated with similar reservations.

Much has been written about the intermarriage of banking dynasties with the aristocracy and such marriages undoubtedly occurred (as indeed they had been doing since the Medici marriages of the sixteenth century), though as might be expected with varying frequency in different countries and at different periods. In Britain it was traditionally more common for a bourgeois daughter to marry an aristocratic husband than for a bourgeois son to marry an aristocratic wife.[65] But Youssef Cassis has shown that by the end of the nineteenth century as many as 24 per cent of leading City of London bankers had aristocratic fathers-in-law, whilst another 20 per cent were married into other banking or adjacent occupations and 1 per cent into industrialist families.[66] For England this is further proof of the social closeness between bankers and landowners and the gulf between both and industry, but it says nothing conclusive about aristocratic hegemony. Furthermore, aristocratic marriages were not always welcomed by families on either side of the social fence. Lord Rosebery's marriage to Hannah Rothschild was forcefully opposed both by his mother and by many of Hannah's male relatives, who stayed away from the wedding.[67] As *Harper's Magazine* disapprovingly remarked, most bankers were less concerned with marriage as a means of upward mobility than as a means of conserving their fortunes; the most desired husband for a banking heiress was another banker, preferably from within the same firm and family.[68] Powerful banking dynasties were formed and survived to produce several generations of successful businessmen, with regular infusions of new blood from outsiders who often subsequently married into the family.[69] The world of international finance, more than any other, depended upon confidentiality and mutual trust, which was best attained through working with close relatives. It also required reliable and speedy acquisition of information from worldwide sources, which was facilitated by close and regular contact among relatives, such as the almost daily letters on business, family and political matters which passed between the Rothschild cousins of London, Paris, Frankfurt, and Vienna.[70]

Conformity to a religious establishment may be seen as another commonly found characteristic of the *ancien régime*, but here again it is difficult to fit bankers into any coherent pattern. In England from the beginning of the eighteenth century bankers had included Tory High Anglicans, Dutch Calvinists, Welsh nonconformists and Jews. The earlier generation of Anglo-Jewish bankers included some Christian converts, but nearly all had converted before they came to England.[71] By the end of the nineteenth century the social pressures to conform to the Anglicanism of the aristocracy were virtually nil. On the contrary, Constance Rothschild, wife of Lord Battersea, would have liked to become a Christian convert, but found that family pressure to remain Jewish was too much for her (particularly as her nominally Anglican husband was indifferent either way).[72] Similarly in France: far from being absorbed into the religion of the aristocracy, Jewish bankers retained a distinct religious identity, and the Haute Banque was often fraught with rumours of sectarian rivalries which spilled over into social and political ones.[73] Even in Austria and Germany, where religious pressures were more powerful, the pressure to convert came often from an evangelistic or radical-populist middle class rather than from the aristocracy.[74]

The fact that many bankers were Jews was everywhere to some degree a barrier to their total integration. Even in England where anti-semitism was less virulent than elsewhere, the glee of high society when the death of Edward VII was expected to remove his friends, the Rothschilds, Sassoons and Cassel, from the court, was undisguised.[75] But anti-semitism was arguably at least as pervasive among industrialists and workers as among landowners and is plainly no indicator of aristocratic attitudes. Nor did it prevent regular business and social contacts between Jews and non-Jews. Its precise effects within business circles in this period remain to be explored.

What perhaps most markedly distinguished bankers socially from aristocrats, however, was their attitude to work and leisure. Many bankers succeeded in doing what many late nineteenth-century industrialists found to be increasingly difficult: they managed to combine landownership with daily attendance at business, and to produce sons who were willing to do the same.[76] In his spare time, Lord Rothschild went hunting and racing, partly because he enjoyed them, but partly also because he believed, as did Walter Bagehot, that the sight of bankers at leisure and play inspired business confidence – surely a profoundly instrumental and non-aristocratic point of view.[77] Moreover, sports like hunting had widely different connotations in different countries: in France hunting was an artificially fostered domain of aristocratic exclusiveness, in England it was a sphere of inter-class solidarity and informal business contacts – a scene in which bankers could exchange information with aristocratic clients.[78] Outside the hunting-field both English and French Rothschilds were pioneers of motor-racing – certainly a rich man's sport, but scarcely a pastime of the old regime. Alfred de Rothschild was a patron of Liszt – one of the most subversive, both musically and ideologically, of nineteenth-century artistic geniuses. Other Rothschilds patronized aspects of 'high culture', such as manuscript collecting and eighteenth-century sculpture, at a time when, as David Spring has shown, the only interest shown by such English aristocrats as the Dukes of Devonshire in their inherited cultural artefacts was in their value in the saleroom.[79] The Rothschilds also patronized low culture in the form of music halls and popular theatre – Philippe de Rothschild being the owner of the *Pigalle*. Many practising bankers were also prominent intellectuals and contributors to the social sciences – such as Sir John Lubbock in ethnology and anthropology, Goschen and Henry Hucks Gibbs in monetary theory and economics.

One feature of the social position of bankers that may seem closely to resemble that of the landed aristocracy was that they were, or were perceived as being, an 'international' class. Like the European aristocracy they tended to marry across national frontiers, owned property in different countries, moved easily among the world's financial capitals, acted as agents for foreign governments and in many cases owned more than one nationality.[80] But this apparent similarity was sociologically and historically deceptive. The internationalism of the aristocracy was a survival from a historical era before the growth of clearly defined national sovereignty. The internationalism of bankers was by contrast a symptom of a new epoch; it was part of a new kind of supranational socio-economic structure that by the early twentieth century threatened to transcend and make obsolete the nineteenth-century boundaries of the nation and the state.

The social and cultural orientation of bankers therefore fits awkwardly into off-the-peg definitions of either aristocracy or bourgeoisie. In all countries they appear to have formed a unique, though varying, stratum of European society: a stratum that combined elements of aristocratic and bourgeois cultures but was reducible to neither. It was a culture that (in spite of the trappings of landownership), was urban rather than rural, functionally progressive rather than reactionary, and combined grand dynastic aspiration with an unpretentious devotion to the ethic of work.

In conclusion: the status of bankers and their relations with other classes varied widely among different European societies; and within each individual society some were more aristocratic than others. In Britain by the end of the nineteenth century the most successful merchant bankers were totally integrated with the indigenous landholding aristocracy, and not simply on the aristocracy's terms – though this did not preclude mutual relationships of fawning and flattery, snobbery and sneering.[81] In Austria, and, less markedly, in Germany they had a more dependent status in relation to courts and government. In France they were an independent elite that was parallel to rather than integrated with the French *noblesse* (it was inconceivable, for example, that Proust's Duke and Duchess of Guermantes would ever have begged for an invitation to the Chateau Lafitte in the way that Queen Victoria eventually begged for an invitation to Waddesdon Manor) [82] Moreover, in each country, the relationship of bankers to the aristocracy seems to have been markedly divergent from that of the bourgeoisie as a whole. Further research might throw light upon the question of just how far social status was causally related to economic function; on whether, for example, the high social status of City of London bankers was functionally related to their estrangement from domestic manufacture; and, if so, why houses which shunned industry in Britain were happy to support it overseas.

We do not seriously suggest that the concept of an 'aristocratic bourgeoisie' should be adopted as a kind of echo to the labour aristocracy, to explain deviant patterns of businessman behaviour! But we do suggest that class labels in this context should be used as dynamic rather than static terms, and that the process by which classes influence and interpenetrate each other should be seen as a genuine (rather than false or diversionary) historical process. We agree with Arno Mayer in thinking that many modern historians have been much too deterministic about class dynamics. But we differ from him in suggesting, not that institutionalized 'reaction' lasted much longer than people have imagined, but that new elites emerged in the nineteenth century which transcended the old regime and could not adequately be described in either aristocratic or bourgeois terms. This analysis seems to fit the case of the leading British merchant bankers, many of whose styles and titles were aristocratic, whose economic practices and sources of income were bourgeois, but whose total status seems to be neither. The relationships among elite groups in each society and the ways in which they wielded power remain open for more detailed scholarly research.

We therefore conclude that class terminology and its application in history should either be confined to ideal types; or, preferably, that it should be reworked and developed to take account of a much wider and more subtle range of historical formations. 'Class' should be seen as open-ended and capable of unforeseeable metamorphosis. That most sensitive noser-out of the nuances of European caste divisions, Marcel Proust, remarked that a *grand seigneur* of the mid-nineteenth century had far more in common with a bourgeois of his own generation than with his aristocratic forebears. Members of both classes had made a social and psychological quantum jump into a new kind of modernity: the 'spirit of the age' occupied 'much more space than caste'.[83] Such a perception aptly describes the position of many European bankers and financiers. It seems far more supportable by empirical evidence than either a narrowly orthodox class analysis or revisionist attempts at resurrection of the *ancien régime*.

NOTES

1 Perry Anderson, 'Origins of the Present Crisis', *New Left Review* 23 (Jan.–Feb. 1964), pp. 26–51; Tom Nairn, 'The British Political Elite', *ibid.*, pp. 19–25.
2 D. Cannadine, *Lords and Landlords: the Aristocracy and the towns, 1774–1967* (Leicester 1980); W.D. Rubinstein (ed.), *Wealth and the Wealthy in the Modern World* (London 1980); W.D. Rubinstein, *Men of Property: the Very Wealthy in Britain since the Industrial Revolution* (London 1981). W.O. McCagg, 'Hungary's "Feudalized" Bourgeoisie', *J. Mod. Hist.* 44 (1972), pp. 65–78; W.D. Rubinstein, 'The Victorian

Middle Classes: Wealth Occupation and Geography', *Econ. Hist. Review*, 2nd ser., 30 (1977), pp. 602–23; W.D. Rubinstein, 'Wealth, Elites and the Class Structure of Modern Britain', *Past and Present* 76 (1977), pp. 99–126; Louis Bergeron, *Les Capitalistes en France* (Paris 1978).

3 Rubinstein, *Men of Property*, p. 44.

4 Cannadine, *Lords and Landlords*, pp. 22–5. Rubinstein, 'The Victorian Middle Classes', pp. 602–23.

5 James Sheehan, 'Leadership in the German Reichstag, 1871–1918', *American Hist. Review* (1968), p. 520.

6 John Röhl, 'Higher Civil Servants in Germany 1890–1900', *J. of Contemporary Hist.* 2, no. 3 (1967), pp. 115–16.

7 Theodore Zeldin, *France 1848–1945*, Vol. I (Oxford 1973), pp. 365–92.

8 D.C. Moore, *The Politics of Deference* (Hassocks 1976), pp. 180–1; Maurice Cowling, *1867: Disraeli, Gladstone and Revolution* (Cambridge 1967), pp. 52–4, 304.

9 D.C. Moore, 'The Corn Laws and High Farming', *Econ. Hist. Review* 18 (1965), pp. 544–61; J.T. Ward, 'West Riding Landowners and the Corn Laws', *English Hist. Review* 71 (1966), pp. 256–72; W.O. Aydelotte, 'The Country Gentlemen and the Repeal of the Corn Laws', *English Hist. Review* 72 (1967), pp. 47–60.

10 Valerie Cromwell and Zara S. Steiner, 'The Foreign Office before 1914: a Study in Resistance', in Gillian Sutherland (ed.), *Studies in the Growth of Nineteenth-Century Government* (London 1972), pp. 167–94.

11 Martin J. Wiener, *English Culture and the Decline of the Industrial Spirit 1850–1980* (Cambridge 1981).

12 Arno Mayer, *The Persistence of the Old Régime: Europe to the Great War* (New York and London 1981), p. 14.

13 E.P. Thompson, 'The Peculiarities of the English', *The Poverty of Theory and Other Essays* (London 1978), p. 85.

14 J.A. Schumpeter, *Imperialism and Social Classes* (Oxford 1951), p. 122; though later in the same volume his argument seems a little different; it assumes aristocratic decline (p. 197ff).

15 Wiener, *English Culture*, p. 13.

16 *Ibid.*, pp. 35–7. It may also be noted in passing that Wiener's thesis and Mayer's thesis are logically incompatible with each other, since if (as Mayer claims) persistence of aristocracy was a European-wide phenomenon, it cannot have been responsible (as Wiener claims) for the unique phenomenon of Britain's industrial decline. But discussion of this wider question lies outside the scope of this chapter.

17 H.H. Gerth and C. Wright Mills, *From Max Weber* (London 1970), pp. 380–1, 386–7; F.M.L. Thompson, 'The Second Agricultural Revolution', *Econ. Hist. Review* 21 (1968), pp. 62–77; Cannadine, *Lords and Landlords*, pp. 24–5 and *passim*.

18 David Owen, *English Philanthropy 1660–1960* (Cambridge, Mass. 1965), pp. 4–5.

19 Mayer, *Old Régime*, pp. 189–274.

20 Asa Briggs, 'Middle-Class Consciousness in English Politics 1780–1846', *Past and Present* 9 (1956), pp. 65–74; and 'The Language of "Class" in Early Nineteenth-Century England', in Asa Briggs and John Saville (eds.), *Essays in Labour History* (London 1967), pp. 59–60.

21 US National Monetary Commission, *The English Banking System* (1910), p. 53.

Nineteenth-century references to private and merchant bankers as a commercial 'aristocracy' abound: see, e.g. William Cobbett, *Rural Rides*, 30 Oct. 1821; Zeldin, *France 1848–1945*, Vol. I, p. 77.

22 J.A. Hobson, *The Evolution of Modern Capitalism* (London 1906 edn.), p. 266.

23 W.D. Rubinstein, 'Modern Britain', in *Wealth and the Wealthy in the Modern World*, pp. 53–64; A. Daumard, 'Wealth and Affluence in France since the Beginning of the Nineteenth Century', *ibid.*, pp. 103–7; V. Zamagni, 'The Rich in a Late Industrialiser: the Case of Italy', *ibid.*, pp. 134–42; Fritz Stern, *Gold and Iron. Bismarck, Bleichroder and the Building of the German Empire* (London 1977), pp. xvii, 5–10, 160–8; Bergeron, *Les Capitalistes en France*, Appendix 1.

24 Walter Schwarz, 'A Jewish Banker in the Nineteenth Century', *Leo Baeck Institute Year Book* 3 (1958), p. 300.

25 W.D. Rubinstein, *Wealth and the Wealthy*, pp. 22, 74–5; A. Daumard, 'Wealth and Affluence in France', pp. 105–7.

26 Fritz Stern, *Gold and Iron*; Lion Feuchtwanger, *Jew Süss* (trans. W. and E. Muir, London 1927). See also F.L. Carsten, 'The Court Jews. A Prelude to Emancipation', *Leo Baeck Institute Year Book* 3 (1958), pp. 140–56.

27 David Farrer, *The Warburgs* (London 1975), pp. 36–62.

28 Zeldin, *France 1848–1945*, Vol. I, p. 81.

29 David Landes, 'The Old Bank and the New: the Financial Revolution of the Nineteenth Century', in F. Crouzet, W.H. Challoner and W.M. Stern (eds.), *Essays in European Economic History 1789–1914* (London 1969), pp. 112–27.

30 Cecil Rhodes MSS, C3A, item 58, Albert Grey to R. Maguire, 24 Oct. 1890; item 179, Lord Gifford to C. Rhodes, 3 July 1891; item 198a, R. Maguire to C. Rhodes, 5 Dec. 1891; C3B, item 20lb, H. Farquhar to C. Rhodes, 20 Jan. 1892.

31 Rothschild Archive. London. RAL XI/114/57.

32 K. Grunwald, '"Windsor–Cassel" – the last Court Jew', *Year book of the Leo Baeck Institute* 14 (1969), pp. 129–32, 134–8; Pat Thane, 'Sir Ernest Cassel 1852–1921', *Dictionary of Business Biography*, Vol. I (New York and London 1984).

33 Charles E. Harvey, *The Rio Tinto Company: An Economic History of a Leading International Mining Concern 1873–1947* (Penzance 1982), pp. 70–4, 106.

34 S.D. Chapman, 'The Evolution of Merchant Banking in Britain in the Nineteenth Century', in *Transformation of Bank Structures in the Industrial Period*, Proceedings of the Eighth International Economic History Congress, Budapest, 1982.

35 S. Adler-Rudel, 'Moritz, Baron Hirsch', *Yearbook of the Leo Baeck Institute* 8 (1963), pp. 34–7.

36 Contrary to the argument of S.G. Checkland, 'The Mind of the City 1870–1914', *Oxford Economic Papers* (1957), pp. 261–78.

37 Wiener, *English Culture*, p. 145.

38 *The Diary of Beatrice Webb, Vol. I, 1873–1892. Glitter Around and Darkness Within*, ed. Norman and Jeanne Mackenzie (London 1982), p. 321.

39 H.N. Brailsford, *The War of Steel and Gold* (London 1914), pp. 220–3.

40 Stern, *Gold and Iron*, pp. xvi–xvii.

41 Mayer, *Old Régime*, p. 129.

42 M. Kent, 'Agent of Empire? The National Bank of Turkey and British Foreign Policy', *Hist. J.* 18, 2 (1975), pp. 375–8.

43 Olga Crisp, *Studies in The Russian Economy before 1914* (London 1976), p. 104; RAL, 130, Alfred de Rothschild to the Paris house, 8 and 10 Jan. 1906; N.M. Rothschild to the Paris house, 9 and 23 Jan. 1906. The Russian loan was successfully launched by Barings in April–May 1906.

44 Kent, 'Agent of Empire?' pp. 377–9.

45 Welby MSS, PRO, T. 250/13, Sir Reginald Welby to Chancellor of the Exchequer (H.C.E. Childers), 29 July 1885; Cromer MSS, PRO, F.O. 633/9, Sir E.N. Baring to G. Goshchen, 11 Feb. 1888; Milner MSS, 27, ff. 72–3, N.M. Rothschild to Sir Alfred Milner, 31 July 1891. On the irritation of the London Banking community with what it perceived as naively unrealistic British government policies towards Egyptian investment, see Edwin Palmer to Milner, 4 April 1896 (Milner MSS, 31, ff. 47–51).

46 RAL, 000/150, memo by Alfred de Rothschild on negotiations with Baron Hermannn von Eckhardstein, 1898–1902, dated 18 Jan. 1912. On similar support for peacemaking among German bankers, see Stern, *Gold and Iron*, pp. 308–9, and Lamar Cecil, *Albert Ballin: Business and Politics in Imperial Germany 1888–1918* (Princeton 1967), pp. 182–213.

47 See, e.g., Welby MSS, PRO, T. 250/13; B.M. Add. MS 48612, Sir William Harcourt to Edward Hamilton, 19 Sept. 1893; B.M. Add. MS 48681, Edward Hamilton's diary, 18 June 1903; L.S. Pressnell, 'Gold Reserves, Banking Reserves and the Baring Crisis of 1890', in T.S. Ashton and R. Sayers (eds.), *Essays in Monetary History* (London), pp. 197–8; Roy Foster, *Lord Randolph Churchill. A Political Life* (Oxford 1981), pp. 194–5, 277, 289, 301–2; Robert Rhodes James, *Rosebery* (London 1963), pp. 367–8.

48 E.g. in renegotiating the Anglo-French tariff agreements, and in putting pressure on Portugal to sell Delagoa Bay. (Dilke MSS, B.M. Add. MS 43912, f.5, Alphonse de Rothschild to N.M. de Rothschild, received 25 Jan. 1882, f. 11, N.M. de Rothschild to Sir Charles Dilke, 16 Feb. 1882, f.12, C. Rivers Wilson to Sir Charles Dilke 17 Feb. 1882. Cecil Rhodes MSS, C3A, items 49 and 58, Albert Grey to Rochfort Maguire, 24 Sept. and 24 Oct. 1890, RAL, 0000/150, Joseph Chamberlain to Alfred de Rothschild, 28 July 1896.)

49 PRO, FO. 633/5, p. 358, no. 483, Sir E. Baring to Sir Philip Currie, 16 April 1891.

50 Harcourt MSS, 166, ff. 113–20, Sir W. Harcourt to Samuel Smith, Oct. 1892.

51 On Goschen's unpopularity with the City, see B.M. Add. MS. 48650, Edward Hamilton's diary, 24 Feb. 1888; US National Monetary Commission 1910, Conference with Lord Swaythling, pp. 91–2; Pressnell, 'Gold Reserves', pp. 213–15.

52 J.A. Thomas, *The House of Commons 1832–1901* (Cardiff 1939), pp. 14–18.

53 Y. Cassis, *Les Banquiers Anglais, 1890–1914: Etude Sociale* (University of Geneva Ph.d. thesis 1982), pp. 248–9.

54 Harcourt MSS, dep. 224, ff.116–7, Henry Riversdale Grenfell to Sir William Harcourt, 11 Nov. 1894.

55 Kenneth Young, *Arthur James Balfour* (London 1963), p. 259.

56 Asquith MSS, 12, ff.32–3, N.M. Rothschild to H.H. Asquith, 14 May 1909; and ff.34–6, petition to Asquith, signed by Rothschilds, Barings, Gibbs, Hambros, Hoares, Morgans, Brown Shipley, etc.

57 Thomas, *House of Commons*, pp. 14–18; Harold Emy, *Liberals, Radicals and Social Politics 1892–1914* (Cambridge 1973), p. 100.

58 Avner Offer, 'Empire and Social Reform: British Overseas Investment and Domestic Politics 1908–1914', *Hist. J.*, 26, 1 (1983), pp. 124ff; S.R. Searle, 'The Edwardian Liberal Party and Business', *English Hist. Rev.* XCVIII, no. 386. Jan 1983, p. 38.

59 Broadlands archives, papers of Sir Ernest Cassel, folder X6, Cassel to Sir Wilfred Ashley, 18 Nov. 1909.

60 These important points are difficult to substantiate in a short chapter, still less in a footnote. The acceptance of such principles is, however, implicit and pervasive in the private correspondence and other papers of the bankers whom we have surveyed, whereas opposition to them is not, whatever predictable reservations bankers may have had about some of the manifestations of liberal democracy in this period. See for example, RAL. 130/3–4, correspondence between the London and Paris cousins, 1909–10, during the Budget crisis; Broadlands archives *op. cit.*, folder XI, copy of letter from Ernest Cassel to King Edward VII commenting on the appointments of Lloyd George and Winston Churchill to the Cabinet. For similar points in relation to Germany see David Blackbourn, 'The Discreet Charm of the Bourgeoisie: Some Recent Works on German History', *Europeans Studies Review* 2 (1981), p. 248.

61 Arno J. Mayer, *Old Régime*, p. 106.

62 H.J. Habakkuk, 'English Landownership 1680–1740', *Econ. Hist. Review* 10 (1939–40), pp. 2–17.

63 Rubinstein, 'Modern Britain', pp. 105–7. W.D. Rubinstein, 'New Men of Wealth and the Purchase of Land in 19th century England', *Past and Present*, 92 (1981), pp. 125–47.

64 David Blackbourn, 'The Discreet Charm of the Bourgeoisie', 2, p. 247.

65 H.J. Habakkuk, 'The Rise and Fall of English Landed Families 1600–1800', *Trans. Roy. Hist. Soc.*, 5th ser., 29 (1979), p. 191; 'Marriage Settlement in the Eighteenth Century', *Trans. Roy. Hist. Soc.*, 4th ser., 32 (1950), p. 24.

66 Cassis, *Les Banquiers Anglais*, p. 222.

67 James, Rosebery, p. 83–6; Cecil Roth, *The Magnificent Rothschilds* (London 1939), p. 87.

68 The Knights of the Red Shield', *Harper's New Monthly Magazine*, Jan. 1874, p. 209.

69 Cassis, *Les Banquiers Anglais*, p. 230–50; Chapman, 'The Evolution of Merchant Banking', p. 28.

70 RAL series XI 85, 86, 87, 101, 105 and 130.

71 E.g. B.O. Bramsen and Kathleen Wain, *The Hambros 1779–1979* (London 1979), p. 46.

72 B.M. Add. MS. 47938, Lady Battersea's diary, summary for 1889.

73 Jean Bouvier, *Etudes sur le Krach de l'Union Générale 1878–1885* (Paris 1960), pp. 146–54.

74 Peter Pulzer, *The Rise of Political Anti-Semitism in Germany and Austria* (New York 1964), esp. chap. 18, 19, 29.

75 Grunwald, '"*Windsor-Cassel*"', p. 153.

76 Adler-Rudel, 'Moritz, Baron Hirsch', pp. 37–8; Walter Bagehot, *Lombard Street* (London 1904 edn.), pp. 270–1.

77 Farrer, *The Warburgs*, p. 45; Bagehot, *Lombard Street*, pp. 270–1.

78 Richard Holt, *Sport and Society in Modern France* (London 1981), pp. 32–6; Raymond

Carr, *English Fox Hunting: a History* (London 1976), pp. 1–2, 50–1, 129, 133, 155, 241–2.

79 D. Spring, paper to the Conference of the Economic History Society, Loughborough, 1980.

80 US National Monetary Commission, *The English Banking System* (1910), p. 57; S.D. Chapman, 'The International Houses: the Continental Contribution to British Commerce 1800–1860', *J. Internat. Econ. Hist.* 6, 1 (1971), pp. 5–48.

81 Compare for example, the sometimes effusively flattering letters that passed between the Rothschilds and the Vernon Harcourts, with the patronizing tone often adopted in Loulou Harcourt's secret diaries (Harcourt MSS), 166 and 167, *passim*; 383, L. Harcourt's diary, 25 July,, 7 Aug. 27 Aug.–19 Sept. (1882). Loulou's private sneers at rich parvenues did not prevent him from marrying the niece of J.P. Morgan.

82 Virginia Cowles, *The Rothschilds, a Family of Fortune* (London 1973), pp. 179–80. It is interesting to note, however, that Proust portrayed Mme Alphonse de Rothschild as a frequent guest at the house of the Duchesse de Guermantes, whereas she was never invited by the Princesse de Guermantes. The difference lay, not in the social status of these two aristocratic ladies (which was identical), but in that one was a woman of 'advanced', the other of 'traditional' views. In other words, modernity of outlook was a more fundamental determinant of certain kinds of social behaviour than aristocracy *per se* (*Cities of the Plain*, trans. C.K. Scott Moncrieff (1929), Part 2, chap. 1).

83 *Ibid.*, p. 114.

10

Problems of Jewish assimilation in Austria–Hungary in the nineteenth and twentieth centuries

PETER HANAK

In his biographical novel Károly Pap, a Hungarian Jewish writer, presents his grandfather Jeremia as a 'wool-dealer'. The sole meaning of Jeremia's existence is his dedication to the *Talmud* and the preparation for returning to the Holy Land. Till the moment of his death, he keeps condemning his sons for their wanton gathering of material wealth and for mingling in the world of the Gentile. The father, a rabbi in Sopron, is, at the same time, a literate man and a businessman, a Hungarian and a Jew who had, by divine grace, been prevented from having to choose in the conflict of dual commitment. And yet the son is compelled, even in his childhood, to revolt against the dualism of hypocritical religious morality and of uncritical business morality. He attempts to reconcile his simultaneous attachment to the Hungarians and the Jews by becoming a writer – understanding and promoting Hungarian culture – only to find his death in a Nazi death-camp in 1944.[1] This is what we call Jewish fate itself (as the critics of assimilation usually argue), the typical and tragic failure of Jewish assimilation in Hungary. And indeed, in the area once belonging to the Austro-Hungarian monarchy, almost one million Jews shared the same fate.

We are presented a different life story in the autobiographical novel of Lajos Hatvany.[2] The son of a corn-dealer, Abraham Deutsch had been a successful merchant; his grandsons became capitalists in Pest, while his great-grandson, Sándor Hatvany Deutsch, grew to become one of the creative talents of Hungarian capitalism. An industrial magnate, he was admitted to the House of Lords and made Veritable Privy Councillor. His son, Lajos, a friend and patron of Ady, a founder of *Nyugat* (a literary journal started in 1908), a biographer of Petőfi, the discoverer of the great twentieth-century poet, Attila József, became a genuine master of Hungarian culture.[3] His cousin, Anna Lesznai, a writer, poet and painter, became an appreciated standard contributor of *Nyugat*, and later on joined George Lukács's Sunday Circle.[4] These were examples of successful lives, the results of the fruitful union of two cultures, an advocate of assimilation may argue. And he would be right, just as his opponent, the critic, was also right, since

235

the number of those who assimilated into the peoples of East-Central Europe and contributed to their civilization comes to no less than hundreds of thousands.

But can a few thousand successful careers or even the tolerated assimilation of a hundred thousand stand as a balance for nearly a million deaths and many millions of injured? The next question would plead the case from another angle: can the course of human progress be measured by the number of the dead? And the historian is, indeed, embarrassed as he faces the dilemma of *numerantur* or *ponderantur*, the classical case of the tragic choice of values between quantity and quality. At this point he feels an irresistible drive to expand the investigation and, besides narrating the story and its outcome, to proceed to an analysis of the whole process and the underlying motivation. He is strengthened in this feeling by his firm conviction that Jewish assimilation is to be treated as part of a greater problem, that of the general European process of migration and the formation of modern nations.

It is an unrewarding task to drown tragedy in cool columns of lifeless figures. And yet the exact analysis of the problem demands this as our next step. Although census data pertaining to nationality in the early nineteenth century are based merely on estimates, their comparison will nevertheless allow us to determine the basic trends. The actual population growth of the various peoples of the monarchy between the early and mid-nineteenth century and 1910 is reconstructed in table 1.

Modern migration and assimilation revealed three great centres or 'melting pots': lower Austria with Vienna as its centre, the Hungarian Great Plain with Budapest, and Galicia. The absorbing capacity of the last two is clearly demonstrated by the tables on population growth. Our calculations show that out of the Hungarian population growth of at least 5 million for the period between 1850 and 1910, approximately one-third, or 1.7 million, derived from assimilation, as a result of the Magyarization of approximately 600,000 Germans, the same number of Jews, and 400,000 Slovaks.[5] The proportions are similar in the Polish case. The Polish census of 1910 counted 810,000 inhabitants of the Jewish faith and 237,000 Poles professing Greek orthodoxy.[6] On the basis of cross-checking our data for the second part of the nineteenth century on the natural population growth and on the migratory margin, we estimate the population increase resulting from the assimilation of Jews, Ukrainians and Germans in Poland to be 1.5 million.

The growth of the German population in the Austrian (Alpine) provinces cannot unambiguously be derived from table 1, as this growth was offset by the dissimilation and decrease in the population of other provinces. But, according to our statistical calculations, in this epoch the Austrian provinces witnessed a heavy Germanization, integrating no less than 1.1 million inhabitants of various nationalities, of which 400–500,000 had been Czechs, 200,000 Jews, and half a

Table 1. *The nations of the monarchy, 1800–1910 (in thousands; percentage in brackets).*

	1800[a]		1851[b]		1910[c]		Annual average growth	
							1800–1910	1851–1910
Germans	5,600	(26.2)	7,871	(25.1)	11,988	(24.6)	0.7	0.8
Czechs	2,600	(12.1)	4,000	(12.8)	6,400	(13.2)	0.8	0.9
Slovaks	1,200	(5.6)	1,854	(5.9)	1,968	(4.0)	0.4	0.1
Serbs	800	(3.7)	995	(3.2)				
Croats	1,200	(5.6)	1,763	(5.6)	3,811	(7.8)	0.6	0.6
(Serbs + Goats)	2,000	(9.3)	2,758	(8.8)				
Slovenes	850	(4.0)	1,172	(3.7)	1,346	(2.8)	0.4	0.25
Poles	1,400	(6.5)	2,056	(6.5)	5,000	(10.2)	1.1	1.6
Ukrainians	1,800	(8.4)	2,940	(9.4)	3,991	(8.2)	0.7	0.56
Rumanians	1,600	(7.5)	2,455	(7.8)	3,224	(6.6)	0.6	0.5
Italians	400	(1.8)	534	(1.7)	802	(1.6)	0.6	0.7
Hungarians	3,400	(15.9)	4,872	(15.6)	10,061	(20.6)	1.0	1.35
Jews	400	(1.9)	1,039	(2.3)	2,246[d]	—		
Others	150	(0.7)	134	(0.4)	150	(0.4)	—	—
Monarchy total	21,300	(100.0)	31,685	(100.0)	50,987	(100.0)	0.75	0.82

Sources: [a]Excl. Lombardy and Venetia, incl. Salzburg, Dalmatia. Estimation, J.C. Bisinger, *General-Statistik des öster-reichischen Kaiserthumes.* vol. 1. *Theil.* (Vienna = Triest, 1807.); S. Becher, *Die Bevölkerungsverhältnisse, der österreichischen Monarchie* (Vienna 1846); A. Kovács, *Développement de la population de la Hongrie depuis la cessation de la domination Turque* (Budapest 1919).
[b]K. Czörnig, *Etnographie der Oesterreichischen Monarchie,* vol. 1 (Vienna 1857), pp. 74–80; idem, *Statistisches Handbüchlein* (Vienna 1861), pp. 44–7.
[c] *Österreichische Statistik. Neue Folge,* vol. 1 (Vienna 1917); *Magyar Statisztikai Közlemények,* 64 (Budapest 1912).
[d] Jewry was regarded as a religious group, not as an ethnic minority.

237

million Slovenes, Croats and others.[7] Considering also the assimilation by the Czechs and the Croats and adding the effects of the continuing migration along linguistic borders, we can assess the number of the assimilated at somewhere between 4 and 5 million throughout the epoch, a number which accounts for more than 10 per cent of Austro-Hungary's inhabitants. By and large we are also able to determine the timing of the waves of migration and assimilation. On the one hand, these roughly coincided with the cycles of economic prosperity – the 'take-off' phases of industrialization; on the other, the waves followed the pogroms in Russia. We may also attempt to define the socio-historical stages of assimilation. The first stage is that of settlement. In this stage, the immigrants or internal migrants retain their original identity, live in their own communities, have business but no social interrelations with the recipient society. The newcomers do not know whether the settlement will be provisional or their lasting home. They are satisfied with their external adjustment to the extent that they take over some indigenous habits and a basic vocabulary of the new language. Immigrant Jews in Hungary typically spoke German or Yiddish mixed with some basic Hungarian words.

The longest and most decisive stage is the second one, the stage of linguistic-cultural and later social integration which one may call the bicultural stage, and which subsumes bilingualism. After a few decades the immigrant Jews of the first or second generation became bilingual: outwardly they used the new language (Magyar, Polish, German); inwardly, in the synagogue, the family, and among friends, their original one. Their culture and attitude became dual; they learned Hungarian poems, literature, history, and ethos but they also knew the Jewish religious and historical tradition, and the Jewish 2,000-year-old folklore. Telling examples of this bicultural mind are specific mixtures of Jewish and Christian holidays. Assimilated Jewish families in Central Europe usually celebrated both Hannukah and Christmas, singing both Jewish and Christian seasonal songs.[8] It was not exceptional for Hungarian Jews to keep Passover together with Easter and to eat matzos with smoked ham.

Bilingualism and bicultural attitudes meant belonging to two communities, a dual commitment. Since belonging to two or more groups, in other words multiple commitment, necessarily implies conflicts, assimilated Jews tried to harmonize the external conflicts and psychic ambivalences. In Austria and Hungary they could do it in the age of liberalism, up to the last decade of the nineteenth century.

The similarly long third stage is that of true assimilation – if nothing disturbs the process. In this stage, the new identity becomes dominant, while attachment to the original community is reduced to sympathy and memories of secondary significance and interest.[9] The assimilation of Central European Jewry was a multi-stage process lasting many generations, and can hardly be examined historically in any other context.[10]

In the first half of the eighteenth century, the centres for Jewish settlement within the monarchy were the Czech-Moravian provinces. During the reign of Maria Theresa and Joseph II, some larger groups were drawn southwards to Hungary. These were joined by the Jewish population of Galicia following the division of Poland. The mass migration of these latter began in the early nineteenth century and was mainly directed to northern Hungary, from whence it branched off to the inner regions of the country. The Czech-Moravian branch spoke German, with occupations mostly in industry and commerce. This rather enlightened branch was well disposed to assimilation. The newcomers brought to Hungary by the Galician 'waves', on the other hand, comprised people with occupations as, for instance, grocers, itinerant vendors or farm labourers. These people retained a strong attachment to the orthodox tradition. Mass immigration into the Austrian provinces began rather late, only in the 1860s. It is also from the Czech provinces that most of the Jewish merchants and intellectuals came to Vienna.

It can be seen from table 2 that the growth of the Jewish population was rather rapid: the average for the first period was 1.8, for the second 1.45 per cent. Disregarding the loss resulting from migration and conversion, this increase well surpassed natural growth. By a modest estimate we may assess the migratory margin for the nineteenth century at 800,000 at the least. Of this number, approximately 250,000 fell to Austria (Galicia) and 550,000 to Hungary. (Since the latter went through Galicia, immigration into Galicia must have surpassed half a million from Polish–Russian territories). As opposed to assumptions usually found in the literature, the stream of immigration lasted until the 1880s and declined only in the two decades at the turn of the century.[11]

The inner migration of Jewry fundamentally altered the structure of settlements. In Cisleithania, the economic and intellectual centre of the Jewish agglomeration shifted from the Czech provinces to Vienna. In Hungary, the number of Jews almost reached that in Galicia, and their significance well surpassed that of the Jews in the north-eastern agglomeration. That this migration was focused on Vienna and on Budapest is, in itself, an indication of the close connection between economic concentration (embourgeoisement) and assimilation. The figures on urban settlement are even more striking: 92 per cent of the Jews in the Austrian provinces lived in Vienna, while 76 per cent of the Galician Jews, 48 per cent of the Hungarian Jews and 45 per cent of the Jews in the Czech provinces lived in towns. In the South Slav provinces 81 per cent of the Jews settled in Trieste and 23 per cent of the Jews in Hungary lived in Budapest.[12] Thus, urbanization throughout the monarchy was greatly influenced by the Jews, just as the Jews were greatly influenced by urbanization.

Data on the occupational structure and the economic situation of the Jews also illustrate their drive towards *embourgeoisement*. In Hungary in 1910, 12.5 per cent of the artisans, 54 per cent of the merchants, 43 per cent of the employees of credit

Table 2. *Growth of the Jewish population within the monarchy*

Region	1787	% Austria's population	% Monarchy's population	1857	% Austria's population	% Monarchy's population	1910	% Austria's population	% Monarchy's population
Alpine provinces	853	0.4	0.2	7,557	1.3	0.7	191,265	14.6	8.5
Czech provinces	68,642	31.0	22.6	131,148	21.0	12.6	140,426	10.7	6.2
Galicia Bukovina	151,302	68.4	49.8	478,160	76.5	46.3	974,814	74.2	43.5
Southern Slav provinces	425	0.2	0.1	4,031	0.6	0.4	7,182	0.5	0.3
Austria	221,222	100.0	—	626,000*	100.0	—	1,314,000	100.0	—
Hungary	83,000	—	27.3	413,000	—	40.0	932,000	—	41.5
Monarchy total	304,222			1.039,000			2,246,000		

* Including people in military service.

Sources: as table 1; Alajos Kovács, *Azsidóság térfoglalása Magyarországon* (Expansion of the Jews in Hungery), vol. 1 (Budapest 1922).

institutions and 20 per cent of the intellectuals were Jewish, and they in turn accounted for no more than 5 per cent of the country's population.[13] The proportion of workers and other personnel within the economically active Jewish population amounted to 34 per cent,[14] surpassing the figures for any other nationality. If, beside the statistical cross-section, we also analyse the sequence of historical development, it becomes quite clear that there is a correlation between the socio-economic position of the Jews and the structural development of capitalism. The Jews in Austro-Hungary primarily pursued local and contracting trades; they were the ones to organize transportation, to finance agriculture and the eventual construction of the railway network. According to the demands of modernization, the intellectuals among them took occupations in the technical fields and in the service sector. Intermediary trade, the credit system, transportation, technology, services: what else do these terms stand for if not for the organic unfolding of the infrastructure upon which industrialization was based? The significant role the Jews played in banking, heavy industry and among the intellectual elite at the turn of the century all contributed to this process.

On the one hand, then, we have the premise – as a verified thesis – that the Jews in East-Central Europe entirely adapted to the main currents of *embourgeoisement*. On the other, we have a no less indisputable premise, according to which *embourgeoisement* in East-Central Europe meant not only economic modernization and social reform, but also the formation and acceptance of national identity. Is it at all possible to conclude from all this that in this great transformation Jewry should have kept its own traditional identity?

The inner logic of the syllogism and the historical facts both seem to deny the grounds for posing the question that way. First of all, the Jews did not constitute a homogeneous community. Within the monarchy there were at least two distinct Jewish populations differing both ethnically and at the cultural level. Secondly, the Jewish population had never been homogeneous in social terms. The more Jewry was integrated into modern capitalist society the more it was divided by class stratification and class conflicts. Thirdly, the great historical transformation which designated Jewry to the vital posts of capitalist commodity production was inevitably accompanied by the spread of enlightened rationalism and the weakening of religious belief, together with growing religious indifference.[15] How could this weakening and split religion possibly have united the heterogeneous Jewish community? And lastly, religious tradition and messianic utopia were no longer enough to cement a modern identity in the age of conquering nationalism when only the isolated and immobile village communities could resist the attraction of emerging new national identity. Possibly considered as a sin by religious orthodoxy or Hassidic messianism, and as narrow-mindedness by the belated wisdom of posterity, the monarchy's Jewry, having already reached the stage of dual commitment at the time of the *Vormärz*, had no other option than to choose a national identity adequate to the age, the place and to its interests and inclinations. The majority were absorbed by the Austro-Germans, the Hungarians and the Poles, while a smaller number became part of the Czech and other Slavic nations.

The option for German identity does not require further explanation. The Bohemian and Moravian Jews spoke German, and their Germanization began back in their original homeland. They had left the Czech land – and to a smaller extent Hungary – as *Deutschjuden* and, settling in Vienna, soon found their proper place in the bourgeois society of the supranational-cosmopolitan city. Their elite was probably influenced by the Baroque life-style of the *Hochadel*, but their assimilation was basically oriented to the *Beamtenadel* and the *Bildungs- bürgertum* (ennobled bureaucracy and educated middle class). These Austrian leading strata were not attached to the German nation, but to the Austrian state and the Habsburg dynasty, or in other words, were not committed to a nation but to a state-patriotic identity.[16] Around 1890, the majority of the 133,000 Jews in the Austrian provinces and of the 100,000 Jews in the Czech provinces, as well as the 5,000 German-speaking inhabitants of Trieste, were adherents of German culture and loyal subjects of the Austrian emperor. The attachment of the Jews to dynastic state-patriotism partly follows from the religious tolerance of the Josephinist Enlightenment, which thoroughly imbued the Austrian ruling elite and bureaucracy in the *Vormärz*. The religious tolerance of the Austrian governments promised some protection to the Jewish citizens against clericalism and traditional forms of anti-semitism.

The motivation of the Hungarian and the Polish Jewry for assimilation is less self-evident. What induced these German- or Yiddish-speaking ethno-religious communities to switch their language, culture and habits? And what made them assimilate to the image of the Hungarian and Polish nobility rather than to the German bourgeoisie of the recipient towns and the Empire? All this began at a time when, before 1867, the ruling authorities used German, and their business connections also tied the Jews to the Austrian and German economic centres. (Of course, this question also applies to the Magyarization of the German population in Hungary; this was not specifically a Jewish problem.)

Omitting the details of the innumerable local variations, my solution derives from the basic fact that in Hungary, in the first half of the nineteenth century, modernization was represented and promoted not by the traditional burghers, but by the nobility and the gentry active in commodity production. And this meant the ethnic assimilation of the old 'middle class' of the town burghers and the Jews. The great figures of the Vormärz, Wesselényi, Kossuth and Eötvös, emphatically urged the linguistic Magyarization of the Jews; in fact they connected assimilation with emancipation.[17]

Since in Hungary and in Poland the numerous nobility kept their leading role and still represented the social model, assimilation to them meant adjustment which, in turn, promised a growing prestige for the newcomers. Magyarization (or Polonization) in itself provided the opportunity to be a real gentleman and opened up the road for careers and profitable relationships. But with the Jewry of the *Vormärz* and the *Ausgleich*, material interest, profit, was not the sole motivation. They were in search of a new identity. The traditional faith no longer satisfied the mobile personality of the nineteenth century.[18] Both the Hungarian and Polish identity, looking back on a great historical tradition and charged with passionate patriotism, were exceedingly attractive. 'Hungary is my motherland,' Franz Liszt wrote in 1838. 'I, too, belong to this ancient race, I, too, am a son of this unruly nation swelled with vital force, destined to a better future.'[19] These lines could have been written by Chopin about the Poles, and the feeling could have been entertained by Pest's banker, Moric Ullmann, or the textile manufacturer, Samuel Goldberger, even if they would not have been able to express it the same way.[20]

The unique Hungarian mixture of the romantic idea of liberty and an enlightened rational liberalism was more attractive to the Jews of the area than Josephinist state-patriotism with its practically useless, cool, non-emotional ideal of the abstract 'public good' (*Gemeinwohl*). The extent to which Hungarian and Polish nationalism was more attractive than Austrian state-patriotism is well demonstrated by the fact that despite the traditional anti-semitism of Polish noble society, only a fragment of the Galician Jews declared themselves Germans (3 per cent in 1910) and the rest registered as Polish (3 per cent as Ukrainian).[21]

The key to the weakness of assimilation in Austria lay in its one-way orientation to the state and in its strong attachment to liberalism, in other words, in the acceptance of a supranational Austrian identity. The traditional upper classes, the 'first society' (*Hochadel*) had never accepted the Jewish *nouveaux riches*, not even the converted ones, although they shared the same supranational patriotism. They had profitable business and political connections with the Jewish middle class, but hardly allowed the admission of Jewish businessmen into the first society and resisted Jewish integration. On the other hand, Jews could not integrate into the German middle class and petty bourgeoisie either. Their state-oriented liberalism provoked German racial nationalism and the fervent anti-capitalism of the competitive German middle strata.[22] Austrian Jews, particularly the middle class, were barred from access to either the traditional upper or lower classes. Their fate was sealed by the decline of the Austrian state-idea and by the deep crisis of free-trade liberalism. The Jewish bourgeoisie became subject to a series of traumatic experiences in political and intellectual life, at the universities, and in professional fields. So Austrian Jewish intellectuals were obviously the first to recognize the frustration of assimilation.[23] Nor was it an accident that a Jewish nationalist organization (Kadimah) was started in 1883 by Jewish immigrant students from Eastern Europe in Vienna.[24]

As a reaction to the growing political and social anti-semitism in the 1890s,

Jewish assimilation in Vienna was hindered and in many cases frustrated. Its various trends parted to spread in all directions. Devoted liberals like Moritz Benedikt, the editor of the *Neue Freie Presse*, or Heinrich Friedjung, the historian, remained faithful to dynastic state-patriotism, resuscitating the dying embers of declining liberalism. Others looked for new ways and ideals of assimilation. A sweeping trend of the desire to assimilation, mostly of socially committed Jewish intellectuals and proletarians, led to the socialist movement. On the basis of sublime ideas of social justice and internationalism they hoped to obtain admittance to the surrounding native population.[25] Joining with the rising working class and identification with its socialist movement were of similar importance for Jewish workers and nonconformist intellectuals as acceptance into the ranks of the bourgeoisie and identification with liberalism were for well-to-do Jewish merchants and bankers.[26]

A specific reaction to expanding anti-semitism was the Jewish self-hatred[27] described by psychologists as a form of psychic defence mechanism (*Abwehrmechanismus*). The despised Jew compensated for his feeling of inferiority by identifying with his enemy through a mechanism of self-humiliation.[28] The problem can also be elucidated from the point of view of social history; the Jewish identity crisis took place at the time of the great revolt of the upper-class Jewish youth against the hypocritical ethics and business mentality of their fathers' generation. (Let me mention only Fritz Mauthner, Georg Simmel, Carl Sternheim, Karl Kraus or the well-known case of Otto Weininger.)[29]

On the opposite side, the most explicit form of Jewish de-assimilation appeared in Vienna at the turn of the last century, and gave birth to an influential trend of political Zionism.[30] Austria had also been the hot-bed of the newly developing modern Jewish national consciousness.[31] And yet the acceptance of an overtly Jewish identity demanded such a destructive self-denial from the Germanized Austrian Jewish elite that only very few chose this route before Nazism. The majority, wounded as they were, chose to remain Austrian, faithful to liberal humanism, and found a refuge in an apolitical psycho-erotic and aesthetic culture, and somewhat later, just before World War I, in the anti-political avant-garde culture.[32]

The assimilation of Hungarian Jewry seemingly advanced resolutely and successfully. From time to time anti-Semitic disturbances flared up (as, for instance, in 1883, during the infamous case of ritual murder of Tiszaeszlár), but these abated in all cases. The Hungarian ruling stratum felt the need to co-operate with the Jews, not only in economic life and in modernization, but in defending the 'idea of the Magyar national state'. This ruling stratum was therefore in no position to deny liberalism; it needed constitutionalism in opposing Viennese centralism and imperial power, just as it could not dispense with assimilation in its effort quantitatively to strengthen the Hungarian nation both in respect of material wealth and of intellectual capacity. And although the conservative elite and the gentry middle class looked at the growing strength of Jewry with increasing hatred and envy, they managed to relegate political anti-semitism to the sphere of conscious self-censorship. They submitted to the *Lex suprema*, which was to preserve the Magyar hegemony and integrity of Greater Hungary.

This double impulse of love and hate led to ambiguous socio-psychic behaviour, to a cognitive dissonance[33] among the majority of the Hungarian nobility, particularly the leading elite. On the one hand they preserved tolerance and liberalism, at least in religious matters and acceptance of the Jews in business and public life. In 1895 a special law was enacted which announced the reception of the Jewish denomination and its reciprocity with the others.[34] On the other hand, they put an ever-growing emphasis on the Christian character of the Hungarian state, favoured explicitly 'Christian' institutions and enterprises, tacitly tolerated anti-liberal, neo-conservative trends. Up to the end of the dual monarchy, however, they could not solve the contradictions of their cognitive dissonance.[35]

Disturbances and split consciousness were not the privilege of the Hungarian elite. The Jews in Hungary were also divided by assimilation itself and by the religious reform accompanying the process. From the 1870s onwards, a large gap came to separate the neologues, the followers of religious reform, and those communities which, although assuming a commitment to the Hungarian *political* nation, strictly adhered to the orthodox tradition. And beyond this split, the presence of a massive population of non-assimilated, Yiddish-speaking Eastern Jewry, numbering about 200,000, also made itself felt in hindering assimilation without, however, contributing to a revival of Jewish national consciousness.

The adjustment to the new social environment caused, nevertheless, great problems of consciousness among assimilated Jews. We can speak of a specific cognitive dissonance in their case also. In public life they had to accept the rules and habits of the traditional middle class, the formalities, parades, the gala dress, the rhetorical style of the nobility, its pseudo-heroic feudal value system. In public life they intransigently exercised their business minds and entrepreneurial spirits, following the bourgeois ethos; they ostentatiously upheld their fathers' German-Jewish names, Goldberger, Deutsch, Weiss, even if these were prefixed by Magyar titles such as 'Budai', 'Hatvani' or 'Csepeli'.[36]

Let me mention two characteristic examples. The head of the Hatvani Deutsch family, owners of sugar factories and of a flourishing finance business, was quoted on the stock exchange simply as Deutsch, but participated in public life under the name of Hatvani Deutsch; while his son, the writer and editor, used only the name Hatvany.[37] Or, when Sigismund Kornfeld, president of the Hungarian *Creditanstalt*, was admitted to the Upper House, he solemnly put on the traditional Hungarian gala dress with a sword he never knew how to wear, and bought 10,000 acres of land, as was proper to a man of his rank. And since Hungarian landowners were entitled to the right of patronage, Kornfeld founded a church as well – a Jewish church – perhaps the only instance of Jewish patronage in Europe.[38]

Assimilation to the nobility and preservation of the bourgeois ethos in business and public life; and Jewish culture in private life – this dualism of behaviour and mentality runs parallel with the ambiguity of the Hungarian recipient strata. The contradictory process of Jewish assimilation and Hungarian reception made the two sides of the same problem: the *embourgeoisement* of a feudal society without native bourgeoisie. Their mutual love–hate was a phenomenon of complementary cognitive dissonance which could not be solved in the age of Austro-Hungarian dualism. The solution – if we can call it a solution – was brought about by the authoritarian 'Christian nationalist' regime of Admiral Horthy, who took power after the fall of the monarchy.

The situation was different again in Galicia. Here, in the dualist era, the state did not officially register Jews as a nationality, nor Yiddish as a distinct language, thus inducing the Jewish masses to choose their allegiance. A majority declared themselves Polish. (In 1910, out of 872,000 Jews, 808,000 registered as Polish – no less than 92 per cent.) No pressure was exerted, so in all probability these people really felt closest to the Poles – which of course, from our perspective, testifies to the relativity of social measurements. It is hard to tell how many of the 800,000 Polish Jews were actually assimilated, though an assessment is facilitated by the census of 1931, when the Hebrew religion and the Yiddish-Hebrew language were separately registered in Poland. Of the 3.1 million Jews, only 372,000 declared themselves Polish, of which 241,000 lived in Galicia, accounting for almost one-third of the 790,000 Jews in the area. These figures point to a more advanced stage of *embourgeoisement* and assimilation in Galicia.[39]

Despite their formal identification with the Poles, the remaining two-thirds lived within the bounds of their traditional socio-cultural community, and although emancipated, their social position and mentality were still tied to the ghetto. Presumably this dualism greatly hindered the assimilation of Galicia's Jewry and contributed to the aggravation of conflicts both among the Jews and between them and the Poles. But there is no real ground for establishing a definite historical correlation between the process of assimilation and the rise of anti-semitism in East-Central Europe. Let us only recall the fact that both the well-assimilated and the non-assimilated Jewish communities were equally destroyed by the German Nazis.

In conclusion: the assimilation of Jewry in the Austro-Hungarian monarchy was a process subject to the general miseries of East-Central Europe. First, in these backward societies, the majority of Jewry adapted to the process of *embourge-*

oisement, to capitalist commodity production and its concomitant mentality. This created a permanent and growing gap between them and the declining strata within the traditional structure of the recipient nation. The new, bourgeois stratification created grave tensions and conflicts all over the world, even in 'Jewless' homogeneous societies. In East-Central Europe, these social conflicts acquired an ideological and emotional anti-semitic charge right from the moment of their birth. This was already apparent during the disturbances in Pest in April 1848.

Secondly, Jews in the monarchy adapted to a declining power, a vanishing reality. In Austria, they submitted to the Austrian state and to the Austrian identity, which involved no national commitment. In Hungary, they yielded to the liberal nationalism of the traditional landowner elite, a nationalism which could afford to be receptive and tolerant only within the bounds of the monarchy, permitting Magyar influence over Greater Hungary. The theoretical and political foundations of assimilation had already been weakened by the Austrian identity crisis at the turn of the century, and were eventually undermined by the dissolution of the monarchy and the ultimate prevalence of the authoritarian–conservative regimes.

Thirdly, the fact that the assimilation of Jewry implied an attachment to the Austrians and the Hungarians naturally produced an aversion among the Czechs, Slovaks, Rumanians, and Croats, reinforcing their old, deep-rooted superstitious anti-semitism. The only exception was Polish Jewry, the majority of which, however, failed to assimilate. The Jews remained an alien body in Polish society, without enjoying the status and rights of an ethnic minority.

Fourthly, in Austria–Hungary and later in the successor states, anti-semitism stood in the way of achieving total assimilation. But the high level of *embourgeoisement* within Jewry rendered a withdrawal to de-assimilation very difficult. Such a step back however would have been the precondition *par excellence* of Jewish national organization and of the development of Jewish national consciousness.

But 'responsibility' for all that happened lies with history, if anywhere. At the dawn of a new age, Jewry had no more real option than did all other nations of the region; modernization was an inevitable necessity, and capitalism could not be confined at the Western frontiers of the monarchy. And capitalism meant *embourgeoisement*, in the course of which there was no way to avoid assuming a given identity with a state or a nation. Up to that point there was no other option. But when the recipient societies arrived at the point of partial or total refusal, that assimilated part of Jewry had a number of options; a choice had to be made, in answer to the partial or total anti-semitism surrounding them. The organic process of free choice was brutally interrupted by German and other varieties of fascism.

Up to this point the historian has attempted to present the story as it was, within a strictly hermeneutic framework. But neither he, nor his readers, will be able to detach themselves from later developments; a reflex conditioned by history itself. The concluding words about the Nazis' brutal genocide can be interpreted as a condemnation of Jewish assimilation, or they can be read as a recollection of a grave but passing tragedy. The mass frustration of Jewish assimilation may lead one to argue for an independent Jewish state as the single solution left for Jewry. Without questioning the rationality of the above interpretations, one may well consider any of the options open to the Jews as a reduction of the self and a loss of values. One could regard the very need to choose as a classical case of Kierkegaard's collision of values, independently of whether one opts for the Jewish state and nation, or for Jewish identity within the diaspora, or for the accomplished assimilation. Beyond doubt, there are serious arguments for the defence of the self, of human dignity and of freedom. After all, *vivere necesse est.*

But others may maintain – as the Romans did – that *navigare necesse est, vivere non est necesse.*

NOTES

1 Károly Pap, *Azarel* (Budapest 1946).
2 Lajos Hatvany: *Urak és emberek* (Men and Gentlemen) (Budapest 1980).
3 William C. McCagg, *Jewish Nobles and Geniuses in Modern Hungary* (Boulder 1972), pp. 70–4, 142–8.
4 Eva Karady and Erzsébet Vezér (eds.), *A Vasárnapi Kör* (The Sunday Circle). (Budapest 1980), pp. 56–8; Erzsébet Vezér, *Lesznai Anna élete* (The Life of Anna Lesznai) (Budapest 1979).
5 Péter Hanák (ed.), *Magyarország története 1890-1918* (History of Hungary) (Budapest 1978) pp. 418–19.
6 The term 'Jewish' had religious, not national, connotations in the monarchy's censuses following 1869. See *Ergebnisse der Volkszählung vom 31 Dezember 1910* (hereafter *Volkszählung 1910). Österreichische Statistik.* New ser. Vol. I. no. 2, pp. 40ff.
7 *Ibid.,* Vol. I no. 1, pp. 60ff.
8 Gershom Scholem tells us a similar story from his own youthful experience. As little children they waited for the "Hannukahmann" – The Jewish Santa Claus – to bring them presents. Gershom Scholem, *Von Berlin nach Jerusalem* (Berlin 1947), pp. 42–3.
9 Peter Hanák, 'Polgárosodás és assimiláció Magyaroszágon a XIX században' (*Embourgeoisement* and Assimilation in Hungary in the Nineteenth Century), *Történelmi Szemle* (Historical Review) 4 (1974), pp. 519–20.
10 Victor Karády and Istvan Kemény, 'Les Juifs dans la structure des classes en Hongrie : essai sur les antécédents historiques des crises d'antisémitisme du XXe siècle', *Actes de la Recherche en Sciences Sociales* 22 (June 1978), pp. 36–7. The authors termed the three stages 'integration', 'acculturation' and 'assimilation' respectively.

11 Alajos Kovács, *A zsidóság térfoglalása Magyarországon* (Jewish Expansion in Hungary) (Budapest 1922), p. 13.

12 *Volkszählung 1910*, Vol. I, no. 1, pp. 38–94, and *Magyar Statisztikai Közlemények* (Hungarian Statistical Review) (New Ser.), 64. Compare with the data in Peter G.J. Pulzer, *The Rise of Political Anti-Semitism in Germany and Austria* (New York, London and Sydney 1964), pp. 346–7.

13 Alajos Kovács, *A zsidósag terfoglalása*, pp. 41–4.

14 Hanak (ed.), *Magyarország története*, p. 465.

15 The basic work on the history of Jewish integration in Hungary is Lajos Venetaner, *A magyar zsidóság története a honfoglalástól az elsö világhaboruig* (The History of Hungarian Jews from the Conquest of the Country till World War I) (Budapest 1922). See also Ernest Márton, 'The Family Tree of Hungarian Jewry', 'Hungarian Jewry: Settlement and Demography', and Nataniel Katzburg, 'Hungarian Jewry in Modern Times', in Randolph L. Braham (ed.), *Hungarian–Jewish Studies* (New York 1966).

16 Peter Hanák, 'Österreichischer Staatspatriotismus im Zeitalter des aufsteigenden Nationalismus', in *Wien und Europa zwischen den Revolutionen (1789–1848)* (Vienna 1979), pp. 325–8.

17 Domokos Kosáry, *Kossuth Lajos a reformkorban* (L. Kossuth in the Vormärz) (Budapest 1946), pp. 229–31, George Barany, 'Magyar Jew or Jewish Magyar?' *Canadian-American Studies*, 8, 1 (1974), pp. 18–20; Istvan Deak, *The Lawful Revolution. Louis Kossuth and the Hungarians, 1848–1849* (New York 1919), pp. xv, 35, 45.

18 For the 'mobile personality' see Daniel Lerner, *The Passing of Traditional Society* (New York 1958), pp. 48–9.

19 Quoted by Béla Pukánszky, *Német polgár magyar földön* (German People in Hungary) (Budapest n.d.), p. 97.

20 For the rapid Magyarization of Jewish bourgeoisie see Jokab Pólya, *A Pesti Magyar Kereskedelmi Bank keletkezésének és ötven éves fennállásának története* (A History of the Origins and the Last Fifty Years of the Pest Hungarian Commercial Bank) (Budapest 1982); Venetaner, *A magyar zsidóság története*, pp. 115, 139–44, 154–62; P. Hanák and K. Hanák, *A magyar pamutipar története* (The History of the Hungarian Cotton Industry) (Budapest 1964), p. 32.

21 *Volkszählung, 1910*, Vol. I, no. 2, pp. 54–5.

22 Pulzer, *Political Anti-Semitism*, pp. 88–91, 144–8; Roy Pascal, *From Naturalism to Expressionism* (London 1973), pp. 67–73.

23 In his basic study on Jewish assimilation Kurt Lewin regards the frustration of assimilation as necessary. Lewin argues that assimilation, by creating new inhibitions and a feeling of uncertainty, eventually distorts the personality itself. Kurt Lewin, *Psycho-Sociological Problems of a Minority Group: Resolving Social Conflicts* (New York and London 1948), pp. 145–58.

24 Moses Landau, *Geschichte des Zionismus in Österreich-Ungarn* (Vienna 1932); Adolf Böhm, *Die Zionistische Bewegung* (Berlin 1937), Vol. I, pp. 99–101; Ludwig Rosenhek (ed.), *Festschrift zur Feier des 100. Semesters der akademischen Verbindung Kadimah 1883–1933.* (Mödling 1933); Hugo Gold, *Geschichte der Juden in Österreich* (Tel-Aviv 1971).

25 Robert S. Wistrich, *Socialism and the Jews* (London and Toronto 1982), pp. 229ff and

242ff. The author explicitly deals with problems of the assimilation of Jews in Austria and Germany. Heinz Lubasz (University of Essex) called my attention to this very important aspect of Jewish assimilation (1982).

26 A typical example can be found in the history of the Viennese family of Victor Adler. A psycho-historical analysis appears in William J. McGrath, *Dionysian Art and Populist Politics in Austria* (New Haven and London 1974).

27 Some references to the huge literature; Theodor Lessing, *Der Jüdische Selbsthass* (Berlin 1930); Kurt Lewin, *Resolving Social Conflicts*, pp. 186–200. Peter Loewenberg, 'Antisemitismus und jüdischer Selbsthass', *Geschichte und Gesellschaft*, 5 (1979); Peter Gay, *Freud, Jews and other Germans* (New York 1978), (particularly the chapter on Hermann Lewi, 'A Study of Service and Self-Hatred'); Gershom Scholem, 'Zur Sozialpsychologie der Juden in Deutschland 1890–1914', in Rudolf von Thadden (ed.), *Die Krise des Liberalismus zwischen den Weltkriegen* (Göttingen 1978); Hans Dieter Hellige, 'Generations-konflikt, Selbsthass und die Entstehung anti-kapitalistischer Positionen im Judentum', *Geschichte und Gesellschaft* 5 (1979).

28 Anna Freud, *Das Ich und die Abwehrmechanismen* (Munich 1973), pp. 85–94; I. Sarnoff, 'Identification with the Aggressor: Some Personality Correlates of Antisemitism among Jews', *J. of Personality* 20 (1951), quoted by H.D. Hellige, 'Generationskonflikt', p. 477.

29 Hellige, *ibid.*, pp. 497–510.

30 Adolf Boehm, *Die zionistische Bewegung* (Berlin 1920).

31 Alex Bein, *Theoder Herzl: Biography* (Vienna 1934); Carl E. Schorske, *Fin-de-Siècle Vienna. Politics and Culture* (New York 1980), pp. 146–62; József Patai, *Herzl* (Budapest n.d.).

32 Schorske, *Fin-de-Siècle Vienna*, pp. 7–22, 302–11; Wistrich, *Socialism and the Jews*, pp. 214–19.

33 The term 'cognitive dissonance' was introduced by Leon Festinger, 'The Theory of Cognitive Dissonance', in W.C. Schramm (ed.), *The Science of Human Communication* (New York 1963), pp. 17–27.

34 *Corpus Juris Hungarici. Articles of 1894–1895* (Budapest 1897), Law Article 42. Article 17 of 1867 declared only the civic equality of the Jews.

35 The great poet, Endre Ady, gives the most apt characterization of this relationship in his article "Korrobori", written in 1917, first published in 1924. Erzsébet Vezér (ed.), *Ady Endre publicisztikai írásai* (Endre Ady's Published Writings), Vol. III (Budapest 1977), pp. 575–7.

36 Hanak, *Magyarország története*, pp. 447–8.

37 McCagg, *Jewish Nobles*, pp. 70–4, 142–8, 158, 182.

38 Radnóti József, *Kornfeld Zsigmond* (Budapest n.d.), pp. 80–2, 108–9.

39 *Drugi powszechny spis ludošci z dn, 9, 12 1931*); *Statystyka Polski*, Ser. C, no. 62 (Warsaw 1937), pp. 22–3, 28–9, 31.

11

Alternatives to class revolution: Central and Eastern Europe after the First World War*

IVÁN T. BEREND

Counter-revolutionary deluges in Hungary, Bulgaria, Germany and Austria

The tragedy of the First World War greatly intensified age-old unsolved social and political contradictions, which deepened into crisis in a number of economically and/or socially backward countries. Attempted proletarian revolution was the response emerging from the confused historical circumstances which followed the war. It triumphed and became permanently established only in Russia. Elsewhere its fate was either suppression after briefly gaining the upper hand (as in Hungary), or else its victory was successfully thwarted. However, revolution is not the subject, but the starting-point of the present study.

An icy, dirty flood of counter-revolution inundated many countries in Central and Eastern Europe in the wake of these hopeful or hopeless revolutionary experiments. In some places a clearer definition of fronts in the class struggle made the counter-revolution reveal itself exceptionally frankly. Although the Hungarian Soviet Republic was suppressed by military force from outside and Budapest was temporarily occupied by Romanian units, in Vienna, Arad and Szeged, even during the months of dictatorship of the proletariat, the organizers of counter-revolution not only formed a government, but with feverish haste drummed up armed detachments, for the most part consisting of army officers and professional NCOs, upper-class members of the former apparatus of oppression and officialdom, and in some places the sons of reliable farmers. When the Czechoslovakian and Romanian armies had completed their work, it was the turn of the counter-revolutionary armed forces gathered around their commander-in-chief, Nicholas Horthy, to play an important role. This was to 'clean up' the country – to punish and exterminate the revolution. Having marched through the area between the Danube and the Tisza and entrenched themselves around Lake Balaton, they not only hanged revolutionary peasants

---

*Translation by M.H.P. McCarthy, MA (Oxon.), L-és-L., F.I.L.

in the acacia groves, not only brought members of the revolutionary Directory to their knees in front of firing squads and incited and conducted pogroms against Jews in Diszel and other villages, but they also ensured that the old class system, re-established partly by occupying forces and partly by the provisional governments, was fully restored. In the midst of the problems facing the state, the changing, powerless governments and the ineffective parliament, these forces not only dominated the situation temporarily, but, following Horthy's entry into Budapest, organized the counter-revolution into a real power. The monarchy was restored, and Admiral Nicholas Horthy was elected regent of Hungary under the threat of armed detachments occupying the parliament building. The real masters of the situation were the members of the units from Szeged. The Union of Hungarian Awakening, led by Gyula Gombos, and other organizations completed these units. They drowned social democratic journalists in the Danube (turning George Bernard Shaw's wry aphorism: 'murder is the extreme form of censorship' into the grimacing face of reality) and dragged hundreds of Budapest citizens to their notorious headquarters, the Britannia Hotel, to be tortured and murdered in order to punish the 'criminal capital'. The same armed forces frustrated with ease two fruitless, weak attempts at return made by Karl Habsburg.

The white terror, which acted as a ruthless open deterrent for two years, killing thousands and driving tens of thousands into emigration, amongst them the cream of the country's intellectual and artistic life, thus organized itself into power.

The same thing took place with similar blatancy in the case of the Bulgarian counter-revolution, although with more legality under King Boris. The government of Professor Cankov, the intellectual leader of the counter-revolution, brought the rightful Stamboliski government down with a coup and ordered bloody revenge. That government's minister of war, General Velkov, the *éminence grise* of the whole decade, maintained the closest connections with the Macedonian terrorists. With the collaboration of Ivan Mihaijlov he ruthlessly ordered the killing of the commander-in-chief, Todor Alexandrov and General Protogerov, those leaders of the Macedonian Revolutionary Organization who had toyed with the idea of Macedonia's immediate or eventual independence. Peasant leaders arriving for elections held under the terror and communists who had risen in arms were mercilessly eliminated (Stamboliski's collaborator Petkov, elected as his representative, having been released from prison to take a seat in parliament, was murdered in the street).

The counter-revolution performed its bloody work in a more covert manner in Germany, where the various Freikorps, unlike Horthy's detachments, did not organize themselves into an independent power. The Freikorps formally accepted the command of the military expert of the majority Social Democrats, Gustav Noske; then, armed with the tactical expertise of the German general staff, and in practice completely independent of the government, they came out onto the streets of Munich, Hamburg and Berlin in the government's name. At the same time, many members of the right wing of the ruling Social Democratic party, aiming at the introduction of genuine, honourable bourgeois democracy, while actually establishing the counter-revolution, criticized Noske and another Social Democrat, the Prussian minister of the interior Wolfgang Heine, for their excessive brutality, and quickly got rid of these colleagues. (They played a particularly embarrassing role after January 1920, the date when the workers, disillusioned at the impossibility of meeting their demands, organized a demonstration in front of the Reichstag building during a debate on a bill aimed at rendering otiose the role played by the industrial councils, and were met by machine-gun fire.) In the meantime the young Republic had to undergo yet another trial of strength: individual groups in the army and internal counter-revolutionary forces openly aimed at seizing power. The 60-year-old monarchist General von Lüttwitz saw the salvation of his country in a strong regime based on the army. While the Freikorps began to be merged into the new Reichswehr, whose numbers were to be limited under the terms of the peace treaty, von Lüttwitz refused to disband the individual units under his direction, and even demanded the dissolution of parliament and the government. On 12 March Captain Ehrhardt marched on Berlin with his unit, which had been ordered to disband. On the following day the government left the capital. While Captain Ehrhardt's brigade marched unchallenged through the Brandenburg Gate and occupied the government quarter, Wolfgang Kapp, who had been secretly directing proceedings, appeared on the scene and appointed himself chancellor and prime minister of Prussia. General von Lüttwitz directed events as head of the general staff. In the eastern territories (perhaps no coincidence) – Silesia, Pomerania, Mecklenburg, Prussia – the military forces quickly linked up with the counter-revolutionary coup, and removed the local Social Democrat administrations. Although in Bavaria the Social Democrat government was forced to resign, in that area the army was unwilling to accept Prussian leadership. Again, in south and west Germany the general mood was against the army linking up with the openly counter-revolutionary Kapp coup, and loyalty was maintained to the central Social Democrat administration.

The general strike throughout the country and the mobilization of left-wing forces resulting from the coup urged everyone to caution. The Kapp adventure collapsed after four days. The counter-revolution could not organize itself into an independent power. Actually, in what we may consider another symbolic event, when on 19 March in answer to the counter-revolutionary coup another workers' rising took place in the Ruhr district and a 50,000-strong Red Army was recruited (no such large armed revolutionary body was formed on German territory in 1919!), once again the Social Democrat government ordered in the Reichswehr. On 2 April the army, including in its ranks units of the Ehrhardt brigade which promoted the open coup, started a bloody settlement of accounts, taking revenge on the working class for the general strike. Then the army was again able to pose as a force for re-establishing order and peace, acting in accordance with the wishes of the legitimate majority Social Democrat government.

The Social Democrat government system therefore represented only one stratum of power in the new republic, which was peculiarly intermixed with other strata – the independent factors represented by the army and the state apparatus, and the counter-revolution covertly built into the system. Even though the counter-revolution was unable to organize itself it was therefore decisively present. It existed as an independent force when the debates on the preparation of the constitution were held under the leadership of Professor Hugo Preuss with the intellectual co-operation of Max Weber, when the democratic elections were held, and when the sittings of the National Assembly, which adopted the democratic constitution of the Weimar Republic, began. Clearly, the Social Democrat government did a great deal towards building up a genuine bourgeois democratic system. On paper the Weimar constitution founded one of the world's most democratic systems. However, in reality it was an exceptionally fragile democracy, the birth of which was conditioned by the conservatism of the independent counter-revolutionary forces, more particularly the army. It was not the much debated Article 48 of the constitution (the special rights conferred on the chancellor in emergency situations, which subsequently ensured that even Hitler had constitutional opportunities) or any other institutional weaknesses which rendered that democracy powerless. It was rather the tense conflict between the adapted institutions and real internal power relationships and determinative social factors which at that time turned even the best of institutional and constitutional prescriptions into empty, futile formalism.

Again, German history following the First World War is a clear example of how the power elite, including the military leadership, regarded open counter-revolution as a particularly necessary evil and, being offered the means to do so by the majority Social Democrats, obstructed its organization into an independent power.

The suppression of the Austrian mass movements shows many similarities. The upsurge of revolutionary forces, the strike in January 1918, the naval mutiny at Cattaro on 1 February (40 warships raised the red flag), the workers' and soldiers' councils formed throughout the country and the establishment of Red Guard units culminated in a left-wing rising as early as 12 November 1918, when a republic was declared. In Austria, sandwiched between two republics of workers' councils, no genuine revolutionary crisis developed, but on 17 April demonstrations and risings broke out which degenerated into bloody clashes. The task of pacification was undertaken by the powerful, majority Austrian Social Democratic Party, which feared the democratic possibilities of any kind of

'Bolshevik adventure', but which was a genuine bourgeois democratic party, aiming at strengthening the interests of the workers. Julius Deutsch, the military expert of the Austrian Social Democratic Party, merged the Red Guards into the new Volkswehr as its 41st battalion, and by swooping on 115 communist officials during the night of 14–15 June attempted to decapitate the leadership of the left-wing opposition. Deutsch's units occupied the inner city of Vienna. The armed forces, drawn up in the Hörlgasse, without hesitation opened fire on the crowds arriving to liberate their leaders. The 20 dead and 80 wounded, left lying in the street, clearly exemplified the limitations of the Austrian Democratic Republic. In this case it should be emphasized that what we face here is not only the counter-revolutionary model familiar from Germany, but also those social realities which obstructed the proletarian revolution. To the hostile rural and city petty bourgeoisie lined up behind the Christian Democratic Party even the Social Democrats, who opposed the possible forces of proletarian revolution, seemed too red and dangerous. At the same time, apart from the Social Democratic Party, no other workers' organization possessed any essential influence, so the amount of revolutionary radicalism depended on what procedures could be effected in the Social Democratic Party. On 17 April the latter collapsed.

It must be added that Hungary, following the classical path of counter-revolution, also shows certain similarities with the foregoing examples. In Hungary also, two years after the white terror had performed its dirty work, its forces were repressed and merged into the apparatus of consolidated state power. The leaders of the circles of military gentry at Szeged, who had made Nicholas Horthy head of state, now relegated him to the second rank, giving place once more to the aristocracy led by István Bethlen and a compact, legitimized and liberalized system of sham parliamentarianism built on a 'unified party'. As Károly Polányi points out, although with considerable exaggeration, when drawing attention to the process by which the former system of government was re-established: 'When the smoke of counter-revolution had dispersed, the political systems in Budapest, Vienna and Berlin did not differ greatly from their pre-war character.'[1]

'Preventive counter-revolutions' – escape to a firm-handed administration

However, the counter-revolutions had to suppress not only revolutions which had actually broken out and mass movements winning power or knocking at the government's gates. The social and political conditions of the post-war years produced a second type of counter-revolution, which to some extent fulfilled a different purpose: the preventive counter-revolution, to use the term invented by Fabri, the Italian revolutionary anarchist theoretician. Fabri applied the expression to Italian fascism, which came to power in 1922. In its wider, basic meaning it refers to the historical situation created by a revolutionary crisis, when the old system has fallen apart, but the revolutionary forces are still too inadequate and weak to win. The preventive counter-revolution, which is capable of organizing force, then fills the resulting political vacuum.

Clearly, in this situation, the man in the street, weary of the shocks and trying changes of the revolution, escapes in his alarm to stability, the comforting certainties of a strong government. Marx long ago made the point very effectively with the example in French history of Bonapartism. Knowing nothing of this, but a contemporary of the events he describes, Thomas Mann with splendid insight recognizes this retrograde tendency, when in a letter dated 5 December 1922 he writes: 'In the name of German humanity... I face the wave of reaction which, just as it did after the Napoleonic wars, is moving across Europe (because I am not thinking only of Germany)... I feel that any kind of obscurantism has a great danger and fascination for men and women, who are tired of relativism and yearn for the path of absolutism.'[2]

However, these preventive counter-revolutions did not merely take advantage of the chaotic conditions of the revolutionary crisis and the relative weakness of the revolutionary forces. They organized force to offer certainty and stability to the petty bourgeoisie and the middle classes (representing large sections and sometimes the majority of society), while at the same time securing the well-to-do, property-owning classes against attacks on the class system and private property. Although these preventive counter-revolutions more than once became inseparably linked with classical counter-revolutions, which suppressed actual revolutions and re-established the class system, they nevertheless differed essentially from the latter. Their social policies did not merely aim at defending the capitalistic class system, and their radicalism showed its ruthless brutality in other fields. In them also the social revolt of the crisis situation was acute. It was no mere empty phrase when these movements described themselves as right-wing 'revolutions'. Unlike the variants of counter-revolution which we may call classical, it was not in the name and under the banner of the old system, private property, the class hierarchy or religion that they opposed the proletarian class revolution. They themselves spoke of crying social injustices, inevitable changes, the need to clean up society, and they came on the scene not just to defend the old conservative values, but with a programme for remedying these shortcomings. In countries where the revolutions had been suppressed, counter-revolutionaries protested against the tardiness of social change. 'They told us,' declaimed Hitler in 1922, 'that they are destroying capitalism... They will annihilate capitalism as a whole, and the whole nation will be free. They fight not against Jewish or Christian capitalism, but against all forms of capitalism.' In reality, he added, Christian capital had gone to ruin, while 'international Jewish money-market capitalism has gained ground in proportion as the others have fallen back... the millions of workers in Berlin have remained the same as they were in 1914 – the same workers, only thinner.'[3] As the foregoing shows, at that time every social programme was alloyed with a 'national' element.

We can regard all this as mere phrases, empty deception of the people, only if we simplify the historical formula to imply that the essential objective of these movements, with their violent and extreme hostility to class revolution, was to defend the capitalistic system. No doubt this was their basic historical role. However, we must not disregard the way in which they linked the defence of the capitalistic society with its transformation; it was precisely this feature which gave the right-wing preventive counter-revolutions their real strength and which, in its most clearly expressed forms, expanded them into powerful mass movements. These movements would be incomprehensible if we ignored the fact that their sails successfully caught the wind of social revolt.

The fascist movement from Germany to Romania

No matter what theoretical construction is used in order to classify phenomena which are most frequently mixed in reality, we must nevertheless draw a distinction between a counter-revolution which opposes class revolution, and those preventive counter-revolutions also called 'right-wing revolutions', 'ultra-conservative counter-revolutions' which, referring to their first successful variant, we generally include under the collective name of fascism, although material differences and distinctions must be noted in individual countries. It should be emphasized that in historical reality everything took place in considerable confusion. From its own ingenuity the Hungarian counter-revolution also 'discovered' and used all kinds of things from fascism, and its features were a pretty good mixture. In the 1920s Italian fascism, filling the vacuum in social power by the organization of force and proclaiming the transformation of society, illustrates this type clearly. In Germany the distinction can perhaps be sensed most vividly: the already described attempts at pure counter-revolution, such as the Kapp coup, arrived on the crest of the stormy revolutionary waves of the 1920s. Then, from those months onwards, although at that time with little success, the fascist-type Nazi movement also tried to ride those same waves.

The German Workers' Party, founded by Karl Hessen and Anton Drexler around 5 January 1919, the date of the Berlin proletarian rising, and joined by Adolf Hitler when he returned from military hospital in September, within a short time changed its name to the National Socialist German Workers Party, coming under Hitler's leadership from 1921 onwards. The majority voting principle ended with the arrival of the new chairman. The party, which opened up its central office at 12 Corneliusstrasse, Munich on 1 November, with a card index showing about 3,000 fully-paid-up members, was based on the leadership principle. When a few months later its terrorists had clashed with the socialist workers in the 'battle of the beer-halls', the Nazi Party's shock troops were officially organized as the Sturmabteilung (SA). The Nazi movement had begun its bloody career. It is true that its impatient leaders provoked a premature trial of strength: Hitler's Munich coup attempt on 8 and 9 November 1923 led not to power, as expected, but merely to Landsberg prison. In this case also the conservative military detachments, under the influence of Ludendorff, co-operated. But this abortive coup, taking place only three years after Kapp's attempt to seize counter-revolutionary power, was not intended to put down or throttle the hardly repressible revolutionary urge in Germany in accordance with the old counter-revolutionary pattern, but to exploit that urgent social driving force for its organizers' purposes, to direct it into their own channels.

With or without coup attempts, fascist-type movements quickly grew up in the majority of Central and Eastern European countries. Hitler's Nazi Party itself, of course, consisted of three parts extending to three countries or, to put it another way, developed in the 1920s as an international organization, with German, Austrian and Sudeten German Nazi sections, the last operating on Czechoslovakian territory. This section not only had great traditions, since its activities dated back to the foundation of the Deutschnationaler Arbeiterbund (German National Workers Association) in 1890, but it also became particularly powerful after the war. J. Havránek states on good authority that the swastika flag could be seen more frequently in Czechoslovakia than in Germany. However, it would be a mistake to equate the fascist movement with Sudeten German Nazism in Czechoslovakia. The first Czech fascist organization (the Central Committee of Czechoslovakian Fascists) was also set up in 1923; two years later General Gajda, who had changed his Christian name Rudolf to the Czech name Radola, organized the National Fascist Community and tried to carry out a coup the following year. In Slovakia Hlinka and principally Tuka, the leader of the movement's right wing, created a powerful basis which gathered broad masses of peasant supporters. In 1925 half the Slovak voters supported them.

Similarly, it would be a mistake to equate the Austrian broader right wing with the Austrian activities of the German Nazi movement. In the 1920s the inner crystallization point of the right-wing social movements was formed by Ignaz Seipel, representing the right wing of the Christian Socialists; the group of intellectuals, organized around K. Lugmayer, J. Messner and particularly Othmar Spann, who proclaimed romantic medieval co-operative political theories; the Catholic youth, opposing parliamentarianism; and above all the Heimwehr, which played an increasingly important role from July 1927 onwards and was preparing a coup. The young Prince Ernst Rüdiger von Starhemberg, who had been a second lieutenant in the 4th Austrian Dragoons during the war, formed a small private army of 700 men, and similar armed counter-revolutionary (so-called policing) units grew up like mushrooms. The military force recruited from these very quickly became independent. As early as May 1920 the Christian Socialist politician Richard Steidle massed the Tyrolean Heimwehr units into a single body. Several years later, increasing in muscle and existing throughout the country, the Heimwehr broadened into an organized paramilitary movement which adopted the ideology of institutionalized anti-semitism.

After 1918, in Romania the University of Iasi became the cradle of right-wing terrorism and of the militant anti-semite, anti-liberal, anti-communist movement. Its young shock troops tried out their wings by organizing anti-Jewish pogroms and breaking up meetings. And when, as late as the middle of the 1920s, the prefect of Iași finally tried to restore order, a young student simply shot him down. The young man's name was Corneliu Zelea Codreanu.

In general, characteristic of all these organizations and movements was the predominance of aggressively nationalistic ideologies, opposed to every kind of liberalism, democracy and workers' movements, propagandizing authoritative social ideas, and going hand-in-hand with the open, crude use of force. Their general organizational model was virtually the incorporation in the party of the paramilitary organizations of shock troops, or purely and simply a party constructed around such paramilitary organizations. Terrorism proved particularly useful in suppressing instinctively rebellious social discontents. It lent to these movements a false revolutionary appearance, a poignancy which forged unity in face of existing institutions. According to H. Arendt's witty summing-up: 'What proved so attractive was the transformation of terrorism into some kind of philosophy, useful for the expression of bitterness and blind hatred, some kind of political expressionism, which used bombs for self-expression.'[4]

National revolutions; did they favour the development of small nations? Czechoslovakia, Yugoslavia, Romania

Any discussion of the responses to the challenge of crisis which matured in a conflict-filled area of backwardness and resulting outward movement must consider not only the attempt at class revolution and corresponding counter-revolutions and 'preventive counter-revolutions' (the fascist 'right-wing revolution'), but also give special attention to the response attempted by national revolutions – possibly the most typical and frequent solution tried in the Central and Eastern European area after the First World War.

The fact is virtually self-evident. Historical processes in this region had been very closely bound up with questions of nationality. The more backward countries of Europe, since the sixteenth century traditionally acting as agricultural and raw materials exporters to the Western European centre, dominated by monetary dependence and the influence of foreign capitalistic interest groups, found themselves in a completely changed position following the First World War. We must not overlook the fact that after several centuries countries in the area were suddenly liberated from the hegemony of traditionally dominant powers. Turkey, the power which ruled the Balkans, became a poor little country seeking to follow new paths, and the Balkan countries were finally freed from half a millennium of oppression. The Czechs, Slovaks, Hungarians, Croats, Poles and Romanians were liberated from the Austrian Empire after almost five hundred years of rule by the House of Habsburg, while the Slovaks, Croats and Romanians emerged from a thousand years of Hungarian domination. The Russian Empire lost its domination of Poland and the Baltic countries. The three powers, therefore, which had held the major part of Central and Eastern Europe under their sway, either finally disappeared as powers, or were expelled from the area.

The victorious Great Powers believed they had an interest in the complete disappearance of the Habsburg Empire and the establishment and support of an independent framework of small or medium so-called successor states arising in its place. Clearly, the victors felt they could exercise superiority more reliably over many small countries divided by a burden of grave antagonisms and disputes. However, although victorious they lacked the necessary strength; while exerting considerable influence with federal ideas, credits and other instruments of policy, their interests and ambitions interfered with one another and proved abortive. Even France, which was now the most influential and strongest of the continental powers had only an indirect influence. A strange, unaccustomed power 'calm' prevailed in an area used to political power hurricanes. And this understandably encouraged and strengthened national ambitions. As Tomáš Masaryk, the champion of Czechoslovakian independence, noted with excessive confidence in his memoirs, written during the 1920s: 'The most recent political developments have favoured the small nations... The independence of even the smallest national unit can be ensured in the new Europe.'[5]

National yearnings and ambitions, suppressed for centuries, suddenly became reality. Only now were several nations able to achieve that main attribute of modern bourgeois development, an independent national state. The new, radical rearrangement of nationalities demanded justice against long-standing oppressions. Under the peace treaty suddenly the whole world was at work on developing new national relationships. The Austro-Hungarian monarchy, with an area of more than 676,000 sq. km and a population of 51 millions, was replaced by the 'residual fragments' (to use Clemenceau's expression) of the collapse – an Austria with an area of about 86,000 sq. km and a population of 6.5 million; Hungary cut down to one-third of its size, with an area of about 93,000 sq. km and a population of 7.8 millions; Czechoslovakia, with an area of 140,000 sq. km and a population of 13.6 million, comprising the territories of Bohemia, Moravia, the former northern Hungarian counties, the Sudetenland

and part of Silesia. These countries found themselves faced with problems in developing their new relationships. However, the situation was similar in Romania, which with the acquisition of Transylvania, the Banat, Bukovina and Bessarabia had increased from not quite 138,000 sq. km to over 304,000 sq. km, the population rising from 7.5 million to 17.6 million souls; similarly, Yugoslavia had replaced Serbia with its 87,000 sq. km and 4.5 million people by absorbing Croatia, Slovenia, the Voyvodina, Bosnia-Herzegovina and part of Macedonia, the result being an area of 249,000 sq. km with a population of 12 million; similar problems faced Poland, which was formed from Polish territory in Russian and German hands, Galicia and parts of Bukovina, the total area being 388,000 sq. km, with a population of 27 million. P. Sugar is therefore right to emphasize '... despite all the differences between the countries in the area, they showed many similarities... they had to create national currencies and reunite their national economies... and in the temporary absence of the dominating superpowers they had to try to integrate their countries in the family of nations.'[6]

In many of these countries national revolutions were established, in some cases a government being formed by independence or separatist movements active before and during the war, without any kind of coup, rising or 'revolutionary' upheaval, power being achieved as a result of the peace settlement, although even in such cases preferably by revolution. The nations of the area, a fairly large number of countries, were capable of realizing the yearnings and ambitions of centuries. They felt that in the new historical situation everything hitherto unsuccessful, neglected or unattainable could now be effected in the changed national circumstances. They hoped that the remedies for the nation's most smarting wounds would contain all the healing ointments for oppression and backwardness. Since the absence of an independent national entity was the main obstacle to bourgeois development, with understandable exaggeration the view arose that this was the sole source of all social and economic backwardness, and every limitation to liberty. The result was an expectation that solving the national question would automatically solve every pressing problem. Genuine national euphoria was experienced, and to many nations it seemed apparent that national revolution would produce a comprehensive, effectual response to the challenge of the crisis. Feverish activity was expended on exploiting possibilities afforded by the war for the emergence of national revolution.

Just like the Russian, Hungarian or German class revolutions, the Yugoslav National Movement, whose antecedents reached far back, received a powerful impetus at the end of the war. The South Slavs living in the Austro-Hungarian monarchy had undergone the constantly increasing national and political influence of organizations formed by South Slav communities and emigrants living in the West, more particularly the Yugoslav Committee founded on 1 May 1915 in London. Then in July 1917 the representatives of the various South Slav nations promulgated a declaration on the island of Corfu stating that 'our peoples form one nation, one in faith and written and spoken language'. In October 1918 the Croat and Slovene leaders, meeting in the National Council, issued a statement emphasizing their loyalty to the idea of Yugoslavia.

The Romanian National Movement flared up at the end of the war. In October 1918 the Romanians of Transylvania set up their National Council, the union of Transylvania with Romania and the foundation of a united Romanian state being proclaimed at Gyulafehérvár (Alba Iulia) on 1 December.

The roots of the Czechoslovak national revolution had wider ramifications, lying closest to the activities of the former Young Czech Party, the work before and during the war of that determined protagonist of pan-Slav Czech independence, Karel Kramař (who was sentenced to death by an Austrian court in 1916), and, last but not least, the career of Professor Tomáš Masaryk, who had cherished the Czech idea when a parliamentary deputy. Masaryk (who had published his first book, *Suicide as a Social Mass Phenomenon of Modern Civilization* in 1881) debated the possibilities of Czech independence with his future colleague Eduard Beneš as early as the autumn of 1914, as they strolled around the ancient streets of Prague after the outbreak of war. In December of that year Masaryk, followed a few months afterwards by Beneš, departed abroad to lay the foundation of an independent Czechoslovakia with the assistance of the subsequently victorious powers. Equally decisive factors were the Czechoslovakian Committee, set up abroad at the beginning of the same year (1915) and the recruitment of the 'Družina', a Czech military unit at first formed as part of the Czarist army. The link-up between the Czech and Slovak prisoners at the end of the war brought into being the independent Czech Legion, numbering more than 90,000, which on 20 March 1917 set up an independent Czechoslovakia, proclaiming the National Council in Paris as its provisional government. In the spring of 1918 the Czech Legion went into action at Chelyabinsk; by taking Penza and Kazan and organizing the defence of the Trans-Siberian Railway it performed services against the Russian Revolution which practically symbolized the confrontation between the national class revolutions. As Poincaré, the French premier, was very soon able to announce at the Paris Peace Conference: 'The Czechoslovakians won their right to independence by fighting in Siberia, France and Italy.'[7] Or, as Masaryk asserts in his book on the foundation of the Czechoslovak state, emphasizing the importance of the internal revolution accurately, but without passing judgment: 'The work performed abroad was decisive. However, that work was brought to fruition by the widespread opposition of the national masses to Austria-Hungary and the revolution which broke out after Vienna had capitulated...'[8]

The Czech National Council proclaimed the independence of Bohemia and Moravia in Prague on 28 October. Two days later at Túrócszentmárton the

Slovak national leaders announced that they were joining the united Czechoslovakian state.

Since national independence had been a precondition of progress from the inception of a capitalistic national economy and bourgeois society, in several countries of Central and Eastern Europe the belated achievement of that independence following the First World War meant the inclusion in their agendas of long-standing, inevitably neglected economic, social, and, last but not least, political aims. In individual cases, particularly in Czechoslovakia, but also in Austria and Turkey, and in Poland during the first half of the 1920s, the national revolution was interwoven with an ambition to imitate the industrialized Western European bourgeois democracies, in order to establish similar social and political systems. On the other hand, during the decade following the war these aims could essentially be observed in varying strength and with varying results in national revolutions in every country in the area.

However, the euphoria of national revolution and bourgeois democratic dreams quickly came into collision in a peculiar, typical way with the re-emergence of the nationalities problem in different form.

The national revolutions would seem to have been propagated not by meiosis, but by unification. Rapid disillusionment was the lot of those small nations which had hitherto existed under the domination of other peoples and were now tearing themselves from their former conditions and seeking more promising ones, with great expectations and a hope of partnership in equality. When the desired South Slav state, for example, or the union of the Czechs and Slovaks were attained, more or less immediately new national revolutions were organized. The long dreamt-of brotherhood of the newly founded states was very quickly found to have snags. On 1 January 1921 Pašić, the head of the Serbian government, put before the recently elected national constitutional assembly a centralist draft constitution – one which ensured Serbian supremacy. As a protest 161 deputies walked out of the assembly with the Croat delegates led by Stjepan Radic, who was seeking not a compromise but a federal solution. The centralist constitution was adopted with less trouble in their absence. Thus began the Croatian national movement against the Serbs.

Similarly, in the newly founded Czechoslovakia, although Professor Masaryk during his return journey from Siberia via the USA had signed the Pittsburgh Agreement in June 1918, thereby accepting the obligation of establishing an autonomous Slovakian parliament possessing judicial independence and safeguarding the official use of the Slovak language in public administration and the schools, these objectives were not attained. In face of the Czech conception of a 'united Czechoslovakia', extremist Slovak nationalist forces stepped into the arena. Although the more moderate wing of the Slovak national movement, the National Party, was satisfied with a claim for greater decentralization, under the leadership of A. Hlinka the proponents of limitless autonomy poured into the Slovakian People's Party. Professor Vojtěch Tuka, the leading figure on the right wing of the party towards the end of the 1920s, even went so far as to throw doubt on the legality of the union between the Czechs and Slovaks. His argument was that the Túrócszentmárton proclamation contained a secret clause relating to union for a period of ten years. Consequently, since Slovak autonomy was not a reality, a *vacuum juris* had arisen which ensured the right of free decision to the Slovaks. Tuka was sentenced to a prison sentence of 14 years on a charge of activities in collaboration with the Hungarian government aimed at dissolving the Republic, but such punishments stoked rather than quenched the fire. The Slovakian national revolution turned to different methods.

In reality, the former Yugoslav and Czechoslovakian national movements did not merely break up into purely Czech and Slovakian, or Serbian and Croatian wings – an exceptional variety of different national minorities was characteristic of the newly founded states.

New multi-national states and internal national antagonisms, new oppression of minorities

Even before the First World War, of course, the question of nationalities had been one of the main social problems of the area. Following the breakdown of the multi-national empires, several nations achieved independence in this part of Europe. However, it was impossible to put the national–ethnical principle into effect consistently, nor was there any desire to do so. National reorganization could not therefore spell the solution of the problem, but rather its re-formulation. In Czechoslovakia and Yugoslavia (Serbs and Croats) two nationalities formed the majority. In the new Polish state 69 per cent of the population was Polish, six to eight nationalities forming about one-third. In Romania 72 per cent of the population was Romanian, while in Yugoslavia a quarter of the country's population belonged to minority nationalities, apart from the Serbs and Croats. In the more homogeneous Hungary and Bulgaria masses of people, amounting to one-third and one-tenth respectively of the countries' populations, had become minorities in neighbouring countries.

Out of the area's total population of 110 million every fifth individual belonged to some national minority. However, many religious differences were not without significance. In Catholic Poland 13 per cent of the population was orthodox and 10 per cent Jewish; in Romania 7 per cent, and in Hungary 5 per cent, were of Jewish origin, while in Bulgaria 14 per cent were Muslims. The religious difference, as illustrated by the example of the Yugoslav Muslims, on more than one occasion led to the establishment of some sort of national minority even in people of identical ethnic origin. It is possible that nearly one-half of the population of the area belonged to various kinds of non-official scattered minorities, fragmented by diverse differences, including religion.

Of course, their problems could not be solved by the League of Nations endeavours to ensure their protection by special minority covenants. These covenants did not relate to scattered minorities and it was usually easy to get around them. Moreover, such 'protection' was of the kind which the minorities were not very anxious to have. Officially the League of Nations merely desired to offer protection against discrimination, its aim being to smooth the path to 'just and gradual' assimilation. As Austen Chamberlain declared: 'the aim of a minority covenant is... to ensure... protective measures and justice, which will gradually prepare them for incorporation in the national communities to which they belong'. Briand was not much more reassuring when he stated the objective to be 'not the disappearance of minorities, but a special kind of assimilation' [9] This is a suitable point at which to quote the apparently unprejudiced opinion of a well-known British scholar:

> In the Polish Republic and the enlarged Kingdom of Romania the Poles and Romanians formed about two thirds of the population. In Czechoslovakia the Czechs and in Yugoslavia the Serbs formed less than one half – that is to say, a smaller proportion than the Russians in the old Russian Empire, or the Hungarians in the old Kingdom of Hungary. All these four States were multinational, while all four wanted to create the impression of being a unified nation state, in which the other nationalities were merely temporarily tolerated guests, the longer-term objective being to assimilate them all in the ruling nation. [10]

This varied national make-up became a source of social tension and former historical injustices brought their reaction with new, merely inverted injustices. The minorities were plagued with reprisals and counter-reprisals; oppression had not ceased – the oppressed and the oppressors had merely changed places. Subsequently rebellion became typical of national minority groups of all sizes, in protest against purposeful assimilation (sometimes by force, sometimes by peaceful patronage), against discrimination in daily life and the proscription of their mother tongues. Countries in the area were inundated by the waves of a minor migration of peoples. Hungarians flooded from Transylvania into Hungary, True, they included mainly former civil servants and members of the intellectual elite, but they numbered hundreds of thousands. Under the exchange of population between Greece and Turkey, about half a million Greeks from Asia Minor entered Greece itself. Several hundred thousand Bulgarians were expelled from Greece (Western Thrace) under the Graeco-Bulgarian exchange of population. About two hundred thousand Bulgarians fled from Yugoslav Macedonia to their mother country, while similarly it is estimated that hundreds of thousands of Turks fled from Bulgaria.

However, the majority were quite unable to escape. About half a million

Hungarians remained in neighbouring Czechoslovakia (most of them in the area of Southern Slovakia, which was almost entirely inhabitated by Hungarians), in Romania (where a huge, homogeneous mass of Hungarians lived in the former so-called 'partium' and on the northern borders of Transylvania) and in Yugoslavia. Significant German minorities were to be found in Poland, Czechoslovakia, Hungary and Romania. Ukrainians lived in Poland and Carpathian Ukrainians in Czechoslovakia. All these sections of the population, lacking national opportunities and rights, became a hot-bed of national revolts.

This was one of the factors which substantially kept the twentieth-century national revolutions clear of the classical path of national transformation by *embourgeoisement* and democracy familiar from Western Europe. The value systems and institutions of the sated, highly-developed bourgeois democracies of Western Europe only exceptionally and occasionally made contact with those of the national independence movements in Central and Eastern Europe, which had experienced long years of oppression only to come into conflict immediately with the varying ambitions of the minority nationalities. Much more often they were violently opposed to those aspects of the West.

At this point attention should be drawn to the fact that national aspirations often conflicted bitterly with class ambitions; in their endangered, backward position the nationalists tended to subordinate every other social aim to the national idea. For this reason the subsequent national awakenings often led not to democracy, but to dictatorship. This process is perhaps most clearly exemplified in Poland.

The case of Poland

After the long period of dismemberment following the third partition, Poland was now re-established on territories returned from the three powers, so not only its political leaders, but the broad Polish masses attached prime importance to the achievement of independence and the establishment of a strong state affording security against dangers sensed from Right and Left. The key figure in events taking place in Poland during the 1920s was Marshal Josef Pilsudski. Originally Pilsudski had been a member of the Polish social democratic movement. Before the war he became the leader of the majority wing of the divided socialist movement gathered around the Polish Socialist Party, which made the liberation of Poland the main plank in its programme (in contrast with the minority wing which, under the leadership of Rosa Luxemburg in the Kingdom of Poland and the Lithuania Social Democratic Party, forming part of Russian social democracy, laid emphasis on the international social revolution). Having fought against Russia on the Austrian side in the war, Pilsudski was empowered to form a government by the Polish Council of Regency set up with Austrian and German assistance in Warsaw on 14 October 1917. At the same time the Polish National Committee, sitting in Paris with the recognition of the

Entente, was led by the conservative Russophile Dmowski. Nevertheless, finally the Great Powers recognized Pilsudski, and the Polish Sejm elected in January 1919 confirmed his appointment, with the full support of the Left and Centre-Left tendencies. The French-style constitution adopted by the Sejm in 1921, conferring supreme power on the legislature and sanctioning only limited ministerial power, resulted in Pilsudski's opposition, resignation, and return to his country home. The power vacuum ensuing in the new Poland progressively enhanced the power of the right wing led by Roman Dmowski, while the National Democratic Party (Endek) became the assembly point for the nationalistic, conservative, anti-semitic and strongly religious middle class, mainly in the formerly Prussian area. In 1926 Dmowski formed the fascist-style Greater Poland Camp, an organization based on the leadership principle, which gathered together the proponents of direct, dictatorial action. An increasingly important role was also played by General Wladyslaw Sikorski. Sikorski had fought with Pilsudski in the Polish Legion of the army of the monarchy during the war and he kept up his connections with the left-wing movements until 1920, but subsequently came forward as a proponent of right-wing military dictatorship. A coup was expected any day in the mid-1920s. Even though all expected Dmowski and Sikorski to lead it, in May 1926, when the leader of the Galician Piast Peasant Party, W. Witos, became head of government, it was Pilsudski who acted first, dissolving the government and removing the prime minister. Even though he was supported in his action by the left wing, before long he had obviously established an autocratic, dictatorial system.

Pilsudski took his bearings from the various centre strata when he strengthened the executive power at the expense of the Sejm and, tolerating the parliamentary system, founded the 'non-party block', which obtained a relative majority in the 1928 elections. Of course, the strengthened central power spelt the enhancement of class domination, however disguised in 'national' or 'non-party' garb. Until his death nine years after the coup, the real power in unstable Poland lay in the hands of Pilsudski and the soldiers around him. Although Pilsudski held a variety of posts, sometimes being prime minister, and sometimes minister of war, during the whole period he kept a firm hand over the army (remaining its inspector-general to the end) and influenced the state bureaucracy strongly by appointing his own nominees to all important posts. However, there can be no dispute that the 'moderate dictatorship' of the military group exercising power was also directed against Dmowski's right-wing opposition.

Understandably, we find extremely contradictory and often confused historical assessments of Pilsudski and his system, as is the case with other autocratic, dictatorial systems in Eastern Europe. Not only his apparent attitude of being above parties and classes and his pronounced all-national character and opposition to the fascist right wing, but also his obvious dictatorial, right-wing tendency and constant shift to the Right, particularly during the second half of his term in office, have evoked varying assessments. According to P. Wandycz, in 1926 Pilsudski directed his coup against the centre-right-wing groups (certainly at that time there was no danger from the left wing in Poland). Another view is that the Pilsudski who strengthened the power of the executive had no thought of fascism or, to quote H. Wereszycki's evaluation: 'we can define the system and government existing in Poland between 1926 and 1939 as semi-fascist', while events in Poland 'were moving from a very moderate dictatorship ... in the direction of an ever-stronger dictatorship', although until 1930 'there can be no question of a fascist-type state system'.[11]

The figure of Pilsudski, typical of the political changes in Poland during the 1920s, who had started out as a socialist, but engineered a coup in the middle of the decade to set up an autocratic dictatorship of soldiers and officials, draws attention more particularly to the powerful connections between these systems and the national cause.

Pilsudski turned his back on socialism for the national cause, his career thus recalling that of Mussolini, the creator of fascism, although the Italian dictator, who had also turned his back on the socialist movement, adopted different methods both in practice and ideology. (The 'Mussolini phenomenon' was fairly typical: many revolutionary socialists or trade-union leaders became fascists, from Roberto Michaels through Arturo Labriola to Hubert Lagardell. However, the individual conversions were only symptomatic.) As a natural consequence of late arrival and backward conditions, the national cause advanced to the forefront with incredible force and ousted other aspirations.

National revolution and 'nationalist revolution'

To some extent, therefore, various obstacles to the belated fulfilment of national aims diverted the twentieth-century national revolutions in Central and Eastern Europe into different paths from those trodden by the national revolutions in eighteenth- and nineteenth-century Europe. We are faced with an endless variety of transitions and mutations. Nevertheless, to understand the phenomenon better we may advantageously add to the concept of national revolution that of 'nationalist revolution'. It must be emphasized that I use this expression to describe national aspirations, often completely legitimate national demands, in cases where the national element develops not in classical democratic form, but in socially retrograde dictatorships of various shades, accompanied by hatred and aggression against other nations. This phenomenon could be observed even where national aims were belatedly achieved and sobering-up after the intoxication of post-war euphoria caused a natural hangover in the national minority movements of the new, multi-national countries. But such an atmosphere sprang up even more naturally as a result of post-war national humiliation and disillusionment. Perhaps this is an unavoidable syndrome in vanquished countries. The wrongs and humiliations inflicted on the vanquished by the treaties of Versailles, Trianon and St Germain, territorial losses and the payment of reparations provoked a natural national reaction, namely revolt against the inescapability of acquiescence (and its propagandists). During this period the people of these countries could hardly share the naively humanistic opinion expressed by Benjamin Franklin about 150 years earlier, that there was never a good war or a bad peace. This was certainly a case of a bad peace after a bad war. Through Germany and Austria spread an oppressive feeling of irrevocable decline and national peril, the loss of achievements attained. They had become fawning debtors to the creditor Great Powers, which were expanding; formerly central empires, they were now little countries without hope. Austria was seized purely and simply by a mood of panic as to its ability to survive. Vorarlberg wanted to join Switzerland, and the Tirol Italy, while opinion ranging from Social Democrat Otto Bauer to the extreme right-wing reaction saw the only way out in a link-up with Germany, the *Anschluss*. As H. Arendt correctly points out: 'Although between the two world wars an atmosphere of disintegration was characteristic of Europe in general, it was nevertheless considerably more perceptible in the vanquished than the victor countries, and found its full expression in the States refounded as a result of the winding up of the Dual Monarchy and the Tsarist Empire.'[12]

Genuine national grievances dominated everything and were represented as the real, final cause of all social and economic problems. It was as if such oppression had become divorced from its social and economic sources and was exclusively the consequence of the wounds suffered by the nation, as shown by the slogan which every Hungarian schoolchild during two decades had to repeat, standing at attention before lessons began: 'Hungary maimed is not a land, but Hungary complete – a heavenly land!'

However in the post-war years serious national problems to some extent affected the victors and vanquished indiscriminately in Central and Eastern Europe. Not only the defeated Germany and Hungary, but victorious Romania and Poland suffered equally from several years of inflation, which was practically uncontrollable everywhere before 1923–4, although there were countries, for example Poland, in which currency stability failed to return until 1927. Confidence in money collapsed in those countries. Inflation destroyed small savings, along with confidence in war-loan bonds, which had lost their value.

Everywhere the constant growth of the preceding decades came to a stop, and incomes could not be restored to the level of the 'days of peace', which was in any case extremely low, although those days already seemed to be a 'golden age' in the eyes of the masses, suffering to the full the storms of deprivation. For both the victors and the vanquished, in Poland as well as in Hungary, the elimination of relative backwardness, the previous feeling of success and progress in the closing of the ranks, vanished to give place to an increasing sense of setback and failure.

Of course, it is easy to fall victim to the view that the national revolutions, or nationalist revolts, originated somehow in the terms of the peace settlement. In reality their roots extended much deeper and farther back in time. The natural begetters of these events were the national risings which followed the First World War (affecting both the victors and the vanquished), and the peculiar development of Central and Eastern Europe (in the wider sense, the historical path typically followed by the backward regions of Europe). The peace settlement merely gave the dormant frustrations the opportunity to burst upon the scene openly, sweeping everything away. Their roots are to be found in economic and social backwardness, the belatedness of national awakening, which consequently interfered with the ruling interests of other nations, the obstacles placed in the way of the existence of multi-national states, or the long-standing frustration of national unity, and the geographical location of the majority of the countries of the area, forced to the periphery of the world's economic and political life. These were frequently accompanied, understandably in view of more recent upheavals, by the denial and loss of all those values which the Western nations, dominant at the centre of the world system, represented as universal. Sternhall is therefore right when he states: 'the new European nationalisms were first and foremost rebellions against democracy and proved to be highly critical of all weakness, inconsequentiality and impersonality in that system: parties were formed with the object of a general rebellion against the values represented by the French Revolution and the legacy of the Enlightenment.'[13]

The national revolutions, and of course the 'nationalist revolutions' therefore mainly represent a specific response, not simply to the peace settlement, but to the obstacles set in the way of development in the past, the defencelessness of the preceding century, the subordinate, peripheral role assumed with the division of labour in the capitalistic world economy developing between the sixteenth and eighteenth centuries, and the resulting obstacles to independent national development (and of course the preceding historic failures concealed behind all these aspects). Non-acquiescence sometimes resulted in an embittered, devastating attempt to break out. Understood in the wider sense, the impulse often connecting the national revolutions and the nationalistic risings after the First World War was an attempt by the outlying areas of Europe to throw off their peripheral role. Similarly, after the Second World War, much more widespread national risings, extending to several continents, represented an elemental attempt by the non-European peripheries to throw off their peripheral role.

Counter-revolutions, nationalist retrograde social uprisings, and their connection with the national revolutions

The national revolutions, therefore, often linked up within themselves and turned into 'nationalist revolutions', although of course behind both forms there lurked belatedness, repression, bars to a national development unable to assert itself. Legitimate national aspirations and real national grievances could become the source of sham solutions. Action and counter-action reinforced one another in the post-war period to bring to the forefront as the main problem in Central and Eastern Europe the national question, the national struggle, the national or nationalist revolutions, which linked up with the most varying trends, from democratic programmes of progressive national development to fascist experiments.

The dividing lines were therefore particularly imprecise and often ran into one another. As Linz stated, referring mainly to the Slovakian and Croatian examples: 'In countries where the nation has not become the state it is sometimes difficult to decide whether we are faced with merely an extremist nationalist movement or a fascist one.'[14] Here we grasp the really decisive reason for such imprecision. Of course, to identify the nation with the state was a natural consequence in all of these movements, which placed national aims and interests above all else, and whose objective was the absolute authority of a state securely raised above all social groups and conflicting interests. In this way the primary national aim was made the vindication of dictatorships, and the brusque rejection and repression of the class struggle.

In theorizing about the sources of unrest we may draw a certain distinction between the socio-political trends of various origins which followed the war, and revolutions (counter-revolutions, fascist-type retrograde social uprisings, national revolutions and 'nationalist revolutions'), but even greater emphasis must now be laid on their extremely numerous, inextricably interwoven connections. This was a straighforward consequence of a fact already emphasized: that an independently established progressive national revolution having connections with bourgeois democracy was perfectly possible, and is shown by history to have been more than once typical of some particular country in Central and Eastern Europe. Such revolutions were nevertheless in the main full of contradictions, and gave the opportunity for counter-revolutions and fascist movements to link their retrograde social uprising with the tide of 'nationalist revolution'.

Of course, the 'pure', independent occurrence of any particular trend can be traced only in the rarest instances, in odd political episodes. In general precisely the opposite was true. Although the pure formula of counter-revolution can be observed, for example, in Hungary following the Republic of Councils, it was nevertheless linked with the social opponents of the old conservative system, and even more closely with the national revolt rooted in the despair following the grave national trauma of the Trianon peace settlement. Nicholas Horthy, who had taken bloody revenge on the proletarian revolution and ensured the restoration of the class system, the large estates and all forms of private property, emerged in national garb, not only to disguise himself, but also because he was able to express the real political problems of the newly independent, although considerably diminished, Hungary. However, the déclassé soldiers and officials of the ruling classes gathered around him were not merely aiming at the restoration of the social conditions embodied in the old dualist system. They would have liked to limit the political power of the aristocracy, nor was a certain reduction of the large estates necessarily far from their minds, particularly if it would have enabled them to effect their own stabilization. However, one of their most cherished aims was to gain control over the economics of 'Jewish capital', the 'Jewish bankocracy'.

The Slovakian and Croatian nationalist–separatist movements, which had become extremely strong in the newly founded states and were essentially 'nationalist revolutions' against the Czech and Serbian national movements respectively, made increasing efforts to ride the forces of social discontent and showed themselves ever more favourable to the retrograde aims of the social revolt, in order to win over the masses and thus decisively achieve the aims of a unified 'national' entity. With their markedly Catholic ideology in contrast to the religious indifference of one ruling nation (the Czechs in Czechoslovakia) and the Orthodoxy of the other (the Serbs in Yugoslavia), these at least equally populist-social, fascist-type trends finally gained ground in the Slovakian movement of Hlinka–Tiso and Tuka, and the *ustashi* movement led in Croatia by Ante Pavelić at the end of the 1920s. Starting as national movements, therefore, often as a logical process resulting from local historical circumstances, these trends became inseparably merged with fascist-type movements. If in no other way, the growing tendency towards such connections is shown by their political dealings, as illustrated by the career of Pilsudski in Poland.

The politics of Central and Eastern Europe during the decade following the war were alloyed with such typical admixtures. After all, the class revolution breaking out at the end of the war was met by the rise of counter-revolutions, tending to fascism and laying the main emphasis on national aims, or trends proclaiming the solution of social problems to be national unity at the expense of foreigners and Jews. Even more generally, national revolutions developed which announced that the automatic solution to every social evil, backwardness, and oppression was a function of the achievement of national aims. The national and social elements took an intermixed, interwoven form, and finally the national element ousted the aims and endeavours of the social revolution.

We can regard it as typical of the history of Central and Eastern Europe in the first half of the twentieth century that social problems were clad in national garb, and posed as national questions. The fact is that the former social and economic backwardness obstructing development created a suitable climate for presenting the two sets of problems as identical. That identification was given out as objective reality, evoking widespread credence and acceptance. In countries where bourgeois development had progressed undisturbed, national development forming an organic part of the process, social fronts and also the social possibilities offered by national development were shown much more evidently and clearly, but so were their limitations.

Due to its belated and peculiar development, therefore, the area of Central and Eastern Europe offered a particularly favourable soil for the proletarian class revolution, the social revolution. More particularly after that revolution was suppressed (except in the Soviet Union), the climate was right for national revolutions opposing it in bitter disappointment and dissatisfaction at the failure to obtain a solution. In individual instances or at different times the national revolutions established bourgeois democratic institutions in independent states for the settlement of hitherto insoluble economic, social and political problems thrown up by history. Very often, however, even starting as 'nationalistic revolutions', they expanded their connections with retrograde social revolts to the point of integration.

Connections between events in Central and Eastern Europe and the general cessation of capitalistic development

I must hasten to add that however closely these phenomena may be specifically and characteristically connected with historical events in the area, they form part of a worldwide atmosphere of change which followed the First World War. Throughout Europe the hopelessness and disillusionment suffered by the various social classes and strata of society were accompanied by an undoubted and obvious general breakdown of old values and, as a result, a sense of bewilderment prevailed. It cannot be concealed that after its successful advance during the preceding century, the forward march of capitalism had now generally come to a stop. Virtually complete stagnation had replaced the huge growth (an average of 3 per cent per annum) taking place in international commerce before the war.

In 1928, the boom year of the post-war decade, one of the most important bourgeois economists of the period, J. Schumpeter, published a study in the columns of the *Economic Journal* under the significant title 'The Instability of Capitalism'. The logic of his argument and his conclusions are exceptionally interesting and significant. Referring to existing historical circumstances he points out at once that a hiatus in political, social or economic policy stability may and in some cases does occur in capitalist countries. However, he distinguishes from such a hiatus those effects which result from the internal operating mechanism of the economic system properly so-called. He takes precisely this aspect as the subject of his examination, and arrives at the conclusion that the capitalistic economic system itself can be regarded as stable (Schumpeter implies that even if the most extreme crisis or even catastrophe should occur, the internal workings of the economy can nevertheless ensure recovery).

However, his argument leads to an interesting conclusion: when examining exclusively the processes and operation of the economy his diagnosis was like that of a doctor, who finds that a patient is not suffering from cancer; all the same, 'this is an insufficient basis for drawing the conclusion that the patient will live for ever. Precisely the contrary; capitalism is at such an obvious stage of transition to something else that there can be no difference of opinion about the fact, but only about its interpretation.' Although capitalism is economically stable, it has nevertheless produced social and intellectual effects not in harmony with its own system or social institutions, and for this reason capitalism 'will be transformed into a system which it will merely be a matter of taste or terminology to call socialism or not, even though this is not an economic necessity, and will possibly even be accompanied by a certain sacrifice of prosperity'.[15] It is worth again emphasizing that these lines were written by one of the best-known bourgeois economists at the height of a boom.

Károly Polányi goes much further; according to him it is a matter of the 'bankruptcy of the market economy'. 'When seeking the causes of the cataclysm we must turn to the rise and fall of the market economy.' In his opinion,

> We can detect the roots of the crisis in the threat of collapse of the international economic system. Since the turn of the century the system had already been operating jerkily and it was finally smashed by the Great War and the peace settlement. This became obvious in the 1920s when there was hardly any internal crisis in Europe which was not rooted in international economics.

He then adds:

> The market economy was born in Great Britain, but its weaknesses caused the most tragic confusions on the Continent... The market economy, free trade and the gold standard were British institutions. Those institutions collapsed everywhere in the 1920s; in Germany, Italy or Austria events merely took a more violent political form and occurred on a more dramatic scale.[16]

Those countries which had risen on the trans-Atlantic trade, the leading capitalistic Great Powers, were of course unwilling to permit the bankruptcy of the world and national economy built on the self-regulating market system (the nineteenth-century form of capitalism), and after the First War World convulsively attempted its revival. In reply, the vanquished countries, where the conflicts took a more dramatic form, fighting against the status quo which was to be their lot in world arrangements, 'quickly discovered the weaknesses of the existing system of institutions... After suffering defeat, therefore, Germany was in a position to recognise the hidden weaknesses of the nineteenth-century system and use them to smash that system more quickly...'[17]

Polányi is partly right in emphasizing that the economic and social roots of the very variously named and organized 'right-wing revolutions' (although we should also include the customary collective term of fascism, referring to the Italian model) lay in the upheavals of capitalism surrounding the First World War. He also correctly draws attention not only to their worldwide effects, but also to the particularly favourable soil which conditions in the defeated countries created for the growth of such right-wing movements. However, he argues that facism cannot be

> deduced from local causes, the national mentality, or historical precedents, as its contemporaries generally did. Fascism has just as little to do with the Great War as with the Versailles peace settlement, Junker militarism, or the Italian temperament. The movement appeared in the vanquished countries... and amongst the victors in Aryan and non-Aryan, Catholic and Protestant, militarist and bourgeois countries.[18]

True. Clearly it is impossible to emphasize any particular factor, or to quote any particular cause. However, reversing the logic of the argument, even less can we invoke a cohesive concatenation of factors and causes, historical processes. Nor did the only universal event to which Polányi refers, the 'bankrupt market economy' everywhere lead to fascism. That happened only in those regions and countries of Europe which had made a late start and were backward, outlying, or forced to the periphery; in the rich countries capitalism made essential changes and transformations which reconsolidated the system.

The ideology of retrograde revolt – the 'rationality' of irrationality

The changed circumstances following the war were not the only factors smoothing the path for retrograde tendencies, dictatorships and fascist movements, which developed in the disgruntled, outlying and late-starting countries of Europe. The foundations had been laid by the ideology of revolt, formulated in the historical circumstances of that region long ago at the beginning of the nineteenth century, and were now quickly gaining substantial strength in the altered situation.

In the post-war decade the fascist and dictatorial governments and movements found support in an ideology already practically fully developed. It should again be emphasized that broadly speaking we are not dealing simply with a system of ideas formed as a result of the war. In fact the fascist ideology (although we cannot speak of a self-contained, cohesive system of economic, political and philosophical views) was essentially formed in every aspect during the four or five decades preceding and partly following the First World War. Its roots reach very far back, in particular further than can be demonstrated by a study of the 'genealogy' of slogans and views proclaimed by the fascist-Nazi movements.

The more backward countries echoed, envied and imitated the bourgeois democratic ideas of the Western European countries, now the centre of world economy, and (though this may sound strange at first) the ideology of the Industrial Revolution, which was the product of the Western system and depicted as universally valid. At the same time, however, rejection of these views and the values they represented became widespread in peripheral European countries. Although certain historical and philosophical works have shown a partiality for trying to discover a system of precedents in the history of ideas, the demonstration of such links is liable to one-sidedness and over-simplification.

The virtually classical formulation, even system, evolved in refutation of the Anglo-French system of values, was produced by the German philosopher and political thinker Johann Gottlieb Fichte. In 1800, a quarter of a century after Adam Smith's doctrine had shaped the West's economics and outlook, Fichte published *Der geschlossene Handelsstaat*, a work which opposed everything Smith had taught. (How significant that this work was republished in Jena in 1920!) As against the liberal-international view and the attitude of maximum individual liberty, Fichte, who had been an enthusiastic apostle of the Enlightenment, but, perhaps as a result of his first experiences of Napoleon's wars of conquest, noticed a considerable discrepancy between ideas and practice, cried out with reference to the backward, even threatened situation in Germany: 'Every individual entity has the right to increase its prosperity.'[19] To this end he preaches the central role of an all-powerful state: 'Only the state can unite the limitless number of people into one single, complete whole.' In contrast with Smith's harmony, arising from free, unlimited individual enterprise, according to Fichte the individual can find his appropriate place only if the state assigns it to him. 'The basic task of the state ... is to place everyone in the field appropriate to him. This can be achieved [Fichte adds] only if the state totally abolishes commercial anarchy, just as it gradually curtailed such policies, and becomes a self-contained commercial state, just as it has become absolute in the fields of legislature and judicature.' On this basis the state can guarantee necessary social security to all. 'No one can become particularly rich, but no one can become poor. All can maintain their position and ensure the secure, equal survival of the whole.' Accordingly a strictly organized corporative economy is needed in which individual uncontrolled enterprise is impossible. Any party entering into any kind of undertaking must seek authorization from the government, and if his activities interfere with those of any branch of industry which has already reached full establishment in accordance with the corresponding regulations, the state will have the exclusive right to refuse permission and direct the initiative to some other field. Every process of production and commerce must be carried out under state control and the sale of all goods which have been produced outside the regulating activities of the state prohibited. In answer to the theory of harmony deriving from freedom, Fichte posits the watchwords *Gesetz und Zwang* (law and compulsion). When discussing Smith, Fichte remarks that the objective of the state's activity is 'the *national* wellbeing, not the individual wellbeing of the few; in fact the greater wellbeing of the latter is often the true cause and the most obvious mark of the nation's greatest destitution...'

In his system Fichte combines strict internal control with equally strict autarchy in international links. 'The subjects of the state must be prohibited from all commerce with foreigners, and such commerce must be rendered impossible.' To this end 'every instrument of international payment, such as gold and silver, which is in the hands of the citizens, must be withdrawn from circulation and replaced by a new internal currency which has value solely and exclusively within the country...' As a result, international trade becomes a state monopoly, and the state will determine the quantity of goods, and even 'which articles must be imported or exported, laying down the quotas of individual articles... Not individuals, but the state must direct this commerce.' Imports, for which the home price must be paid, quite independently of the price internationally, are regarded by Fichte as simply a 'transitional' necessity which must be reduced each year. 'Consumers' demands for foreign goods will decrease from year to year, since home production provides the same articles or useful substitutes... home production and industry, no longer left to blind chance, but directed with planning and statistics, will constantly grow, so that home-produced goods will take over from foreign products.' At the same time the state makes use of all instruments, collective foreign exchange, possible loans, and so on, in order to purchase every necessary article, a machine for copying, a raw material unobtainable at home, so that 'a national economy independent of foreign countries is no longer merely a necessity, but the basis for the greatest possible prosperity'. Fichte emphasized that he considered it impossible to keep all these steps separate and put them into effect partially, independently of one another. The state cannot allow itself to become enriched by restricting foreign exchange unless it creates the logically self-contained commercial state, regulates trade, fixes prices, and guarantees conditions for all. Otherwise property will become a matter of uncertainty, dreadful chaos will follow, and embittered humanity will rise in revolt against the dishonest system of government.

Clearly, very quickly in a nation thus self-contained,

> national honour will reach a higher level and a much more clearly defined national character will form, since of course the members of such a nation will merely live amongst themselves, having very little contact with foreign countries. By such institutions they will maintain their own way of life and customs, and live in love pledged to their native country.

In his analysis of *Der geschlossene Handelsstaat*, R. Butler wrote: 'This embryonic socialism for the nation is already National Socialism.'[20] There can be no disputing that this is a permissible comparison, but the relationships can be spread over a wider period, and such views harmonized with other paths followed by revolts against backwardness. For this reason it is worthwhile quoting here the words of Professor H. Waentig in the preface to his new edition of Fichte's book, which appeared in 1920: 'Fichte was not only the first German socialist, ... the first German social democrat, but a democrat in the noblest meaning of the word.'[21]

Misinterpretations? One-sided misunderstandings? Or can Fichte's formulation of his rejection of dominant values be at one and the same time the 'ancestor' of an organized capitalism reduced to obedience (to which post-war Social Democracy stood so close) or of all kinds of state capitalism – any variant break-away, including the fascist solution?

Presumably the latter, just as can the ideas of the practical economist and propagandist of railways, Friedrich List. List followed the political thinker and philosopher Fichte by about four decades and his thought is directly related intellectually to Fichte's. In his famous and very influential book *Das nationale System der politischen Ökonomie*, published in 1841 (Louis Kossuth used it as his 'bible'), List constantly tests Adam Smith's views against the backward situation in Germany. According to List, Smith and his school had three basic faults:

> Firstly, impartial *cosmopolitanism*, which neither recognises the national element, nor takes the satisfaction of the national interests into account; secondly, dead *materialism*, which is always mainly interested in the exchange value of things, ignoring intellectual and political values and the interests of the present and future... thirdly, disorganising particularism and individualism... However, between each individual and the whole of humanity stands the *nation*, with its own language and literature, its own origin and history, its characteristic usages, its legal and institutional systems... society, which a thousand threads of interest and thought unite to make a single independent whole.[22]

He compares industrialization carried out under state direction in German circumstances with the powerful Great Britain which arrived on the scene early and had great advantages, with its liberalism, free trade and international trading system based on those advantages. List emphasizes: 'The intellectual strength, state earnings, intellectual and material forces of self-defence and the secure establishment of national independence grow hand in hand with the creation of industrial power.' Then he adds:

> In times when the technical and mechanical sciences exert such an enormous influence on the method of waging war... when successful self-defence depends to such an extent on whether the masses of a nation are rich or poor, intelligent or stupid, energetic or sunk in apathy; whether their sympathies lie exclusively with their homeland or partly with foreign countries... the value of industry must be judged from the political viewpoint.

Friedrich List urged backward German capitalism in its own interests to abandon liberalism and substitute state activity, to abandon free trade and adopt rigorous protective tariffs, to reject commerce based on 'mutual advantages' in favour of self-supporting industrialization to supplement imports. In this connection it is interesting to quote Marx's criticism of List, that German conditions lagged far behind the modern age or any connection with a developed economy or a corresponding political system. According to Franz Mehring's interpretation:

Marx's objection to List's argument is that he measures the backwardness of German conditions from the distant viewpoint of French and British socialism. The progressive nations argue about the bases of the modern state empirically, but in Germany, where such bases are still non-existent, the criticism of such bases is mainly a matter of their reflection in philosophy.[23]

The assessment was correct. However, precisely his realization that the 'bases of the modern state' were lacking in Germany led List to associate the adoption of imports – supplementary protectionism – with the strengthening of national independence. In his view, therefore, protectionism was not an eternally valid principle. List emphasized that the exclusive policy of supplementing imports represented an advantage to backward countries in the historical, transitional period of industrialization – it was valid for a period of closing up of ranks. However, the nationalistic variant of the national idea suddenly emerges when this same Friedrich List, with his 'new values', his lofty dismissal of 'dead materialism', his talk of the interests of a backward, still weak Germany, formulates the aims of voracious German capitalism. He understands German unity to include Belgium and Denmark, plus Holland which he declares to be 'German territory, having regard to its origin and the language of its population'. He speaks of *Ergänzungsgebiete* – complementary territories as necessary to Germany as 'the breath of life', spheres of interest in Central and Latin America, areas of interest in Eastern Europe and the lower Danube Valley, and future German colonies in Australia, New Zealand and the islands of the Pacific.

The romantic philosophical, political and economic thinking of Central and Eastern Europe took root in the peculiar soil of a region of backwardness and late arrival. And subsequently a characteristic crop sprang from that soil.

The ideology of the backward: a front formed between 'proletarian nations' and 'capitalistic nations'

To prove the relationship, in spite of a difference in time amounting to decades, let me establish a direct link between these views and the 'revolt on the peripheries'. National rebellions in the late-starting, backward countries represent perhaps the most characteristic ideology of the beginning of the twentieth century, the epoch when the classes negated and rejected confrontation within the nation and declared the conflict to lie *between* nations, more precisely 'proletarian nations' and 'capitalistic nations'; this seemed merely a widening in scope, but in reality altered the whole concept. The protagonist of this view, the Italian Enrico Corradini, set forth his views in a speech concerning 'national socialism' given before the first nationalist congress held at Florence in December 1910: 'Just as the socialists taught the proletariat the importance of class struggle, we Italians must now teach the importance of international struggle.' In his eyes Italy was a proletarian nation in both the material and moral sense and could achieve status only through unavoidable combat and struggle. Adopting this theory, Italian fascism consciously turned to the historical fact of backwardness, late arrival, and servitude to better developed and stronger countries. The socio-economic and political effects of European backwardness therefore became a recognized ideological element in the theory of fascist revolt and the basis of its practical programmes.

It is less well known that the national revolt of the Nazi movement also, in fierce opposition to the humiliation of the peace settlement, with its very typical technique of half-truths employed arguments characteristic of developments in Central and Eastern Europe. In his speech, 'The Free State or Slavery', Hitler applied the following historical argument: 'Europe began to fall into two parts, Western Europe on the one hand, and Central and Eastern Europe on the other. At first Western Europe took the lead by a process of industrialization. Masses of agricultural workers, farmers' sons, or ruined farmers themselves flooded into the towns and brought into being the fourth estate...' In comparison, industrialization was slower in Central and Eastern Europe, the movement of peasants to the towns went slowly, and the formation of industrial centres and a fourth estate took longer. Of course, in Hitler's way of thinking the differing paths of development in Western, Central and Eastern Europe was important because of the Jewish question and the role played by the Jews. There was a relatively small number of Jews in Great Britain and France, while 'there were more Jews both in Eastern Europe and in Germany'; in this way Hitler linked the historical truth of different paths of development in these two parts of Europe with the mendacious theory that their differences in social development were due to differing Jewish influence.[24]

However, I consider it particularly important that the backward, poor-nation theory (just like Fichte's system) cannot be related exclusively to fascist theory, but must also be defined with respect to national revolts on the European periphery, which varied greatly in character or were even democratic in trend. Certainly the most typical proof is the Turkish variant of national revolutionary theory. The ideologues of the Turkish movement, in contrast with the fascist system of rejecting class and class struggle and caricaturing the Jewish question, developed their own theory of the 'Third World' type, to use today's expression. (It is worth noting that this preceded by several decades certain theories which originated in the Third World only well after the Second World War.) The ideology of the Turkish Revolution of the 1920s did not reject or negate the existence of the class struggle, which it considered decisive only in the industrially developed countries. The Turks stressed that the second contradiction of the modern world, equal in importance to class struggle, was the glaring contrast between 'poor countries' (colonies, semi-colonies, agricultural and raw-material-exporting countries) and 'rich countries' (the 'metropolises' where advanced high technology was concentrated). While the answer to the first contradiction is class struggle, the second contradiction can be solved by a national liberation struggle; it would of course be an illusion to imagine that class struggle can solve the second contradiction also. The Turkish avant-garde and ideologues gathered around Mustafa Kemal (Atatürk) moreover regarded the Turkish Revolution as the beginning of an epoch internationally. They emphasized that an age of national liberation movements was inaugurated by the Turkish Revolution in 1919. According to their assertion: 'The transition from a colonial economy to a national economy will be put into effect for the first time in history in Turkey.'[25]

At its inception, therefore, the ideology of revolt in backward countries shows many basic points connecting it with fascist ideology.

The facts are thus; J. Gregor, clearly demonstrating the effect of the 'proletarian nation' theory in Italian fascism, concludes from his general analysis that fascism is a dictatorship of the kind 'which suits a partially developed or backward national community lacking status in a period when intensified international struggle for position and status is in progress.'[26] By a different route E. Weber came to a similar conclusion regarding the Romanian example; he linked the fascist ideology not so much with a middle-class reactionary movement as with the general problems of backward countries.

These assertions can of course easily be disputed, and they have provoked sharp criticism. For example, John Weiss argues that Weber takes the ideological manifestos too seriously, more seriously than the people making them. Turkish demagogy obviously derived its power from explosive tension caused by backwardness, deprivation, and rejection of the prevailing European systems of values. Nevertheless, it would be a great mistake to forget the counter-revolutionary content of the various forms of fascism and dictatorships, their connections with ruling elites, or the services which they performed in defence of the class system. It would be an error to mistake the stock phrases of demagogues for reality. All the more so, since in the words of the expanded Executive Committee of the Communist International in 1923: 'Fascism shows its true nature after coming to power, when its policies serve the interests of the industrial capitalists.'[27]

Drawing distinctions between slogans and reality, superficial appearances and the facts of history does not justify our ignoring the genuine links which existed between the ideologies of retrograde social revolts, dictatorial systems, fascist movements, and backwardness, deprivation, and disgruntlement.

NOTES

1 K. Polányi, *The Great Transformation* (Boston 1957), p. 23.
2 Thomas Mann, *Selected Letters, 1889–1955* ed. & trans. R. and C. Winston (Harmondsworth 1975), p. 201.

3 Baynes, N.H. (ed.), *The Speeches of Adolf Hitler April 1922–August 1939* (London 1942), p. 7.
4 H. Arendt, *The Origin of Totalitarianism* (London 1958), p. 332.
5 T.G. Masaryk, *The Making of a State: Memories and Observations 1914–1918* (London 1927), p. 371.
6 P. Sugar, 'Conclusion', in P. Sugar (ed.), *Native Fascism in Successor States 1918–1945* (Santa Barbara 1971), p. 147.
7 Quoted in Masaryk, *The Making of a State*, p. 265.
8 *Ibid.*, p. 367.
9 Quoted in C.A. Macartney, *National States and National Minorities* (London 1934), pp. 272–3.
10 H. Seton-Watson, 'Nationalism and Multi-national Empires', in *Nationalism and Communism: Essays 1946–1963* (London 1964), pp. 23–4.
11 H. Wereszycki, 'Fascism in Poland', in Sugar, *Native Fascism*, pp. 85, 89.
12 Arendt, *The Origin of Totalitarianism*, p. 268.
13 Z. Sternhall, 'Fascist Ideology', in 'W. Laqueur (ed.), *Fascism* (Harmondswoth, 1979), p. 339
14 J.J. Linz, 'Some Notes Towards a Comparative Study of Fascism in Sociological Historical Perspective', in. W. Laqueur (ed.), *Fascism*, p. 28.
15 J. Schumpeter, 'The Instability of Capitalism', in N. Rosenberg (ed.), *The Economics of Technological Change* (Harmondsworth 1971), pp. 41–2.
16 Polányi, *The Great Transformation*, pp. 23, 30.
17 *Ibid.*, pp. 28–9.
18 *Ibid.*, p. 237.
19 Here, and in the following Fichte quotations, see J.G. Fichte, *Der Geschlossene Handelsstaat. Ein philosophischer Entwurf als Anhang zur Rechtslehre und Probe einer künftig zu liefernden Politik* (Jena 1920).
20 R. d'O. Butler, *The Roots of National Socialism 1783–1933* (London 1941), p. 44. (A handwritten annotation in the original: 'I used this volume for demonstrating the systems of Fichte and List.')
21 H. Waentig, 'Fichte'. Preface to new edition of Fichte's *Der geschlossene Handelsstaat* (Jena 1920), p. xvi.
22 Here and for the following references to List, see F. List, *Das nationale System der politischen Ökonomie* (1841).
23 E. Mehring, *Historical Materialism* (Budapest 1979), p. 94.
24 Domarus, *The Speeches of Adolf Hitler*, pp. 22–5.
25 Articles by Sevket Güreyya (Aydemir) and Vedet Nedim in June and August 1932 numbers of *Kadro*. Quoted by Fikret Adanir, 'Statism' – Discussion in Turkey during the World Economic Crisis', *Kadro* 1932–34'. Paper given at the conference of the Institute for European History, Mainz, December 1979.
26 A.J. Gregor, *The Ideology of Fascism: the Rationale of Totalitarianism* (New York 1969) p. xiii.
27 Minutes of the conference of the extended Executive of the Communist International, Moscow, 12–13 June 1923, Hamburg, quoted in D. Eichholtz and K. Gossweiler (eds.), *Fascism: Research, Attitudes, Problems, Polemics* (Berlin 1980), p. 26.

12

Vicissitudes of feudalism in modern Poland

ANTONI MĄCZAK

The main thesis of this chapter is that feudalism took a rather peculiar shape in early modern Poland; that it exerted its influence for a longer time than in most European countries; that it strongly coloured capitalist relationships in the nineteenth and twentieth centuries; and that some recent socio-economic phenomena are still curiously reminiscent of early modern feudalism.

I cannot comment at length upon the origins of feudalism in Poland and its development in the Middle Ages; this has been done many times.[1] At the turn of the fifteenth and in the early sixteenth century, the Polish economy, society and state show traces which are familiar to every student of Central and Western Europe. Only from that period did the public institutions of Poland (and since the Union of Lublin, 1569, of the Commonwealth of Poland and Lithuania) begin to change and to take a turn quite different from that characteristic of Western Europe, and in fact different from almost all other European countries.

In 1948 the Marxist notion of feudalism was still little in use in Poland, but some historians wished to adapt the concept of 'feudalism' (until then connected principally with the high Middle Ages in the West) to Polish conditions. Tadeusz Manteuffel then observed that Polish–Lithuanian society from the sixteenth century settled into a shape familiar to students of Carolingian times.[2] This conclusion has been neither accepted nor contradicted by any scholar since. However, it ought to be regarded as an important suggestion of some peculiarities in what might be called the periodization of social relationships. While basic economic conditions of life, and lord and peasant relationships in the Commonwealth, did not deviate from those characteristic of the neighbouring countries, the internal structures of the Noble Estate and of their state were taking distinct forms. This opinion has been endorsed recently by Perry Anderson. According to him, 'the feudal State it [Poland] produced provided a singular clarification of the reasons why Absolutism was the natural and normal form of noble class power after the late Middle Ages.'[3] And absolutism had no chance in Poland.

283

It is difficult to explain thoroughly why this was so. Counter-factual reasoning has found no place in Polish historiography, either economic or political. However, several arguments may be outlined here. The factors involved were both accidental and structural in nature. Descendants of Wladyslaw Jagiello (died 1434) had no clear hereditary rights to the throne, and had to haggle for the consent of the nobility by means of generous charters for the whole Noble Estate. After the dynasty died out in 1572, the free election of kings shattered the power of the throne and deprived the royal person of much of his inherited charisma. In the meantime there were powerful structural factors at work. In the fifteenth and sixteenth centuries few rulers escaped problems with the Estates. The Polish Estates were atypical in that townspeople played virtually no role. As Gottfried Schramm has pointed out, this was not a uniquely Polish situation.[4] But Poland was a vast country and her kings did not keep her divided into separate *pays légaux*, and therefore were unable to play off one against another as did the Hohenzollerns. Unlike successful European princes, the Jagiellons were more often than not short of cash and – what is much more important – they never built an efficient fiscal machine.

Nobody has seriously and thoroughly discussed the consequences of particular social hierarchies and structures for the development of the Commonwealth. The multitude of gentlefolk should be regarded as a secondary factor: petty noblemen never played an active political role and might be compared to simple freeholders or to Prussian *Freie*. They enjoyed fully only their legal freedoms and shared (some only in part) the fiscal ones, but the biggest assets – duty-free exports and imports of goods – were turned fully to account only by the greatest landowners.[5] On the other hand, the lesser nobles were in search of social promotion and could easily be exploited by their bigger neighbours as servants and officials. In the given political structure the king did not take as much advantage as the magnates from the squires' willingness to serve. The highly democratic parliamentary system was not matched by similar equality of wealth and prestige. A recent study of the power elite of Poznan and Kalisz *voievodships* (counties) between 1587 and 1632 (the reign of Sigismund Vasa), has revealed the existence of about 280 officials, from top-rank senators of national importance to petty judges and judiciary officials, as well as repeatedly re-elected members or speakers of the regional Diet.[6] The top nominations depended on the king himself, but the ruler could not elevate upstarts in the face of a popular decision in the local Diet or against the wishes of the whole elite group. Lesser officials were duly elected by the whole body of noblemen. In the long run, this power elite gained politically at the expense both of the king and of their constituency. Less successful landowners were able to carry on exerting political power if they enjoyed prestige due to their firm establishment in their area. However, the whole group was clearly acquisitive and successful on the land market.

During the whole early modern period and in most parts of the country, landed property was increasingly concentrated. This took place not only where there was no substantial core of noble landed estates of large size already in the later middle ages (Prussia, Masovia).[7] During the late sixteenth and early seventeenth centuries the middle stratum of the gentry was decimated and in some parts subsequently as good as wiped out, or rather bought up. Lesser nobles were made dependent upon their wealthier neighbours and this meant the breakdown of the political independence of the gentry. The parliamentary power struggle that in the 1560s had seemed to be fully won by the Executio-Iurium movement for the rights of the middle gentry (or the lesser strata of the power elite?) was eventually determined at the district level and by socio-economic factors like profitability of landed estates and market in landed property.

Political equality within the Noble Estate was doomed by the vitality of the clientage. As Tadeusz Manteuffel saw it,

> the disruption of authority suffered by Poland at the turn of the sixteenth century... caused, first, the independence of the great lords; secondly, their taking over of governmental functions within their estates; thirdly, the creation of a personal relationship between the magnates and the gentry based on the pledge of loyalty (servingmen bound to their masters by the ceremony of handshake), sometimes also strengthened by tenure for life by the grace of the lord; fourthly, the spread of conditional property in the form of endowments granted to the handshake-servants.[8]

All of this was strongly reminiscent of the feudal forms of the high Middle Ages in the West rather than of the changes which in modern times were leading the more advanced societies to capitalism.

The legal and constitutional system made a particularly important contribution to this development. Whereas the great lord was becoming 'not so much a citizen of the Commonwealth as the absolute ruler over a territory, sometimes large, sometimes less so, within its borders', the freedom of the king to choose his ministers and other dignitaries was strictly limited to persons of already high economic and political standing. The leaders of the House of Deputies in the sixteenth century were likely to be promoted to senatorial rank and to be granted royal domains as leaseholds for life. Such a system was detrimental to the 'democracy of the gentry', as Polish historians call it. In the seventeenth century grass-roots political movements degenerated into anarchic rebellions (*rokosz*) and were to a large extent manipulated by the magnates. The clientage was not without its virtues on a local level and in matters of law and order but turned out disastrously in the sphere of national politics. There are good reasons for connecting all of this with the size of the country, with its weak system of communications[9] and with sharp divergences of regional political and defence interests. Whereas kings were elected for life, the local potentate not only seemed to be, he *was*, the backbone of stability for his clients and lesser neighbours. The Radziwills, the Sapiehas, and a score of their peers were as dynastically strong as any family upon one of whose members had been bestowed the crown and the sceptre.

Too little attention has been paid to the system of operation of institutions in Poland–Lithuania or to the social structure of bodies of officials. The Commonwealth lacked mechanisms which contributed to the consolidation of states in early modern Europe. Royal servants with large judicial and administrative powers (*starostowie grodzcy*) were already in the later sixteenth century losing their particular status and becoming as good representatives of local power elites as any other local dignitaries. The precious balance of local and central influences so characteristic of the English Justices of the Peace was never the lot of their counterparts in Poland–Lithuania. And officialdom there never settled into a corporative shape like, say, *parlements* in France. Officialdom never carried on internal struggles between various bodies of different social standing, so characteristic of France and typical of all states where bureaucracies were composed of simple commoners, patricians and true nobles.

Between 1772 and 1795 the Commonwealth endured three partitions culminating in the disappearance of the state from the political map of Europe. There has been much discussion among Polish historians concerning the origins, causes and the inevitability of the partitions. From the mid-nineteenth century each generation of Poles has taken over this problem, translated it into their own terms, used it for their particular goals, as well as studied it according to the rules of scholarship. Nowadays there is more oral than printed discussion. Should we focus upon the whole history of the Commonwealth from the vantage point of its sorry ending? Many Polish historians believe that we should not; no Czech, they argue, studies the Bohemian sixteenth century as a road leading to the White Mountain in 1620.

So far as the fate of feudalism is concerned, two principal sets of questions emerge. First, how the Polish nobility adapted themselves to the new power systems they had to live with, and to subordinate to; second, how the society and economy reacted to capitalist impulses in the nineteenth century. Both questions can hardly be answered in two or three paragraphs. Most Polish–Lithuanian magnates easily turned into aristocrats and courtiers in Berlin, Vienna and St Petersburg, thanks to their wealth, connections, and to what might be called *horror vacui*: they were simply needed as pillars of society in the territories acquired by the partitioning powers. Unless they became security risks because of their Polish patriotism, they were safe from persecution. On the other hand, they were expected – at least by conservative circles – to employ their wealth and prestige in the national cause. While Polish aristocrats lost their political power with the dissolution of the Commonwealth (they could win it only as individuals within the framework of a partitioning monarchy, and there were outstanding cases of such success), they remained socially and economically well established. Unlike the landowners in Upper Silesia, none of their Polish counterparts owned deposits of minerals worth mentioning, so they concentrated on agriculture, forestry and connected industries. If one may risk a generalization, the aristocrats – or rather great landowners – were more prone to risk commutation of labour services and emancipation of tenants than lesser owners. To make a long story short, ownership of large landed estates provided the most important assets although it did not make the landowners immune to crises. Inherited prestige, conservative patriotic myths[10] and wealth brought to that group certain political profits even during the 20-year period of independence (1918–39). Polish industry, heavily dependent upon foreign capital, needed both money and big names; the latter were readily available.

The last chapter about this social group is still to be written: perhaps it will be a study of the remarkable social adaptability and highly differentiated fates among a once ruling class. Probably the most outstanding case is that of the Radziwills who are, in their numerous branches, great landowners in Africa, socialites in the United States, as well as citizens of the People's Poland, professional intellectuals, and active members of Independent Trade Union *Solidarnosc*.

Less wealthy landowning groups found it more difficult to cope with political and economic hardships from the eighteenth century onwards. In 1777 in Prussia and 1781 in Austria, and 1864 in Congress Poland, feudal ownership of land and the personal dependence of tenants and the landless poor upon their lords was abolished.[11] While general and rapid reforms had to be forced by the state upon reluctant landowners, many among them were seeking their own optimal solutions. For lesser owners even commutation of services could be fatally expensive. Started from the mid-eighteenth century by enlightened landlords, commutation was tried in the following decades even by some of the less wealthy as an act of the lord's grace towards his tenants and as a private contract. As a rule, landlords tended to maintain a profitable and flexible ratio of services and money rents according to their own current needs and their tenants' economic potential. In some places, the proximity of early centres of industry made strict forms of serfdom and labour services obsolete. Political changes in the period 1772–1815 left hardly a corner untouched. For example in parts subdued by Prussia the sudden accessibility of credit, hitherto unknown, led the Polish gentry into bankruptcies: they had borrowed heavily but did not use their loans for productive investment, and unexpectedly wound up broken by the terms of payment (Napoleon took over from the Prussians all these claims).

Hard lessons were not ignored (even if bankruptcies were generally attributed to Prussian slyness). Transformations in the management of estates corresponding to commutation of services, enclosures and the emancipation of peasantry, which in some parts of the West had been spread over centuries, in Poland (and in some other Eastern countries) occurred over just decades or even had to be accomplished almost at once.

We cannot discuss here the process of primitive accumulation of capital or the particular traits of capitalism in Poland. What remains to be told is the fate of the petty gentry. That very numerous social class seemed to have little to lose, and yet it lost much. Once unruly voters and retainers of the magnates, petty noblemen (having no serfs) lost their voting rights in 1791. After the partitions, new rulers were reluctant to acknowledge their noble status. In the Kingdom of Poland (Congress Poland) there were hundreds of villages inhabited almost exclusively by petty noblemen unable to prove their noble status. On the other hand, successful capitalists were striving for hereditary titles and coats-of-arms. The noble life-style dominated over the bourgeois one, and the struggle between these value systems is one of the basic themes of Polish literature of the post-1863 era. The fate of the gentry, poorly equipped to cope with the political reality of the late nineteenth century, with structural changes in agriculture and agrarian crises, and unable to find appropriate positions in capitalist society, contributed to a curious idealization of the loser, the unsuccessful and of the misfit idealist. This trend, in Polish literary tradition, is by no means extinguished.[12] Reliable quantitative data concerning the 'social genealogy' of the intelligentsia have been produced only recently and a discussion is now under way, but it seems very likely that it was the noble myth and ethos, more often than not unmatched by personal wealth and chances of social advancement, that was instrumental in creating that social stratum.

In the countryside, enfranchisement reforms did not create anything approaching social equality and they left barely touched some remnants of the feudal system. These were the perseverance of the near-subsistence sector of the economy, and the continuation of ancient social relationships, independent of progressive bourgeois legislation (the Code Civil of Napoleon was in force in Congress Poland). Subsistence farming was not in itself feudal, of course, but its remarkably wide diffusion and intensiveness created major obstacles to the development of capitalism and contributed to the preservation of feudal, or rather semi-feudal, bonds. An even more powerful obstacle to the development of capitalism was a peculiar gap between the estate (successor of the manorial farm) and the (peasant) farm. The reforms only modified a little, but did not remove, differences of social conditions. It was much easier for a town bourgeois to settle down as a landowner (and from the mid-nineteenth century the differences between noble and commoner landowners were narrowing) than for an enriched farmer to become recognized as a person 'of quality'. In general, the Polish peasant would not recognize himself in the literary portrait of his French counterpart painted by Honoré de Balzac.

In independent Poland all differences of orders and all hereditary titles were duly abolished. Peasant political parties and farmers' co-operatives led in many respects to the social emancipation of the peasantry. They could hardly improve the structure of land ownership. The enfranchisement of the peasantry had robbed them (directly or indirectly, there were portentous regional differences) of a part of their land, and during the late nineteenth century there continued a trend towards greater polarization of peasant property. In 1921, 24.9 per cent of land under cultivation belonged to dwarf-farms of less than 5 hectares (64.7 per cent of all agricultural properties). Only 1.8 per cent of owners had farms of 20–100 hectares, and 0.6 per cent of over 100 hectares (respectively 10.3 and 27.2 per cent of cultivated land). The agrarian reforms of the 1920s and early 1930s did not bring about much change, although 2,423 thousand hectares of large property were subdivided and sold to 630,000 small owners. All of this contributed to some of the principal causes of the very limited development of a market economy. According to M. Kalecki and L. Landau in 1934, only 54 per cent of the national income passed through the market (65 per cent of consumed income). The market consumption of peasants and labourers was only a little over 22 per cent of their total consumption.[13]

All of this should be borne in mind when we pass to the next – and up to now the last – chapter of the history of feudalism in Poland. We do not argue that some sort of system of that kind was reintroduced in Poland in the later 1940s, but that some socio-economic features, characteristic of pre-capitalist times, reappeared as sometimes secondary but hardly unimportant attributes of the new order.

The post-war land reform of 1944–5 wiped out the landlord class and subsequently was executed with excessive zeal, so that numerous *kulak* owners of much less than 50 hectares found themselves landless. A short if violent wave of forced collectivization succeeded but few of the collective farms were to survive the deep 'thaw' of October 1956: only 17 per cent, about 1,530 in all. And yet, in spite of the violent fate of the country during both World Wars, in spite of two reforms of landed property, of changes of the frontiers of the nation and despite collectivization, one element in the agrarian economy remains constant: the persistence of small farms. In 1921, farms of up to 5 hectares constituted 65 per cent of all farms; in 1950 in the People's Poland they formed 57 per cent of individual farms; in 1970 the corresponding figure was 59, and nine years later 60, per cent.[14] The government tried to cope with the social and economic consequences of these facts in various ways. It tried to impose taxes in kind and compulsory deliveries of grain, and to compel farmers to sell to the state various kinds of crops and animals through sophisticated contract systems.

The student of the feudal economy can easily perceive analogies between some of its characteristics and contemporary Polish agriculture. One needs only a certain degree of generalization. Whereas there were once thousands of feudal owners of peasant and demesne farms, today state agrarian farms (PGR) are run by the state, the same state which pursues particular policies towards private farmers. There is a close analogy to a particular trait characteristic of the relationship between the state and the (independent) trade unions. This was clearly brought home in the summer of 1981 by Bronislaw Geremek: *Solidarnosc* has a particular scope and forms of activity because it represents its members on a nationwide scale not against numerous employers (as has been the case under capitalism) but against a single employer.

This single partner with a voice decisive in all legal and economic matters disposed of a powerful and monopolistic, if clumsy, agro-business system. And yet it could not (and cannot, because this is current history) use methods familiar to the owner of serf-labour manors. He did not dispose of the field labour of farmers, it is true, because he needed it in rapidly developing industry. Also, the mechanization of agriculture in the twentieth century has changed the situation: in serf-labour times demesne farms depended heavily upon the quality and quantity of farmers' tools and draught animals.

And yet the state faced problems very similar to those the early modern Polish landowner had to solve. The uneasy living together of large state-owned and subdivided private farms was in many respects analogous to conditions made familiar to English-speaking scholars by Witold Kula's *Economic Theory of Feudalism*.[15]

First, the state strives to take over the largest possible part of agrarian produce. During the six-year plan (1951–6), alongside buying up of grain, it introduced compulsory deliveries. In 1953 they reached (according to Anderzej Jezierski) 85 per cent of peasants' 'marketable' grain (total produce less seed and household consumption), 51 per cent of potatoes, and 50 per cent of pigs or cattle.[16] Although some of these figures seem lower than in the eighteenth or early nineteenth centuries, strict comparisons would not make sense here.[17] On the other hand, the structural analogy between compulsory deliveries and feudal rent in kind are clear. In this connection one may recognize the gradual evolution of the purchase system by the state as one more commutation of the rent in kind: in 1955 compulsory deliveries made up 70 per cent of grains taken and bought by the state from peasants; in 1970 only 27 per cent. For potatoes, corresponding figures were 84 and 38.[18] After obligatory deliveries had been abolished in 1971, the problem of rents was reduced to that of the differences between the prices paid by market customers and those fixed by the state.

Secondly, both critics of the system and the 'establishment' of the post-Gierek era fluently condemn the wastefulness of that system, and the sorry, miserable results of costly investments in state-owned farms. Once more the student of contemporary Polish agrarian policy should be reminded of its ages-old antecedents. This policy is hardly irrational, or rather it has its particular social rationale. The absurdly inflated apparatus of agro-business and easily tolerated corruption may be interpreted as manifestations of the helplessness and low efficiency of the economic system. However, they are successful as a means of passing the heavy costs of maintenance of thousands of local state servants onto the shoulders of both producers and consumers. Exactly the same has been said about the monumental administrative systems of early modern large estates. And yet both systems were 'rational' only when they remained closed to themselves. Once exposed to competition with their more efficient rivals, they could hardly evade exposure of their fallacies.

The third analogy is more of a societal than an economic nature. Notwithstanding their motivation and official rationale, until recent years (the late 1970s) there remained multiple forms of debasement of the social position of the peasantry. Together with private craftsmen and shopkeepers, private farmers were deprived of a free health service, and of a social security system equal to that of state-employed people;[19] in 1976 they were not granted rations of sugar equal to allocations for the rest of the population. In the early fifties private village industries had been wiped out thoroughly and state-owned plants or state-controlled co-operatives were never able to fill that gap. There is more than a shadow of analogy between that decision and the liquidation of tenants' mills, village ironworks and independent shops in the late sixteenth/early seventeenth centuries.[20] The landlord strove at monopoly of grain turnover and was taking over the lucrative sector of village industry. In both cases there was a tremendous waste of the means of production. In the twentieth century this has led to grave market shortages and in recent times even to ecological problems.[21]

Long after the ruling Polish United Workers' Party renounced mass collectivization, the administration and particularly the local administration, remained reluctant to strengthen the farmers' rights to their soil. This has been proven in 1979 by Waldemar Kuczyński,[22] and strongly confirmed in 1980–1 by the dramatic struggle of small farmers for plots that had been taken away from them.

Whereas in the seventeenth or eighteenth century the landlord had good reasons to subordinate tenant farming to his own demesne farming because it made him the owner of almost the whole product of his estate, a roughly similar tendency on the part of the state was obviously fallacious. Without much success, it was strongly countered from several quarters as being contradictory to national interests. In both spheres – of agrarian policy and of social privilege – one may trace analogies to feudal, or rather pre-capitalist, relationships. In both, that relapse borders upon the ludicrous because principles of socialism have been accepted by the nation and expectations of welfare still run high.

One more analogy with the pre-industrial, pre-capitalist economy can be drawn in respect of the money economy. Both the, say, seventeenth and the later twentieth century deviate from the yardstick of 'free-market economics'. And both deviate in the same direction. In pre-partition Poland money was operational in regulating the contacts of the landed estate with its outer world; it secured to the landlord the means of paying for conspicuous (mostly imported) luxury goods and it was necessary for pursuing his political goals. Inside the estate, marked prices hardly served for measuring the value of goods that were not for sale.[23] Kula has exposed the sophisticated and/or brutal means used by estate administration against any contacts by tenants with markets and customers outside the estate's borders. Some scholars are prone to call that a particular deviation of mercantilism, in the service of the sovereign landlord.

Now, until 1980, by interpreting the official propaganda one might argue that the state commercial policy was based on principles of mercantilism: the development of exports and production for exports, imports limited to vital necessities plus goods and machines, stimulating the national economy and its foreign trade potential, reasons of state being the guiding principle.[24] Revelations of the 1980s totally destroyed this image. In many respects a close comparison of foreign trade priorities in different ages simply makes no sense. However, if one employs the Marxist criterion of class interest, in both cases one can easily trace important common features: foreign trade strategy directly serves the ruling group. In the seventeenth century, against the protests of economic thinkers, along with a monumental monetary crisis and the petering out of foreign demand for Polish grain, imports of silks, woollens, spices and other luxuries were increasing. After the dramas of December 1970 – shipyard workers' protests, the Gdansk-Gdynia massacre and the fall of Mr Gomulka – the import policy was much more sophisticated and complex. However, there is no doubt that individual decisions, the location of new enterprises, the selection of contracting parties, and the choice of goods for import were to a large extent determined by subjective – in contradistinction to the public – interests. On the other hand, it is easy to be carried away by colourful anecdotes.

In order to avoid that danger, let us keep to facts and administrative decrees. A good key to understanding how the group privileges of the 1970s worked is ruling 58 of 11 July 1975 of the minister of foreign trade and maritime economy[25] 'concerning the release from customs inspection of goods carried by some persons crossing the state frontier': 25 categories of state and party dignitaries *and members of their families* were exempted. A close examination of their list (still secret) may lead to better understanding of the composition of power elites. The historian is struck by the similarity of that charter to clauses of the Statute of Piotrkow (1496), that exempted the nobility from export duties on their own needs. It has already been stressed that such a privilege was vitally important only for the upper stratum of that order.

In the same article in *Zycie Warszawy* several other privileges are enumerated, such as a 'right' to unrepayable loans of up to 500,000 zloty, the opportunity to buy foreign currencies at beneficial rates, free redecoration and refurbishing of homes. Popular wisdom easily throws in further benefits: special shops, coupons for sought-after goods, and so on. The fantasy of the people can hardly compete with the vivid imagination of the administration.

Popular consciousness does not endorse such practices. This is the key to analogies and differences between the periods compared. What in the *ancien régime* issued from the very essence of the society of orders in its particular Polish form, is perceived today as a manifestation of corruption, as a caricature, or both. This is due to the short constitutional experience of the inter-war period, to a prevailing myth of the nature of Western societies, and also to a true (if rarely conscious) acceptance of general principles of socialism. It is in this light that the gap between theory and reality becomes so dramatic.

The Polish public cannot compare these facts with manifestations of power abuse abroad. One knows little about the Mafia, Camorra and the abuse of political power in the Mezzogiorno; here and there some arguments, which in feudal conditions were normal or acceptable, in certain conditions rouse popular indignation. This is particularly true of political patronage and judicial immunity.

Ruling 58 was one such privilege of immunity granted to the whole Estate (family members included!). Unlike the old Polish nobility, strictly hereditary and formally closed, the privileged group of today reminds one rather of a *Beamtenadel* of absolute monarchies. This corresponds well with the strong centralizing tendencies of the People's Republic. There are numerous proofs of individual immunities as well: public prosecutors overlook some misdemeanours, malfeasances and felonies, and many similar things have been said and written recently about judges. This makes a particularly stark contrast with the value of quotas of fines that the ministry of justice was imposing upon particular Courts of Justice; justices were appreciated according to their financial achievement... [26]This was roughly similar to the practice of manorial courts which treated fines as a form of feudal rent. The ruling group did not forget to secure some privileged rights to acquire land in the form of secret but ruthlessly enforced reservation of purchase rights on most sought-after residential quarters and resorts. Virtually nothing has been disclosed about tax immunities.

Political patronage needs much serious research hitherto impossible to pursue. In the Florence of the *Duecento*, in sixteenth-century Scotland, in Lithuania two centuries later, clientage constituted the cornerstone of the political systems. It was petering out where absolutist institutions developed or parliamentary democracy was established. Wherever either royal power or societal control weakened, the field of activity was open for clientage, for cliques and various other informal hierarchical groups. They find the best soil where public substance can be exploited. A biographer of Mayor Richard Daley of Chicago has shown how the Democratic 'machine' dominated and exploited the municipal administration.[27] Contributions to the 'machine' were rewarded by municipal jobs or commissions. This remote case shows that the exploitation of public resources and opportunities by political groupings are widespread and characteristic of various systems. So far as the two ages of Poland's society and state are concerned we come back to the comparison of the archetype and its caricature. The nobility was well aware that theirs was the state, and that they were the state. A much more narrow group, later called the magnates, divided up a large share of state property (income from Royal Domains first of all) and did it according to law. After 1945, the economic activity of the state increased the sphere open for corruption and in the past decade exploited it out of all proportion.

These recurrences of and relapses into the past in the domain of power, find their counterpart in the reactions of the people. Readers of the press in Poland in 1981, already familiar with information about Latin American peons or Portuguese small farmers struggling for land, were astonished to find scanty but strange news about private farmers in Poland seizing pieces of land belonging to state farms. After the first wave of strictly censored information in the mass media, some newspapers reported that local authorities 'have been obliged to reconsider all applications of private farmers concerning restitution of [their] land that had been seized illegally or with glaring injustice...'[28] Another newspaper reported the land hunger of small farmers from Swiebodzin, bordering upon a state farm extensively cultivated on about 24,000 hectares. The conflict was described in a form well known to the student of early modern agrarian history.

These analogies with a remote past – and are they only superficial? – are leading to situations in which the public interest is identifiable with that of the farmer and antithetical to that of the power elite. The earliest and the loudest manifestation, the *cause célèbre* of agrarian conflicts, took place in the autumn of 1980 in the south-east corner of the country in the Bieszczady Mountains. A peculiar sit-in strike of farmers protested against a large *chasse gardée* for VIPs laid out some time before, and protected by severe game laws. 'The Ustrzyki strike is known all over the world,' wrote a poet-protester in January 1981, 'The brave people of Bieszczady shall sweep away all the filth and dirt.' Its author, a former machinist and party instructor, was fired from his job in a state farm (which was in 1980 over £500,000 in the red), and became a prominent member of the solidarity of private farmers'. Ghosts of the Sheriff of Nottingham and King John, and the spirit of Robin Hood, were hovering over Bieszczady Forest, in AD 1981.

Awareness of a particular moral–political insanity is widespread, if one may conclude from letters to editors of the more open and outspoken newspapers and journals: 'A cynical interest group, appearing as Pomet [an enterprise] is building its settlement of "second homes" (so called *dachas*) in the Wielkopolska National Park, against the law and two decisions of the Ministry... It appears that these gentlemen, who may be compared to ancient *feudal nobility* hold cheap the restoration', wrote an outraged reader in September 1981.[29]

Does that mean that feudalism ought to be overthrown once more, after the blows dealt to it by the nineteenth-century emanicipation and reform legislation of the independent Republic, and the *coup de grâce* of the land reform of 1944–5? There is something in that, but by no means everything. If one accuses the participants in power and privilege of feudalism, it is nothing but an inversion of an interpretation much liked by the 'establishment' itself. 'Every society has an explanation for evil. In the West it is largely a religious one. In the Communist societies the official explanation is largely a secular one: "remnants" of influence from the prior social order or "class enemies" are blamed for anything that goes wrong.'[30] In Poland there is an intellectual tendency to trace some features of the 'national character' from early modern traditions of nobility.[31]

Corruption and abuse of power are as good a subject of study as any other and ought to be explored thoroughly as a basic and an applied practical problem. One should not confine oneself to them alone, just as one cannot explain the nature of the British state and society (or can one?) from the fact that there even a princess pays for her own tickets for public entertainment.

'At the root of all the evil in our economy are market shortages,' wrote a columnist in October 1980.[32] This was an overstatement of a truth, as always when one uses the emphatic words: everything, always. He was right that such shortages 'undermine public morals'. I have tried to show how the 'morality of market gaps' does not only open the way for mass misdemeanours. However, it would be a mistake to examine these problems only as economic evils; all these anachronisms, manifestations of a 'renewal', or remnants of feudalism are closely connected with the structure of power.

'*Polonia hodie iacet et laborat*', wrote Philipp Oldenburger in 1675, 'Which Esculap will step forward who may find a medicine for this malady?'[33] One hopes he will be a family doctor.

NOTES

1 Cf. J. Fedorowicz *et al.* (ed.), *The History of Poland until 1863* (Cambridge, forthcoming).
2 T. Manteuffel, 'Problem feudalizmu polskiego' (The Problem of Polish Feudalism), *Przeglad Historyczny* 37 (1948), pp. 62ff.
3 P. Anderson, *Lineages of the Absolutist State* (London 1975), p. 298.
4 G. Schramm, 'Adel und Staat. Ein Vergleich zwischen Brandenburg und Polen-Litauen im 17 Jahrhundert', paper presented at conference of West German and Polish historians in Toruń, April 1981 (in press).
5 A. Maczak, 'Money and Society in Poland and Lithuania in the Sixteenth and Seventeenth Centuries', *J. European Econ. Hist.* 5, 1 (1976), pp. 77ff.
6 E. Opaliński, *Elita władzy w województwach poznańskim i kaliskim za Zygmunta III*

(The Governing Elite in the Poznan and Kalisz Voivodship under Zygmunt III) (Poznań 1981), chap. 1.

7 A. Maçzak, 'Zur Grundeigentumsstruktur in Polen im 16 bis 18 Jahrhundert', *Jahrbuch für Wirtschaftsgeschichte* (1967).

8 Manteuffel, 'Problem feudalizmu polskiego', p. 62.

9 U. Augustyniak, *Informacja i propaganda w Polsce za Zygmunta III* (Information & Propaganda in Poland under Zygmunt III) (Warsaw 1981), *passim*.

10 There were also more or less radical, or populist, anti-myths, particularly popular with partisans of peasant political groups. An early protest song from the 1830s ('Hail, lords and magnates') became a sort of anthem of the peasant movement until very recently. One stanza ran as follows:
> The landlord class is like an old harlot
> Who has lost all her charms...
> We won't be allured by the grace of that old hag.

11 J. Blum, *The End of the Old Order in Rural Europe* (Princeton 1978), and my comments concerning his treatment of Poland in *J. European Econ. Hist.* 8, 3 (1979), pp. 777–81.

12 Cf. essays by Professor Janusz Tazbir, in particular 'Pochwa "nieudacznika" i nagana kariery w literaturze polskiej' (Praise of the Unsuccessful and the Rebuke of Success in Polish Literature), *Spotkania z Historia* (Warsaw 1979), pp. 239–52; this essay has unleashed an interesting and fruitful literary discussion in *Kultura*.

13 *Mały rocznik statystyczny, 1937*, p. 66; for Kalecki and Landau's calculations see p. 60 and bibliography in footnote.

14 *Mały rocznik statystyczny, 1937*, p. 64; *idem., 1958*, p. 110; *idem., 1981*, p. 157.

15 W. Kula, *An Economic Theory of Feudalism* (London 1976).

16 A. Jezierski, *Historia gospodarcza Polski Ludowej 1944–1968* (Warsaw 1971), p. 198.

17 The best recent monograph on the servile farm in early nineteenth-century Poland is that of J. Kochanowicz, *Pańszczyźniane gospodarstwo chłopskie w Królestwie Polskim w I połowie XIX w* (The Servile Peasant Holding in the Kingdom of Poland in the First Half of the Nineteenth Century) (Warsaw 1981).

18 *Mały rocznik statystyczny, 1971*, p. 182.

19 On the other hand, in the late 1970s farmers became heavily assessed for compulsory social security charges without adequate benefits. This led to general dissatisfaction and local farmers' protests.

20 Cf. B. Zientara, *Dzieje małopolskiego hutnictwa zelaznego. XIV-XVII wiek* (The History of Iron founding in Malopolska in the 14th–17th Centuries) (Warsaw 1954), pp. 190ff.

21 On the grain trade in early modern times, see Kula, *An Economic Theory*. After 1945 the destruction of village mills based on water power and using small dams probably contributed to the inadequacy of the water supply in the Polish countryside. Shortage of water – dry household wells – is very common and has become one of the principal problems of Polish agriculture and cattle breeding. It is being increased by some recent ill-considered industrial projects, chiefly strip mines.

22 W. Kuczyński, *Po wielkim skoku* (After the Great Shock) (Warsaw 1979). In 1981 this book was reprinted by an official publishing house in Poland.

23 Kula, *An Economic Theory*; A. Maczak, 'Preise, Löhne und Lebenshaltungskosten im Europa des 16 Jahrhunderts', *Wirtschaftliche und soziale Strukturen im saekularen*

Wandel. Festschrift für Wilhelm Abel zum 70 Geburtstag, Vol. II. (Hanover 1974), pp. 322–6; see p. 326 for a comparison of regional salaries in the twentieth and sixteenth centuries. The late Professor Jan Rutkowski made a penetrating analysis of these questions in his unfinished work, *Badania nad podziałem dochodów w Polsce w czasach nowożytnych*, Vol. I (Research on the Division of Incomes in Poland in Recent Times), (Krakow 1938).

24 For a different approach to contemporary 'mercantilisms' see I. Wallerstein, 'Socialist States: Mercantilist Strategies and Revolutionary Objectives', paper presented to 5th Annual Conference on Political Economy of the World-System, Madison, Wisc., May 14–16, 1981.

25 *Zycie Warszawy*, 31 October–1 November 1981. Article by W. Markiewicz, 'The Equal and the More Equal. Ruling No. 58'.

26 *Polityka*, No. 22 (30 May 1981). Article by S. Sołtysiński, 'The Court of Justice is a Business'.

27 M. Royko, *Boss. Richard J. Daley of Chicago* (New York 1971).

28 *Zycie Warszawy*, 7 September 1981; *Dziennik Ludowy*, 8 September 1981.

29 *Kultura* (13 September 1981), letter to the editor. 'Restoration' (*odnowa* literally, renewal) is a key word in contemporary Polish political parlance; it means the return to the proper 'Leninist principles' in state and party politics on the one hand, and the (equally vague) rule of justice, democracy, and common sense in economic leadership on the other. Some journalists, tired of that much-repeated word, asked: 'Did what is about to be restored ever exist?'

30 Ross Terrill, 'Gang of Four in Satan's Role', *International Herald Tribune* (2 October 1980).

31 J. Tazbir in *Kultura* (16 August 1981).

32 *Sztandar Młodych* (2 October 1980).

33 P.A. Oldenburger, *Thesauri rerum publicarum pars secunda* (Geneva 1675), p. 73.

ACKNOWLEDGMENTS

In recent years I approached this subject several times, each time in a different way. This was due not only to changes in my own opinions, but also to massive new material produced in recent years and months, particularly concerning the latter part of this chapter. While I did not always follow the suggestions made to me, I am indebted for comments from participants in the seminar on agrarian societies in transition to capitalism (Institute of History and Institute of Economic History, Uppsala University) in February 1980; of the conference sponsored by La Société d'Études sur Féodalisme in Trier in May 1981, and to Warsaw University students of history, who recently, whilst on strike, commented upon my free lecture. A similar text – an earlier version – will appear in a collection of papers from the Trier conference, *Feudalism in Poland: Heyday – Survival – Revival. Sixteenth to Twentieth Century*; this paper, with some changes, was also due to be published at Christmas 1981 in the Warsaw weekly *Kultura*.

The Editors are grateful to Antony Polonsky for his assistance with the final preparation of this manuscript.

Index

Abensour, M., 148
Aberystwyth, creation of, 207
absolutism, 256, 283
Ady, Endre, 235
Agulhon, Maurice, 156, 159
Alexandrov, Todor, 252
Allgemeine Deutsche Arbeiterverbrüderung, 95, 102
Allgemeiner Deutscher Arbeiterverein, 95
anarchists: American, 146; French, 143, 146, 149–50, 151, 153, 155, 157, 159–62; Spanish, 175–9 *passim*, 180, 182, 184, 186–7, 189
anarcho-syndicalists, Spanish, 181, 182, 185, 186
Anderson, Perry, 215, 218, 283
Anscele, Belgian delegate to London Congress (1888), 145
Anschluss, 269
anti-semitism, 223, 227, 242, 243, 244–5, 246, 247, 259, 267; *see also* pogroms
appièceurs (home-based tailors), 71, 73–4
appondeurs (weavers' assistants), 160
apprenticeship system: British, 122; German, 108
Arbeiter, definition of, 96–7, 98
Arendt, H., 259, 269
aristocracy, 2, 3, 8–9, 215, 216; and bankers, 221, 225–9; and middle classes, 197–9, 201, 208–9, 217–19; Polish, 284–5, 286–7, 293, 294; role in industrialization and urbanization, 199–200, 202–8; values and practices, 197, 201, 216, 218, 225; *see also* landed society
Arkwright, Richard, 124, 208
Arnold, Matthew, 218
artisans, artisanal ideals, 4–6, 48, 67–9; *see also* craft workers; tailors

Ascaso, Francisco, 187, 188
association, 38–9, 59, 67; *see also* sociability
Association Fraternelle des Ouvrières Lingères, 79
Atelier, L', 42, 46, 47, 54–5
atelier social, 67
Au rendez-vous de la Rade tavern, Paris, 49
Austria, 28, 222, 228, 254–5, 258–9, 260, 263, 269, 287; *see also* Austro-Hungary
Austro-Hungary, 260; Jewish assimilation in, 235–48

backward-nation theory, 279–81
Bagehot, Walter, 227
Baird family, 210
Balfour, Arthur, 224
banditry, 19
Bank of England, 220–1, 223
bankers, British and European, 219–29; economic position and power, 220–2; role in political systems, 222–5; social and cultural life, 219–20, 225–9
Bar-le-Duc (Meuse), France, weavers' strike, 154
Barcelona, regionalist and working-class movements in (1890–1930), 173–90
Baring family, bankers, 210, 219, 221, 223; Edward Charles, first Baron Revelstoke, 224; Everard, 224; Hugo, 224; Maurice, 224
Barrow-in-Furness, creation of, 203–4
Battersea, Lord, 227
Bauer, Otto, 269
Bavaria, 253
Beasley, Ammon, 135, 136
Bebel, August, 95, 104, 175
Bedford: 7th Duke of, 201; 13th Duke of, 202
Bell, Richard, 136

Benedikt, Moritz, 244
Beneš, Eduard, 262
Benôit, Joseph, 39, 57
Béranger, Pierre Jean de, 46, 58
Berger, John, 178
Berlin: bankers, 220; proletarian rising (1919), 257
Bethlen, István, 255
Bieszczady, Poland, farmers' protest, 294
Bilbao, May Day celebrations, 175
Birmingham building-trades' strike, 123
Bismarck, Otto von, 222, 223
Blackpool, creation of, 206
Blanc, Louis, 70, 78–9, 84
Blanco, Ramón, 176
blanket-makers' strike, Cours (Rhône), 163
Blanquists, 149
Bleichröder, Gerson von, 220, 222
Bloch, Ernst, 31
Blyth and Tyne Railway, 204
Bohemia, 261, 262
boot and shoe industry, British, labour relations in, 131
Bordat, Toussaint, 160
Bordeaux, *cercles* in, 44, 48
Born, Stephan, 95
Boulton, Matthew, 124
bourgeoisie, 2, 15, 16, 17, 25–6; and aristocracy, 197–9, 201, 208–9, 217–19; class consciousness of, 216; Jewish assimilation in Austro-Hungarian, 239–41, 242, 243, 245, 246–7; sociability, 38–9, 44, 48, 49, 51, 54–5; relation to working classes, 18, 20, 21, 196–7; view of the family, 82, 84–5
Bournemouth, creation of, 206
Brailsford, H.N., 222, 223
Brentano, Lujo, 99
Briand, Aristide, 265
Bridgewater, 3rd Duke of, 202
Bridgewater Canal, 202
Brindley, James, 202
Britain, 27, 28; bankers, 219, 220–1, 222, 223–5, 226–9; class structure, 195–7; development of capitalism, 22, 23, 278; labour movement, 20–1; *see also* British industry; landed society
British industry, structures of subordination in, 119–38
Brittany, celebration of May Day in, 165
Brochard mill, Vienne, workers' demonstration at, 155, 161
Brunet, militant joiner from Paris, 164
Budapest, 236, 239, 247, 251, 252
Bulgaria, 252, 264, 265

Burlington, Lord (later 7th Duke of Devonshire), 203–4, 205, 206
Bute: 2nd Marquis of, 204; 3rd Marquis of, 204, 208

Cabet, Étienne, 67, 68, 69, 83; *Voyage en Icarie*, 148–9
Café de la Redoute, Lyons, 58
cafés, as centres of French working-class sociability, 42–3, 48
canal building in Britain, 202, 203
Cankov, Professor, 252
Canler, Louis, 51
Cannadine, David, 205
capitalism, 14, 15, 22, 23, 107, 247, 278; crisis of, 33, 273–5
Captain Swing rising, 19
Cardiff, development of, 204
Carlyle, Thomas, quoted, 207
Carrington, 6th Lord, 197
Casanova, Rafael, 179
Cassel, Sir Ernest, 219, 221, 224, 225, 227
Cassis, Yussef, 226
Catalonia, 173; language, 174; nationalism, 178–9, 182, 184–9; Regionalist League, 184
Catholic Church: in Austria, 258; in Czechoslovakia, 272; relations with workers' associations in France, 45
Catholic countries, ritual and folklore in, 174, 175, 176
Cattaro, naval mutiny at, 254
'Cercle de la Tour de Nesle', Paris, 55
Cercle des Ouvriers de Nuits (Côte d'Or), 53
cercles, 39, 41, 48–9, 52–6
Chamberlain, Austin, 265
Chamberlain, Joseph, 200–1
chambrées, 40–1, 57, 156
chambrettes, 41
change, process of, 2, 16
'Chicago martyrs', trial of, 145
child labour, 74, 175, 176
China, social revolution in, 27
choral societies, French, 46–8, 49, 56
City of London financiers, 217, 221, 222, 223, 224–5, 226, 228–9
civil disobedience, in Spain, 185, 187, 188
Civil Guard, Barcelona, 177
civil service, British, 216
Clacton, development of, 206, 207
class, 3, 14–15, 16, 32, 111, 196, 217; relations, 21, 137, 217–18, 229; structure, English, 195–7; struggle, 20, 32, 37, 54, 159, 189, 196; *see also* class consciousness
class consciousness, 14–15, 32, 58–9, 108, 123, 164, 178, 216

Clermont-Ferrand, May Day procession, 158
Clifton family of Lancashire, 206
coal-shipping docks, British, 203–5
Cobden, Richard, 198, 208
Codreanu, Corneliu Zelea, 259
Colbert, Jean Baptiste, 22
Coleman, D.C., 208
collective: agreements, 128, 130, 132;
    bargaining, 125, 133, 136, 137
colonial system, imperialism, 23, 25
Comas, Francisco, 175, 181, 182, 183–4
*Combat (Le), organe quotidien des
    Travailleurs Socialistes,* 151
'Communist League', Germany, 95
Communist Party: French, 27; Italian, 27;
    Spanish, 185, 187
conciliation and arbitration system, Britain,
    130, 132, 136
confection, see ready-made clothing industry
co-operative system, 3, 5, 6, 38, 50, 67, 69, 73,
    101, 102; co-operative communities, 79
Corn Laws, 198, 216
Corpus Christi procession, Barcelona,
    bombing of, 179–80, 189
Corradini, Enrico, 279
cotton industry, English, 199, 215
counter-revolution, 251–7, 271, 272, 281; in
    Austria, 254–5; in Bulgaria, 252; in
    Germany, 252–3; in Hungary, 251–2, 255,
    257
country houses, Victorian, 210–11
Cracroft, Bernard, 198
craft unions, 100, 103, 104
craft workers, craft traditions, 2, 3, 5, 77, 78;
    British, 6; German, 95–112; importance in
    early labour movement, 6–7, 67, 69, 95–6,
    98–112
Croats, 237, 238, 247, 260, 261, 262, 263,
    264, 271, 272
Cromer, Evelyn Baring, 1st Earl, 223
Cuban War of Independence, 179
Cumberland, coalfields of, 203
Curwen family, of Cumberland, 203
Czechoslovakia, Czechs, 236, 237, 238, 247,
    260–1, 266, 272; Czech Legion, 262;
    Czechoslovakian Committee, 262; Czecho-
    Moravian provinces, 239; fascism in, 258;
    independence, 262–4; *see also* Slovakia

Daley, Richard J., 293
Dawpool, Cheshire, 211
Deroin, Jeanne, 83
Deutsch, Abraham, 235, 245
Deutsch, Julius, 255
Deutsch, Sándor Hatvany, 235

Deville, Gabriel, 147
Devonshire, Dukes of, 227; 7th Duke (Lord
    Burlington), 203–4, 205, 206
dictatorial systems, 266, 267, 275, 281
Diputació Chapel, Barcelona, 186, 187
division of labour, 74, 96, 105, 121–2, 123,.
    127, 128, 131, 132, 137, 270; Marx's view
    of, 28, 29, 30, 121; sexual, 69, 71, 75–6, 85,
    86
Dmowski, Roman, 267
Dobb, Maurice Herbert, 22, 23
docks, British: coal-shipping, 203–5; labour
    relations, 132–3
Dommanget, Maurice, 147
Dormoy, Jean, 145, 159
Doyet-les-Mines (France), May Day
    demonstration, 158–9, 161
Drexler, Anton, 257
Dupont, Pierre, *Le Chant des Ouvriers,* 50
Durruti, Buenaventura, 187, 188
dye-workers' circular to employers, Lyons,
    151–2

Eastbourne, development of, 205
Edmonston, Gabriel, 147
Edward VII, King of England, 227
Egypt, British business enterprise in, 221, 223
Ehrhardt, Captain Hermann, 253
eight-hour day, campaign for, 144, 146–7,
    150, 154, 156, 158, 164, 175, 176, 177;
    'Eight Hours Song', 158
electrification revolution of 1900s, 221
Emancipation, L', 150
employment contracts, British industry, 122
Enfantin, Prosper, 81
Engelhardt, Ulrich, 103
Engels, Friedrich, 14, 20, 24, 25, 26–7, 29, 43,
    57
engineering industry, British, 122, 129, 132
English Revolution of 1640s, 25
Eötvös, József, 242
Estat Català, 185, 187, 188
Ewington, signalman on Taff Vale railway,
    135
Executio-Iurium movement, Poland, 285

Fabri, Italian anarchist theoretician, 255
factory proletariat, 2, 98
family in nineteenth-century France, impact of
    reorganization of work and pressures of
    wage labour on, 67–87
fascism, 247, 257–9, 271, 272, 274–5, 281;
    Czech, 258; German, 257–8; Italian, 255,
    257, 268, 279–80, 281; Polish, 267–8
Fay, Sam, 136

Federation of Industrial Unions, Barcelona, 183
Federation of Labour Syndicates, Barcelona, 183
Fédération Nationale des Syndicats ouvriers, France, 145, 153
female labour, regulation of, 74, 175, 176
feminism, 69, 79–81
Feuchtwanger, Lion, *Jew Suss*, 220
feudalism, 14, 16, 22, 33, 208, 216; in modern Poland, 283–95
Fichte, Johann Gottlieb, *Der geschlossene Handelsstaat*, 276–8, 280
Fleetwood family, and development of Fleetwood, 206
flower-vendors of Barcelona, 177, 180, 181, 186
folkloric rituals, 173, 174, 186, 187, 189
Ford, Henry, 127
Fourier, Charles, 67, 68; Fourierism, 55, 56
Fourteenth of July holiday, 157, 165
Frachon, Benoît, 145
France, 27, 101, 137, 216, 260; bankers, 220, 221, 223, 228; labour movement, 101, 143; *see also* French Revolution; garment trades; May Day; sociability
Franco, Francisco, 174
Franco-Belgian metalworks, Raismes, May Day demonstration at, 153
free-masonry, French, 52
free trade, 217, 224, 243, 278
Free Unions, Barcelona, 181, 182
Freikorps, Germany, 252–3
French Revolution, 22, 24, 25, 51, 143, 164, 220, 270
Freud, Sigmund, 28
Friedjung, Heinrich, 244
Friendly societies, mutual associations: French, 44–6, 49, 54, 73; German (*Kassen*), 95, 103–4, 106, 108
funerals, as collective ritual, 173, 174, 175, 181, 182–4
Furness Railway, 203

Gajda, General Rudolf (Radola), 258
Galicia, 236, 239, 246, 261, 267
garment trades, Parisian, 68–87
Garraf terrorists, Spain, 187, 188
gas industry, British, labour relations in, 132–3
Gay, Desirée, 79, 80, 81
Gelu, Victor, 45, 47, 52–3
Gerando, Baron de, 56
Geremek, Bronislaw, 290
Germany, Germans, 137, 216, 223, 266, 269,

278–9; bankers, 220, 221, 228; counter-revolution in, 252–3; craft workers, 95–112; Liberal Party, 100; Social Democrats, 100, 252–3, 254; *see also* Nazism
Geslin, Claude, 165
Gibbs family, bankers, 224; Alban, 224; Henry Hucks, 228
Girondists, 24
Giuliano, Salvatore, 19
goguettes, 46–8, 54
Gombos, Gyula, 252
Goschen, George, 223–4, 228
Grand National Consolidated Trades Union, 122
'Great Day', notion of, 163–4
'Great Depression', 127, 133, 164, 221
Greece, 265
Gregor, J., 281
Grenfells, merchant bankers, 224
Griffuelhes, Victor, 165
Guesde, Jules, 150
Guesdists, 143, 145, 146, 150–1, 153, 155–6, 157, 161–2
guilds, trade: French, 44–5, 49; German, 97, 98, 101–2, 108
Guinguette de l'Ascension café, Marseilles, 52–3
Guinness family, 210
Guizot, François, 45
Gyulafehérvár (Alba Iulia) proclamation of united Romania, 262

Habsburg, Karl, 252
Habsburg dynasty, 242, 260
Hambros banking house, 219
Hamburg, Germany, 98, 103, 220
Handwerk, Handwerker, definition of, 96
Handwerksgesellen, 95–112 *passim*
Handwerksmeister, 96, 97, 98, 99, 101–2, 104, 106, 108
Harcourt, Sir William, 223
Hatvany, Lajos, 235, 245
Hatvany-Deutsch family, 245
Havránek, J., 258
Heimwehr, Austria, 258–9
Heine, Wolfgang, 253
Helps, Arthur, 124
Henry, Marius, 152, 163
Hessen, Karl, 257
Hilferding, Rudolf, 222
Hilton, John, 23
Hirsch, Moritz de, 219, 221
historical materialism, 13–14, 17, 27, 28, 29, 33
Hitler, Adolf, 254, 256, 257, 280

Hlinka, Andrew, 258, 264, 272
Hobsbawm, Eric, 1–2, 13–34, 199; *The Age of Capital*, 19, 25, 29, 215; *The Age of Revolution*, 2, 19, 29, 215; *Bandits*, 19, 31; *The History of Marxism*, 13, 25; *Industry and Empire*, 19; *The Jazz Scene*, 19; 'Karl Marx and the British Labour Movement', 20; *Labouring Men*, 19; 'Lenin and the Aristocracy of Labour', 30; 'Marx, Engels, and Politics', 25, 26; *Primitive Rebels*, 19, 31; *Revolutionaries*, 19, 26; 'Society since 1914', 20
Hobson, J.A., *The Evolution of Modern Capitalism*, 220, 222
Holdernesse (Londonderry) House, Park Lane, London, 203
Home of the Hirsel, Lord (Alexander Frederick Douglas-Home), 197
homeworkers, household production, 98; in Parisian garment trades, 69, 70–9 *passim*, 81
Hörlgasse massacre, Vienna, 255
Horthy, Admiral Nicholas, 246, 251–2, 255, 271
Hottinguer bank, France, 220
household production, *see* homeworkers
Hugo, Victor, *Les Misérables*, 50, 58
Hungary, 236–47, 260, 264, 265, 266, 269; counter-revolution in, 251–2, 255, 257, 271–2; Jewish assimilation in 235–47 *passim*; liberal nationalism of, 243, 247
Huskisson, William, 126

Iasi University, Romania, right-wing terrorism at, 259
Iglesias, Pablo, 175
industrial relations in nineteenth-century Britain, 119–38
Industrial Revolution, 22, 23, 109, 121–2, 123–4, 196, 199, 209, 215, 275; *see also* industrialization
industrialization, 22, 99, 101, 102, 107, 121, 124, 196, 217; and craft traditions, 97, 104–5, 106; role of landed aristocracy in, 199–200, 202–5, 207–8, 209
inflation in Europe in 1920s, 269
Ismay, Thomas, 211
Italy: Communist Party, 27; fascism in, 255, 257, 268, 279–80, 281

Jacobins, 39, 54, 58
Jagiello dynasty, Poland, 284
Jeansoulin oilworks, Marseilles, attack on, 155, 160
Jews, 264, 272, 280; assimilation in Austro-

Hungary, 235–48; as bankers, 226–7, 241; *see also* anti-semitism; Yiddish; Zionism
Jezierski, Anderzej, 290
Johnson, Christopher, 73
Jones, Gareth Stedman, 86
Josephinist Enlightenment, 242, 243
journeymen: in French tailoring trade, 70, 72, 73, 77; German, 95–112 *passim; see also* journeymen brotherhoods
journeymen brotherhoods, 97–8, 99–101, 103–4, 106, 108, 109
József, Attila, 235
Juiferrant, Le (Eugene Sue), 55
July Monarchy, France, 44, 45, 46
Junkers, 217, 226

Kadimah, 243
Kalecki, M., 289
Kalisz, Poland, study of power elite in, 284
Kapp, Wolfgang, 253, 257, 258
Kassen, see friendly societies
Kemal, Mustafa (Atatürk), 281
Knights of Labor, USA, 145
Knox case (1913), 136
Kornfeld, Sigismund, 245–6
Kossuth, Louis, 242, 278
Kramař, Karel, 262
Kuczyński, Waldemar, 291
Kula, Witold, *Economic Theory of Feudalism*, 290, 292

'labour aristocracy', 123, 217, 222, 225
labour law, British, 125–6; 1799 Act, 125; 1824 Act, 126; 1825 Act, 125
labour movement, 6–7, 8, 16, 20, 55, 67, 68; American, 143, 145; British, 6, 20–1; French, 101, 143; German, 95–112; Spanish, 179, 185
Labriola, Arturo, 268
Lagardell, Hubert, 268
Landau, L., 289
landed society, English, 195–211, 215, 216, 218, 226, 228
Lassalle, Ferdinand, 95, 104
Lavigne, Raymond, 144, 145
Le Bon, Gustave, 149
Le Play, Frédéric, 73
League of Nations, 265
Legre, Parisian tailor, 85
Lenin (Vladimir Ulyanov), 15, 18, 22, 24, 26, 28, 29, 222
Leroux, Pierre, 148
Lesznai, Anna, 235
Leveson-Gower, Granville, 1st Marquis of Stafford, 202

Leveson-Gower family, 200, 202
Liebknecht, Wilhelm, 95, 104
linotype machine, impact of introduction of, 129–30
Linz, J.J., 271
List, Friedrich, *Das nationale System der politischen Ökonomie*, 278–9
Liszt, Franz, 227, 243
Lithuania, 266, 283, 293
Liverpool and Manchester Railway, 202
Livesey, George, 133
Lloyd George, David, 224
loi Guizot (1833), 56–7
Loire *département*, France, May Day celebrations, 156
Loire river, May Day boat trip, 165
London Congress (1888), 145
Londonderry, Frances Anne, Marchioness, 207
Londonderry, 3rd Marquis of, 124, 203, 207, 208
Lonsdale, Earls of, 203
Louis Philippe, King of France, 53
Lubbock, Sir John, 228
Ludendorff, Erich von, 258
Lugmayer, K., 258
Lukács, George, 235
Luton Hoo, Bedfordshire, 210
Lüttwitz, General von, 253
Luxembourg Commission (1848), 70
Luxemburg, Rosa, 266
Lyceum Theatre bombing, Barcelona, 179
Lyons, France: May Day celebrations (1890), 151–2, 153, 154, 158; working-class sociability, 39–40, 41, 44, 53, 55, 57
Lytham St Anne's, Lancashire, creation of, 206

Macedonia, 252, 261, 265; Macedonian Revolutionary Organization, 252
Macià, Francesco, 185, 187, 188
McKenna, Frank, 134
Maison du Peuple, concept of, 55
managerial ideology, nineteenth-century British, 123–4, 137
Manchester, 202, 216
Mancomunitat (federation of Catalonian cities), 184
Mann, Thomas, 256
Manteuffel, Tadeusz, 283, 285
Marlstone House, Berkshire, 211
Marseilles: locations of sociability, 41, 44, 45, 47, 52–3; May Day demonstrations, 157, 158, 160
Martin, Pierre, 160, 161

Martinez Anido, General Severiano, 186
Marx, Eleanor, 175
Marx, Karl, 20, 23, 32, 105, 216, 222, 256, 278–9; and craft traditions, 97, 98, 102–3; on 'formal' and 'real' subordination, 120–1; *Introduction to the Critique of Political Economy*, 13, 16; philosophy of humanity, 28–9, 30; theory of class, 14, 15, 16, 217; theory of the state, 25, 26–7; view of war, 24
Marxism, 13, 14, 15, 17, 29, 34, 86, 283; French, 143, 151; myth in, 32–3
Maryport, Cumbria, 203
Masaryk, Professor Tomáš, 260, 262, 263
Massach, Domingo, 188
Master and Servant Law, British, 126
May Day: French celebration of (1890), 149–65; invention of, 143–9; in Spain, 175–9, 186, 188, 189
Mayer, Professor Arno, 216, 218, 219, 222, 223, 225, 229
mechanization of industry, effect of, 121–2, 123, 129–30, 154; *see also* science and technology
Mehring, Franz, 278–9
Meinertzhagen, Daniel, 222
Messner, J., 258
Meyrick family, 206
Michaels, Roberto, 268
Michel, Louise, 160
Michelet, J., *Journal*, 43
middle classes, *see* bourgeoisie
Midland Railway, 134
migration of European peoples, 236, 238
Mihaijlov, Ivan, 252
millenarianism, 31, 164
miners, French, May Day demonstrations by, 158–9, 162–3
minorities, oppression of, 264–6
Montlucon, France, May Day celebrations in, 157, 158, 159
Moravia, 239, 261, 262
Moss, Bernard, 101
Munich coup attempt (1923), 258
Muslims, Bulgarian and Yugoslav, 264
Mussolini, Benito, 268
mutual associations, *see* friendly societies

Nairn, Tom, 215, 218
Napoleon III, Emperor (Louis Napoleon Bonaparte), 25, 220
Narbonne, France, May Day celebrations in, 156
National Confederation of Labour (CNT), Spain, 183, 185

National Federation of Printing and Kindred Trades, Britain, 131
national revolutions, 30, 259–64, 266, 268, 270–3
National Socialist German Workers Party, 257–8
nationalism, 3, 29–30, 243, 247, 259; 'nationalist revolutions', 268–73; *see also* national revolutions
Nazism, 246, 248, 257–8, 280
New Domesday Book of 1873, 211
Newcastle-on-Tyne, coal and trading interests, 205
Niboyet, Eugenie, 77
Nieuwenhuis, Domela, 175
non-violence, doctrine of, 50
North Eastern Railway, 136
Northumberland, 4th Duke of, 204, 205, 207, 208
Northumberland Docks, River Tyne, 204–5
Noske, Gustov, 252, 253
nuclear war, threat of, 24, 33
Nyugat, 235

Odessa, pogroms in, 223
Oldenburger, Philipp, 295
Orient Express, 221
Ottoman Empire, 221, 223
output, restriction of in British industry, 131, 132
overseas investment, European bankers' interest in, 221, 223, 224, 229
Overstone family, 210
overtime working, control of in British industry, 122–3, 130, 131
Owen, Robert, 124
Ozouf, Mona, 147

Palmer, Samuel, 211
Pap, Károly, 235
Parent-Duchâtelet, A.J.B., 83
Paris: May Day celebrations (1890), 156, 162; Peace Conference, 262; Universal Exhibition (1889), 145; working-class sociability, 41, 42, 43–4, 47; *see also* garment trades
Parti Ouvrier Français, 143, 150 158, 159; *see also* Guesdists
Pasić, Nicholas, 263
paternalism in British industrial relations, 124–5, 132, 133, 134, 135–6
Pavelić, Ante, 272
Peel, Sidney Cornwallis, 224
Perdignier, Agnicol, 45
Périer brothers, bankers, 220
petitions to the authorities, workers', 146, 157, 158, 176

Petkov, Dmitri, 252
piece-work, piece-rates, 112; in British industry, 124, 127, 128, 129, 130, 131; in Parisian garment trades, 72, 74, 76, 77, 78, 79, 81
Pilsudski, Marshal Josef, 266–8, 272
Pittsburgh Agreement (1918), 263
pogroms, 223, 238, 252, 259
Poincaré, Raymond, 262
Poland, Poles, 237, 239, 260, 261, 264, 266–8, 269; feudalism in modern, 283–95; Jewish assimilation in, 242–3, 246, 247; nationalism, 243, 263, 267; population, 236, 237; United Workers' Party, 291
Polányi, Károly, 255, 274–5
political patronage, 293–4
politics: and banking, 222–5; and history, 33
Pompey Theatre bombing, Barcelona, 182
Possibilists, 143, 149–50
Poznan, Poland, study of power elite, 284
Prat de la Riba Serra, Enrique, 184
premium bonus system, British industry, 128, 129
Preuss, Professor Hugo, 254
Primo de Rivera, General Miguel, 174, 181, 184–5, 186, 188
Producteur, Le, 148
profit-sharing system, British industry, 133
Prolétariat, Le, 150
propaganda, early use of, 150–1
prostitution, 83–4
protectionism, 223, 224, 278, 279
protest movements, early working-class, 5, 7, 68, 69, 73, 107
Protogerov, General, 252
Proudhon, Pierre Joseph, 68, 82, 86
Proust, Marcel, 164, 228, 229
Provence, *chambrettes* in, 41
Prussia, 253, 285; aristocracy of, 216, 218, 226, 287
pseudo-gentry, British, 209–11
Puig i Cadafalch, Josep, 184

Radic, Stjepan, 263
Radziwill family, 286, 287
Rafa, Josefa and Rosita, 175, 180, 181, 182
Ragionieri, Ernesto, 21
railways, British, 215; classes of passenger compartments, 195; industrial relations in, 133–7
Raismes, France, May Day demonstrations in, 153
Ramblas, Barcelona, 176, 177, 178; bombing at flower-market (1905), 180, 189
Raventós, Salvador, 183

reading societies, French, 51, 54, 55, 56
ready-made clothing industry (*confection*), Paris, 69, 71–2, 77–8
red flag, as class symbol, 158, 161, 175, 176, 184
Red Guards, Austria, 254, 255
Reform Acts, Britain, 198, 199, 216
Regionalist League, Catalan, 184
Reichswehr, 253
religious holidays, and socialist collective ritual, 173, 174, 189
religious minorities, 264–6
Rémusat, Charles de, 47, 57
republicanism: French, 159; German, 223; Spanish, 178, 179, 182, 183, 185, 189
resort towns, British, 202, 205–7
restrictive practices, British industry, 119, 128
Révolte, La, 160
revolution, revolutionary change: failure of proletarian, 17, 27, 30, 33, 251; French *fin de siècle* vision of, 162, 163–4; in Third World, 26, 27; revolutionaries and reformists, 31; war as agent of, 24–5, 27, 33, 251; *see also* counter-revolution; national revolutions
Revolution: of 1830, 25, 59; of 1848, 17, 18, 25, 30, 70, 74, 97, 99; *see also* English; French; Russian
Revue des Deux Mondes, 47
Ricardo, David, 217
Rice, Tim, 197
Richardson case (1912), 136
Rio Tinto Company, 221
rituals, civic, and patterns of resistance in Barcelona (1890–1930), 173–90
Roanne, France, May Day celebrations at, 155, 156
Romania, Romanians, 237, 247, 259, 260, 261, 262, 264, 265, 266, 269, 281
Rosebery, Lord, 226
Rossel, André, 145
Rothschild family, 210, 219, 221, 223, 224, 226, 227–8; Alfred, 227; 1st Baron, 227; Constance, 227; Hannah, 226; of Paris, 220, 225, 227; Phillipe, 228
Roubaix, France, May Day demonstrations, 154, 163
Rubinstein, W.D., 209, 211
Ruhr workers' rising (1920), 253–4
Russia, 29, 223, 260, 265, 266; *see also* Russian Revolution
Russian Revolution, 16, 27, 251, 262
Rutland, 10th Duke of, 197

St Germain, Treaty of, 269
Saint-Leger-des-Vignes, France, quarry-

workers' demonstration, 154
Saint Monday, 105, 111, 122, 150
Saint-Pavace (Sarthe), France, workers' demonstration, 153
Saint-Quentin, France, May Day celebrations at, 157
Saint-Simon, Henri de, 164
Saint-Simonians, 67, 69, 81, 83, 148, 151
San Jordi Day celebrations, Barcelona, 175, 185–8, 189
Sanjuanada plot, Spain, 188
Sapieha family, 286
Scarborough, Earl of, 206
Schramm, Gottfried, 284
Schumpeter, J.A., 218, 273–4
science and technology, impact on labour relations, 120, 127–30, 134–5
Scotland, industrial relations in, 130, 131
Seaham Harbour, creation of, 203
seamstresses (*lingères*), Parisian, 69, 76–7, 78–84, 85, 86
Second International, 144, 175
secret societies, French, 49–50, 51–2, 54
Seguí, Salvador, 175, 181–3, 184, 186
Seipel, Ignaz, 258
Senhouse family of Cumberland, 203
Serbia, Serbs, 237, 261, 263, 264, 265, 272
Sète (Cette), Hérault, France, workers' demonstrations, 41, 160
Sewell, William, 59, 101
Shaw, Norman, 211
shop stewards' committees, 137
signalmen, railway, 134, 135, 136
Sikorski, General Wladyslaw, 267
Silesia, 253, 261, 287
Simon, Daphne, 126
Skegness, creation of, 206
Slovakia, Slovaks, 236, 237, 247, 260, 262; nationalist movement, 263–4, 271, 272; Southern Slovakia, 266
Smith, Adam, 122, 215, 276, 278
Smith banking dynasty, 224
sociability in nineteenth-century France: bourgeois, 38–9, 44, 48, 49, 51, 54–5; locations and types of association, 39–51; working-class, 38, 39–60
social democracy, 27–8, 99, 107, 150, 277–8; Austrian Social Democratic Party, 254–5; German Social Democrats, 100, 252–3, 254
socialism, 29, 30, 31, 33, 102, 148, 244
Société de Bienfaisance de St Laurent, Marseilles, 45
Société de l'Union des Travailleurs du Tour de France, 44, 47
Société des Babouvistes, 47
Société des Jacobins, 47

Société des Montagnards, 47
Solidarnosc trade union, Poland, 286, 290
South Africa, British investment in, 221
Southend, creation of, 206
Sozialdemokratische Arbeiterpartei (SDAP), 95
Sozialistische Arbeiterpartei Deutschlands (SAP), 95
Spain, 175, 185, 189; *see also* Barcelona; Catalonia
Spann, Othmar, 258
Speyer, Sir Edgar, 224
Spring, David, 227
Stafford, Lord, 202
Stalin, Joseph, 28; Stalinism, 29
Stamboliski, Alexander, 252
Starhemberg, Prince Ernst Rüdiger von, 258
state, theory of the: Fichte's, 276–7; Marxist, 25, 26–7, 28, 29
state-patriotism, 242, 243, 244
Statute of Piotrkow (1496), 292
Steidle, Richard, 259
Stephen, Sir James Fitzjames, 126
Stern, Fritz, 220, 222–3
Sternhall, Z., 270
strikes: in Britain, 123, 125, 126, 130, 133, 134; in France, 41, 43, 45, 69, 72, 73, 156, 162–3; in Germany, 95, 97, 106, 109–12; notion of international general strike, 145–6; in Spain, 176, 177, 180, 181, 185
Strutt family, 208, 210
subordination: Marx's categories of 'formal' and 'real', 120–1; structures of, in British industry, 119–38
Sudetenland, 258, 261
Sugar, P. 261
surplus value, Marx's labour theory of, 16, 32, 120
Swaythling, 2nd Baron, 224
Sweden, British investment in, 221
Sweezy, Paul, 23
Swiebodzin, Poland, land hunger in, 294
syndicalists, Spanish, 181, 182–3
Szeged, Hungary, 251, 252, 255

Taff Vale Railway, 134–5, 136
tailors, custom tailoring, France, 40, 69, 70–1, 72–6, 77, 81–3, 85
Takahashi, 23
Tavernier, Josephine, 160
taverns, as locations for French workers' sociability, 41–3, 46, 49, 56
terrorism, 259; in Barcelona, 179, 188, 189
textile workers, French, militancy of, 152–3, 163
Third International, 28

Third World, 26, 27, 30, 33, 280
Thivrier, Christou, 158
Thizy, France, fear of May Day demonstrations, 152
Thompson, E.P., 217, 218
Thompson, F.M.L., 218
'Three Eights', 7, 147
Tirol, 269
Tiszaeszlar affair (1883), Hungary, 244
Tivoli Theatre meeting, Barcelona (1890), 176, 177, 178
Tortelier, Parisian delegate at 1888 London Congress, 145
Toulon arsenal, revolutionary workers of, 54
trade unions, unionism, 59–60; English, 99, 100, 124, 126, 132, 133, 135, 136; French, 54; German, 95, 99–101, 103, 106, 112; Spanish, 181, 182; *see also* craft unions
Transylvania, 261, 262, 265, 266
Trelazé (Maine-et-Loire), workers' militancy at, 160, 164
Trianon Treaty, 269, 271
Tribune des Femmes, La, 69
Tristan, Flora, 41–2, 50, 55, 59; *L'Union Ouvrière*, 54
Troyes, France, May Day procession, 154, 157, 158
Truquin, Norbert, 40
Tuka, Professor Vojtěch, 258, 264, 272
Tuke, Sir Anthony, 202
Turkey, 260, 265; Turkish Revolution, 263, 280–1
Túrócszentmárton proclamation, 262–3, 264
Tyne Improvement Commissioners, 205

Ukrainians, 237, 266
unilinearism, 14
Union of Hungarian Awakening, 252
United States of America, 28, 137; Federation of Labor, 144; labour movement, 143, 145; railways, 221
Ure, Andrew, 121, 122
ustashi movement, 272
Ustrzyki farmers' strike, Poland, 294
utopianism, 31–2; utopian socialists, 67, 82, 83, 85–6

Valencia Conspiracy (1928), 188
Vandenesse, France, woodcutters' May Day demonstration, 153–4
Vane-Tempest, Frances Anne, 203
Varagnac, André, 147
Veiras, Denis, *L'Histoire des Sévarambes*, 147
Velkov, General, 252
Vernet, Armandine, 163

Vernon (Eure), France, building workers'
    May Day demonstration, 153
Versailles, Treaty of, 269, 280
Vestey family, 197
Victoria, Queen of England, 228
Vienna, 236, 239, 242, 243, 244, 251, 255, 262
Vienne (Isère), France, May Day
    demonstration at, 155, 158, 159–61
Villermé, L.R., 56, 82
Voix des Femmes, La, 77, 83
Volkswehr, 255
Vormärz, 241, 242, 243

Waentig, H., 277
Wandycz, P., 268
war: as agent for social revolution, 24–5, 27,
    33, 251; First World War, 27, 251, 273,
    274–5; Second World War, 27
Warburgh banking house, Hamburg, 220
Watney family, 210
Watt, James, 124
Webb, Sidney and Beatrice, 99
Weber, E., 281
Weber, Max, 29, 32, 107, 218, 254
Wedgewood, Josiah, 122, 124
Weimar Republic, 254
Weininger, Otto, 244
Weiss, John, 281
Wereszycki, H., 268
Wernher, Sir Julius, 210
Wesselényi, Miklos, 242
Westminster, Duke of, 197, 215
white-collar workers, British, 20
white terror, Hungary, 251–2, 255
Whitehaven, Cumbria, 203
Wiener, Martin J., 216, 218, 219, 221
Witos, W., 267

Wolowski, Professor Louis, 57
women: capitalist exploitation of, 83–4;
    nineteenth-century French working-class,
    42, 43; position in socialist countries, 29;
    role in May Day demonstrations (1890),
    155, 178; workers in Parisian garment
    trades, 67–9, 71–2, 74, 75–87; *see also*
    feminism
Women's National Workshops Commission,
    France, 79, 80
worker autonomy, independence, 5, 6, 123,
    127, 130–1, 132, 134
workforce discipline, 121, 122, 123, 124, 125,
    133; law as agent of, 126
working class: consciousness and unity, 3, 4,
    6, 15, 50, 58–9, 108, 123, 164, 173;
    exploitation of, 29, 30, 107, 127, 132, 133;
    Hobsbawm's critique of, 17–20; image of
    the family, 4, 82–6
working hours, control over time, 122–3, 124,
    127, 130, 131, 132, 134; *see also* eight-hour
    day; overtime
workplace: British tradition of resistance at,
    119, 121, 127, 137; as location of sociability
    in France, 39–40
workshop production, Parisian garment
    trades, 70–1, 72–3, 74, 75, 76, 77, 79, 80,
    84
Wyatt, Benjamin and Philip, 203
Wynyard, Co. Durham, 203

Yiddish, 238, 245, 246
Yugoslavia, 261–2, 264, 265, 266, 272; South
    Slavs, 261–2, 263; Yugoslav National
    Movement, 261, 264

Zionism, 244, 248

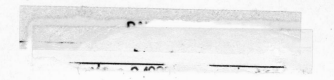